**CREATIVE
LICENSE**

CREATIVE
LICENSE

The
Law and Culture
of Digital Sampling

KEMBREW MCLEOD AND **PETER DICOLA**

with Jenny Toomey and Kristin Thomson

Duke University Press
Durham and London
2011

Printed in the United States of America on acid-free paper ∞
Designed by C. H. Westmoreland
Typeset in Warnock by Copperline Book Services, Inc.
Library of Congress Cataloging-in-Publication Data appear on the
last printed page of this book.

CONTENTS

ACKNOWLEDGMENTS

This book benefited from the insight and generous assistance of many individuals. First, we would like to thank Jenny Toomey and Kristin Thomson for their enormous contributions. As the executive director of Future of Music Coalition (FMC), Jenny introduced the two of us to each other in 2005 and helped in the conception of the project. In addition, she secured funding for the work, participated in all of the planning, conducted many of the interviews, and helped us edit the first draft. As research and education director of FMC, Kristin managed the editing process for the first draft and arranged for informal but extensive peer reviews. Since then, Kristin has read and commented on draft after draft over a three-year period; we owe a lot to her skill as an editor.

Sam Howard-Spink, now a music-business professor at New York University, conducted some interviews on our behalf in 2006. We had great conversations with—and received valuable advice from—Peter Jaszi and Patricia Aufderheide, both of American University. Their work on licensing and fair use in documentary films inspired this book. We also want to thank Benjamin Franzen, Kembrew's documentary partner on the film *Copyright Criminals*. The film, which serves as a kind of multimedia companion piece to this book, is the source of some of the interviews found herein.

We would like to thank all of our interviewees, who are listed in appendix 1. This book samples liberally from the way our interviewees expressed themselves, but it also relies on the understanding and ideas they conveyed.

The efforts of our informal peer reviewers in reading the first draft were invaluable. Each of them took the time to read a book-length manuscript and provided detailed line-by-line comments as well as advice on the big picture. The informal peer reviewers for our first draft included Whitney Broussard (entertainment attorney), Ann Chaitovitz (intellectual property attorney and former FMC executive director), Jeff Chang (hip-hop historian and music journalist), Jane Ginsburg (law professor, Columbia Law School), Dina LaPolt (entertainment attorney), Jennifer Lena (sociology professor, Vanderbilt University), Jessica Litman (law professor, University of Michigan Law School), Walter McDonough (entertainment attorney, FMC cofounder, and FMC counsel), David Sanjek (director, BMI Archives), Siva Vaidhyanathan (media professor, University of Virginia), and Marcy Rauer Wagman (entertainment attorney, media arts professor at Drexel University, and founder of MAD Dragon UNLTD). We want to give special thanks to Jessica Litman—one of Peter's advisors at the University of Michigan Law School—for her encouragement to turn this project, which started its life as a sort of policy white paper, into a scholarly book with a narrative arc.

Later drafts and excerpts benefited from comments from Andrew Koppelman (law professor, Northwestern University); Robert Merges, Suzanne Scotchmer, and the students attending the fall 2008 intellectual property seminar at the University of California, Berkeley, School of Law; and Matthew Sag and the students attending the fall 2009 intellectual property seminar at DePaul University College of Law.

We would like to thank the two anonymous reviewers who read the manuscript twice for Duke University Press. Their suggestions and enthusiasm were of great help to us.

We would also like to thank those who participated in or otherwise facilitated various panel discussions we have held about sampling, including Tony Berman, June Besek, Hope Carr, El-P, Peter Jaszi, Peter Jenner, T. S. Monk, Jo-Ann Nina, Siva Vaidhyanathan, and the following members of Public Enemy: Chuck D, Hank Shocklee, Keith Shocklee, and Harry Allen.

One of the chapters in Peter's dissertation concerned sample licensing, and thus advice from his committee at the University of Michigan made its way into this book. Big thanks to chair John DiNardo, Jim Adams, Omri Ben-Shahar, Mark Clague, and Justin McCrary, and especially to Rebecca Eisenberg, who along the way provided advice about many different papers on sampling.

We had the benefit of great research assistance from Samantha Joyce, Zane Umsted, Mike Mario Albrecht, Puja Birla, Evelyn Bottando, Gina Giotta, Kristen Norwood, Kim Robinson, Rachel Avon Whidden, Nathan Wilson, and Jennifer Zoller.

Also, thanks to the world's most rockin' literary agent, Sarah Lazin, who advised us on contractual matters.

Three foundations made our work possible: the Nathan Cummings Foundation, the Ford Foundation, and the John D. and Catherine T. MacArthur Foundation. We are grateful to Claudine Brown at Cummings, Orlando Bagwell at Ford, and Elspeth Revere at MacArthur for their work and support of our work. Kembrew would also like to thank the University of Iowa and the University of Iowa Faculty Scholar Program for their financial support.

Finally, we especially want to thank everyone at Future of Music Coalition for helping us to obtain funding and to make this project happen, including Michael Bracy, Jean Cook, Nicole Duffey, Chhaya Kapadia, and Casey Rae-Hunter.

We also would like to thank those at Duke University Press who shepherded this project into publication, most notably editorial director Ken Wissoker, editorial associate Leigh Barnwell, design manager Cherie Westmoreland, copy editor Jean Brady, assistant managing editor Tim Elfenbein, publicity and marketing assistant Amanda Sharp, and senior publicist Laura Sell. The index was created by J. Naomi Linzer Indexing Services, and was paid for in part by the Book Subvention Fund of the University of Iowa Office of the Vice President for Research.

INTRODUCTION

In 2008, Girl Talk, the musical project of Gregg Gillis, released an album titled *Feed the Animals* on a small independent American label named Illegal Art. Gillis is a biomedical engineer turned laptop computer remixer who creates music with "samples" of other musicians' work—a technique that incorporates portions of existing sound recordings into a newly collaged composition.[1] Sampling can be done using a variety of media and methods, including cutting up magnetic audiotape on analog equipment, physically manipulating vinyl records on a turntable, and remixing sounds using digital technologies like computers or drum machines, among other techniques. De La Soul's Pasemaster Mase describes sampling as "taking sounds and meshing them together and putting them all in time, to come up with something totally different." The underground producer Kid 606 explains sampling's appeal in the following way: "It's like Legos. If someone said, 'Here's a bunch of Legos, put them together,' you have something to work with—as opposed to, 'Here's a bunch of plastic, mold it, and then start building it.'"[2]

Over the course of Girl Talk's *Feed the Animals*, Gillis pieces together musical fragments from the work of over three hundred recording artists. In doing so he effortlessly joins together (like Lego blocks) music from traditionally isolated genres: metal riffs run alongside love songs from the 1970s and West Coast rap; today's pop gets down with R&B from the 1960s and classic rock. With its hundreds of easily recognizable musical snippets, the album is part parlor game, part dance party soundtrack, and part love letter to four decades of popular music. After its release *Feed the Animals* received dozens of positive reviews, ranging from the agenda-setting hipster music website Pitchfork to mainstream publications like *Rolling Stone* and the *New York Times*. In the wake of this buzz-making attention, Gillis embarked on a successful world tour, in which he played in increasingly large concert venues and music festivals as he went along. Given all this, *Feed the Animals* could be considered a successful release if not for one problem: Gillis did not get permission to use any of the songs he sampled—which means he and his record label could be sued for tens of millions of dollars in damages.

Gillis is but one of many who makes new music from old songs. As a still-developing musical method, sampling has played an increasingly prominent role in the creation of popular music over the past quarter century, and it has developed in a variety of ways. For instance, Girl Talk uses fairly long samples to create a mash-up of two or three recognizable songs at a time—as opposed to some of the hip-hop songs from the late 1980s that typically combined many more musical fragments at once, often rendering the original sources unrecognizable. Whatever their aesthetic choices, sampling artists all share an important concern: according to the recording industry, it is unlawful to sell or even freely distribute sampled music unless everything is licensed. Therefore, *Feed the Animals* might be illegal under current copyright law.

Most everyone knows that duplicating an entire CD and selling copies to strangers is copyright infringement. Perhaps less well understood is the fact that sampling—copying a few seconds of a single song and integrating it into a new song—can also be infringement, depending on the context. In fact, using those few seconds might infringe *two* different copyrights—one for the musical composition (the notes and lyrics) and one for the recording of that song (the sound stored on a CD). We will explain this aspect of copyright law in more detail in chapter 3, but for now it is useful to think of song as a coin that has two copyrightable sides: the composition and the sound recording. Therefore, because Girl Talk sampled parts of over three hundred songs to make *Feed the Animals*, Gillis may have infringed more than six hundred distinct copyrights. But then again, maybe he didn't. According to most press accounts—and our own correspondences with Gillis and his label—

Girl Talk and Illegal Art believe that *Feed the Animals* is legal under the fair use doctrine. We will discuss this legal doctrine in some detail in chapter 4 and in later chapters, but for now we offer the following brief overview.

Fair use is one of many exceptions and limitations on copyrights in the United States, and it allows individuals to use elements of existing works without permission and yet not violate the law—in certain circumstances. Fair uses include, but are not limited to, "criticism, comment, news reporting, teaching, scholarship, or research."[3] Quoting from a book in the course of reviewing it is a classic example. But fair use can also include "transformative" uses of existing works,[4] a category that might well include some forms of sampling. To determine whether a particular use is fair, courts consider four factors, including whether the use is commercial, whether creative rather than factual elements of the existing copyrighted work were used, how much of the existing work was used, and whether the market for that work has been harmed. Courts evaluate fair use on a case-by-case basis, thereby making the doctrine sensitive to context but also unpredictable to the extent that corporations hesitate to rely on it as a defense to copyright infringement.

As the *New York Times* noted in an article on Gillis, "Because his samples are short, and his music sounds so little like the songs he takes from that it is unlikely to affect their sales, Gillis contends he should be covered under fair use."[5] As of this writing, any dispute remains a mere possibility. Despite the easily recognizable snippets of songs from many high-profile—and some frequently litigious—artists, Girl Talk has yet to be sued for sampling a copyrighted work without a license.

It is an open question whether Girl Talk should have obtained licenses, whether Gillis's fair use defense would hold up in court, or some combination of these outcomes—depending on the particular sample at issue. Sampling prompts many other questions, the answers to which depend in part on samplers' position (or lack thereof) in the mainstream music industry. As a matter of law, must these musicians get licenses for everything they sample? As a matter of policy, should they have to? What procedures do sampling artists use to secure licenses on musical compositions and sound recordings? What business, legal, and aesthetic factors affect whether it's possible to obtain licenses? Perhaps the most interesting question is *why* it is so difficult to obtain licenses, or "clearance," for many of the samples contained in sample-based records. In this book we explore the answers to these questions by providing historical, legal, and cultural contexts that we hope will promote an informed debate over sampling, as well as a better understanding of it.

THE ART OF SAMPLING

A lot of people look at hip-hop sampling as doing
what be-boppers did—taking standards of the day and putting
a new melody on top of it.—GREG TATE

Like any musical technique, sampling can be used well or used poorly. Most people can clearly hear the bass line to Queen and David Bowie's "Under Pressure" in Vanilla Ice's "Ice Ice Baby" or much of Rick James's "Superfreak" in MC Hammer's "U Can't Touch This." Critics of sampling often cite such songs (which borrow lengthy hooks or choruses) to dismiss sampling as an illegitimate creative method. Surely, few would argue that these are particularly imaginative uses of musical samples— though this approach has certainly resulted in fun, sometimes-classic party records, as well as mega-selling hits. These simplified examples, however, do little justice to the complex rhythms, references, and layers of sound that sample-based music can achieve. In the late 1980s, recording artists like De La Soul, A Tribe Called Quest, the Jungle Brothers, Public Enemy, and the Beastie Boys constructed single songs from multiple brief, often unrecognizable musical quotations. More contemporary artists like RZA, DJ Shadow, the Avalanches, and El-P today employ a similarly dense style of sampling.

During the 1970s, hip-hop DJs used the turntable as an instrument that could manipulate sound, and thus transformed the record player from a technology of consumption to one of musical production. And in the 1980s, hip-hop producers built on these turntable techniques by using digital samplers to distill dozens of sampled sound sources into a single new track. "We'd grab a conga sound. We grabbed trumpet sounds, violin sounds, drumbeat sounds, and remanipulated them and created our own music," says Mix Master Mike, a member of the Beastie Boys and the DJ crew Invisibl Skratch Piklz. Sampling has had a leveling effect on music making by allowing virtually anyone to make music, even those without formal training. "You don't have to learn how to play guitar," says Steinski, a pioneering remix artist. "You don't have to know nothing. All you have to do is get a sound editing program for your computer, and you're right there. You can make the next big record in the world."

The innovations of pioneering hip-hop artists dramatically changed the way popular music is created and have forced us to rethink what counts as creativity in a digital world. As Gillis, in discussing the ways that music fans, amateur music makers, and professionals are using digital technologies to remix and share music, tells us, "People are interacting in others' lives, and music is becoming a lot more democratic." Similarly, iMovie, YouTube, and the like have altered our relationship with technology and cultural production by providing consumers with the tools to become producers (or "remixers") of and distributors in their media environments. Today, a thirteen-year-old can make music with samples, and plenty do. "I think because of the way kids are raised now, your average kid sits in front of the TV with a remote control and *click, click, click, click, click, click,*" the rapper Mr. Lif says in explaining how remix culture has touched so many aspects of contemporary life. "It's the same way you're going to think musically. You're going to be like, 'OK, here's the theme from *Diff'rent Strokes,* here's Kermit the Frog, here's a Sally Struthers infomercial,' you know what I mean? It all becomes the same thing, and I think that's what's happening with music too."

The clashes over sampling that emerged in the late 1980s anticipated both today's remix culture and the legal culture that is largely at odds with it. Therefore, it's not much of a stretch to say that the hip-hop DJs of the 1970s helped plant the seeds of some key debates that are currently raging over intellectual property. This is one reason why our work in this volume primarily focuses on hip-hop. We start in chapter 1 by describing the so-called golden age of sampling, a term that refers to a moment in time in the late 1980s and early 1990s when artists had more freedom to create sample-based music. The legal and administrative bureaucracies of the music industry had not yet turned their attention to hip-hop, which was considered a passing fad. This vacuum allowed many hip-hop artists to make music the way they wished, without a proverbial (or literal) attorney looking over their shoulders. And the music they made was groundbreaking.

In chapter 1 we use the golden age as a case study that clearly demonstrates what can go wrong if we don't properly understand how copyright law can act as a de facto cultural policy. By this we mean that the law encourages some forms of creativity and discourages others—a subtler form of what happens in communist societies, with their official decrees concerning state-sanctioned art. Actually, the existence of a cultural policy is not a bad thing, as long as the members of a society have a chance to shape it. The situation we face today, in the context of sampling, is one where we let private institutions impose constraints on the production of art, with little or no input from actual creators. We should also point out that copyright was conceived as a kind of cultural policy from the very beginning, given that the U.S. Constitution charged Congress to make laws to "promote the progress of science and useful arts."[6]

The framers of the Constitution never understood intellectual property as equivalent to physical property, and instead viewed it as a limited right designed to encourage and sustain the production of cultural and scientific works. Built into this design was a balance between the needs of individual creators, users, and (more generally) society. But by the early 1990s, in the realm of musical sampling, courts and music industry professionals allowed copyright owners' perspective to trump all other understandings of copyright law. That's when the trouble started. We wrote this book with the idea that the relatively recent past can offer us lessons on how to not repeat the same mistakes in the near future.

In chapter 2 we move from the particular to the general by widening the frame to discuss the broader history of musical collage across time and genres. Despite the shock of the new that digital sampling delivered, this technique is merely the latest manifestation of a rich musical tradition previously found in jazz, folk, bluegrass, and blues. Over the past century, however, the expansion of copyright law, the rise of the music industry, and the introduction of new sound recording technologies have served to make matters more complicated.

CONFLICTS OVER SAMPLING

You can't just have a record made up of other people's records and not pay them for it.—KEN FREUNDLICH, music attorney

The musicologist Joanna Demers notes that "with the rise of disco, hip-hop, and electronic dance music, transformative appropriation has become the most important technique of today's composers and song-writers."[7] This statement encapsulates two key facts about sampling: it is commercially important and musicians in a wide variety of genres engage in it. There is also a fascinating tension embodied in the phrase that Demers chooses to describe this method. Much of the legal, cultural, and economic difficulty accompanying the proliferation of sampling stems from the tug of war between the positive connotation of the adjective "transformative" and the more negative connotation (at least in legal circles) of the noun "appropriation." One's attitude toward sampling depends on one's aesthetic, ethical, and perhaps legal point of view. As we discovered in our research for this book, it can also depend on one's position in the relationship between the artist who samples and those who are sampled.

In chapter 3 we examine several categories of positions within the music industry—positions created by copyright law and music-business practice—and the variety of perspectives individuals can have, even within each category, on disputes over sampling. We also relate a series of rich narratives in chapter 3 that describe particular instances of sampling and illustrate the competing interests at stake: publishing companies, record labels, remixers, artists who are sampled, sample licensing experts, and so on. This chapter underscores the diversity and the complexity of opinions about sampling, for there is no single monolithic position that exists on either side of the equation.

Conflicts about sampling have their roots in the fundamental relationship between musicians past and present. Musicians do not reinvent the twelve-tone scale used in Western music but rather borrow it from previous generations. Instrumentalists often use major-seventh chords, play in 4/4 meter, and perform on instruments with unique timbre like the violin and the piano. No musician living today invented those things. Someone (or some group of people) did once invent chords, meter, and musical instruments, but that was long ago. In the time since, millions of people have used those musical ideas, instruments, and traditions to make their own musical contribution. Music is not unique in this regard; all creativity occurs in this way. Writers, composers, artists, and inventors all make use of ideas—and particular applications of those ideas—that others created before them.[8] For example, to write this book we have made use of the English language, employed various words (and arrangements of words) coined by others over the centuries, displayed the influence of other scholars' research, and wrestled with ideas that our interviewees put on the table—often quoting them while doing so.

To keep the chain of creativity going, copyright law prevents anyone from owning the rights to certain abstract musical ideas.[9] As DJ Vadim points out, "You can't own a B-flat or a B-sharp or a C minor or a C major on a keyboard, on a guitar, or what have you." But the boundary between ideas too abstract to be owned and particular expressions of ideas that one can copyright can still be disputed. Difficult examples from music abound. What about a distinct eight-note melody using some of the twelve tones of the scale? Or a specific five-chord progression that includes a major seventh chord? Or a complex rhythm played in a 6/8 meter? Or the unique timbre achieved by the skill of a particular flutist, pianist, or violinist? Because mining the past for inspiration is so commonplace, and takes so many different forms, all musicians have a strong interest in the ability to use existing music as source material.

Controversies start when musicians use specific melodies, chord progressions, rhythms, or timbres found in existing music—and sampling is a major example of this kind of boundary dispute in copyright law. In chapter 4 we discuss the most prominent of the judicial decisions that have determined how copyright law applies to specific disputes over sampling. These decisions provide an important explanation of how and why the industry developed a system to handle sampling that generally requires licensing and thus encourages copyright holders to demand payment for most uses of the works they own, even the shortest and most unrecognizable samples. For better or worse, licensing is now standard practice in the music business today.

WHY PROTECT SAMPLES WITH
COPYRIGHT LAW?

*To lift someone else's riff and then call it your own—
that's stealing—unless it's a quotation, in which case you'd still
owe a percentage, in my opinion.*—DAVID BYRNE

So why protect samples with copyright law? From the downstream creator's perspective, it may seem odd or even retrograde to put a roadblock in the way of new music. But recognizing ownership of existing music does not necessarily prevent musicians from incorporating elements of older works. Although copyright owners do have the right to simply deny permission, not all of them use that right. Instead, what ownership really means in many instances is the right to negotiate a license at a price that the owner finds acceptable. Thus, copyright protection for samples often boils down to the difference between getting no compensation when a subsequent artist samples your composition or recording and getting some amount of compensation that you bargained for. To us, a successful licensing transaction means that the owners of existing compositions and recordings receive compensation, when it is deserved; the creators of new, sample-based works get to make their art; and both parties have reached an agreement.

Such voluntary, mutually beneficial deals are the core of what is socially desirable, according to economic theory. And, described in that abstract way, licensing might sound pretty good. Recognizing ownership and control over samples allows society—in theory, anyway—to tap into the benefits that copyright law is supposed to have in general. Lawyers and economists over the past two centuries have justified copyright law with arguments along these lines. By protecting creators from competition from those who would sell exact (or substantially similar) copies of their work, copyright siphons financial rewards from the public to creators in the form of higher prices.

For example, when Merge Records released the album *Neon Bible* by the Arcade Fire, federal law prohibited any other company from selling exact copies of that album. This allowed Merge to set its own price, which was influenced by factors such as how much money fans of the Arcade Fire were willing to pay for CDs or downloads of the album;

the interest of fans in competing bands' albums; and, more indirectly, other forms of entertainment besides listening to the Arcade Fire. If the price Merge set had to take copycat record companies into account, which offered identical copies of *Neon Bible* (or close substitutes), then that price would be much lower. Enhanced financial rewards allow musicians to anticipate the opportunity to recoup, and possibly surpass, the money and time they spend creating. In this way, copyright provides incentives to create. Some economists go even further by arguing that copyrights also maximize the value of works even after they are created.[10]

But as everyone knows, including economists, the real world is much messier than economic theory. The economic analysis of law, for instance, has focused on the idea of "transaction costs," meaning the money, time, and other resources that parties must expend to reach a deal, such as a licensing agreement. The idea of friction in physics can be a helpful metaphor for transaction costs: we operate a large economic machine, but some energy gets lost as the gears grind against each other. The work of the Nobel Prize–winning economist Ronald Coase has in many ways launched the study of transaction costs. Although lots of interesting theoretical work builds on his ideas, the problem is a dearth of empirical work that studies the factual details of real-world transactions. Coase has implored economists to work with lawyers, sociologists, and those in other disciplines "to understand why transaction costs are what they actually are."[11]

This book is in part inspired by Coase's charge. In chapter 5 we attempt to document the tangled reality of sample licensing. In our interview research, which we describe in more detail below, we asked questions like the following: How easy is it to find the owner of the preexisting work? How long does it take to reach an agreement? Does licensing always occur when it would be socially beneficial to allow the creation of a new work that incorporates existing works? How do these concerns impact the aesthetic decisions that artists who sample make? In sum, how well does the sample clearance system really function? The answers to those questions should shape our view about whether, how, and when we want copyright law to insist that musicians obtain a license to sample. If licensing were straightforward and smooth, we might be confident that protecting samples with copyright will generate the desired benefits. But if—as happens to be the case—the process of sample licensing is fraught with difficulties, we should question whether the system that copyright law and the music industry have generated for clearing samples is a desirable one.

COPYRIGHT AS A CONSTRAINT ON CREATIVITY

By discouraging copying, [copyright law] discourages the historically very important form of creativity that consists of taking existing work and improving it.—WILLIAM LANDES and RICHARD POSNER, *The Economic Structure of Intellectual Property Law*

Copyright law's benefits come with costs—economic and otherwise—as many commentators before us have noted.[12] Some of the costs fall on consumers, such as those who have to pay more for albums like *Neon Bible* than they would if copycat record labels could legally enter the market. A host of copycats would offer lower prices to poach sales from Merge and from each other. Higher prices also lead some people who would have bought the album at a lower price to decide not to buy it. The lost enjoyment of those whom higher prices discouraged from buying the album is another cost of having copyright law. Our specific focus in this book is on those who want to draw on previous songs and use (at least parts of) these creative works as building blocks—and the costs that come with that effort. In economic terms, as William Landes and Richard Posner have put it, copyright increases the "cost of expression."[13] Copyright protection converts what would otherwise be a free input into a costly input. This insistence on compensation may be a desirable thing for copyright law to do, but it nevertheless has important consequences for creativity.

Copyright presents a tradeoff between providing incentives for creators and granting access to both the public and other creators. Some of the costs of licensing copyrighted music are the same as they would be for any economic input—for instance, when a bakery makes bread it has to pay for the flour and yeast. But the full cost of expression that results from other musicians' copyrights includes costs that differ from those involved in a simple transaction for the baker's ingredients. You cannot go to a store and buy sample licenses off the shelf. Nor is it easy to set up a relationship with a regular supplier of sample licenses, at least not in the way that bakeries contract with foodservice companies to deliver staples on a regular basis.

The transaction costs of licensing existing copyrighted works are almost certainly higher than the transaction costs of a bakery's purchase of the ingredients for bread. For example, to clear all the samples on *Feed the Animals*, Gregg Gillis first would have to figure out which samples require licenses under copyright law.[14] More practically, he would need to figure out which samples the music industry expects him to clear as a matter of business custom. For each of the samples requiring a license, he would determine who owns each copyright (a huge problem on its own), and then gain permission from the owners of both the sound recording copyright *and* the composition copyright.[15] Each discrete, private negotiation—and there would have to be at least six hundred in this case—takes time and money paid to intermediaries. The costs of engaging in these licensing transactions pile up. Some copyright owners might simply deny permission, thereby forcing Gillis to rearrange or even abandon the songs, which could have both financial and artistic costs.

For those negotiations that succeeded, Girl Talk would have to pay the licensing fees (on top of the transaction fees associated with hiring sample clearance experts who have the industry connections that can make a deal possible). Once in a while a sample might come for free, but prices can escalate quickly to tens or even hundreds of thousands of dollars, especially for samples of well-known songs, which are exactly the types of tunes Gillis sampled. And any instances in *Feed the Animals* where Gillis sampled a source that itself contains multiple samples—like Public Enemy's "Bring the Noise"—would compound all these expenses. For instance, he would not only need permission from Public Enemy's song publisher and record company, but also those who hold the rights to the songs that are sampled within "Bring the Noise" (including a notoriously litigious publishing company named Bridgeport Music). Even if Gillis diligently secured the sound recording and composition publishing rights for all the identifiable samples used in "Bring the Noise"—but had not cleared the rights for an obscure sample that had previously gone undetected—he could be sued. Ignorance of a copyright infringement is not an adequate defense.

Similar problems are already creating headaches for filmmakers, television producers, game designers, and other media makers who want to license sample-based music for their projects. As the producers of the movie *I Got the Hook-Up* discovered—when they included a hip-hop song from the early 1990s that, unbeknownst to them, contained an uncleared sample—licensing failures can cause multimillion dollar losses. (The *Bridgeport Music v. Dimension Films* suit was brought forward, and won, by Bridgeport.) Because music is a basic building block for all kinds of media texts, the labyrinthine sample clearance system is a concern for media makers of all stripes. This system often demands that one obtain a towering stack of licenses—often referred to as "license stacking" or "royalty stacking"—a problem that also arises with types of intellectual property other than music.

In his book *The Gridlock Economy*, the law professor Michael Heller presents a sobering example of how the need to license patented genes and other pharmaceutical "inventions" has hindered the development of life-saving drugs. A drug company executive told Heller that his researchers "had found a treatment for Alzheimer's disease, but they couldn't bring it to market unless the company bought access to dozens of patents. Any single patent owner could demand a huge payoff; some blocked the whole deal."[16] The drug is still sitting on the shelf, even though it could have benefited millions of people and generated millions more dollars, Heller writes. We recognize that digital sampling and drug manufacturing are on two very different planes of social importance, but the legal and bureaucratic pressures of licensing cause analogous problems in both areas. Exacerbating the gridlock phenomenon is the increased duration of copyright law. Copyrights in the United States now last for the life of the author plus seventy years or, for works with corporate authors, ninety-five years after publication or one hundred and twenty years after creation, whichever is shorter. Longer copyright terms mean a taller stack of licenses to negotiate.

In the context of these legal and bureaucratic constraints, in chapter 6 we describe the impact of the sample clearance system on creativity. Musicians can respond in many ways to the burdens of licensing. For example, a musician might choose to quote a short phrase from an existing song by rerecording that short phrase rather than sampling the existing recording directly. Another musician might abandon particular projects entirely. Others might go to huge lengths to disguise what they have taken from other musicians, and many more might decide to distribute it through more "underground" distribution networks. Regardless of how would-be samplers respond to the costs of licensing, copyright law and traditional music industry practices have shaped their choices, whether in the foreground or the background. Put another way, artists who sample pay some price—either in terms of creative constraints, limited distribution options, exorbitant licensing fees, or all of the above.

In chapter 6 we also attempt to measure the impact of the changes and adjustments musicians make in response to the sample clearance system. To get at that question, we ask whether commercial record labels could release albums from the golden age of sampling (described in chapter 1) under the modern licensing system. Others have asked and answered this question before, but never in a sustained empirical manner. In looking at two sample-heavy albums released in 1989 and 1990—the Beastie Boys' *Paul's Boutique* and Public Enemy's *Fear of a Black Planet*—we estimate that they probably would *not* be released today without taking a significant loss on each copy sold. (And this is assuming that all the samples contained on those albums could be cleared successfully, which is highly doubtful.) These fiscal and legal realities deter the creation of collaged compositions containing multiple samples, thereby stunting the development of an art form in its relatively early stages.

A BALANCING ACT

The limited scope of the copyright holder's statutory monopoly, like the limited copyright duration required by the Constitution, reflects a balance of competing claims upon the public interest: Creative work is to be encouraged and rewarded, but private motivation must ultimately serve the cause of promoting broad public availability of literature, music, and the other arts.—The U.S. SUPREME COURT in *Twentieth Century Music Corp. v. Aiken*

As a society we want to reward musical creativity and encourage more of it. When composers or recording artists take existing musical ideas— perhaps adding some new elements—and combine all of the elements in sufficiently original ways, we offer their creations copyright protection. This is one way we facilitate the efforts of musicians, their record labels, and publishers to make money from music. And we don't stop at protecting whole creations—we also protect certain portions of them. At the same time, we want future composers to be able to use some elements from previous music without permission. Thus, copyright must perform a balancing act by brokering a compromise between compensation and access.

The controversy over sampling in music is part of a larger set of debates about how legal and bureaucratic institutions regulate new technological innovations and their creative uses. For instance, in a narrow 1984 decision the Supreme Court effectively legalized the videocassette recorder (VCR).[17] But a decade later Congress mandated that digital audio tape (DAT) devices be outfitted with anticopying controls.[18] Courts and Congress have thus played a large role in the success and failure of these respective technologies and the companies that invested in them. The VCR achieved a near-universal adoption rate in households, while the DAT was essentially extinct by the mid-1990s. On the other side of these disputes over new technologies, the owners of copyrighted content will reap rewards or suffer losses depending on the decisions that courts and Congress make.[19]

The advent of digital technology has made the musical technique of sampling even more prevalent, thus contributing to the continuing stream of sampling-related controversies. Although sampling presents issues about creativity distinct from those presented by the VCR, technological advances have put analogous pressure on copyright law to strike a new balance between the parties that sampling affects. Sampling implicates the interests of the copyright owners (including the original songwriter, his or her publisher, the recording artist, his or her record label, and anyone else who owns a copyright interest in a sampled song); the artists who have sampled; and the listening public. The current rules for separating copyright-protected elements from unprotected elements determine whether an instance of sampling requires a license (and usually payment). Thus, the rules governing sampling reflect the balance our society has struck between earlier musicians and subsequent musicians who wish to use existing music as source material.

Copyright law draws the line between the copyright-protected elements of music and freely available elements differently depending on the kind of musical borrowing. Using a single note or quoting a brief phrase from an existing composition is free if you don't take too much.[20] Employing the style or displaying the influence of another musician (say, writing a folk ballad inspired by Woody Guthrie) is not an infringement as long as the song is not substantially similar—in a legal sense—to another musician's song. Copyright law also contains a compulsory license for cover versions—a compromise between songwriters and subsequent recording artists and their labels. Congress struck this particular balance over one hundred years ago in the Copyright Act of 1909. Recording a cover version of another songwriter's composition costs pennies per copy and does not require permission, which means that performers are free to reinterpret a song in whatever style they wish as long as they don't significantly alter the lyrics.[21] (For instance, changing a pronoun from he to she is fine, but changing the words of a chorus is probably not.)

But not all creative uses of previous work are treated equally. Some types of musical borrowing have few legal restrictions, but other forms have many. The creative freedoms associated with brief quotation, mimicry of style, and cover versions often don't apply for those who wish to sample fragments of sound recordings. This makes digital sampling a relatively costly form of borrowing, and in this sense copyright law discriminates against sampling as compared to other kinds of borrowing. It might have justification for doing so, but copyright law as applied to sampling constrains the forms that expression can take. It also constrains the ultimate content of that message—something that causes concerns rooted in the First Amendment and in free-speech values more generally.[22]

With this in mind, in chapter 7 we examine several proposals for reform. Some proposals require government action; others rely on private institutions and actors. Throughout the chapter, we seek a set of complementary solutions that are practical, uphold the value of compensating musicians who are sampled where appropriate, and reduce the extent to which sample-licensing burdens creativity. Ultimately, the process of deciding who should end up with what rights and what compensation ought to involve consultation with all parties that have something at stake—which is what we attempted when choosing our interviewees. Finally, in the conclusion we propose a thought experiment that isn't as pragmatic but suggests a way to move outside the constraining boxes of copyright's conventional wisdom that limit our options.

In our research for this volume we discussed sampling and sample licensing with over one hundred prominent stakeholders—a diverse assembly of interviewees who provided us with everything from informed commentary to raw, opinionated passion. We talked to musicians who sample, musicians who have been sampled, and musicians who have been on both sides of this issue during their careers. We also talked to music lawyers, industry executives, sample clearance professionals, public-interest group representatives, law professors, musicologists, music historians, and music journalists. Direct quotes from these interviews are regularly woven into our analysis because we feel it is important to report our interviewees' points of view in their own words.

In doing so, we set out to craft a comprehensive study that maps the field of sampling in all its complexities and contradictions. A great deal of the recent discussion about these issues has simplified the landscape in an effort either to defend the status quo or to undermine the existing sample license clearance system. Also, much of this work lacks a sustained empirical component, which is something that perpetuates false assumptions and oversimplifications that could be corrected by simply asking a participant in the sample clearance system. We did not, however, take everything our interviewees said as gospel, because we found that more than a few of these insiders frequently recited apocryphal stories that earlier academics and journalists have been guilty of propagating. We hope this book will help end this recursive cycle.

Although we weren't able to find a true consensus among our interviewees about how to properly fix the sample clearance system, we did find there is a near-universal opinion that the system is broken. Of course, opinions vary about the degree to which the system is inefficient as well as the resulting creative consequences of this inefficiency. It is clear, however, that the sample licensing system and collage-based forms of creativity are in conflict. We have attempted to understand the nuances of that conflict, and our interviews have greatly enhanced our understanding of this subject. This is one of the central reasons why the interviewees' words provide the backbone of this study. Like a musical collage, this volume mixes together this source material with our own legal, economic, historical, and cultural analysis to create a richer text—a collage of words that both describes and enacts the technique of sampling.

1

THE GOLDEN AGE OF SAMPLING

In this chapter we compare and contrast two key moments in hip-hop music's evolution in order to illustrate how the emergence of the contemporary sample licensing system impacted creativity. First, we examine the golden age of hip-hop, when sampling artists were breaking new aesthetic ground on a weekly basis. Following that, we explain how legal and bureaucratic regimes forcefully constrained the creative choices that hip-hop producers could make. The rise and fall of sampling's golden age—roughly between 1987 and 1992—offers evidence that illustrates why we should care about sampling as a fruitful musical technique. As we mentioned in the introduction, recent history can provide us with a lesson about what happens when we don't make carefully considered policy decisions about copyright and creativity.

Paul Miller, a.k.a. DJ Spooky, notes that some of the key albums and artists from the golden age include De La Soul's *3 Feet High and Rising*, Pete Rock & C. L. Smooth's *Mecca and the Soul Brother*, and Public Enemy's *It Takes a Nation of Millions to Hold Us Back*, among others. We can add to that list many other classic albums from the Jungle Brothers, Queen Latifah, MC Lyte, Boogie Down Productions (BDP), and Eric B & Rakim, to name but a few. "These albums had a rich tapestry of sound, a variety of messages," notes the media studies scholar Siva Vaidhyanathan. "They were simultaneously playful and serious, and they really stand as the *Sgt. Pepper's* or *Pet Sounds* of hip-hop." And as the MC and producer Mr. Lif observes, "The difference between hip-hop production in current times and in the 1980s during the golden era—it just allowed so much more freedom. Like, you didn't think about, 'You couldn't sample this, or you couldn't sample that.'"

So, for instance, when BDP released their debut *Criminal Minded* in 1987, they didn't ask AC/DC whether they could sample "Back in Black" on their classic song "Dope Beat." Instead, BDP just did it, despite the fact that the hard rock group has since become known for turning down sample requests (or, for that matter, refusing to allow its music to be sold online). "To this day I don't know why AC/DC didn't sue us for that song," frontman KRS-ONE told the journalist Brian Coleman. "That's all samples. I'm probably incriminating myself, but nothing on *Criminal Minded* is cleared."[1] A few years later, artists like KRS-ONE would no longer be able to fly under the radar like they used to. The golden age was an important moment during the development of hip-hop as a musical art form, and it opened up a range of artistic possibilities that largely weren't censored by legal and economic interests.

SAMPLING'S GOLDEN AGE

> Sampling was a very intricate thing for us. We didn't just pick up
> a record and sample that record because it was funky. It was a collage.
> We were creating a collage.—HANK SHOCKLEE

The standout records of the golden age were created at a time when hip-hop was still considered a flash in the pan by the larger music industry. This attitude gave many hip-hop artists the opportunity to make music exactly as they imagined it, without restrictions. This was particularly true of De La Soul, a group that hailed from the African American suburbs of Long Island, a region that also produced Public Enemy. De La Soul consisted of Pasemaster Mase, Trugoy, and Posdnuos—a threesome that was augmented on their first three classic albums by the producer Prince Paul. His former group Stetsasonic was signed to Tommy Boy Records, an important independent hip-hop label that released records by Naughty By Nature, Queen Latifah, and many other popular hip-hop acts. But it was De La Soul that was the jewel in the label's crown in the late 1980s, particularly because they were able to match their experimental approach with platinum sales.

"They had an aesthetic of taking everything and the kitchen sink and throwing it into the blender," states the hip-hop historian and journalist Jeff Chang. "So, you didn't just have George Clinton, the Meters, and the usual funk stuff you would expect on a record. You'd have French language records. You'd have the Turtles. You'd have Led Zeppelin. You'd have Hall and Oates. You'd have all kinds of crazy things coming out of the mix, and it sounded the way like a lot of people heard pop culture at that moment in time." The title of their first album came from a sample they snatched from Johnny Cash's hit from the 1950s "Five Feet High and Rising," during which Cash sings, "Three feet high and rising, ma." ("Dave's father had that record," says Posdnuos, referring to the group member known back then as Trugoy.)[2]

"I definitely, *definitely* was taken aback by what De La Soul did," says the hip-hop journalist Raquel Cepeda. "They just went ahead and took whatever moved them." Prince Paul echoes Cepeda when he says, "We went in there to have fun and experiment, and with De La, we could literally do *anything*."[3] The creative field was wide open, with no significant legal or administrative fences yet erected. One can also place the Beastie Boys' densely packed sophomore record, released in 1989, into the same experimental category. "Look at the *Paul's Boutique* record," says the current Beastie Boys DJ, Mix Master Mike. "That was sample mastery right there. Those records were just *full* of samples." Although there is no accessible paper trail that confirms what was sampled, or how many samples *Paul's Boutique* contains, somewhere between one hundred and three hundred is a safe guess.[4]

The Dust Brothers' John Simpson, who co-produced *Paul's Boutique*, details the creative processes and the technologies—rudimentary by today's standards—involved in making that record. "The people who worked at the studios thought we were crazy at the time, 'cause they had never seen anybody make songs that way."[5] Simpson explains that they would build a song starting from one sampled loop of instrumentation that was then layered with other loops and bursts of sound. The Beastie Boys and the Dust Brothers would then painstakingly sync each of the other loops up with the first one, spending hours getting the layers to sound good together. It was a laborious process, Simpson says, explaining that "if you knew which tracks you wanted playing at any given time, you typed the track numbers into this little Commodore computer hooked up to the mixing board. And each time you wanted a new track to come in, you'd have to type it in manually. It was just painful. It took *so* long. And there was so much trial and error."[6]

Not only was it time consuming to put the parts together, the search for musical materials was also laborious. As Miho Hatori—one half of the now-defunct duo Cibo Matto, who used numerous samples in their work—tells us, "We were always buying records, *searching, searching,* and then sometimes we find, 'Oh, a Silver Apples record!' And then we find this one very short part, 'There, *that* bass line!'" This process of searching for sounds is called "crate digging," and it is central to sample-based music. "To find the right one or two seconds of sound," Hatori says, "that's a lot of work." Trugoy of De La Soul explains the haphazard ways he looks for potential samples as follows: "I could be walking in the mall and I might hear something, or in a store, something being played in the store, and say, 'Wow that sounds good.' Or a sound in an elevator, you know, elevator music, 'That sounds good.' If it sounds good and feels good, then that's it. It doesn't matter if it was something recent or outdated, dusty, obscure, and, you know, weird."

Although those records by De La Soul, the Beastie Boys, and others are justly revered for their sampling techniques, no one took advantage of these technologies more effectively than Public Enemy. When the group released *It Takes a Nation of Millions to Hold Us Back* in 1988, it was as if the work had landed from another planet. The album came frontloaded with sirens, squeals, and squawks that augmented the chaotic backing tracks over which frontman Chuck D laid his politically and poetically radical rhymes. Their next record, *Fear of a Black Planet*, released in 1990, is considered culturally so important that the *New York Times* included it on its list of the twenty-five most significant albums of the last century. Additionally, the Library of Congress included *Fear of a Black Planet* in its 2004 National Recording Registry, along with the news broadcasts of Edward R. Murrow, the music of John Coltrane, and other major works.

In the final pages of this section, we examine Public Enemy's creative processes during this period in order to glimpse what was possible creatively and to understand what was lost when the golden age came to a close. Public Enemy was, and still is, deeply influential for a wide variety of artists who followed them. Public Enemy's production team, the Bomb Squad—Hank Shocklee, Keith Shocklee, Eric "Vietnam" Sadler, and Chuck D—took sampling to the level of high art while keeping intact hip-hop's populist heart. They would graft together dozens of fragmentary samples to create a single song collage. "They really put sound and noises together and made incredible music," De La Soul's Posdnuos says. As a contemporary of Public Enemy who hailed from the same area and drew from a similarly wide sonic palate, he tells us, "Public Enemy reminded me a lot of what we were doing, obviously in a different way. But you can listen to their music and hear something else for the first time."

The group's music was both agitprop and pop, mixing politics with the live-wire thrill of the popular music experience. Matt Black of the British electronic duo Coldcut, which emerged around the same time as Public Enemy, remembers the impact of their song "Rebel Without a Pause." It was one of the many tracks on *It Takes a Nation* that featured repetitious, abrasive bursts of noise, something that simply wasn't done in popular music at the time. As Black tells us, "That noise—what some people call the 'kettle noise'—it's actually a sample of the JB's 'The Grunt.'" Public Enemy took that brief saxophone squeal (from a James Brown spin-off group) and transformed it into something utterly different, devoid of its original musical context.

"It was just so avant-garde and exciting, and heavy," Black says. Chuck D tells us that part of the intention behind transforming the sounds was to disguise them, but that wasn't the primary purpose; mostly they wanted to make something fresh. "We wanted to create a new sound out of the assemblage of sounds that made us have our own identity." Chuck D says, "Especially in our first five years, we knew that we were making records that will stand the test of time. When we made *It Takes a Nation of Millions to Hold Us Back* we were shooting to make *What's Going On* by Marvin Gaye and when we made *Fear of a Black Planet* I was shooting for *Sgt. Pepper's*."

Behind the boards was Hank Shocklee (widely credited as the architect of Public Enemy's aesthetic), who served as the director of Public Enemy's production unit, the Bomb Squad. "Hank is the Phil Spector of hip-hop," says Chuck D, referring to the producer from the 1960s who perfected a sonic approach known as "the wall of sound."[7] In Public Enemy's hands, sampling was now a tremendously complex choreography of sound that reconfigured smaller musical fragments in ways that sounded completely new. "My vision of this group," says Hank Shocklee, "was to have a production assembly line where each person had their own particular specialty." Jeff Chang explains that the members of the Bomb Squad had worked out an elaborate method that involved the group members bringing into the studio different types of sounds. "They're figuring out how to *jam with the samples*," says Chang, "and to create these layers of sound. I don't think it's been matched since then." The Bomb Squad's success hinged on the fact that each member brought a different approach to making music, crafting sounds, and working with technology. "I'm coming from a DJ's perspective," says Hank Shocklee. "Eric [Sadler] is coming from a musician's perspective. So together, you know, we started working out different ideas."

Public Enemy's distinctive sound grew out of the push and pull between Eric Sadler, who often advocated for a more traditional, structured approach to songwriting, and Hank Shocklee—who "wanted to destroy music," as Chuck D put it. "When you're talking about the kind of sampling that Public Enemy did," Hank Shocklee says, "we had to comb through thousands of records to come up with maybe five good pieces. And as we started putting together those pieces, the sound got a lot more dense." In some cases, the drum track alone was built from a dozen individually sampled and sliced beats. The members of Public Enemy treated audio—from singles, LPs, talk radio, and other sources—as a kind of found footage that could be spliced together to create their aural assemblages.

"We thought sampling was just a way of arranging sounds," says Chuck D. He explains that Public Enemy wanted "to blend sound. Just as visual artists take yellow and blue and come up with green, we wanted to be able to do that with sound." Hank Shocklee adds, "We would use every technique, no different than in film—with different lighting effects, or film speeds, or whatever. Well, we did the same thing with audio." Even though the group was working with equipment that was rudimentary by today's standards, they made the most of the existing technologies, often inventing techniques and workarounds that electronics manufacturers never imagined.

"Don't Believe the Hype" on *It Takes a Nation* is another notable example of the Bomb Squad's aural experiments. It was, according to Hank Shocklee, "one of the strangest ways we made a record. We were looking for blends in particular records; so I might be on one turntable, Keith on another, and Chuck on another turntable at the same time." As Chuck D elaborates further: "We would go through a session of just playing records, and beats, and getting snatches, and what Hank would do is record that whole session. You know, 95 percent of the time it sounded like *mess*. But there was 5 percent of magic that would happen. That's how records like 'Don't Believe the Hype' were made. You would listen to sixty minutes of this mess on a tape, and then out of that you would be like, 'Whoa! What happened right here?'"

They used the same approach when constructing Public Enemy's next album, *Fear of a Black Planet*. "It's completely an album of found sounds," Chuck D says. "It was probably the most elaborate smorgasbord of sound that we did." He describes how he spent at least one hundred hours listening to various tapes, records, and other sound sources in search of samples for the album. As the group's lyricist, Chuck D needed to fit the snatches of sampled songs, radio snippets, and everything else into his lyrics so that his rhymes and those sounds would weave together to create a theme for the album. "There were hundreds of sampled voices on that album," Chuck D explains. Pointing to the album's opening track, "Contract on a World Love Jam," he says the song holds "about forty-five to fifty voices" that interlock and underscore the album's message with a forceful sonic collage.[8]

Regarding Public Enemy's musical complexity, the DJ and producer Mr. Len points to a particular track, "Night of the Living Base Heads," from *It Takes a Nation*. As Mr. Len says, "If you really listen to that song, it changes so many times." Kyambo "Hip Hop" Joshua—who started out in the music industry working for Jay-Z's Roc-a-Fella Records in the mid-1990s, and who now co-manages Kanye West's career—echoes Mr. Len. "It was common to have multiple samples in a song, like on Public Enemy or N.W.A. albums," Hip Hop says. "If you was to go into those records, you could look at one record and you'll see five or six samples for every song. There was more changeups and drums was changing on different parts, and samples was changing."

"I'm a big Public Enemy fan," Girl Talk tells us. "Even on the subconscious level I think it really affected me—just understanding sampling as an instrument and understanding the way people make their music like that." And MC Eyedea adds, "One of the reasons why we don't like most modern hip-hop is because we can listen to [Public Enemy records], and their arrangements are so much more complex than *anything* today." During hip-hop's golden age, artists had a small window of opportunity to run wild with the newly emerging sampling technologies before the record labels and lawyers started paying attention. "It was definitely a time when sampling artists could get away with murder and we just—we *did*," says Coldcut's Matt Black.

On Public Enemy's *It Takes a Nation of Millions to Hold Us Back*, Chuck D raps about white supremacy, capitalism, the music industry, and—in the case of "Caught, Can I Get a Witness?"—digital sampling: "Caught, now in court 'cause I stole a beat / This is a sampling sport / Mail from the courts and jail claims I stole the beats that I rail . . . I found this mineral I call a beat / I paid zero." Our interviewees told us that no one bothered to clear the many fragmentary samples contained in Public Enemy's classic song "Fight the Power," which was featured in Spike Lee's *Do the Right Thing* (even though that film was released by a large movie studio and the soundtrack album was on a major label). As Chuck D explains, "It wasn't necessary to clear those albums, *Fear of a Black Planet* and *It Takes a Nation*, because copyright law didn't affect us yet. They hadn't even realized what samplers did." The music producer El-P waxes nostalgic: "It was just this magical window of time."

THE END OF THE GOLDEN AGE

Once the money came in and said, "Yo, you can't keep doing this,"
all the momentum just kind of dropped out. It was like the bottom fell
out the bucket. And those cats were saying, "Man, that's our style. Now
you're telling me that our style's too expensive?"—MR. LEN

Of course, not everyone stitched together their samples like Public Enemy did. There were plenty of songs from the golden age that merely looped the hook of an earlier song, and it was this type of sampling that began provoking legal action. For example, the influential old-school rapper T La Rock (and one-time EPMD label mate) points to the "I Shot the Sheriff" sample—which provides the backbone of EPMD's "Strictly Business." Referring to the sampled performance by Eric Clapton, T La Rock says, "I don't care who you are, you *know* where that loop is from. And there's a few songs like that in their records." Those reservations aside, he is still a fan of EPMD, and he acknowledges that even a simple loop can work its magic if used the right way. Nevertheless, this kind of sampling made T La Rock uncomfortable back then, when few hip-hop artists had concerns about copyright.

"There were some producers who really had no originality," T La Rock says. "It's as if they took the whole song. They sampled so much out of that record that there was no real production there. That's the problem I had with a lot of the producers that sampled. They didn't try to contact the person and say, 'Hey, you know, I want to make some type of publishing deal or something like that.' And for years and years and years, this went on and on under the radar, you know?" In EPMD's case it wasn't far enough below the radar, because many of the original artists tracked them down and demanded payment. "We never cleared any samples on the first album," EPMD's Erick Sermon chuckles. "People would just come after us after they knew we had sampled them. Eric Clapton wanted ten thousand dollars, Roger Troutman wanted five thousand. They didn't even sue us back then—we just paid them and that was that."[9]

With the commercial success of a number of hip-hip albums in the late 1980s, the music industry had begun to see the genre as not just an inner-city fad but as a solid source of sales revenue. With commercial validity also came increased scrutiny over samples. During the early 1990s—after a wave of lawsuits we will address in chapter 4—the legal landscape radically changed. This shifted the ground beneath the feet of hip-hop artists. "By 1994, when we made *Muse Sick-N-Hour Mess Age*," says Chuck D, "it had become so difficult to the point where it was impossible to do any of the type of records we did in the late 1980s, because every second of sound had to be cleared." Another thing that occurred by the early 1990s was that the cost of clearing samples—and the legal risks of *not* clearing samples—had significantly increased. As Harry Allen, a hip-hop journalist who has long been affiliated with Public Enemy, observes, "Records like *It Takes a Nation of Millions* and *3 Feet High and Rising*, we would have to sell them for, I don't know, $159 each just to pay all the royalties from publishers making claims for 100 percent on your compositions." Allen's hypothetical $159 CD refers to the cumulative costs associated with tracking down the owners and obtaining the proper licenses to clear the one hundred to two hundred samples on each of those early Public Enemy albums.

Many of the musicians, lawyers, and record company executives we interviewed have made similar claims regarding the costs of licensing numerous samples in a single composition. Danny Rubin, who runs a firm that clears samples for artists and record labels, tells us that today it is impractical to license songs with two or more samples. Given this, no wonder that the Beastie Boys never attempted to follow up on *Paul's Boutique*'s densely layered collages. On the Beastie Boys' album from 1992, *Check Your Head*, they used drastically fewer samples, and traditional instruments comprised most of that album's instrumental bed. "The way I always heard it," says Money Mark, who played keyboards on *Check Your Head* and later albums, "was that their accountant told them that they couldn't make any money with all those samples, so they tried a different route." [10] Mario Caldato Jr., who worked as a recording engineer on *Paul's Boutique*, estimates that 95 percent of the sounds on that record came from sampled sources, and that "they spent over $250,000 for sample clearances."[11]

As Posdnuos of De La Soul remembers, "I think *Stakes Is High* [1996] was the first album we recorded where we actually sat down in the beginning of the album, and the record company went through a list, 'Well, George Clinton is in litigation with Westbound [Records], so don't mess with his stuff right now.' Or, you know, 'Serge Gainsbourg, you sampled him for the second album, but his estate—he died, and his family's trying to get control of his estate—don't mess with him.' Or, 'George Harrison don't like rap, don't mess with him.' We actually had a list of people *not to touch*." And De La Soul's Trugoy complains, "You kind of have to do the work before you even do the creative end of things. That's what's kind of messed up about sampling, in some cases. You know, when you create a song and you think, 'All right, this is hot, this is it, right here.' And then you hand the work in to the lawyers to go clear. And either the numbers are just so crazy that you don't want to pay that kind of money, or some people just clearly say outright, 'No, you know, you're *not* using my stuff.' It kind of spoils the creative process."

By the 1990s, high costs, difficulties negotiating licenses, and outright refusals made it effectively impossible for certain kinds of music to be made legally, especially albums containing hundreds of fragments of sound within one album. Reflecting on the current state of the art of sampling, Kyambo "Hip Hop" Joshua says, "Now it's like, 'I like that beat. I'm just gonna use this one Isley Brothers sample, and that's it.' . . . It ain't that complex no more." And Mr. Len adds, "Nowadays, because of people getting into trouble with samples, or having to pay a lot for more than one sample, it's forced a lot of people now to rework their styles. To me, it took a lot away from where the music could have gone." Given the cumulative effect of multiple expensive samples and administrative hassles, one can see why the sample-laden albums like Public Enemy's *It Takes a Nation*, De La Soul's *3 Feet High and Rising*, or the Beastie Boys' *Paul's Boutique* (all released in 1988 or 1989) couldn't be made today—or at least couldn't be distributed through legitimate channels.

With the golden age of sampling long gone, the music industry's conventional wisdom recommends clearing even the most fragmentary uses. For example, on Jay-Z's song "Takeover" (from his album *The Blueprint* from 2001), the rapper felt compelled to get permission to use a single word in his lyrics. Hip Hop—one of the managers of Kanye West, who produced the music for "Takeover"—told us that Jay-Z's record label got clearance from David Bowie not because West sampled a sound recording but because of the way Jay-Z uttered a single word. In the song, he raps, "I know you missin' all the FAAAAAAAME!"— imitating the phrasing from Bowie's 1975 hit "Fame"—"Nigga, you LAAAAAAAME!" Significantly, this didn't provide the hook of "Takeover"; Jay-Z just said it once in passing in the middle of a verse. It's the kind of referential vocal phrasing that occurs all the time in music. Copyright law actually permits such "sound-alike" recordings. But in the risk-averse world of the major labels, the rules are different:

> HIP HOP: Like when he said, "Fame," that was an interpolation of a David Bowie record. Jay didn't sample that record, but he said it just like David said it, in the same context.
>
> KEMBREW: Are you saying that you have to get permission if you end up sounding like David Bowie when you just say the word "fame"?
>
> HIP HOP: Yeah, if you *sound* like him. . . . If you say a hook like somebody else said it, or you say a phrase like somebody else said it. Sometimes it can be a short saying, and [the copyright owners] will be like, "Okay, whatever." Like Jay might start a record off singing a little bit of Biggie verse, and depending on how long that verse is determines whether the person who owns it wants to come in and say, "Hey, we want a percentage of that," or, "Don't worry about it."

Many artists, scholars, and critics have argued that the growth of twentieth-century jazz music would have been similarly stunted if the jazz musicians of the time—who regularly riffed on others' songs—had to obtain permission or a license from music publishers for the use of every sonic fragment they improvised upon. Others disagree that the sample clearance system has had any negative impact on creativity. One of these dissenters is Dean Garfield, vice president of anti-piracy at the Motion Picture Association of America (MPAA), who formerly worked for the Recording Industry Association of America (RIAA). He doesn't believe that the requirement to clear samples hindered anyone's music. "If one person doesn't clear a snippet, you could just use another snippet from someone else who would clear it," says Garfield in denying Chuck D's assertion that the sample clearance system changed the way Public Enemy made music. "I think Chuck D may say that today because he finds it convenient to say that. But it's not true."

SAMPLING CONTROVERSIES HEAT UP IN THE NEW MILLENNIUM

The other person who was being sampled, their attorneys got up and said, "Well, hey, where's my piece?" That's when all the lawsuits started happening.—SHOSHANA ZISK

The copyright conflicts that began swirling around sampling in the 1980s certainly haven't gone away. Indeed, the disputes have only intensified and expanded in recent years. And it is probable that they will continue, because every major label likely owns and distributes numerous ticking time bombs waiting to be ignited by a copyright infringement lawsuit. A quarter century of nonstop sampling undoubtedly has produced a very large number of uncleared samples that are embedded in hundreds of albums released by major labels. Even though some of them have been discovered, many of our interviewees believe that a huge number have gone undetected—for the time being, at least. Lawsuits can arise long after a sample-based album was made.

The potential for sampling lawsuits increased after the *Bridgeport Music v. Dimension Films* case of 2005, a case we mentioned in the introduction that centered around an N.W.A. song from 1991 titled "100 Miles and Runnin'." This gangsta rap song was used in the film *I Got the Hook-Up.* The song sampled two seconds and used three notes from a guitar solo taken from the Funkadelic song "Get Off Your Ass and Jam." The sample was looped by N.W.A. and repeated intermittently throughout the song, where it was placed fairly low in the mix to provide a texture rather than a central hook. A federal appellate court concluded that N.W.A.'s use was an infringement of the law and infamously declared, "Get a license or do not sample." The floodgates opened after *Bridgeport* with several high-profile lawsuits targeting classic hip-hop albums such as Notorious B.I.G.'s *Ready to Die* and Run-DMC's *Raising Hell*. Both of these albums, important contributions to hip-hop culture, were removed from record store shelves and from online vendors after copyright infringement suits were filed.

The Notorious B.I.G. case centered around a sample of "Singing in the Morning," a song by a funk band from the 1970s named the Ohio Players, which Biggie and the producer Sean "Puffy" Combs (a.k.a. Puff Daddy, P. Diddy, or Diddy) sampled for the title track of *Ready to Die*. They were found liable for infringing the copyright of both the sound recording, which was owned by Westbound Records, and the underlying composition, which was owned by Bridgeport. After the injunction, *Ready to Die* could no longer be sold lawfully, and the trial court also awarded over $4 million combined to Westbound and Bridgeport. The plaintiffs and defendants could not reach a licensing agreement in the wake of the lawsuit, and thus the only way *Ready to Die* could return to the legitimate marketplace was to remove the offending sample and completely remaster the album, an expensive proposition. While the new version of "Ready to Die" still features Biggie's smooth vocal flow— which is part of the album's appeal—a side-by-side comparison demonstrates that the reworked version loses something aesthetically.

One of the more unexpected sample-related lawsuits in recent years— perhaps reflective of the post-*Bridgeport* landscape—was the lawsuit brought by the Knack in 2006. The Knack alleged that Run-DMC sampled the guitar riff from their hit from 1979, "My Sharona," without permission in the rap group's track from 1986 titled "It's Tricky." The lawsuit was unanticipated because even though "It's Tricky" was a Top 40 radio and MTV hit, the guitar sample had gone undetected by the band for twenty years. If one pays close attention to the two songs, one can hear the similarity; however, a lot of rap and rock fans surely missed this Knack sample because it was detached from its original context. The reworked Knack riff embedded in the Run-DMC song is so minimal and generic that it could come from almost any new wave song from that era. There was nothing particularly unique about it.

Another interesting twist in the Knack versus Run-DMC lawsuit story was that the primary hook that runs through "It's Tricky" actually derives from a different song from the same era: Toni Basil's "Mickey." According to the recollection of DMC, one of the group's two MCs, they got the idea for "It's Tricky" from a rhyming routine done by the old-school rap group the Cold Crush Brothers, in which "they'd use a melody from another record and put their names and words in there." Explaining how Run-DMC's song was based on Basil's "Mickey," DMC states, "I just changed the chorus around and we just talked about how this rap business can be tricky to a brother."[12] If you are familiar with both songs, compare "Hey Mickey, you're so fine / You're so fine you blow my mind, hey Mickey!" with "It's tricky to rock a rhyme / To rock a rhyme that's right on time, it's tricky!" Same cadence, rhyme scheme, and nearly identical sing-along hook. It is somewhat ironic that the song that Run-DMC borrows much more from was *not* the one that caused them legal hassles, in part because of the way the law treats distinct forms of musical borrowing quite differently.

The Knack versus Run-DMC lawsuit and others like it have implications for any major or independent record label that has ever put out a sample-based album, as well as movie and television studios, other content providers, and music distributors (both online and off). For instance, when the Knack sued Run-DMC it also sued iTunes—Apple's online music store—as well as Amazon, Napster, Yahoo, and others that sold either CD or MP3 copies of the song. The lawsuit alleged that these distributors were also liable for copyright infringement, despite the improbability that any of these companies was aware of the sample or knowingly conspired to distribute an infringing product.

This kind of legal "gotcha" game has turned into a bankable business strategy. Kyambo "Hip Hop" Joshua tells us about a friend of his who represents a widely sampled music catalogue. This person makes a nice living extracting money from downstream users and distributors who have not secured licenses for samples of the copyrighted music he controls. Hip Hop says that his friend is strategic about the way he goes about licensing his copyrights. "What I mean by that is he'll do a license with someone who wants to release a record, and he limits to album-only rights, which means you can only release the record," Hip Hop says. "Then a song from that album gets licensed in a commercial or a movie and—lo and behold—now he can go to the movie company or the advertising company and require them to license it, even though that movie company had no idea what was going on, and they assumed everything was okay."

Hip Hop reminds us that one doesn't need to know about a potential infringement in order to be liable for it. This was the situation in *Bridgeport* when the production company Dimension Films included N.W.A.'s "100 Miles and Runnin'" in its movie *I Got the Hook-Up*. Even though producers and executives at the movie company likely had no idea that N.W.A. had embedded an unauthorized sample in its song, Dimension was still liable for copyright infringement because it had not obtained permission for its indirect use of the sample in its film.

SAMPLING AS A HARBINGER OF FUTURE CONTROVERSIES

A wide range of critical commentary, mostly awful but some brilliant, has exploded on the Internet, as more have come to master the remix capabilities of digital technologies. . . . The potential of this technology is extraordinary. Its artistic potential is obvious; its political potential is just beginning to be glimpsed. . . . Yet this form of speech —remix using images and sounds from our culture—is presumptively illegal under the law as it stands.—LAWRENCE LESSIG, "Free(ing) Culture for Remix"

Beyond the ticking time bomb that film studios, television companies, music retailers, and other distributors face as a result of unlicensed samples lies another set of licensing quandaries. These complex scenarios result from two now-familiar technological developments. The first, personal computers with widely available and even preinstalled software, allows people to edit music and video in ways that were impossible or prohibitively expensive in previous decades. The second, Internet connectivity (especially the advent of broadband), allows people to distribute widely the fruits of their creative production at an extremely low cost. Together, these technological advances make it easy to access a copyrighted work; combine it with other copyrighted works, which may themselves incorporate still other copyrighted works; add one's own sounds or images; and distribute the recombined product across the world in seconds, making thousands of copies in the process.

This sequence of events—once the domain of entertainment industry professionals alone—is now an everyday occurrence that can be accomplished by amateurs. But can modern copyright law and current licensing practices handle so-called user-generated content? Digital sampling has a lot in common with YouTube's plethora of videos that often remix existing material. Both trends reflect the plummeting cost of sophisticated recording and editing software. As the hip-hop journalist Jeff Chang explains:

> Sampling is the kind of technology that's really shifted the way that people consume and produce culture. It used to be the kind of thing where a record company would have a record to produce, and they'd put all kinds of money behind it, and they'd send it down to you, the consumer, and you were supposed to passively accept it and buy it and enjoy it and dance to it—*Saturday Night Fever*, or whatever. Instead, these days what you have is people that are listeners and fans of the music being able to do their own remixes with technology, to do their own mash-ups, to do their own versions and to redo this type of stuff and to put that out into the world. So, the consumers have become producers, and this has taken a lot of power away from the record companies.

Understandably, the owners of copyrighted material are interested in asserting whatever legitimate rights they have regarding how their works are used. We know that copyright law protects the music industry from copycat record companies that sell exact or substantially similar copies of the original work. But can copyright law protect the music industry from competition that comes from its own customers, that is, the general public?

Copyright law, whether through Congress or the courts, has already reacted to the power of contemporary personal computers and network technology on multiple fronts, most prominently in the area of file sharing. The act of downloading and uploading copyrighted files is understood to violate the law.[13] Under certain conditions, the makers of file-sharing software will be liable for contributory infringement based on the illegal activity of their users.[14] Perhaps this approach has struck an acceptable balance and allowed a legitimate market for downloaded music to develop on iTunes, Wal-Mart, Rhapsody, eMusic, Amazon, and other sites. Or perhaps the law has unnecessarily stifled the music-spelunking delight of services like the original Napster and merely pushed underground whatever forms of file-sharing software are currently in existence.

Whatever one's conclusion about the correct policy, the dispute over file sharing forced the law to react to technological change and grapple with the complex issues involved in it. Lawsuits have also forced the courts to respond to sampling, which presents quite distinct legal issues from file sharing. But, with some exceptions, courts have not addressed sampling in a thorough or farsighted way. Instead, courts helped bring the golden age of sampling to an end, often without attention to the consequences for creativity. Anyone intrigued by the potential for remix culture to change entertainment, or even to change our public discourse, has an interest in seeing both public and private institutions address digital sampling in a more productive and realistic manner.

Battles over how copyright should respond to technological change, cultural trends, and new musical practices cannot be settled in an abstract way based on extreme points of view on either side. Only by studying the history of sampling and working toward a compromise among all competing interests can we find a path toward a sensible copyright policy that can govern remix culture. An engagement with particular practices in the real world will allow us to find the right balance between copyright and the public domain, between licensing and unfettered use, and between compensation and access. In this spirit, chapter 2 places digital sampling in its proper context within the larger history of sound collage in its many diverse forms.

2

A LEGAL AND CULTURAL
HISTORY OF SOUND COLLAGE

Fundamentally, sampling is a form of the fine arts practice of collage, but one that is done with audio tools rather than scissors and glue. Collage itself is a hundred-year-old artistic practice, and it flourished throughout the first three-quarters of the twentieth century. Visual artists such as Marcel Duchamp, Pablo Picasso, and Robert Rauschenberg regularly appropriated from images and texts made by others; similarly, writers like T. S. Eliot, James Joyce, and William Burroughs cut up other people's words in their literary experiments. Paul Miller, a.k.a. DJ Spooky, points to other areas of art and culture that use collage as their primary creative method. "Sampling usually is viewed as a musical thing," he says, "but if you look at the art world, for example, you have Andy Warhol taking photographs and painting them. You have different photographers taking certain scenes and reconstructing them, digitally. It all implies a layer of collage and pulling together bits and pieces."

Don Joyce of the group Negativland, who studied collage in school during the 1970s before joining the group, says that "the first instances of what could be called collage happened in the late-nineteenth century, with people taking photographs of different things and cutting them up and pasting them into what would become a postcard for the tourist trade." As he explains further, "You would have a picture of the horse and wagon with a giant cucumber on it, late-1800s humor, or a huge fish in the back of wagon—a juxtaposition of different things to make funny little pictures." These sorts of collage practices were popular during the nineteenth century, though collage—as a recognized "artistic" method—was not properly canonized until the beginning of the twentieth century when the avant-garde art movement known as Dada emerged. With the popularization of the phonograph occurring the same time that Dada shook up the art world, the seeds of sound collage had been planted.

SOUND COLLAGE IN POPULAR MUSIC AND THE AVANT-GARDE

We were cutting up classical music and making different size loops, and then I got an engineer tape on which some test engineer was saying, "Number nine."—JOHN LENNON, on "Revolution #9," quoted in Barry Miles, *Paul McCartney*

The first documented use of the phonograph for anything other than straightforward playback occurred in 1920, when the experimental composer Stefan Wolpe performed a piece that used eight gramophones playing different records at a variety of speeds.[1] Between the years 1922 and 1927, the French composer Darius Milhaud would vary the speeds of multiple simultaneously running phonographs in order to generate a collage-like effect. Several other avant-garde composers flirted with the possibilities afforded by the phonograph in the 1920s, but these experiments ultimately generated little direct impact on avant-garde music composition techniques.[2] Although one could hardly call these efforts a movement, it was at this point that the method began.

A few decades later, the American composer and conceptual artist John Cage used the phonograph to produce, in his words, "hitherto unheard or even unimagined sounds."[3] In addition to manipulating the phonograph and radio, Cage also experimented with magnetic tape, crafting a piece he called *Imaginary Landscape No. 5* in 1952. Cage's instructions asked for any forty-two records to be "treated as sound sources, rather than being what they were."[4] This was a radical move at the time, though the technique is par for the course in popular music production today. Other Cage works that arranged "found" sound fragments included *Williams Mix* and *Fontana Mix*, both of which used everyday sounds such as street noise, coughing, swallowing, cigarette smoking, and other ephemera.[5]

Musique concrète—an important, pioneering sound collage technique—was developed in Europe during the late 1940s and 1950s. The phrase was coined by the engineer and radio announcer Pierre Schaeffer, who began experimenting with recorded noises captured on magnetic tape shortly after the Second World War.[6] As the art historian Glenn Watkins writes, "Pierre Schaeffer's *Étude aux chemins de fer* (1948), a three-minute early classic of its kind, assembled and juxtaposed the sounds of railway trains for a 'concert of noises' that was broadcast over French radio."[7] During the mid-1950s, many musicians and composers, such as Karlheinz Stockhausen, were attracted to this compositional strategy.

"The early history of electronic music was closely allied with tape," writes Watkins, "and editing techniques involving splicing and overlay were by definition akin to notions of collage investigated in painting, literature, music, and the cinema in the early decades."[8] A decade after Stockhausen began his work, James Tenney, a young American musician and composer, created a piece titled *Collage #1 (Blue Suede)* in 1961. He reworked portions of Elvis's rendition of the rockabilly classic "Blue Suede Shoes" by slowing it down, chopping it up, and altering its tempo.[9] He wasn't sued for this, most likely because his work came from so deep within the esoteric sound-art world.

Within popular music, the earliest example of quoting directly from a sound recording was Bill Buchanan and Dickie Goodman's hit from 1956 "The Flying Saucer," the first of many "break-in" records the two created (Goodman also created several "solo" records, working through the late 1980s). "The Flying Saucer," a skit about an alien invasion as told through then-current rock 'n' roll hits, was composed by Buchanan and Goodman on a reel-to-reel magnetic tape recorder. "Buchanan and Goodman cut up hits of the 1950s," says Don Joyce, who heard the recordings as a kid. "They were all little spliced up bits of song that can be used with a narrator so it was a song lyric that would finish the narrator's sentence, as a little joke."

Imitating the radio broadcasts of *War of the Worlds*, Buchanan and Goodman use a fake radio announcer who is interrupted by short fragments from pop songs—something that creates a jarring, goofy collage of sound: "Radio Announcer: The flying saucer has landed again.

Washington: The Secretary of Defense has just said . . ." Then Fats Domino breaks in, singing, "Ain't that a shame." Elvis appears, as do many other stars. The record sold over a million copies and inspired a host of imitators. A few song publishers went after Buchanan and Goodman by filing copyright infringement lawsuits. The duo's legal problems prompted them to release the totally unauthorized piece "Buchanan and Goodman on Trial" later that year.

This delirious single swiped the *Dragnet* theme, among many other popular songs from that era. Buchanan and Goodman cast Little Richard as their defense attorney, and he argued before a jury of Martians. Taking the bait, four labels (Imperial, Aristocrat, Modern, and Chess) and two performers (Fats Domino and Smiley Lewis) filed for an injunction to prevent the sale of all Buchanan and Goodman recordings. They also asked for $130,000 in damages. But Judge Henry Clay Greenberg denied the injunction because he believed that the single was clearly a parody and not a violation of anyone's copyright. The judge stated that they "had created a new work," rather than simply copying someone else's music.[10]

"I think that is pretty much where the lawsuits began," says Don Joyce. "I don't think any of the classical composers got sued for using anyone else's music, but as soon as collage appeared in popular music, you had a mass commodity that was worth a lot of money. People got protective about it and proprietary about it." The British sound artist Scanner observes that today there is a certain amount of freedom in the visual art world when it comes to appropriating copyrighted material. "You can simply get away with a lot more in terms of reference points than you can with sound," Scanner says. "The lawyers seem to be a lot faster with their running shoes to get to the musicians than in the art world."

The Beatles' "Revolution #9" is perhaps the most widely heard example of the avant-garde technique of *musique concrète*. The basic rhythm for "Revolution #9," released in 1968, was built from the sound of twenty tape loops pillaged from the archives of EMI, the Beatles' record label, and they worked several other sound sources into the lengthy eight-minute, twenty-two-second track.[11] Although the Beatles obviously had implicit approval to chop up EMI's material, it is highly unlikely that the Beatles paid any royalties or secured formal permission from the original performers or song publishers. (For the famous *Sgt. Pepper's* album cover—the picture-perfect definition of collage—it is unclear as to whether the group or its label secured copyright permissions for all the photos they appropriated from; they did, however, get signed photo releases from all the living celebrities who appeared on the cover.)

Though credited to Lennon and McCartney, "Revolution #9" was composed solely by Lennon and Yoko Ono. The pair went on to feature similar cut-and-paste techniques throughout several of Ono's solo albums, as well as on their collaborations *Two Virgins* (1968) and *Wedding Album* (1969). Despite her undeserved reputation as a groupie, Yoko Ono was an important figure in the avant-garde art world at the time. Before meeting Lennon, she had performed with Ornette Coleman, La Monte Young, and John Cage. She also had deep ties with the Fluxus movement, an art scene in the 1960s that, according to a manifesto from 1965, was "the fusion of Spike Jones, Vaudeville, gag, children's games and Duchamp."[12]

In collaboration with seminal avant-garde figures, Ono launched what became known as the Chambers Street Series—ground zero for New York's experimental art and music scenes in the early 1960s. "The sound collage thing I did," she tells us, "I collaged it myself. In *Yoko Ono/Plastic Ono Band*, if you listen to it again you will hear that I did an incredible amount of collage. . . . Most people think that the *Plastic Ono Band* record was improvisational, with adlibs, but I just made it *sound* like that. When you listen to 'Greenfield Morning,' you will see that it was a very, very aggressive collage that was done."

Brian Eno and David Byrne's *My Life in the Bush of Ghosts*, released in 1981, is another key album that music critics frequently cite as bringing sampling and sound collage into popular culture. On this record, Talking Heads frontman David Byrne and the pop experimentalist (and soon-to-be U2 producer) Brian Eno appropriated a plethora of voices and sounds. It is very much a logical extension of the earlier avant-garde sound collage tradition, one that includes Ono, Stockhausen, Tenney, and others. "Oh yes," Byrne tells us, "we were both aware of *musique concrète*—and of course pieces by Steve Reich, Alvin Lucier, and others that used a recorded voice as the raw material were known as well." Here Byrne refers to "new music" pioneers such as Steve Reich, whose piece *It's Gonna Rain* incorporated two recorded tracks of a street preacher shouting "It's gonna rain" that ran simultaneously, though slightly out of synch.[13] The piece clearly influenced *My Life in the Bush of Ghosts*.

Even though the album didn't have a massive impact in terms of chart success, it nevertheless influenced a wide range of musicians, including DJ Spooky, who tells us, "Probably my favorite album, looking at early sampling, is *My Life in the Bush of Ghosts*." Working when digital recording technologies had yet to be refined, Eno, Byrne, and their engineers laid down their tracks on analog equipment, synchronizing the vocal "samples" manually. Their stature in the music industry gave Eno and Byrne access to good recording studios and the money to pay for the necessary equipment that allowed them to craft their collages. But for those who could not afford this luxury, a new wave of consumer electronics and home recording equipment allowed a D.I.Y. sound collage scene to bloom during the 1980s.

THE CONTEMPORARY SOUND
COLLAGE UNDERGROUND

I've always seen myself as an editor of life—just by the very fact that I'm cutting, pasting, rearranging, and layering. I like the idea that I'm in control of various elements, putting them together in a way that I don't think they have gone together before.—VICKI BENNETT

The Tape-beatles formed in Iowa City, Iowa, in 1986, though the key members have since relocated to Prague, where they remain active as a creative unit. "When we started we really wanted to do the kind of work that anyone could do in a bedroom," says John Heck, a founding member. "Our sources were radio, television, and vinyl LPs. We had a cassette player, a cassette recorder; we had a simple Sony reel-to-reel tape deck." In the 1980s, home-recording devices became relatively inexpensive and available to more people, which is one of the reasons why sound collage exploded during that time. Lloyd Dunn—another member of the Tape-beatles who also published a highly regarded series of photocopied 'zines titled *Retrofuturism* and *Photostatic*—explains the origins of the group's name as follows: "What we wanted to do was exploit the possibilities of recording and audiotape, and in a sort of cheeky move, to pay homage to the Beatles and their studio recording experiments in the 1960s."

In another mischievous move, the Tape-beatles adopted the phrase "Plagiarism: A Collective Vision" as their de facto motto. They also claimed to have trademarked the word "plagiarism," and, to top it all off, their logo consisted of the AT&T "globe" logo with Mickey Mouse ears attached.[14] Although the Tape-beatles were certainly aware of avant-garde sound collage traditions, Dunn says that their attitudes and positions on collage largely stemmed from their engagement with popular culture. He tells us that that "our first impulse in getting together was to form a pop music group that didn't play any instruments." He further describes the Tape-beatles' methodology in a way that echoes statements made by many of the artists we interviewed: "Essentially, we tried to build our work around home stereo equipment, because one of the things that we wanted to say was that this was an egalitarian effort."

Similar in spirit to the Tape-beatles, the West Coast sound collage collective Negativland began self-releasing records in 1980. Mark Hosler, the group's unofficial spokesperson, tells us that they were simply teenagers reacting to a media-soaked environment. "There was also something that was really appealing to us about taking sounds from our world around us. And this wasn't an intellectual thing, and it wasn't a political thing," Hosler says. "I was only sixteen years old. It just sounded really cool . . . and there was something that was really appealing about taking things out of their context, and putting them in a new context." Being mostly teenagers when the group first got together (aside from Don Joyce, who is older than the other members), Negativland initially didn't know much about avant-garde composers like Cage, Tenney, and Schaeffer.

"I was doing radio first, before Negativland," Joyce says. "I was kind of into the whole idea of taking things and editing them, using them in some new way. And then Negativland came along and it fit right in." His radio show *Over the Edge* began in 1981 at the Berkeley-area station KPFA, which broadcasts at 59,000 watts and covers half the state of California. As Hosler recounts, "KPFA had all kinds of reel-to-reels, tape decks and turntables, and auxiliary inputs and mixers, and extra studios with microphones and you could put callers on the air." After absorbing Joyce into the group, Negativland took full advantage of the radio station and its equipment. "Immediately, we just started playing four records at once and turning everything backwards, and stopping and starting stuff, and bringing in tape loops, and putting the phone callers on the air," says Hosler. Today, Negativland has over two-dozen CD releases to their name—including the classic *Escape from Noise* from 1987—and they continue to broadcast the longest-running free-form radio show in North America.

Compared to his contemporaries, the Canadian composer John Oswald took the appropriation of popular works to an extreme, at least with regard to the quantity of sources he draws upon. His work recalls James Tenney's *Collage #1 (Blue Suede)*, in that Oswald recombines recognizable segments of well-known songs in an unapologetic manner, a method he calls "plunderphonics."[15] The point of the plunderphonic technique is to create some sort of recognition before the musical segment cuts out and another brief sample is introduced—thereby causing some sort of confusion, disorientation, or cognitive dissonance. Since the mid-1980s, Oswald has released several plunderphonic works, the most interesting of which is *Plexure* (1993). The album's artwork is a visual collage of the album covers for Bruce Springsteen's *Born in the USA*, Bobby Brown's *Bobby*, and Garth Brooks's *The Chase*. This combination creates a sort of pop-music Frankenstein's monster, which in turn acts as a metaphor for the compositions contained within. For this work Oswald plundered hundreds of Top 40 songs from the 1980s and 1990s and pieced them together like a jigsaw puzzle to produce a jarring but flowing nineteen-minute CD.

Like the artists mentioned above, or perhaps more so, the British collage artist Vicki Bennett balances her avant-garde sensibilities with a dose of goofiness. As the British experimental-music magazine *The Wire* observes, "Unlike others working in similar audio-collage terrain, her work largely sidesteps the opportunity for social commentary (think back to such classics of the genre as Steinski & Mass Media's 'The Motorcade Sped On' or Negativland's *Escape From Noise*) and plunges instead into a freeform, unfolding imaginary landscape that is liberally peppered with slapstick."[16] Bennett—who performs under the name People Like Us—demolishes the demarcations between high and low culture as well as "seriousness" and "humor" in music. As Negativland's Mark Hosler observes, "A great example is Vicki Bennett's work, People Like Us. Her work tends to be wacky and weird and goofy and fun to listen to, and not so clearly a critique of anything in the way I think our work is."

Today, Bennett works with both sound and moving images, but when she began doing collage work around 1989 she realized that analog video editing suites were financially far out of her reach. Video was not yet something one could do on a home computer, which is perhaps another reason why sound collage exploded before its moving-image equivalent. As a result, she says, "I defaulted to sound and bought an Amiga computer," referring to the brand popular among computer enthusiasts in Europe. By chance, the person who sold her the computer had already installed sound programs on it, including a piece of "tracker" software that functioned as a sequencer that could arrange samples. "So I bought a cartridge sampler and started working with samples, and at the same time I was working with a mixer and doing lots of layered sounds." It was around this time that she began listening to collage-based works by artists like Nurse With Wound and Negativland. "I wasn't aware of any movement going on," Bennett says. "That was before the days of the Internet, when it wasn't so easy to do a search of things."

Today's sound collage underground is diverse and decentralized, with many individuals doing similar work. As such, this section should be understood as a brief overview—a sampling, so to speak—of some of the more notable figures that have emerged in the past quarter century. A full accounting of this scene would need to include Wobbly, Evolution Control Committee, and several others. For brevity we will close the section with another British artist, Robin Rimbaud, who is better known as Scanner. Rimbaud chose his stage name because he began his sound-art career by sampling cellular telephone conversations, shortwave radio broadcasts, and other ephemera snatched from the airwaves with a scanner.[17] Like many of the underground sound collage artists we interviewed, Scanner tells us pop music and the avant-garde influenced him equally. "I think there's been a very clear link between the more academic compositional world of collage and the popular music world," Scanner says. "I've grown up living between the two. I grew up listening to awful glam rock records that my brother played me, and Beatles records. In listening to my more experimental music, I realized there was a relationship between the two. There's a very clear relationship."

"SAMPLING" IN OTHER CONTEXTS

> Look at how every great poet made culture, how Homer
> made culture. It's all about collage. It's about taking the bits and
> pieces of your influences and forging them into something
> newer and stronger.—SIVA VAIDHYANATHAN

Musical borrowing practices touch many areas of cultural life, and thus go far beyond the rarified worlds of avant-garde sound collage. "The thing that's really interesting about sampling is that we all do it," argues Jeff Chang, author of *Can't Stop Won't Stop* and other books on music and culture. "We'll pick up a catch phrase, or we'll hear a song and we might sing it again on the street, or that kind of thing. And the technology has allowed us to be able to immediately go to those source thoughts, source ideas, source moments, and to actually work with them creatively." Matt Black, co-founder of the seminal British cut-and-paste group Coldcut, believes that sampling operates as a metaphor for the way people participate with culture more broadly. "You could say that humans are just sampling machines," he tells us. "We all learn by taking in what we hear and see and trying to imitate it, and output it again. That's how we learn to speak. That's how we learn to paint and make music as well."

We can find plenty of evidence of musical borrowing in the European classical and art-music tradition. Brahms's First Symphony borrowed musical phrases from Beethoven's Ninth Symphony. After listeners noted the strong resemblance between the middle strain of the main theme of the finale to his symphony and the middle strain of Beethoven's "Ode to Joy," Brahms snapped, "Any jackass can see that." One can also hear elements of Beethoven's Ninth in Mendelssohn's *Lobgesang*, as well as in a great deal of Wagner's body of work. And in composing the introduction to his Third Symphony, Mahler swiped a major theme from Brahms's Beethoven-biting First Symphony—converting it into minor mode but keeping the melodic structure intact. When someone pointed out to Mahler the fact that those two pieces were so similar, he echoed Brahms's earlier retort by saying, "Any fool can hear that."[18]

The hip-hop journalist and activist Harry Allen states, "I've never heard a completely original musical idea, *from anyone*. Most musicians will say that the best musicians copy." Debussy was another composer who is widely acknowledged to have borrowed heavily, such as in "Golliwog's Cakewalk" from his *Children's Corner* suite (1906–1908). By cutting and pasting, and by moving back and forth between American ragtime music and Wagner's *Tristan*, Debussy's piece anticipates the "postmodern" forms of composition that would become common by the late twentieth century.[19] The composer Charles Ives, in his *Flanders Field* (1917), set John McCrae's wartime poem "Flanders Fields" to music that interpolated several songs familiar to Ives's audience: "Marseillaise," "America," and "Columbia, Gem of the Ocean." As Glenn Watkins writes of the listening experience: "Memory, nostalgia, and fantasy potentially flood the listener, and composite citation encourages intertextual interpretation without freezing the message."[20]

Igor Stravinsky often borrowed from traditional folk music, particularly in his work *Le Sacre du printemps* (1911–1913). In Watkins's book *Pyramids at the Louvre*, he quotes Stravinsky as saying, "Whatever interests me, whatever I love, I wish to make it my own."[21] The anxiety that haunts many modern artists—an anxiety that they are actually creating nothing new under the sun—is something that has been pervasive within Western culture during the last two centuries. Stravinsky confronted this "anxiety of influence" by using in his own work methods of adoptive transformation and appropriation. In his autobiography *My Musical Life* an irritated Stravinsky addressed music critics who, "having noticed, both in *The Snow Maiden* and *May Night*, two or three melodies borrowed from collections of folksongs (to notice they were powerless, as they were ill-acquainted with folk creation), proclaimed me incapable of creating my own melodies."[22]

Stravinsky was one of many European composers who borrowed from folk melodies. Another notable appropriator was Johannes Brahms, who was quite obsessed with the songs of his youth. He arranged well over two hundred folk tunes in his lifetime, and some of these melodies found their way into his art song compositions, such as *Sehnsucht*. Brahms's most significant and highly regarded use of folk song material was his *Deutsche Volkslieder* for voice and piano. The biographer Malcolm MacDonald writes that they are "a series of miniature masterpieces worthy to stand with any of his art songs of the same period."[23] Brahms loved these little works as much as his major compositions, perhaps more so.

Walter Ong, in his classic book *Orality and Literacy*, argues that print culture attempts to close off intertextuality by emphasizing the importance of a pure text that is supposedly untainted by the influence of other texts.[24] Of course, this is an impossibility—a fiction generated by this anxiety of influence. Traditional folk singers, for instance, did not share this uneasiness about the "originality" of the songs they performed; there was no framework in which they could even conceive of such a thing.

The impulse to appropriate from—and intervene in—popular culture was prominent in the folk music that emerged in the first half of the twentieth century. By recycling folk melodies and adding his acerbic words to them, Woody Guthrie fought for the rights of workers and battled the rich folks through song. As Guthrie wrote in his journal of song ideas, for example: "Tune of 'Will the Circle Be Unbroken'— will the union stay unbroken. Needed: a sassy tune for a scab song." In another episode, Guthrie discovered that a Baptist hymn performed by the Carter Family, "This World Is Not My Home," was popular in migrant farm worker camps. But he felt the lyrics were politically counterproductive. The song didn't deal with the day-to-day miseries forced upon workers by the capitalist class but instead told them they'd be rewarded for their patience in the next life. It was basically telling the workers to accept hunger and pain and not fight back.

For Guthrie that innocent-sounding song was evil and insidious, so he mocked and parodied the original. He kept the melody and reworked the words to comment on the material conditions of the world that many suffered through.[25] The result, "I Ain't Got No Home," is a great example of how appropriation—stealing, borrowing, whatever you want to call it—is a creative act that can have a political and social impact. Woody Guthrie and other folksingers drew from the culture that surrounded them and transformed, reworked, and remixed it in order to write songs that motivated the working class to fight for a dignified life. Instead of passively consuming and regurgitating the Tin Pan Alley songs that were popular during the day, Guthrie and other folk singers created, re-created, and commented on culture in an attempt to change the world around them.

Similarly, during Medieval European carnivals, peasants would sing street songs to the tune of serious church hymns. Christmas carols also became fodder for secular songs that sometimes ridiculed those in power.[26] Of course, parodies aren't always so high minded. There is a long tradition in many folk music traditions of irreverent and silly appropriations, especially in some strains of Yiddish American music. Mickey Katz was a parodist whose professional peak in the United States occurred in the 1950s, when he recorded a series of "anarchistic, irreverent, and wildly ethnic klezmer parodies of mid-century popular songs," as Joshua Kun writes in *Audiotopia*.[27] For instance, Katz transformed the country singer Tennessee Ernie Ford's hit "Sixteen Tons" (1955) into an ode to kosher delis—"You load sixteen tons of hot salami / Corned beef, rolled beef, and hot pastrami."

The Jewish singer also rewrote Patti Page's "Doggie in the Window" by turning it into another deli-themed ditty, "Pickle in the Window."[28] Even though Katz's spoofs were whimsical, there was an element of resistance in his songs—particularly the anti-assimilationist streak that was evident in his parodies. Kun writes that not only did they "work at the level of lyrics, they also involved significant Jewish musical interruptions of pop style. Typically about halfway through each parody, Katz would overturn whatever style he was playing and suddenly lead his band, without any warning to the listener, into a spirited klezmer *freilach*." He then adds, "These jarring, often violent klezmer 'breaks,' not at all unlike the role of the break in jazz or hip-hop, served as loud Jewish musical ruptures within the pop structure and style of each song."[29]

THE BLACK ATLANTIC

> You can also look at the blues and, for that matter, you can look at anything. Melodies have always been borrowed.—SAUL WILLIAMS

The practice of appropriation is an important aspect of African American music, from blues and jazz music to the black folk-preaching tradition that reaches back two centuries. Within these cultures, music and words were treated as communal wealth, not private property. African American religious music, from its very beginnings, was built on borrowing—whether in speaking of Sister Rosetta Tharpe or anonymous church singers lost to time. The ethnomusicologist Cheryl Keyes writes that during the trans-Atlantic slave trade, Africans were forced to learn a new culture and language: "In the face of this alien context, blacks transformed the new culture and language of the Western world through an African prism."[30] For instance, slaves commonly fused African folk melodies with the Christian lyrics forced upon them by their white owners, allowing them to create the appearance of assimilation while secretly holding onto elements of their culture.[31]

Oral tradition was central to African American culture partly because American laws forbade slaves from learning to read or write; as such it contributed to the ethic of sharing in various forms of black music. It's doubtful that blues artists such as Leadbelly "wrote" every single song for which they were assigned a copyright; Leadbelly's song "In the Pines," for instance, has antecedents in the nineteenth century.[32] John Lee Hooker's "Crawlin' King Snake" was based on a recording by Tony Hollins made in 1941, which was in turn rooted in a song that Blind Lemon Jefferson recorded in 1926, "That Black Snake Moan."[33] And Willie Dixon in his autobiography described how Chuck Berry's "Maybellene" was based on a country song named "Ida Red." Dixon convinced Berry to simply change "the country & western pace" of the original and give it more of a rhythm and blues feel. With that slight change, the song became Berry's first hit.[34]

Jeff Chang talks about the tradition of quoting that is rooted within African American music. "I think sampling is in line with that tradition," he says. "You've got new generations of artists quoting older generations of artists, just to show that they've got the knowledge, the bona fides, to be a part of the culture." Sampling is also an extension of the call-and-response tradition; it's a kind of musical dialogue that has existed within African American music for centuries. Invoking this call-and-response tradition, the pioneering hip-hop DJ Grandmaster Flash once described the work of the DJ as a dialogic act: "That's what mixing two songs together felt like," says Flash. "A question and an answer. One song would ask, the next one would respond."[35] And Jeff Chang adds that "sampling itself is an embodiment of this active process of engaging with history."

Musicians who were part of the African diaspora not only copied each other's musical ideas but also did so across geographic boundaries. Paul Gilroy in his book *The Black Atlantic* argues that music is one of the key vehicles of cultural exchange—one that is both multidirectional and dialogic. Members of the African diaspora who were spread across the Atlantic regions of North and South America, Western Europe, and Africa have been "listening in" and responding to each other for years.

For example, American jazz musicians imported the styles of Brazilian bossa nova in the late 1950s; for another, Nigerian Afro-beat pioneer Fela Kuti borrowed from James Brown's funk experiments of the late 1960s (which, in turn, had their roots in African rhythms).

Referring to Gilroy's concept of the Black Atlantic, Christopher Dunn writes in *Brutality Garden*—his book on the Brazilian musical movement from the 1960s named Tropicália—that "together with Cuba, Jamaica, and the United States, Brazil has been a key producer and receiver of musical forms of the Afro-Atlantic world."[36] There is a long tradition of appropriation in Brazilian music and culture, which has a lot to do with the nation's diverse religious and cultural influences being drawn from European, African, and indigenous groups. This ethic of appropriation found its most vivid expression in the modernist Brazilian poet Oswald de Andrade's "Manifesto Antropófago," or "Cannibalist Manifesto," first published in 1928. In it, Andrade argued for an aesthetic strategy that devoured both foreign and domestic cultural texts, transforming them in the process.

The cannibalism metaphor resonated within Brazil for many decades afterward. The Brazilian singer Caetano Veloso claimed that Tropicália, the musical movement that brought him to fame, was a kind of "neo-cannibalism" that emerged within, and commented on, the turbulent period of the late 1960s.[37] The collectively created album *Tropicália, ou panis et circencis* (1968) was an aural pastiche that combined the talents of Veloso, Gilberto Gil, Gal Costa, and the eccentric rock-fusion group Os Mutantes. "Instead of working as a group in order to develop a homogeneous sound that would define a new style," Veloso says in explaining the ideas that underpinned the album, "we preferred to utilize several recognizable sounds from commercial music, making the arrangements an independent element that would clarify the song, but also clash with it. In a way, we sought to 'sample' musical scraps and we used the arrangements as ready-mades."[38] Discussing both Tropicália and contemporary Brazilian music, David Byrne points out:

> They're not the only ones to [appropriate]. Uniquely, though, they made it transparent, visible, and part of the content. You can hear the bricolage happening. I think in many countries you had a generation who grew up with both the local and sometimes traditional music and also the music of the multinational corporations—the Anglo pop tradition that for some time

dominated the globe. They love elements of both: of rock, techno, tango and samba, and they feel free to mix them all together. It flows every which way too, with their recordings influencing the rest of the world as well.

As Alexander Weheliye writes in his book *Phonographies*, "By enabling disparate audiences in a variety of locations to consume black music, sound technologies assured that local calls and responses would differ according to spatio-temporal coordinates, facilitating the emergence and reconfiguration of numerous cultural practices. The phonograph's recalibration of locality effected changes in its relation to other vicinities rather than erasing the local altogether."[39] It is in this sense that American hip-hop, jazz, and blues are deeply connected to 1960s Brazilian pop, 1970s Jamaican reggae, and 1990s jungle (a British subgenre of dance music that featured what are essentially sped-up hip-hop breakbeats dosed with a strong West Indian influence). All are elements of this "Black Atlantic."

Jamaican reggae, in absorbing many influences and, importantly, heavily influencing other forms of music, is significant in its tendency toward boundary crossing. Hip-hop was directly shaped by the aural innovations of dub, which is a largely instrumental version of reggae that created the template for the modern remix. In dub, the studio engineer— including those such as Lee "Scratch" Perry, King Tubby, or Scientist— is as much a composer or creator as the guitarist, vocalist, bassist, or drummer who recorded the song. These producer-engineers invented "versioning," which in Jamaican music refers to the practice of releasing different versions of an original recording. This is done by dropping out or reworking the vocals and instrumentation on a soundboard's mixer, extending certain sections of the song, and sonically reinventing other elements of a recording through the use of various gadgets and effects pedals.

The "versions" created by the Jamaican producer-engineers were then disseminated to popular reggae DJs, such as U-Roy, who played them at their parties. Jamaican sound systems were mobile parties that moved from place to place on the island, and the center of attention was the DJ, who often served as an MC as well. For instance, they "toasted" (a precursor to rapping) over the versions and mixed them up with other records they spun. Other musicians and producers regularly copied these versions, and they often scored hits that were little more than slightly modified renditions of a previously released song. The proliferation of these versions had as much to do with Jamaica's very loose copyright laws at the time as it did with the musical culture from which reggae sprang. As Chuck D tells us, "The whole Jamaican reggae vibe is about how that rhythm doesn't really belong to anybody, but belongs to *everybody*. Same thing in hip-hop. There are some rhythms that kind of belong to everybody and not just one person, you know?"

The reggae artist Mikey Dread explains that even in the "Wild West" that was the Jamaican record industry—especially when dub reggae emerged in the 1970s—producers, artists, and labels feared piracy of their own work. They were nervous about releasing a pure instrumental record because someone else would almost certainly come along and re-release it with new vocals on top of it, getting a free ride. "So they have to put something somewhere in the dub," Dread says. "You don't want a man to take your riddim and go voice it straight like it's his—you have to put your trademark in there to stop the pirates!"[40]

Deeply intertwined are the rise of dub—with its infinite versions— and the ascendancy of the hip-hop DJ. "Versioning is still a central practice of Jamaican pop," the musicologist Michael Veal writes. "As in hip-hop, digital sampling of older music plays an important role in Jamaican music, with the canonized musical gestures of the 1960s and 1970s (horn riffs, the trademark drum rolls of roots-era drummers, or the exclamations of particular DJs) reappearing to provide formal punctuation, timbral variation, and de facto historical grounding."[41] The journalist Greg Tate tells us that there were many Jamaican immigrants in New York City, and he notes that DJ Kool Herc brought this sound-system culture with him from Jamaica to the South Bronx. The participants in hip-hop culture in New York City and reggae culture in Kingston were listening to each other, though the cultural flow from Jamaica into the United States was more pronounced.

Dub reggae also fundamentally altered the British music scene beginning in the 1970s—yet another cultural flow within the Black Atlantic. "We have a huge West Indian community," says DJ Vadim, speaking of the Caribbean immigrants who settled in London, where he now lives. During the 1970s, reggae influenced musicians working in other genres; take, for instance, Eric Clapton's cover of Bob Marley's "I Shot the Sheriff" or the Clash's punk-reggae fusions. In England, a prominent sound-system culture was imported from Jamaica, where

DJs toasted over reggae instrumentals in outdoor parties. "I'm not saying England invented hip-hop," says DJ Vadim, "but I'm saying it came across to England very easily. We have such a huge black music scene in London, it's such a cosmopolitan city."

THE HIP-HOP DJ AND THE ORIGINS
OF DIGITAL SAMPLING

By ignoring the rules, hip-hop artists came up with a whole
new way of thinking about music.—DJ SPOOKY

In the early days of hip-hop a few important DJs had large followings in each of their districts throughout the South Bronx. The Jamaican immigrant DJ Kool Herc was the most popular of these early hip-hop DJs in the 1970s. He is credited with developing and elaborating upon two new musical methods that others would emulate.[42] Herc isolated the percussive breaks (known as breakbeats) that were popular with dancers, and he mixed them into one long musical collage. "Essentially what they were all doing is they were beat miners," Greg Tate tells us. "They were mining old records for those break sections."

T La Rock, a DJ and MC who lived in the South Bronx during the 1970s, explains to us that breakbeats are "the really funky part of the record. It was isolated in the middle of the whole song, and we would look for that one particular part in the record." He says that they would buy two copies of the same record, and then mix the two records back and forth. "Once the breakbeat ended, we used what's called a cross fader on the mixer to bring in the same beat," T La Rock says in explaining how DJs would use their electronic gear to go back and forth between the music on two turntables. "That's how we extended the breakbeats and made a longer piece." He tells us that these hip-hop DJ events happened at local parties they threw in the streets and parks, as well as in community centers. "Just picture an apartment building with a community center on the first floor, in the back where the kids would go and hang out," he says. "We would play in places like that, and also apartments. Sometimes it would be somebody's birthday party or something like that, and other times it would just be an empty apartment."

There was another creative practice that complemented the DJ's method of cutting up music: the "pause tape." T La Rock says that before he and his friends got their hands on two turntables and a mixer, they would use a cassette deck with a pause button to string breakbeats together. "Once that breakbeat plays, we would stop it, pause it, bring the needle back to the beginning of that breakbeat, pause it, and then release the pause so that the breakbeat would keep playing." Whether it was cassette decks, turntables, or—later—digital samplers, hip-hop artists made their electronic equipment do things for which the equipment was not originally intended, opening up new creative possibilities in the process.

Even if they were not formally trained on a traditional instrument, the best of the early hip-hop artists knew a lot about music. DJ Kool Herc, for instance, had an encyclopedic knowledge of breakbeats as well as a music collection and booming sound system to match. He tells us, "I quickly realized that those breakbeats were making the crowd go crazy. So I just started digging deeper and deeper into my record collection, ya know? As long as I kept the beat going with the best parts of those records, everybody would keep dancing. And the culture just evolved from that." As a very complicated form of musicianship, DJ-ing requires a great amount of dexterity. Harry Allen reminds us that DJs work within a very small amount of space on a vinyl record, which means that they can't be off by millimeters: "We're talking about very tiny distances on a record," he emphasizes.

As MC Eyedea, one half of the duo Eyedea & Abilities, observes, "The turntable is the newest instrument. Turntables are more rhythmically complex than any other instrument, based on the fact that what you can do with a fader and your hand playing at the same time." Other DJs who built on Kool Herc's innovations began expanding the possibilities that two turntables could offer—particularly Grandmaster Flash, who went even further than Kool Herc in his turntable wizardry.[43] Starting in 1974, Flash attended every Kool Herc party he could, and he carefully observed Herc to try to figure out what the master DJ was doing right, and wrong. "It hit me," Flash remembers, "whatever Herc was doing, he wasn't doing it on time. One song dropped out, but it wasn't on the right beat with the next one. He would pick up the needle and drop it on the vinyl—first on one turntable and then on the next—taking a chance that he would land on the break."[44]

Flash understood the dancers' need for the beat to stay on time, and so he figured out how to apply his engineering and electronics skills to fix this problem. "A simple toggle switch let me hear what was on each turntable," said Flash. "At school, we called it a SPDT—single pole, double throw—switch. I didn't have one on my mixer, so I took some crazy glue and glued one on." This allowed Flash to, as he put it at the time, "lock these beats up and keep the shit going!"[45] But in order to keep the beats flowing, they needed records.

The hip-hop DJs of the South Bronx scored their beats from a variety of obscure sources, including a small specialty store in New York City named Downtown Records. Located in the Forty-Second Street and Sixth Avenue subway station, it had "a million records in a million different places," as Grandmaster Flash put it.[46] He remembers there were records in the bins, racks, stacks, shelves, counters, walls, ceiling, and in boxes and crates: modern jazz, sound effects records, oldies, and more. "Everywhere I turned, there was something cool I couldn't get in the Bronx—white boy music like the Steve Miller Band and Spooky Tooth, Jeff Beck and Steely Dan . . . talk about righteous beats! Crazy beats from the Philippines and India with sounds I didn't know a human being could make."[47]

Another legendary DJ who frequented that store was Afrika Bambaataa. "If you've ever had the fortune to see Afrika Bambaataa mix," says Greg Tate, you'll see "the way he can move between bits and pieces of records and create these incredible medleys in a short period of time." Grandmaster Flash marvels at the depth of Bambaataa's record collection and musical knowledge. During parties on the Bronx's East Side, Bambaataa would throw on the *Pink Panther* theme song, but with a drum beat underneath, and he could get the crowd moving to the Rolling Stones, Aerosmith, the Beatles, Grand Funk Railroad, Led Zeppelin, and even the Monkees. As Flash recalls, "Then he'd play five songs in a row that would have you scratching your head, saying: *'Who the hell was that?'*"[48]

Tom Silverman, who would go on to release Afrika Bambaataa's "Planet Rock" and dozens of other hip-hop classics on his label Tommy Boy Records, recalls the first night he saw Bambaataa rock the crowd:

> I heard about Afrika Bambaataa in 1979 through a record store, Downtown Records, which was down in the subway station in Times Square. I used to go there because they had a great doo-wop section, a great oldies collection, and they had opened a new room called "the breakbeat room." It was a tiny

room and there was a record player, and a young guy named Roy would play records there for the kids that would come in. They were great records like "Scorpio" by Dennis Coffee, or the Eagles' "The Long Run." There were all different kinds of records—some were rock records and some were pop records and some of them were R&B and funk records. Kids would come in, two or three at a time, and they'd chip in and they'd buy a bunch of records. And they were *expensive*. And these kids were coming in from the Bronx and chipping in all their money together to buy records as a team so they could share the records. I asked them, "How do you know about these records and why are you buying them?" They said, "Because we DJ." They said, "There's this guy in the Bronx whose name is Afrika Bambaataa."

So I asked around, and Bambaataa used to buy records there too. Roy and some other people told me about him and that he DJ-ed a certain night of the week at this club called the T-Connection on White Plains Road. So I went up to hear him in the Bronx. . . . There was a stairway against the wall that went up to a balcony, and up on the balcony was Afrika Bambaataa with his DJ setup. On one side of him was Jazzy Jay and on the other side was DJ Red Alert, and they were handing him records he would ask for. I went closer and said hello to him and watched what he was doing. I was looking at the records, and half of them had the label steamed off so you couldn't see what they were—or they had tape over them—and some of them had little pin marks in different places on the record so they knew where to put the needle down. He played "Big Beat" by Billy Squire, which is sort of a big arena rock guy, and Kraftwerk, which was kind of electronic new wave. And to hear that in the Bronx in front of an all-black young crowd was very surprising; it was mind blowing to hear and see these kids totally appreciating every kind of music. Then Bambaataa cut in "Mary Mary" by the Monkees, and I said, "Wow, is there anything this guy won't play?"

The working methods of DJs like Afrika Bambaataa illustrate the analogous relationship between selector and composer, between turntablist and instrumentalist. The legal scholar Imani Perry argues that this practice produces what can be thought of as a metacomposition, one that stretches across the course of an evening.[49] "To Herc, a DJ set was one continuous piece of music," Grandmaster Flash observes in his autobiography. "My man was composing something. And if he was a composer, that went for me too. I went home and reexamined my records; how did Bob James connect to James Brown? Would Mongo

Santamaria work with the Meters? I'd hear a piece of one song and a piece of another and would imagine the two pieces playing over each other. Or one right after another—*on time*."[50] Disco DJs obsessed about the same things.

DISCO AND THE RISE OF THE REMIX

A lot of disco remixes were mash-ups, right?—DREW DANIEL

As in hip-hop, being a good disco DJ hinged on how smoothly and creatively one could segue from one song to another. With two turntables and a mixer, the early disco DJ Francis Grasso of The Sanctuary would blend the beats together, allowing the music to flow from song to song, forming a larger whole. That whole formed a dynamic relationship between the DJ, the crowd, and the music.[51] Other pioneering disco DJs like David Mancuso, who presided over The Loft, shared similarly eclectic tastes with hip-hop DJs like Afrika Bambaataa, DJ Kool Herc, and Grandmaster Flash. Mancuso approached music with open ears, mixing together disparate genres with only one thought in mind: Will the song make people dance? He threw into this musical stew Rare Earth (Motown's first white act), the soulfully psychedelic music of the Temptations (from their late-1960s and early-1970s period), War (and other Latin-influenced acts), and the polyrhythmic Afro-pop of Olatunji.[52]

Francis Grasso probably had more of an impact on disco and the art of mixing than anyone else. He viewed songs not as self-contained entities but as parts of a blended, nightlong set—an experience that links the DJ, the dancers, and the music together within a space and across time. He pioneered beat matching—the act of synchronizing the tempos of two different songs to create a seamless mix from one song to the other.[53] By today's standards, or even the standards of the late 1970s, the early disco DJs had only primitive equipment at their disposal. When disco was in its prime, computers were large machines that filled whole rooms in office buildings; they were not designed to edit music. The DJs mixed the music live, manually—with two turntables, a mixer, and some imagination. There were no pitch controls on the turntables to allow DJs to bend tempos and create transitions from one song to another. So Grasso had to invent creative workarounds, such as manually slowing a record's speed with his finger.[54]

One way Grasso transformed dance music was by using two copies of the same record to seamlessly switch back and forth between the same song—moving from one section to another without missing a beat. Another technique that Grasso introduced to the dance club world, one that is still used by hip-hop DJs today, is the "slip cue." Typically, a mat sits between the rotating turntable and the record itself, allowing the DJ to manually hold the record stationary as the turntable rotates beneath it. That way, a DJ can release a record at a precise time, on an exact beat.[55] Some disco DJs also used reel-to-reel tapes to "edit" or reconstruct songs—kind of like the hip-hop pause tapes created by T La Rock and others in the South Bronx during this era. On tape they prerecorded cross fades, segues, and mixes to supplement what they did on the turntables but in ways that would be impossible to pull off live.

As with dub reggae pioneers such as King Tubby or Lee "Scratch" Perry, early disco DJs were among the first to popularize the notion that there was nothing permanent or fixed about an original recording.[56] Of course, recording studio engineers had previously mixed and remixed songs, but the key difference was that consumers—not elite engineers hired by a band or record company—could now participate in reworking a song. By the late 1970s, the standard dance music tropes of extended mixes—elongated introductions, fade-outs, and instrumental or percussive breaks—made their way from the disco DJ booth to record stores in the form of twelve-inch singles. The difference between twelve-inch singles and the traditional seven-inch ones—which had dominated the singles market for the previous thirty years—wasn't simply in the amount of music each format held. Indeed, the twelve-inch single also embodied a very different philosophy about how music could be consumed.

Music released on seven-inch singles was typically composed and recorded for the needs of commercial radio, which meant that a song had to be short enough for radio program directors to fit in many songs per hour. The twelve-inch single format—with its extended percussion breaks, dynamic shifts in melodies, and wider grooves that could make the bass go boom—is tailored for dancers who want to be pushed to the limits of exhaustion and euphoria.[57] "Take a record like [Dennis Coffey's] 'Scorpio,' which had this fantastic drum beat," says The Loft's David Mancuso. "We'd always mix it back and forth, take a really good break, and make it longer. That's where a twelve-inch came into play. The record companies could take a record and extend it and give the people what they wanted."[58] Twelve-inch singles steadily gained in popularity throughout the 1970s, especially after Tavares released its crossover hit "Heaven Must Be Missing an Angel" on this format. Many others followed, like the Walter Gibbons–remixed version of Double Exposure's "Ten Percent," which reworked the original three-minute version into a nine-minute mix filled with percussive beats and long instrumental passages. This formula became a staple of the twelve-inch format.

Tom Moulton was another remix innovator who helped change the complexion of pop music. Even though Moulton wasn't a DJ, he was nevertheless familiar with what went down in dance clubs, because he was a regular at discos on Fire Island and in New York City. There, he paid attention to what made the dancers go crazy, what bored them, and what gave the denizens of the dance floor a much-deserved break. He deconstructed songs by boosting the hooks, lengthening instrumental passages, building layers of rhythms that beefed up the percussion breaks, and other tricks. Moulton made his first major mark on the music industry when he remixed three relatively short songs into a lengthy medley of Gloria Gaynor's first album, *Never Can Say Goodbye*. The mix spanned the entirety of side two. Moulton dropped another musical bomb when he reworked a legendary disco-funk track by the B.T. Express, "Do It (Til You're Satisfied)," by extending the song from its original three-minute running time to a six-minute jam.

Moulton combined the instincts of a music fan with the sophistication of a studio engineer. On his remix of Dan Hartman's "Instant Replay," for instance, he added sonic flourishes like whirring background sound effects, treated vocals, the inevitable percussive build to a climax, and an unforgettable instrumental break section. He brought out the best in the original recording by, for instance, using the drum breaks as a structuring transition from one section to the other. And Moulton's remix of Andrea True Connection's "More, More, More" is the man at his personal best. Midway through the song, he dropped the vocals and virtually all the instruments out of the mix, leaving just percussion, bass, and piano. For those seven seconds, we hear an electrifying break, one that was sampled, looped, and used as the foundation of the Canadian pop group Len's hit from 2000, "Steal My Sunshine." Arguably the most compelling part of "More, More, More" wasn't part of the song as it was originally recorded—it came instead from Moulton's remix.

Not only were [samplers] expensive, but they were limited in what they could do—they could only sample two seconds at a time.—CHUCK D

Given hip-hop's collage-heavy roots, it is fitting that the first recorded rap song—the Sugarhill Gang's hit from 1979, "Rapper's Delight"—borrowed heavily from a disco song that was popular that summer. As hip-hop shifted from a live medium to a recorded one, "Rapper's Delight" significantly influenced and altered the way hip-hop sounded. Before its release, hip-hop music was made by DJs spinning and manipulating records while the MC spit rhymes. For their hit song, the Sugarhill Gang used a studio band that replayed the basic instrumental track from Chic's disco hit, "Good Times." It technically wasn't a sample of the original sound recording, for "Rapper's Delight" features what would later be called a "replay." Nevertheless, it provoked a lawsuit against the Sugarhill Gang—something that underscores how copyright conflicts have been embedded in the DNA of hip-hop since the very beginning of its recorded existence.

For about four years, "Rapper's Delight" provided the blueprint for how to make a hip-hop record.[59] With the exception of "Adventures of Grandmaster Flash on the Wheels of Steel"—which exclusively used records as its source material—the live, funk-band sound dominated. This fundamentally changed when Run-DMC put out their debut single in 1982. This hip-hop group stripped down the music to simple drum-machine beats, sparse keyboard embellishments, bass lines, scratch sounds, and the occasional live rock guitar. In doing so, they changed the way recorded hip-hop music was produced. Additionally, Run-DMC was among the first groups to overtly use a DJ on a hip-hop record. If you listen closely to their song "Peter Piper," you can hear the pops and crackles of a vinyl record, which was unheard of before hip-hop rewrote the rules of popular music.[60] Run-DMC effectively pushed hip-hop into its next evolutionary stage, where the act of cutting preexisting records into a new recording was embraced, and made transparent. It was the next step toward the era of digital sampling.

"What happened at that time was that a bunch of things collided, which together changed pop music," says Coldcut's Matt Black. "The invention of house music was one of those things. The idea that DJs could make records was another thing. And, the advent of cheap technology like sequencers and samplers was probably the single most significant factor." Still, Black notes that samplers were quite expensive in the early 1980s, and only well-off musicians could afford them. As Public Enemy's Hank Shocklee recalls, "I think at the time the only thing that could capture a sample or a recording was in a keyboard called the Synclavier, and that was a $300,000 machine. The only way you could get access to one was in professional recording studios." Soon, however, those prices dropped. Harry Allen reported in 1988 that the Akai S-900 cost $2,500, and the sampling drum machine the Emu SP1200—which is to hip-hop producers what the Fender guitar is to rock bands—went for about $3,000.[61]

The Wu-Tang Clan's production mastermind RZA remembers that, by 1988, hip-hop producers were increasingly using samplers, "but as usual," he remembers, "I couldn't afford one."[62] Although $3,000 is much less than $300,000, it was still far out of reach for many aspiring hip-hop producers. In the late 1980s RZA obtained his first sampler—a department-store machine made by Casio, the first model the company put on the market. Speaking to the limitations of the technology at the time, RZA explains that the machine could only store two seconds of sound. To bypass this, he would increase the turntable speed so he could import more musical information into those two seconds, and then slow the playback as much as possible. This degraded the quality of sampled recording but it gave RZA and other producers more time to play with—and it also created a certain "dirty" digital sound that appealed to hip-hop fans and artists at the time, and continues to do so today. "I had a few neighborhood hits like that," RZA recalls.[63]

The Casio SK-1, the mass-market sampler RZA used back in the day, was featured in 1986 on an episode of *The Cosby Show* (on which Stevie Wonder was a guest). "Bill Cosby really jump-started hip-hop culture," half-jokes the Roots' ?uestlove. "That one *Cosby* episode, every well-known producer I know, that's the event that changed their lives, but everybody is just ashamed to say it. That was the first time America got to see a sampler."[64]

Hip-hop artists radically rewired the way that we understand how music can be made, a fact that the hip-hop activist and journalist Harry Allen recognized early on. In 1988, Allen, who is often referred to as Public Enemy's Media Assassin, wrote a prescient piece in the *Village*

Voice titled "Hip-Hop Hi-Tech." In this essay Allen argues that hip-hop is, intrinsically, electronic African American music that speaks to a "particularly modern comfort with, and access to, electronic technology." Discussing the emergence of digital samplers and drum machines in the 1980s, Chuck D tells us that hip-hop artists used these new machines in ways the manufacturers didn't necessarily anticipate. This is a point echoed by Harry Allen when he notes that "hip-hop humanizes technology and makes it tactile. In hip-hop, you make the technology do stuff that it isn't supposed to do."[65] This can only be achieved with technological know-how, a fact that is echoed in a comment from Wu-Tang's RZA, who remarks, "In hip-hop, you must master the technology."[66]

Allen notes that it is fitting that Joseph Saddler—better known as Grandmaster Flash—did not attend a traditional music school to learn his craft. Instead, he went to Samuel Gompers Vocational School to become an electronics technician. "I wasn't interested in the actual making of music," Grandmaster Flash recalls. "Beats and grooves were cool, but I wasn't one of those guys who picked up an instrument and instantly knew what to do. But electronics were different. Electronics drew me in."[67] Flash's comments about making music with an electrical engineer's perspective resonate with something Public Enemy's Hank Shocklee said in 1988, quoted in Allen's *Village Voice* essay: "Who said that musicians are the only ones that can make music?"[68] For many traditional musicians at the time, that statement amounted to heresy.

TECHNOLOGY CHALLENGES PREVIOUS CONCEPTIONS OF CREATIVITY

Sampling is like the color red. It's like saying,
"Is the color red creative?" Well, it is when you use it creatively.
It's not when it's just sitting there.—HARRY ALLEN

When digital samplers first emerged in the 1980s, detractors referred to sampling as "groove robbing" and argued that it was a form of aural plagiarism,[69] or that it was just plain "stealing."[70] As one entertainment lawyer diplomatically said at the time, "It may be flattering to have the underlying works used for sampling purposes, but it's still taking." Another lawyer representing an artist who had been sampled stated that it "is a euphemism in the music industry for what anyone else would call pickpocketing."[71] In addition to the "stealing" allegations, some in the industry threw around a term that packed an even heavier rhetorical punch—namely that sampling was "uncreative." For example, Mark Volman, a member of the rock band from the 1960s named the Turtles (who famously sued De La Soul for sampling his group)—bluntly said, "Sampling is just a longer term for theft . . . Anybody who can honestly say sampling is some sort of creativity has never done anything creative."[72]

The recording artist T. S. Monk, son of the jazz legend Thelonious Monk, emphasizes the amount of work that goes into recording a track that would have an appeal for sampling artists: "We must remember that we are talking about intellectual property when we talk about sampling." He continues by stating:

> I'm a musician, I made R&B hit records in the late seventies and eighties. I did four-month lock-outs at [the recording studio] Hit Factory. What were we doing? We were going over an eight-bar phrase and saying, "Damn should this be on an upbeat? Should it be on a downbeat? Is the bass a little loud, should it come down?" And working and working. So that little eight-bar phrase might have been the result of three or four or five days—or if you talk of a group like Steely Dan, eight or ten months work. I'm talking *work*. I'm talking getting up and going to the studio at 10 o'clock and sitting back and listening to that, and play it again. And take twenty-seven, and take eighty-five, and play it again and mix it. Work, work, work.

Tom Silverman, the founder and CEO of Tommy Boy Records, recalls that during the 1980s "a lot of musicians were really pissed off about sampling. Bob James is another one who didn't like to be sampled, *ever.*" In the late 1980s there was no shortage of traditional musicians who were disturbed by this new musical trend. As the entertainment lawyer Anthony Berman, who was working in the music industry when sampling emerged, remembers, "The view on the traditional side was that sampling is a very lazy way of making music, of songwriting." The engineer Bob Power, who recorded many classic hip-hop albums, recalls that a lot of engineers at the time believed hip-hop simply wasn't music. "I have to say, honestly, I think that there was an unconscious element of racism," Powers says. The technical recording community was a white-boys club then and, to a great extent, still is now. "At the time, I think that a lot of the engineers didn't want to get with what was coming through the door."[73]

These "traditional" musicians, engineers, and other industry figures thought these young upstarts were essentially cheating and not putting any creativity into their music. As Digital Underground's Shock G—whose MTV hit "The Humpty Dance" sampled George Clinton's legendary funk group Parliament-Funkadelic—remembers, "As far as sampling is concerned, a lot of musicians and artists from the past generation thought that our generation wasn't doing enough work." Speaking sympathetically from the perspective of a sampled drummer, Harry Allen observes, "Knowing how long he took to work on that drumbeat, to get that drumbeat to where it was, and you're just going to go— *bink*—and just take it right off the record? It almost seemed rude."

The funk artist Mtume attacked sampling for these very reasons during the 1980s. He referred to it as "Memorex music," invoking both the cassette tape brand and also the specter of a lazy new generation of artists who simply hit the *record* button to make their music. This criticism from Mtume and other older artists prompted the hip-hop group Stetsasonic to pen a reply in the form of their 1988 hit "Talkin' All that Jazz."[74]

> Heard you on the radio
> Talkin' 'bout rap
> Sayin' all that crap about how we sample . . .
> You criticize our method of how we make records
> You said it wasn't art, so now we're gonna rip you apart . . .
> A sample is a tactic
> A portion of my method, a tool
> In fact it's only of importance when I make it a priority
> And what we sample is loved by the majority
> But you are a minority, in terms of thought
> Narrow minded and poorly taught

Daddy-O, Stetsasonic's MC, further explained his position on sampling when he told an interviewer that "sampling's not a lazy man's way. We learn a lot from sampling; it's like school for us."[75] Mtume and Bob James notwithstanding, not all older artists hated sampling. George Clinton tells us that he felt at the time that sampling was just a new way to make music, and he recalls that many people from earlier generations dismissed his own group as being uncreative. "My mother called us [Parliament-Funkadelic] lazy too," Clinton says. "She said we vamped. We just got on the groove and we just held it—held a groove for twenty minutes. She said we were lazy. [laughs] . . . Kids love it when [parents] hate it." T. S. Monk identifies another established musician who appreciated hip-hop when it was first emerging: the legendary drummer Max Roach. "Because I'm a music educator," Monk says, "I've heard a lot of people rag on the hip-hop community. But the first person to tell me, 'You know these hip hop kids are onto something,' was Max Roach, in 1985."

Unease about the role of new technologies is nothing new. The sound artist Vicki Bennett observes that the history of music and technology is one full of anxiety and conflict between the old and the new. "Before people were freaking out about sampling, they were freaking about the invention of the synthesizer and how it was going to destroy orchestras," Bennett says. "And on a similar level, much earlier, the industry was freaking out about mass duplication." Lloyd Dunn of the Tapebeatles also puts the disruptive role of reproductive technologies in a broader historical context. "Ever since photography in the nineteenth century," he says, "artists have had to face the notion that there are suddenly machines that are able to produce—*reproduce*—nature better than they could." Shock G offers the following analogy: "Perhaps it's a little easier to take a piece of music than it is to learn how to play the guitar or something. *True,* just like it's probably easier to snap a picture with that camera [looks at camera] than it is to actually *paint* a picture. But what the photographer is to the painter is what the modern DJ and computer musician is to the instrumentalist."

We ask T La Rock if, back in the mid-1980s, he thought about copyright issues. "Yes. That's why I said I was hesitant using samples. Did you ever hear my *Lyrical King* [1987] album? Well, then you see there's not that much sampling going on in that album. . . . I just didn't want to. You know, it just kind of felt like stealing." Nevertheless, there is at least one prominent sample on his classic "It's Yours," which was recorded with Jazzy Jay from Afrika Bambaataa's crew. As T La Rock remembers, "So when Jazzy Jay came aboard, he pulls out a record ["The Champ," a song by The Mohawks from 1968], which I had. He let that beginning go and sampled it," says T La Rock. "I was a little reluctant to use a sample, because I really wanted everything to be live. I think you should know that. Well, we used it, so that's a sample that was used on that record," he shrugs.

Even though copyright wasn't on everyone's radar in the 1980s, norms about "stealing" nevertheless existed, and they shaped the creative practices of hip-hop artists. As T La Rock explains, "There's a word that was used in hip-hop and rap. It's called biting. If someone says a rhyme and this person took a piece of his rhyme, they'd say, 'You bit. You bit his rhyme.'" For instance, on Tuff Crew's song "Feel So Good" (1988), one of the group's MCs quips, "Don't try to bite this beat because it's copywritten." (Missy Elliot echoed the sentiment in her hit "Work It" (2003): "Copywritten, so don't copy me.") The Tuff Crew lyric carries a certain irony because the song and the album on which it appears—the stellar, largely forgotten *Danger Zone*—probably contain several uncleared samples. The sampled beat they are rapping over *is* copyrighted, but not by Tuff Crew. However, they still feel proprietary about the old breakbeat that they sampled because they did the work that goes into digging for old sounds.

"It was a competition, you know, who had the better beats, who had the better breakbeats," says T La Rock in discussing how it was considered bad form in the early days of hip-hop to "bite" a beat from another crew. He adds, "People would come over to you while you're DJ-ing and look over your shoulder, look at the name of the record and run out and get it." This is why Silverman remembers that Bambaataa had obscured the labels on the vinyl records he spun, and why Grandmaster Flash did the same: they were protecting themselves from shady beat biters. Thus, even in a culture based on musical borrowing, there were still norms of originality, authorship, and ownership.

The musicologist Joe Schloss, author of *Making Beats: The Art of Sample-Based Music*, explains some of the principles underlying beat mining and crate digging: "When you sample something you're also at the same time saying, 'I discovered this rare record.' It's very closely tied to ideas of record collecting." Part of the creativity of sampling is in having a deep musical knowledge not just of certain songs but also *every part* of those songs. Schloss also emphasizes the codes and ethics that underpin the acts of sampling and digging for old records. For instance, it's taboo in the hip-hop production world to sample a sound or a record that another hip-hop artist has already used, especially if it's a fairly obscure song that has been revived by, say, a well-known DJ. "This audio archeologist has discovered this rare thing that nobody's ever heard before," Schloss says, "and then you come along a week later and are going, 'Look, I discovered it also.' Nobody is going to care about that as much."

POP EATS ITSELF

I'm sure we will continue doing it and from time to time get into trouble because of it, but [sampling] has always been only a part of the process of how we put our records together and not the reason for them existing.—KLF COMMUNICATIONS

Over the course of the 1980s, the cut-and-paste remix culture kick-started by hip-hop DJs from the South Bronx had spread far beyond New York City's five boroughs. The former Sex Pistols manager Malcolm McLaren dabbled in the hip-hop aesthetic with two fairly well-received twelve-inch singles released in 1983, "Buffalo Gals" and "Double Dutch." Other British artists like Coldcut and the KLF further mutated hip-hop's musical core, as did the cartoonishly subversive Pop Will Eat Itself—whose name referred to the cannibalistic tendencies that run through sample culture. However, the most unlikely outsiders to make a distinct, lasting impact on hip-hop itself were two white ad men named Douglas DiFranco and Steven Stein—Double Dee & Steinski, respectively. Together, they produced a series of twelve-inch singles in the mid-1980s now known as "The Lessons."

Steinski had been attending hip-hop shows around New York since 1981, and he turned Double Dee onto the scene as well. "We had been going to the Roxy quite a bit," Steinski says, "and we understood what a hip-hop remix could be. We were seeing the cream of the hip-hop DJs in the world every weekend—Red Alert, Afrika Bambaataa, Jazzy Jay, DST, just to name four off the top of my head." Double Dee & Steinski started their collaboration in 1983 when Tommy Boy Records held a promotional contest that challenged the entrants to remix the recently released single "Play That Beat, Mr. D.J." by G.L.O.B.E. and Whiz Kid. The grand prize consisted of a Tommy Boy Records shirt, Tommy Boy's back catalogue, and $100. At the time, Stein was working as an advertising-copy supervisor at the firm Doyle Dane Bernbach, and DiFranco worked in a commercial recording studio that produced radio ads, which gave him an extensive knowledge of audio editing techniques.

"One of Douglas's producer friends read in *Billboard* about Tommy's contest and suggested that he and I enter it," Steinski says. They hauled a bunch of records and other sound sources into the studio, and finished their collage in a weekend. Instead of simply remixing the original, Double Dee & Steinski pulled the song apart and put it back together, adding several elements not in the original. Their contest entry was called "The Payoff Mix," which retroactively became known as "Lesson 1." It included spoken-word recordings, a Little Richard song, dialogue from movies, and even voices from the National Aeronautics and Space Administration—as well as snippets of contemporary hits, including Culture Club's "I'll Tumble 4 Ya" and Herbie Hancock's "Rockit," among other recordings. "Douglas would listen to something and he'd go, 'Oh, okay, we need to edit that down and slow it down a bit, and add an extra beat here,'" Steinski remembers. "Douglas was the expert, expert, expert. What I added was ideas and thoughts, along with his ideas and thoughts."

The dance and hip-hop music legends Jellybean Benitez, Arthur Baker, and Afrika Bambaataa served as contest judges, and were supplied with pizza and beer for their efforts. "Lesson 1" was the clear and obvious winner, and the judges reportedly burst into applause at the song's conclusion. "It was great," says Tommy Boy CEO Tom Silverman, "but they ended up creating a record that would never be legally released." His company's attorney was sure it would provoke a lawsuit, "So we released it to radio stations promo only," Silverman says, telling us that they only serviced it to radio stations, not record stores.

"Lesson 1" became one of the first "illegal" radio hits, though for radio stations playing the song it might not have been illegal, despite the ridiculous number of unauthorized samples they used. Silverman explains that the "blanket license" that radio stations must purchase—in exchange for the right to play whatever songs they want, without restriction—allows for radio DJs to play medleys, song excerpts used for bumper music, and other such uses.[76] Because of that technicality, Double Dee & Steinski's collage record went into heavy rotation on radio stations throughout the country, particularly on the East Coast. "Tommy Boy felt that there must be a way to capitalize on this, so it was like, 'Let's clear them,'" Steinski remembers. "So we came up with a list of everything we had used and their poor lawyer [Ricky Ducker], god rest his soul, tried to clear it. A week and a half later, he looked like somebody beat him up, and he came in and put the paper down with one check mark, a lot of question marks, and a bunch of X's. And he was like, 'It ain't never gonna happen.'"

Within a couple years, Double Dee and Steinski completed a trilogy of "Lessons," the third of which was called "The History of Hip-Hop" and was based around Herman Kelly's "Dance to the Drummer's Beat"—a breakbeat staple for early hip-hop DJs. "It was for a project, and it was to accompany a book about Hip Hop," Steinski says. "When we finished, someone woke up and went, 'Hey! Maybe we should find out about clearing that song, 'Dance to the Drummer's Beat.' Herman Kelly—who was the owner, still is, of the copyright and the composer of the song said—'Gosh you should've spoken to me earlier.' I think he wanted like a billion dollars or something. That never came out as intended either."

"The Lessons," as they came to be known, were underground hits, not only in the United States but across the Atlantic Ocean. As Silverman remembers, the series "created a lot of noise, and it also established them internationally." And Matt Black notes that "Double Dee & Steinski's records—Lessons 1, 2, and 3—were so important in kicking off the sampling revolution." The British-based, Russian-born DJ Vadim adds, "People were sampling before that, but Coldcut and Double Dee & Steinski changed everything. Those records would take rock and roll records, pop records, funk, reggae, rock, heavy metal, classical, Indian, world music, and then blend them together. . . . So, in five minutes, and you could hear sixty tracks."

Steinski grew up listening to the Buchanan and Goodman cut-in records, which also mixed spoken word with snatches of popular songs. "I remember hearing it when I was a kid," Steinski tells us, "and it did make a big impression on me because it was like, 'Man, this is crazy. What is this? It's a combination of a radio broadcast and music, and it's funny. What is this?' But as time went on, I was listening to all kinds of shit—you know, Talking Heads, Laurie Anderson, Karlheinz Stockhausen—as well as comedy records and religious records and all kinds of other things." After amicably parting ways with Double Dee, Steinski continued to make records, most notably "The Motorcade Sped On," credited to Steinski & Mass Media (in this case, "Mass Media" isn't a stage name but rather a tongue-in-cheek reference to the mass media, with which Steinski collaborated).

"Motorcade" remixed television and radio broadcasts of the John F. Kennedy assassination, throwing in snatches of JFK speeches—including his "I am a Berliner" speech—and the song is introduced by Ed McMahon trumpeting, "Heeeeeeere's Johnny," from *The Tonight Show with Johnny Carson*. Steinski says that he found a lot of that source material on vinyl—there's a whole subgenre of JFK-assassination LPs—which he pulled from his collection. It was an influential record, particularly in Britain. The *New Musical Express*, which is sort of like the British *Rolling Stone*, pressed up the "Motorcade" record as a flexidisc, and stapled it to the front of their magazine. "I got a big, big, big story with pictures and a huge interview," Steinski says, "and that really helped me out in England a lot. People still say, 'Oh, yeah, that's the first thing of yours I heard.'"

As Coldcut's Matt Black tells us, "I was into hip-hop, and Double Dee & Steinski's records sparked something in me that said, 'Hey, this is fucking cool. We've gotta do this with a four track.' So, that was the original inspiration." In 1987, Coldcut recorded and self-released its debut twelve-inch single, "Say Kids, What Time Is It?"—which mixed James Brown's "Funky Drummer" with a song from the Disney film *The Jungle Book*, along with a couple dozen other elements. Matt Black sent the first Coldcut single to Steinski, who remembers, "I think it came with handwritten inscription that said, 'We made this because of you.' I listened to it, and I went, 'Wow, this is great! Oh my God, that *Jungle Book* thing. That's awesome!' So yeah, I was very impressed." Another British sound artist, Scanner, remembers those early Coldcut singles fondly: "What was very important about Coldcut, and still is important, is that they brought a popular aesthetic to what could still be deemed as academic aesthetic. It's almost *musique concrète* with a beautiful breakbeat underneath it, and a cheeky melody that makes you want to dance."

Coldcut was well aware at the time that Double Dee & Steinski's records were probably illegal if sold in record stores. "Those records were never able to be legally released, and we were aware of these records," Matt Black says. "They used to say on the label, 'For Radio Use Only,' but they were not to be commercially sold." Black was also aware that his own albums had the same questionable legal status. "We just said, 'We're going to have to do it ourselves and do five hundred copies and pretend it came from America.' We actually went through every copy with a soldering iron and burned out the matrix number which identified it as a British pressing so that we could claim that they came from the States—and thus make the pursuit of our ass more difficult."

In the mid-to-late 1980s, many mainstream British pop and rock groups embraced sampling in ways that their American peers had not. Pop Will Eat Itself (a.k.a. PWEI) was one of those bands, and by their third album they made the transition from a rock band to a group that was largely sample-based. And they took it to the extreme. For instance, *This Is the Day . . . This Is the Hour . . . This Is This!* features a head-imploding array of samples: Eric B & Rakim's "Paid in Full"; Jimi Hendrix's "Foxy Lady"; Salt 'n' Pepa's "Shake Your Thang" and "My Mike Sounds Nice"; Tears for Fears' "Shout"; Mantronix's "That's Right"; Pink Floyd's "Bike"; The Wonder Stuff's "Astley's in the Noose"; Public Enemy's "Yo! Bum Rush the Show," "Terminator X to the Edge of Panic," and "Bring the Noise"; Faith No More's "We Care a Lot"; and Love & Rockets' "Jungle Law." That album also samples from the following films: *Dirty Harry, Evil Dead 2, Robocop, The Deer Hunter, The Island of Doctor Moreau, Casablanca*, and *The Warriors*. It also includes samples of a Rice Krispies TV commercial, *Super Bowl XXII*, and the classic American TV series *The Twilight Zone*—just to name a few.

Released in 1989, *This Is the Day . . .* came out in the United States and in Europe on a major label, and so it is hard to believe that the record company was clueless about its content. The most amusing appropriation by PWEI was their use of the word "take" from Mel & Kim's cheesy Europop hit from the 1980s, "Respectable." The original song's refrain went "Take us or leave us," but on PWEI's song "Hit the Hi-Tech Groove" they only sampled the word "take" from the lyric and turned it into a chant: "Take! Take! Take! Take!" During "Preaching to the Perverted," PWEI's lead singer Clint Mansell sings, "So we steal, so what? / So far so good / We're Robin Hoods." The band's T-shirt featured a re-mixed PEPSI logo that morphed the trademark into PWEI (the phrase "Sample It, Loop It, Fuck It, Eat It" surrounded the logo). As Mansell stated in an interview from 1994, "I must admit we don't go hunting people whose samples we use because if you ask them they just tend to be awkward about it. If you don't ask they hardly ever notice you've used them."[77]

However, when it came to pushing copyright law to the outer limits, no one did it with as much style and perversion as Bill Drummond and Jimmy Cauty, an anarchic British pop duo that adopted several pseudonyms: The Timelords, The Justified Ancients of Mu Mu, the JAMS, and the KLF. Between 1987 and 1992 they racked up seven Top-10 hits in the United Kingdom—even crossing over in America with the songs "3 A.M. Eternal" and "Justified and Ancient," the latter of which went to number one in eighteen countries.[78] Those super-cheesy singles are the main reason why they are remembered in the United States, if they are remembered at all, as a novelty techno-pop act. The KLF's brief but widespread popularity obscured their radical and hilariously subversive critique of the culture industry—like a goofy Theodore Adorno whose praxis involved a drum machine.

To this end, the KLF practiced an aggressive brand of provocation that predated both Public Enemy's early forays into the copyright debates and Negativland's impish copyright activism (which was prompted by lawsuit in 1991 for daring to sample and satirize the rock superstars U2). The KLF's debut album, *1987 (What the Fuck's Going On?)*, made extensive and provocative use of samples from the Monkees, the Beatles, Whitney Houston, and ABBA—with the album's liner notes claiming that the sounds were liberated "from all copyright restrictions." In this respect, the KLF were pop music's first "illegal art" ideologues, though they were loath to be pigeonholed as mere copyright criminals. Drummond and Cauty were megastars compared to the relatively obscure sound collage collective Negativland—whose de facto spokesman Mark Hosler says, "We've never had a hit single, but we had a hit lawsuit!"

While the KLF are by no means *the* central characters in this narrative, they nevertheless were among the first to widely circulate self-conscious critiques of copyright, authorship, and ownership to a broad audience. "They knew what they were doing," says the British sound artist Scanner. "They came from an art-school upbringing and followed what in the sixties one would call détournement—where you'd be sort of turning things back on themselves. And that's what the Dada artists did as well." Even though they embraced the pop aesthetic, the KLF could also make an unholy noise, like they did on their single from 1987 "Whitney Joins the JAMS," in which they abducted the voice of the pop diva Whitney Houston by forcing her to "join" their group. (Fittingly, the word *plagiarism* is derived from the Latin term for "kidnapping," which adds an interesting dimension to the parent-child authorial metaphor.[79]) "Oh Whitney, please please, *please* join the JAMS," shouts Drummond over the *Mission: Impossible* theme song, a drum machine, and various other samples—adding, "You saw our reviews, didn't ya?" Then, after more coaxing from Drummond, a snippet of Houston's "I Wanna Dance with Somebody" finally breaks through the cacophonous collage with a little help from their sampling machine. Drummond, in delivering the song's punch line, exclaims, "Ahhhhh, Whitney Houston joins the JAMS!"

When the legal threats against their *1987* album began flying, KLF quickly released—almost as if the whole affair had been planned from the beginning, which it probably was—an edited version of this copyright-infringing album. The edited version of *1987* deleted or truncated all offending samples and included instructions for how consumers could re-create the original version by using old records: "If you follow the instructions below you will, after some practice, be able to simulate the sound of our original record. To do this you will need 3 wired-up record decks, a pile of selected discs, one t.v. set and a video machine loaded with a cassette of edited highlights of last weeks 'Top of the Pops.'"[80] Today, with home computers making cheap editing technologies widely available, it is possible to follow their instructions fairly easily. But in the 1980s it wasn't a feasible option, which only made the joke funnier.

The critical elements of the KLF's aesthetic brings us full circle to sampling's roots in the avant-garde. But the KLF also made internationally popular music, and as such provides just one of many possible examples that sampling isn't an elitist (or ghettoized) technique. Thus, conceptual art and pop culture coexist in sample-based works (shades of Andy Warhol). Sampling stands alongside allusion, quotation, and reinterpretation as part of the modern musician's toolkit for responding to and building upon previous musicians' work. As a technique, sampling reflects the ingenious innovations of musicians across geography (especially the Black Atlantic) and genres (especially classical, jazz, hip-hop, electronic, and dance). We have recounted many reasons why copyright law and the music industry cannot implicitly dismiss sampling as "uncreative." This chapter's largely cultural and aesthetic account of sampling provides a foundation for the rest of the book. With chapter 3 we shift to a discussion of the legal and business aspects of sampling and explain how various music-industry institutions fit into the issues surrounding sampling's rise.

3

THE COMPETING
INTERESTS IN SAMPLE LICENSING

The rich history of musical collage, of which digital sampling is a part, speaks to the value and pervasiveness of musical borrowing (or appropriation, if you prefer). But, as we suggested in the introduction, sampling has sparked a great deal of legal controversy. While sampling should be understood as an art form, that classification does not answer the legal question of whether samples must be licensed. In this chapter we explain the competing interests that sampling implicates, and we demonstrate, based on our interviews, how absurdly complicated the arguments among these competing interests can become. Before we can explore the issue's complexity, however, we must bring copyright law back into the picture—for it shapes the initial bargaining positions of each competing interest group and reflects the balance that society has struck over the use of copyrighted materials.

MUSIC COPYRIGHT

You have to clear the master side and the publishing side for each sampled song. The more songs you sample, the more of an administrative mess it becomes. It's crazy.—TOM SILVERMAN

Music copyrights come in two basic kinds: musical compositions and sound recordings.[1] A musical composition copyright applies to the notes, chords, melodies, and other underlying structures of a piece of music.

A sound recording copyright applies to the particular performance of the singers and instrumentalists captured on vinyl, tape, hard disk, or other formats. We use the terms "musical composition" and "sound recording" in their legal sense, while we employ more colloquial terms like "song," "track," "source," and "piece [of music]" to refer to the unified whole consisting of a composition and a particular recording of it. ("Song" has a certain association with "composition"—hence the term "songwriter"—but in popular parlance "song" also often refers to a composition and a recording or performance together, as many quotes from our interviewees illustrate.) This division in usage allows us to write simpler sentences like "artist X sampled song Y" without always reiterating that there may be two separate copyrights in the music sampled from.

The two kinds of music copyrights can coexist simultaneously in the same piece of music, and they often do. Thus, every piece of music that is created involves two potential copyrights.[2] In the United States, musical compositions have been eligible for copyright protection since 1831, but sound recordings have only received federal copyright protection since 1972 (some states, like California, had laws protecting them before 1972). Historically, both composers and recording artists have transferred their copyrights to publishers and record labels, respectively, in return for promotion and a share of the proceeds.

The distinction between musical compositions and sound recordings predates even Tin Pan Alley, but that era of songwriting helps explain what's going on. When George Gershwin and Ira Gershwin wrote and published "Someone to Watch Over Me" in 1926, their publisher received a musical composition copyright. The Gershwins would receive royalties from sales of sheet music and phonograph recordings of their composition. But when Ella Fitzgerald recorded "Someone to Watch Over Me" in 1959, she received no copyright to transfer to her label. (She and her label could still earn money from record sales, just without copyright protection.) If she had recorded the song after February 15, 1972, however, her record label would have received a sound recording copyright, while the Gershwins' publisher would have retained its musical composition copyright just as before.

Under today's law, each song can simultaneously give rise to both a musical composition copyright and a sound recording copyright. The two copyrights are separate and are designed to accommodate an industry in which songwriters and recording artists are different people. For example, Prince wrote the composition for "Nothing Compares 2 U," which Sinéad O'Connor recorded in 1990 on her album *I Do Not Want What I Haven't Got*. Prince's publisher (Warner Chappell Music) received the musical composition copyright for this song, but O'Connor's record label (Chrysalis) received a sound recording copyright for her rendition. The two separate copyrights can also go to the same person's publisher and record label, as when artists write and record their own songs. The composition copyright in Prince's song "Little Red Corvette" belongs to his publisher (Warner Chappell) and the sound recording copyright in his own recorded performance of that song belongs to his record label (Warner Bros. Records).

Copyright holders get certain exclusive rights with respect to a work: reproduction, distribution, public performance, public display, and creation of derivative works.[3] These rights are subject to various limitations and exceptions; notably, for example, copyrights are limited in time, limited to expression rather than ideas, limited to substantial takings, and subject to users' rights of fair use.

SAMPLE LICENSING

You have to get permission. That's just the way the world works.
—DEAN GARFIELD

Sampling means that the sound recording itself is being used, and it is usually taken from a vinyl, compact-disc, or MP3 copy of the recording. But the underlying notes, chords, melody, and rhythm of the song are also an inseparable part of the sample. Thus, sampling implicates *both* copyrights in the song being sampled. Sampling artists will sometimes infringe both the musical composition copyright and the sound recording copyright in the song being sampled.

Why only sometimes? Not every sample necessarily infringes a copyright, for three basic reasons. First, some of copyright's limitations and exceptions (such as the doctrine of fair use) mean that certain samples of copyrighted works are lawful even without the copyright owner's permission. Second, other limitations and exceptions to copyright (such as the time limit on each copyright) mean that copyrighted works can enter the public domain, becoming free for anyone to sample or use in other ways as they wish. Third, copyright owners can voluntarily specify that certain unauthorized uses of their works are permissible, or even donate their works to the public domain. But if a sample does violate one or both copyrights in a song, then the sampler must obtain permission or a license from the owner(s) of each copyright infringed. (We discuss the lawsuits determining what kinds of samples infringe musical composition copyrights, sound recording copyrights, or both, in chapter 4.)

The two types of music copyrights allow for two kinds of musicians to make money. When a song is sold (for instance, on a compact disc) or licensed (for instance, to be played on the soundtrack of a television show), there are two distinct copyrights whose owner(s) may have a right to receive compensation.[4] To complicate matters more, as Danny Rubin points out, "Most of the time the copyrights aren't owned by the artists." In one important sense, copyrights are like other kinds of property in that they can be sold or licensed to others. Because copyrights are transferable, different people—even people who have no relationship with each other—can own the musical composition and the sound recording. Because composers and recording artists often transfer their respective copyrights to corporations (that is, publishers and labels), copyrights can later change hands through mergers or bankruptcies. Copyright owners may even split each copyright and its accompanying exclusive rights into parts; for example, co-writers of a song often do so. Over time, copyrights may be passed down through a long, complicated chain of different owners.

WHO GETS THE MONEY?

My question is, well, "Who is it actually benefiting?"
Is it benefiting the original artists that have made the song in the
first place or is it benefiting somebody who just happened to be a
holder of certain contracts?—HANK SHOCKLEE

In part because of the two kinds of music copyrights, and in part because copyrights can be divided and sold, following the money through the music industry has always been a complicated task. For instance, who gets money from the $18.98 paid for a new CD? People are often astonished to hear that the musicians typically only end up with roughly

10 percent of the retail price, if that.[5] But retailers, publishers, record labels, managers, lawyers, and producers have to get paid, too. So how does the money flow, and to whom, when one artist licenses a sample of another artist's music?

The answers to these questions depend on the details of both music-industry contracts and copyright law's specific provisions. Music-industry contracts can be complex and far from straightforward, as evidenced by the giant stack of papers presented to the members of Wilco by their record label, as depicted in the film *I Am Trying to Break Your Heart*. The band—perhaps unwisely—started reading, gave up, shrugged, and signed. (Their lawyer probably had a look off-camera.) Moreover, music copyright is among the most convoluted areas in copyright law because of the compromises that Congress has brokered among music and technology companies over the last century. One compromise, for example, specifies the actual number of pennies a songwriter is entitled to receive for each recording sold with his or her composition on it. That same provision allows musicians to record cover versions without permission under certain conditions. Musicians who sample currently lack the benefit of such a compromise.

The terms of musicians' contracts reflect a mixture of industry customs, idiosyncratic negotiations, and the bargaining power of composers and recording artists relative to that of publishers and record labels. The provisions of music copyright represent the answers that Congress has come up with to difficult questions about fairness, creativity, and the workings of the music business. Some decisions, as applied to sampling, may seem reasonable, while others may seem out of whack. In this section, we run down all the different parties that might receive the revenue from a sample license, and we explain some of the relevant copyright provisions along the way. This effort will illustrate how the current system for licensing music samples fits into the larger context of music copyright.

Recording Artists

As we mentioned earlier, recording artists traditionally have signed contracts with record labels to sell their sound recordings. These record-label contracts have provisions in them determining how much money from sample licenses goes to the record label and how much goes to the recording artists. One common arrangement would involve the recording artist receiving 50 percent of the revenue from licensing the sound recording copyright for sampling, subtracting some possible deductions.[6]

But would a recording artist really receive that much money? Or is the story more complicated? As the attorney Anthony Berman says, "It's a very interesting question who gets the money from sampling. It's all about the money, right? Sadly, a lot of time, it's not artists who get the money." There are a few possible reasons why a recording artist who is sampled might not receive any licensing revenue. For example, they or their record label may grant permission to sample without charge. A particular sample may not take enough of their recording to infringe their copyright, or may be fair use.[7] However, a more common reason that artists do not receive any money when their sound recording is licensed for sampling is because their record label "recoups" the money—that is, charges it against earlier expenditures the label made on behalf of the artist.[8]

Royalties from sample licenses are generally applied against recoupable amounts by the record label. If an artist is in the red and another artist licenses a sample of their work, then that payment is applied to the sampled artist's label debt. This may move them closer to being in the black—but they will not receive a check until they are fully recouped. It is not uncommon for recording artists to never recoup, meaning that aside from the rise and the fall of the calculations on their negative balance sheet they receive no money from any licensed samples of their music.[9] The reverse is also true: unrecouped recording artists who sample put themselves deeper into debt. Bill Stafford, a licensing expert from the publishing side, explains that record labels charge sample-licensing fees to the sampling artist's account: "If the artist is in an unrecouped position, which on average about 85 to 90 percent of them are, the label has just a further deficit for that artist. So they just go a little further in the red." Licensing costs could also come out of a recording artist's advance.

Supporting Musicians Who Are Not Copyright Holders

Another group of artists who participate in recordings get paid differently. Some members of a group may not be the "featured artist" on a sound recording or the co-author of a musical composition.[10] Similarly, some musicians who play on a recording might be session musicians, who also do not typically count as featured artists or co-authors. Clyde Stubblefield was one of the two main drummers in James Brown's band in the late 1960s, and he played on many famous recordings, such as "Cold Sweat" and "Say It Loud, I'm Black and I'm Proud." He received a salary for his employment in the band, but James Brown was the featured artist on recordings and did not generally grant co-authorship on compositions to his drummers—who, arguably, were the most important part of his band. As a result, Stubblefield has received no money from samples.

Studio Producers

According to the music lawyer Donald Passman, in addition to receiving a flat fee for their work recording an album, many producers' contracts allow them also to receive royalties—or "points"—when a sound recording is licensed for other uses.[11] Their royalties come out of the recording artists' contractual share of the royalties. But some producers' contracts allow them to get paid from "record one"—even before the recording artist has recouped.[12] This follows the logic that a producer is not benefiting from many of the advance costs (like tour support and video budgets) that might keep an artist unrecouped. Perhaps this is a reasonable arrangement. But it means that a producer who has points on a record that is sampled often has a better chance of receiving money from a sample license than the recording artist does.

Record Labels

Because most recording artists transfer their sound recording copyrights to record labels as part of their contracts, the record labels ultimately control most licenses for sampling sound recordings. A license for sampling a sound recording is a type of "master use license," which in record-industry jargon is a reference to the "master tapes" (or just "masters") of a sound recording. Bill Stafford told us that "there is a real market incentive for labels to license, both so that their own clearances come through from other labels, as well as to make the income." The twin incentives of reciprocity and revenue got the license revenue flowing by the 1990s, after it became clear that sampling often involved copyright infringement in the eyes of the law. As Don Joyce of Negativland says, "There's a whole industry built up around licensing now, getting clearance rights. Every label has offices that do that, and it has become a big income stream."

In the drama swirling around sampling in hip-hop, many interviewees identify record labels and music publishers as the culprits. This has been the experience of EL-P, who is both an artist and an independent record company owner. He attributes the problems with sample licensing to the obscure intermediaries who control many copyrights. "It's usually not the people who created the music," says El-P. "It's not. It's usually someone else who owns the music, who swallowed the shit up, you know, who bought them and a million other groups in some merger." On this note, the artist manager Michael Hausman adds, "I personally feel that a lot of the problems with sampling and copyright come up because you don't have artists talking to each other. You might have artists talking to publishers, or artists' representatives talking to publishers or their representatives." Thus, record labels do much of the negotiating over sample licenses—and collect a significant share of the revenue.

Composers and Songwriters

A compulsory license, known as a "mechanical license," applies to reproductions of musical composition copyrights only.[13] The term "mechanical royalties" (or "mechanicals") refers to the royalty paid to the owners of the musical composition copyright (that is, composers, publishers, or both) from the sales of sound recordings of renditions of copyrighted compositions. Congress sets the royalty rate, which at the time of this writing is 9.1 cents per copy.[14] Despite the statutory limit, mechanicals are a relatively reliable income stream for musicians—which means musicians who compose are more likely to receive revenue than are recording artists.

Songwriters typically receive 50 to 75 percent of the revenue generated by their musical compositions, which includes revenue from sample licenses.[15] But not every sample of a song infringes the musical composition copyright—for instance, one court held that sampling a three-note pattern did not constitute infringement.[16] But many samples that borrow larger chunks of a composition do infringe. When a sample would infringe an artist's musical composition copyright, and when the sampling artist obtains a license to use the composition, the resulting revenue can be meaningful for a songwriter. Anthony Berman says that the sample licensing "certainly created a big jump in the revenue streams of copyright holders." So, for musicians who compose, sample licensing adds another source of revenue to the more traditional ones, such as the licensing revenue from renditions of their compositions (including their own versions).

This situation can benefit songwriters and composers greatly, especially in terms of their career arc. Sample licenses can generate income after a musician has passed the peak of his or her commercial success—or even after a musician has died. As Dina LaPolt, who represents the estate of Tupac Shakur, says, "If they sample Tupac, there's a master use royalty that gets paid and there's also a music publishing royalty that gets paid. And on top of that, because it's a derivative work, it increases our catalogue on an artist that's otherwise deceased." LaPolt continues by noting, "So, when I started with the Tupac estate, we had, say, 200 songs; maybe now we have 290 songs on an artist who's been dead for ten years."

The licensing of samples, then, has two sides. While it has created complications and expenses for musicians who sample, the sample clearance system has also generated meaningful revenue for musicians who get sampled (especially composers), their publishers, and their record labels. Successful musicians who had excellent legal representation at the right time and who own the rights to their work—not necessarily a large percentage of artists—are in an especially good position to exploit the revenue streams from sample licenses. However, the music lawyer Whitney Broussard points out an important distinction: "This is much more likely to be true for modern contracts than older ones."

Publishers

As we explained earlier, many songwriters sell or license their copyrights to a publisher (some songwriters form their own publishing companies). Publishers administer musical composition copyrights to oversee the licensing of songs and some of the revenue that flows in. When a song is recorded—or sampled—under a license, the publisher receives a royalty and usually splits it with the songwriter.

But not every songwriter signs the same contract or retains the same rights with respect to their musical composition copyrights. The music attorney Shoshana Zisk, who has worked with Parliament-Funkadelic mastermind George Clinton, explains one unfortunate scenario. "I don't believe that George Clinton received any money, at least in the publishing," she says. "The publisher came out and said, 'I haven't paid you anything and I'm never gonna pay you anything 'cause you don't own your copyrights.' . . . So George never got paid in the publishing, but I think [he did get paid] for the master. . . . He's currently auditing both record companies that had put out most of his hits for not paying him properly. So I'm not certain if he really saw a whole increase in money based on the sampling."

Copyright Aggregators

Copyrights are, in some ways, commodities like other kinds of property (though there are other important ways that the property analogy does not hold water). As we mentioned earlier, copyrights can be sold, licensed, and divided. Sometimes publishers and record labels split up the rights to a song, meaning that they sell rights to portions of the revenue generated by a copyrighted work. They can divide rights geographically, for example, between the United States and the rest of the world. Sometimes they transfer the whole copyright to another company. Publishers and labels can also go out of business, meaning that other companies will administer the bankrupt entity's copyrights.

Songwriters can also sell, license, or divide their share of the royalties (usually 50 to 75 percent), and the same applies to the rare recording artists who retain their copyrights. Companies that take over copyrights from the original songwriter, publisher, recording artist, or record label and accumulate them are called copyright aggregators or, to use a more derogatory term, "sample trolls."[17] In the *Bridgeport v. Dimension Films* case mentioned earlier (and to be discussed in detail in chapter 4), the plaintiffs were not the original copyright owners. Although it was a track by George Clinton's Funkadelic that N.W.A.

allegedly infringed, Clinton had not retained copyright in either the composition or the recording. He was not the plaintiff in *Bridgeport*. This experience and others led George Clinton to advocate the following: "When you sample, make sure that [you know] who's getting the money. That way you can make sure that the person that wrote it or performed it gets it when you sample each other's music. Otherwise somebody else will get it. And that's the great tragedy of the whole thing. We haven't gotten hardly any of money from that—you know, from the sampling. And this guy [the owner of Bridgeport Music, Inc.] has over $100 million. You know what I'm saying?" In this view and in general, Clinton advocates a greater understanding among artists about the parties to sample licenses. We will return later to the theme of the relationship between sampling artists and those they sample, but Clinton's story also shows how copyright aggregators can complicate the issue of figuring out who gets the money.

Lawyers and Other Intermediaries

We have surveyed the music-industry players who receive the revenue from sample licenses. But to generate such revenue, someone has to negotiate the sample licenses. And this is where the lawyers come in. As Chuck D succinctly puts it, "At the end of the day, lawyers never lose money; they gain from both sides going back and forth." Law firms, the in-house legal departments of the record labels, and the sample clearance houses (which can also facilitate sample licenses) do not receive revenue directly from licenses. But they do get paid for making transactions happen and thus make up part of the cost of having a sample clearance system in the first place. In other words, when a sample license generates revenue for copyright holders it also generates transaction costs, which are paid to lawyers or sample clearance professionals. Sometimes the transaction costs for clearance exceed the profits generated by a newly created sample-based recording.

The revenue from sample licenses can take a number of paths. Each sample funnels some money to many of the seven groups described above. And often times the transactions can become quite complex, as when musicians choose to sample a song that already has one or more samples embedded in it.

I have one client that calls it "mailbox money," because
when he's sampled, the check just floats into the mailbox, so he says,
"Oh, mailbox money—from a song I wrote twenty years ago,
thirty years ago." So, it's great!—ANTHONY BERMAN

When sampling first emerged, many musicians, record companies, and publishers were uneasy about it, but that soon changed. "It turned out that all the traditional people who were so miffed by this way back in the early days," says the entertainment lawyer Anthony Berman, "realized that there was a *huge* amount of money to be made." Berman explains that musicians can increase their chances of receiving compensation for their labor by owning the publishing rights to their compositions. "Publishing is the name of the game of the record business," he says. "My advice to clients, artists, is to hold onto your publishing. If your music is used in a commercial or film, or as a sample, it could be a windfall for you decades later."

The soul music pioneer Sam Cooke was one of the few black artists from the 1950s and early 1960s who owned many of his own composition copyrights. Another Chicago native, Curtis Mayfield, followed in Cooke's business-savvy footsteps. Mayfield's funk records from the 1970s are sampled often, which provide an ongoing stream of revenue for the deceased musician's widow and ten children. Mayfield—who wrote "People Get Ready," "Freddie's Dead," "Superfly" and other classics—not only owned his own publishing unit but his own record label as well. This allowed him to control the copyrights to both his compositions and his sound recordings—a setup that was extremely rare, especially for an African American musician of Mayfield's generation. In 1990, just as other musicians began to sample his music, Mayfield was paralyzed in an accident that left him unable to sing. Despite his expensive medical bills and loss of performance income, "sampling let his family be financially secure," explains Marv Heiman, the executor of Mayfield's estate.[18] That financial security hinged on Mayfield owning not only his publishing but his masters as well.

Most of the artist representatives we spoke with argued for the importance of sample-license revenue to the musicians they represent. As the manager Michael Hausman emphasizes, "It's important for us to get paid for these things; it's our livelihood. I wake up every day and go to work in order to further the careers of our artists." Dina LaPolt also argues for the importance of this revenue stream. "I think a lot of rap artists that get sampled," she says, "they know how much money it generates. So they encourage other artists to sample their materials as well." LaPolt's comments suggest that some musicians—who can end up both sampling and being sampled during their careers—are seeing the financial value of a market for samples.

Musicians themselves may also have ethical reasons to support the flow of revenue to sampled musicians and other recipients of sample-license revenue. As De La Soul's Posdnuos says, "You know, we understand that if you sample someone, you should pay for it. If someone wants to get paid for it, I understand. They made it." And Bobbito Garcia says, "If you were sampling Pee Wee Ellis, you know, he was an incredible jazz musician. He was a phenomenal funk musician. I mean, this guy played music for twenty to thirty years. You're sampling such a sophisticated level of musicianship." These musicians' rationale for supporting licensing emphasizes fairness to the sampled artist more than the prospect of generating revenue for themselves.

Dina LaPolt also explains a fairness rationale in the following way: "Everybody in the music industry has made a nickel an hour at some point in their life. So if you are all of a sudden on the other side of the table where someone's sampling you, then you've definitely come home. It's your time to rise. And people need to pay. So if you sample Shirley Bassey—like Kanye West did—pay her. *Pay*." Kyambo "Hip Hop" Joshua, one of Kanye West's managers, also believes that it is fair to pay the copyright holder for the use of samples, as his client does. Hip Hop just sees sampling as another expense in the business of making and selling music. If, for instance, an artist comes from a region of the United States that doesn't typically use many samples—which is true of many styles of southern hip-hop—then he argues that such an artist can spend more money on top-tier producers like Timbaland or the Neptunes. He makes an analogy between a musician who samples and a musician who likes to play with top-notch session musicians, or record in premium studios, or fly to certain locales in order to capture a certain feeling. "That's expensive," he says. "When you think of sampling, to me, it's just an expense. If that's your key component to your sound, it's like you gotta take that sacrifice."

Hip Hop got his start in the business by clearing samples for Jay-Z's first album, and he watched from the inside as Jay-Z's career skyrocketed through the 1990s and 2000s. Jay-Z's first huge crossover hit was "Hard Knock Life (Ghetto Anthem)," which distinguished itself by interlacing Jay-Z's hardcore rhymes with a sample from the musical *Annie*. When the record came out, the effect of hearing a familiar recording of children's voices in a hip-hop song was for many listeners both jarring and intoxicating, and it is this quality that arguably made "Hard Knock Life (Ghetto Anthem)" a hit. "A sample might have sounds and vocals—and atmosphere, and all these different things on the record—that will now be in your record," Hip Hop says. He continues, "If Jay didn't pay for the 'Hard Knock Life' sample, his whole career could have been different." By investing in this *Annie* sample, Jay-Z received handsome returns in the form of a hit single and a career that increased in its momentum. Needless to say, Jay-Z felt it was worth the expense.

SAMPLING STORIES

I just want my name on it, saying that's Clyde playing. The money is not the important thing.—CLYDE STUBBLEFIELD

The question of whether the money goes where it should can be difficult to answer in a straightforward way. In order to illustrate the divergent answers to that query, here we will offer the stories of five performers: the singer-songwriter Suzanne Vega; "the world's most sampled drummer," Clyde Stubblefield; the funk maverick George Clinton; Aerosmith and Run-DMC's collaboration on "Walk This Way"; and the strange case of Jay-Z and the folk-song collector Alan Lomax.

Tom's Diner Is Open for Licensing

Suzanne Vega's a capella song "Tom's Diner," from her biggest-selling album, *Solitude Standing* (1987), has been the basis for numerous remixes. Tupac sampled it and retitled it "Dopefiend's Diner," and other hip-hop artists who have sampled Vega's track include Public Enemy, Nikki D, Lil' Kim, and the oddly named Mormon Ghetto Projectz.

Michael Hausman—who is now Vega's manager, though he wasn't at the time "Tom's Diner" was released—observes that her song has been "sampled dozens and dozens of times that we know of, and probably hundreds of times that we don't know of." It all started in 1990 when two underground British music producers, calling themselves DNA, put Vega's vocals atop a beat sampled from Soul II Soul, a British dance group popular at the time. Vega's "Doo doo doo doo" at the end of the original a capella version was retrofitted as the hook for the new version of the song, which was released to club DJs as "DNA featuring Suzanne Vega."

Instead of suing DNA, A&M Records—which owns the master of "Tom's Diner"—licensed the song and released it as a legitimate single. It reached the Top 10 in the British and American music charts. The track became so popular that it spawned a companion album that compiled multiple sampled and replayed versions of Vega's song, all of which were licensed, including a one-off collaboration between R.E.M. and Billy Bragg (who recorded under the charming moniker Bingo Hand Job). According to her manager Michael Hausman, Vega likes the fact that this song has had a sort of perpetual life in various versions; she finds it kind of flattering, even when a reworked version diverges dramatically from her original version.

Discussing Tupac's "Dopefiend's Diner," Hausman states: "I don't think [Vega has] ever turned down anything, and this particular version is pretty aggressive, and I guess you could maybe call it a bit violent. But she's open to it because she sees it as his interpretation. It's not even like he's doing her song. He's just using her melody and her recording as an element of his song, and she approved it." He adds, "When DNA sampled 'Tom's Diner,' I don't want to say it launched her career—but it was a major, major driver in her career. It exposed her to millions and millions of people, but also she's made money from the airplay. And it sold more records, so she's also earned money from that. She certainly has made money from licenses of that sample to all the various people."[19]

Clyde Stubblefield and the Pitfalls of Being a Session Musician

In situations where licensing occurs as it did with Vega's "Tom's Diner," today's musicians pass on to older artists some of the money generated by new sample-based songs. Not only do sampled artists benefit financially through licensing fees, but their careers can also receive a boost in the present day, as in the case of both James Brown and George Clinton. Unfortunately, some sampled musicians are neither featured artists nor copyright owners. One example of this is Clyde Stubblefield, whose drumming drives many of the James Brown samples used in hip-hop records. When asked what his favorite breakbeat is, Chuck D replies, without hesitation, "You have to always look in the James Brown catalogue and find something, either 'Funky Drummer' or the 'Cold Sweat' break"—two seminal (and heavily sampled) songs that Stubblefield played on.

In the 1970s, hip-hop DJs mined regularly from James Brown's records, as did the hip-hop artists using digital samplers in the 1980s. In Stetsasonic's "Talkin' All That Jazz," mentioned in chapter 2, Daddy-O rapped, "Tell the truth James Brown was old 'til Eric B came out with 'I Got Soul,'" referring to hip-hop artists Eric B & Rakim.[20] In the case of James Brown, by the mid-1980s the music of Soul Brother Number One was considered by many to be irrelevant. His records piled up in dusty cut-out bins and used-record racks throughout the country, and they were ignored by the next generation of music consumers who rejected the albums as their parents' music. But when hip-hop artists began sampling Brown's 1960s gems "Give It Up and Turn It Loose," "Funky Drummer," "You Know I Got Soul," and other funk jams, he sounded fresh again. Sampling gave his music and career a new life.

Chuck D explains the impulse shared among sampling artists when they feel compelled to borrow from older records: "When those old musicians created magical moments, you had four or five guys that were *the best*. Sampling allowed the best magical moments to be duplicated." One of the musicians who created those moments was Clyde Stubblefield. When Grandmaster Flash started DJ-ing in the 1970s, he carefully studied the album credits on the records he liked so that he knew which musicians to look for when digging through record-store racks. Flash thought that everyone in James Brown's band was obviously very talented, "but Clyde Stubblefield was the baddest. First time I ever heard 'Funky Drummer,' I started looking for his name on anything I could find. If Clyde played on a Lawrence Welk record, I bought it."[21]

During the second half of the 1960s, when James Brown's band churned out the funk classics that later became staples of sampling,

Stubblefield was one of two primary drummers in the group (the other was Jabo Starks). To provide a better understanding of the labor that went into creating "Funky Drummer" and "Cold Sweat"—two of the most sampled songs ever—Stubblefield tells us about the recording sessions that produced those tracks. The band recorded "Cold Sweat," credited to James Brown and Alfred "Pee Wee" Ellis, at King Studios in May 1967, during one of James Brown's creative and commercial peaks. As Stubblefield recalls, "I just started playing [imitates drums], and the bass player came in [imitates bass line], and then the guitar player came in [imitates guitar]. So the rhythm was there and James Brown came in and heard it and said, 'Yeah, I like that!' Then he started putting lyrics on top, [sings, quoting from 'Cold Sweat'] *'I don't care . . . '* Then they put the horns on it, and we had a song! [laughs] And I started it!"

This is a pretty typical description of the creative process used by many funk and soul bands of that era. Musicians would vamp and improvise until they settled into a groove that provided the foundation of a song. Ironically, Stubblefield doesn't even really like "Funky Drummer"—the song or the memories surrounding it. While recording that song he was in a bad mood, which apparently wasn't uncommon for those who worked for the mercurial James Brown. "We were going into the studio in King's studio in Cincinnati," says Stubblefield. "I wasn't up to playing that day, I didn't want to go into the studio—I didn't want to do nothing. So I got into the studio and just played, played a drum pattern, people joined in, and that's where 'Funky Drummer' came from." Stubblefield continues by stating, "When I set out I just played a beat, something simple, and everybody joined in. And then Brown came in and put the lyrics to it and it was called 'Funky Drummer.' Next thing I know all the rap artists was using it, sampling it."

"Even when it came down to James Brown," Chuck D observes, "there was a whole arrangement of musicians—like Clyde Stubblefield and Bootsy [Collins]—that might have ad-libbed and come up with something that James Brown got credit for." It is Clyde Stubblefield's syncopated drumming style that is attractive to many artists who sample, and oftentimes his drum patterns are the only elements of James Brown songs that get sampled (as opposed to horn blasts, vocal grunts, and the other aural qualities associated with Brown's records). Reminding us of the collective approach used to craft those classic songs during the second half of the 1960s, Stubblefield says, "It's all of our song, in a sense.

We all put our own little techniques, our own little feeling in it, so it belongs to everybody." But in reality—legal reality—it clearly doesn't belong to everybody. And in James Brown's case, the song credits and, subsequently, the copyrights belonged to him.

As Stubblefield insists, in speaking about his heavily sampled drum pattern, "That was mine. [James Brown] didn't tell me what to play. I played what I felt, but *he owned it*." Stubblefield shakes his head as he tells us that there are so many groups that have sampled his drumming. "But I haven't gotten a penny for it yet," he adds, with a good-natured laugh that covers up what is surely decades of bitterness from being ripped off by the music industry. Even though Stubblefield may have come up with the famous rhythms he played, the combination of copyright law, contractual arrangements, informal agreements, and traditional industry practices meant that he received no copyright and thus no royalties. In other words, he was paid for his time as a session musician, just like most of the other members of Brown's band—an injustice that has nothing to do with copyright law and everything to do with how Brown ran his business dealings.

This is one key reason Stubblefield hasn't been paid for the hundreds, probably thousands, of times "Funky Drummer" has been sampled in dance, pop, and hip-hop songs. It's also the reason why his name does not appear in the liner notes of albums that sample his beats, as he wishes. "I never got a 'Thanks,' I never got a 'Hello, how ya doing?' or anything from any of the rap artists," Stubblefield says. "The only one I got a thanks or anything from was Melissa Etheridge." Far too many sidemen and a surprising number of featured artists from funk, soul, and R&B's golden era have found themselves in Clyde Stubblefield's unfortunate position. Many innovative artists contributed greatly to the development of popular music during that time, but they didn't receive any copyrights as a condition of playing music professionally. Although some musicians who retained their copyrights reaped rewards through sample licensing—Curtis Mayfield is a notable exception—many more, like Stubblefield, weren't so lucky.

George Clinton Gets Ripped Off

Many musicians—hip-hop artists and otherwise—view sampling as a technique that can revive lost or forgotten music that has been relegated to the literal and metaphorical used-record bins. In the 1980s, record companies disregarded the aesthetic importance of this music, which meant that Parliament-Funkadelic records remained out of print until artists began sampling them on songs like De La Soul's "Me, Myself, and I." Major labels eventually realized that their catalogs of black music—which the labels had typically treated as disposable commodities—were worth making available to the public. "At the time that a lot of hip-hop producers started sampling George Clinton, his records weren't available commercially anymore," Jeff Chang says in explaining how sampling reinvigorated the musician's career. "So, hip-hop literally re-introduced the world to George Clinton and Parliament-Funkadelic." As George Clinton adds, "I was glad to hear it, especially when it was our songs. You know, it was the way to get back on the radio."

Clinton did at one time own the copyrights to his music. But in a classic case of shady music-industry shenanigans, he lost ownership of much of his catalog in the early 1990s. "George Clinton, because of the absurd nature of the labor politics in the music industry, does not own his copyrights," states the media professor Siva Vaidhyanathan. This loss stemmed from an allegedly fabricated contract that transferred many of Clinton's composition copyrights (on songs recorded before 1983) to Armen Boladian of Bridgeport Music, a copyright aggregator. This document—which a New York court ruled was a cut-and-paste job—relieved Clinton of his publishing rights for a ridiculously small sum of money, despite the fact that these copyrights were extremely valuable.

"After a certain amount of time," says Brian Zisk, a friend of Clinton's, "George realized that this other guy was claiming all his rights and he wasn't being paid on any of his music." Clinton himself puts it more bluntly: "The guy just stole them. He just signed his name on the piece of paper and sold it to the other record company." The full story is more complicated, since Boladian wasn't just some stranger to Clinton. In addition to owning Bridgeport, Boladian founded the label Westbound Records, which released some of Clinton's Funkadelic albums (and was a co-plaintiff in *Bridgeport Music v. Dimension Films*). Accusations flew from both sides: Clinton allegedly borrowed money from Boladian, while Boladian allegedly engaged in fraudulent accounting.[22]

Clinton lost the case, perhaps because Boladian hired the same powerful lawyer that George W. Bush used in 2000 to win the Florida election debacle. After Boladian secured control of Clinton's catalog, Zisk says, "He filed over eight hundred lawsuits against people suing them for using George's work without his permission." One defendant was Clinton himself—for sampling *his own song.* "Yeah, I got sued for sampling my own stuff. In fact, I still have a suit pending," says a bemused Clinton. Boladian also sued Public Enemy for using an extremely fragmentary Parliament-Funkadelic sample in their song "Bring the Noise."[23] "He's suing everyone under my name," says Clinton. "He sued Public Enemy for $3 million for one song, so we got on CNN with Chuck and Flav and said that it wasn't me."

Fortunately, in 2005 George Clinton's legal team successfully brought a separate lawsuit and regained control of four of the albums he lost. They still hope to win back the remaining albums that Clinton feels are legitimately his. As Vaidhyanathan puts it, "That means from now on he will actually benefit from the work he did in ways that he hasn't before. That means that when artists want to build upon his work, they're going to be dealing with another artist. This is a good thing in general."

Aerosmith and Run-DMC Take a Walk Together

Just as hip-hop sampling delivered the music of James Brown and George Clinton to a new generation, Run-DMC helped expand Aerosmith's audience in the 1980s with their collaborative take on "Walk This Way." Despite the fact that rock music directly descends from rhythm and blues, the type of arena rock that Aerosmith popularized in the 1970s had a predominantly white fan base. When the producer Rick Rubin suggested to Run-DMC that they cover the song, the idea worked for the rap group because their DJ, Jam Master Jay, had been using the song's opening beat for years in their live performances. Partly with the idea of helping Run-DMC cross over to white rock fans, Rubin then enlisted Steven Tyler and Joe Perry to perform on Run-DMC's 1986 remake of their song.

Before they began their collaboration, the members of Run-DMC hadn't familiarized themselves with the rest of the song, including the verses and chorus. In fact, before their face-to-face meeting, Run-DMC thought Aerosmith's name was Toys in the Attic (the title of the Aerosmith album that contains the song "Walk This Way"). "When Steven

Tyler came into the studio," recounts DMC, "Jay was cutting up [Aerosmith's original version of] 'Walk This Way' and he said, 'Here's what we used to do with your record.' And Steve said, 'Yo, when are you gonna hear *me*?' and Jay looked up and said, 'We never get to hear you. After this guitar riff, it's back to the beginning.' And Steve thought that was amusing."[24]

Run-DMC had previously enjoyed a minor hit with the rock-infused "King of Rock," but their collaboration with Aerosmith resulted in a major hit on M T V and Top 40 radio. Sales of *Raising Hell* broke one million copies, the first hip-hop album to cross that barrier. The success of "Walk This Way" put Run-DMC on the popular culture radar, and it placed Aerosmith—who was more or less washed-up at the time—*back* on that radar. Aerosmith also had a big payday by earning royalties on Run-DMC's record sales and radio airplay. This early rap-rock collaboration provides a fairly straightforward example of sampling's financial benefits, but because it is part of the music business, the paper trail can get far more complicated (to the point of ridiculousness). More often than might be expected, people who have had absolutely nothing to do with the creation of a song have reaped its financial rewards, as is the case with our final example.

Big Pimpin' with Alan Lomax

Our most head-spinning story involves an odd couple: the legendary song collector Alan Lomax—whose Depression-era recordings for the Library of Congress documented hundreds of obscure American folk and blues songs—and Jay-Z, one of the biggest-selling hip-hop artists of all time. In an unlikely turn of events, these two iconic figures became songwriting partners on one of Jay-Z's best songs, "Takeover," from the album he released in 2001, *The Blueprint*. How did a dead white guy who used to record nineteenth-century folk songs end up receiving a songwriting credit on a Jay-Z recording released at the start of the twenty-first century? And why does someone like Clyde Stubblefield receive no compensation when James Brown is sampled, while the estate of Alan Lomax—who didn't have a hand in writing the songs he recorded—gets paid?

To answer this, we need to chart a genealogy of Jay-Z's "Takeover," a case study that highlights the bewildering ways that copyright law deals with art, the operation of sample licensing, and the music industry's troubling relationship with race. In *The Blueprint*'s liner notes, "Takeover" is credited to Jay-Z, the lyricist, and Kanye West, the song's producer and creator of the song's sample-based musical bed. As we discussed in chapter 1, Jay-Z paid out what we assume was a flat fee to say the word "fame" the way David Bowie phrased it in his hit song of the same name. The other rights holders who have a stake in the song publishing of "Takeover" include The Doors' Jim Morrison, John Densmore, Robby Krieger, and Ray Manzarek; KRS-ONE and Rodney Lemay, a.k.a. Showbiz, who produced "Sound of Da Police"; Eric Burdon and Bryan Chandler from the Animals; and, yes, Alan Lomax.

Even though there are so many co-authors, Jay-Z and West only sampled two sound recordings. The first is The Doors' "Five to One," which provides the song's main sampled riff, and the second is the song "Sound of Da Police." When Jay-Z and Kanye West sampled the sound recording of the Doors' song "Five to One," they had to get permission from both the Doors' sound recording owner, Elektra Records, as well as the four members of the Doors who wrote the composition. Because there are no other record labels, songwriters, or publishing companies that control "Five to One," the permission issue was a simple one. The second sample is a fleeting six words from KRS-ONE's "Sound of Da Police": "Watch out! We run New York." Even though "Takeover" samples less than two seconds of KRS-ONE's vocals, Jay-Z nevertheless had to license all of the other elements sampled in the remaining four minutes and seventeen seconds of KRS-ONE's song. Such is the rule according to the music industry's sample clearance system.

The track by KRS-ONE samples a performance by Grand Funk Railroad, a white American hard-rock band popular in the 1970s. What further complicates this genealogy is the fact that Grand Funk Railroad didn't even write the song that KRS-ONE sampled. Instead, it was a cover version of "Inside Looking Out," which was written by the British rock act from the 1960s named the Animals—or, we should say, it was *kind of* written by the Animals. In actuality, "Inside Looking Out" as performed by the Animals was actually a rewritten version of "Rosie," a nineteenth-century folk song that was "collected, adapted, and arranged"—and copyrighted—in 1934 by Alan Lomax and his father, John. The Animals' "Inside Looking Out" features a new musical arrangement and additional lyrics by Eric Burdon and Bryan Chandler, the two central musicians in the group, but Lomax is also listed as a copyright owner on this composition.

Of course, all this still raises the question *why* Alan Lomax is listed as an author on "Inside Looking Out," or even on "Rosie." During the Great Depression, many collectors who recorded folk songs for the Library of Congress, including the Lomaxes, often published them under their own names.[25] There is a long tradition of this sort of practice in the music industry. For instance, the British folk song collector Cecil Sharp attached his name to the copyrights of a number of the traditional folk songs he collected, including "The Battle Hymn of the Republic" and the classic folk song "Old King Cole"—a song that Oscar Brand sarcastically writes was "old when London Bridge was still a plank and 'Beowulf' was the Book of the Month."[26] And thus Alan Lomax, much like his contemporaries and predecessors in the "song catching" business, staked a claim to a song he had no hand in writing.

To summarize: In the 1930s, Alan Lomax copyrighted the nineteenth-century folk song "Rosie." In the 1960s, the Animals rewrote the song as the newly titled "Inside Looking Out," to which they added Lomax as a co-author. Grand Funk Railroad then covered the song a few years later, and KRS-ONE sampled it in the 1990s. Therefore, the Animals' Eric Burdon and Bryan Chandler—as well as Alan Lomax—got a songwriting credit on KRS-ONE's "Sound of Da Police." They received this credit and partial ownership despite the fact that the rapper only sampled very brief guitar riff played by Grand Funk Railroad. The sample neither provides the central hook for his song nor is it very audible in the mix. Nevertheless, it's enough for Lomax to become a co-writer on two classic hip-hop tracks: "Sound of Da Police" and "Takeover," which sampled the KRS-ONE track from the 1990s.[27]

This case underscores several contradictions—racial, economic, and musical—at play in sample licensing. The history of the twentieth-century American music industry is also a history of the exploitation of African American artists by whites. It was not uncommon for a black songwriter to have his or her name replaced by a businessperson or musician with more legal and economic resources but little or no involvement in songwriting. For instance, Elvis Presley reportedly didn't write a single song in his life, but his name appears on the publishing credits of several songs he recorded. Alan Lomax's hip-hop songwriting credits are an uncomfortable reminder of this legacy. Aside from the sticky racial politics, this case also underscores another dynamic at work. The process of adaptation and transformation that occurred during the evolution of the original song "Rosie" is a great example of how the folk music process works—or, we should say, used to work.

INTERGENERATIONAL MUSICAL DIALOGUES

Hip-hop brings back old R&B
If we would not people could have forgot.
—STETSASONIC, "Talkin' All That Jazz"

The example of Jay-Z and Alan Lomax raises an important question for contemporary artists: What happens when an enterprising hip-hop producer comes along in ten years and tries to pay tribute (or disrespect) to Jay-Z by sampling "Takeover"? He or she will have to get permission not only from both Jay-Z's publishing company and record company, Def Jam, but also from the many parties who control the copyrights to the songs sampled in "Takeover." If one of those parties says no, or demands an exorbitant fee, the new song will be denied a legal existence. As more and more modern music incorporates samples from past songs—including songs that themselves contain samples—life is growing increasingly difficult for remix artists. By the same token, sampling can leave the creators of classic songs from the past, such as Clyde Stubblefield, feeling as though they received nothing in return.

Given this, it's important to recognize that sampling isn't just an economic exchange but also an intergenerational one in which younger musicians engage with and recontextualize earlier forms of music. Through the first half of the twentieth century, blues and folk musicians regularly retooled the lyrics, melodies, and songs of previous musicians. From the perspective of some copyright owners and musicians, copyright offers a desirable tool for exerting control over such uses of existing music. However, copyright law slows the folk process of music making by preventing some elements of copyrighted compositions, absent permission or a license, from being legally transformed any further. Copyright can freeze the development of melodic themes and lyrics by stamping the name of an author on a "final product." It can also prevent current artists from engaging with musicians from the past through the technology of digital sampling.

Sampling artists draw on deep musical and cultural traditions that are connected to the sounds they sample, whether they are referencing a specific figure like James Brown or a funky decade like the 1970s more generally. "That's what's cool about sampling," says Drew Daniel, one half of the experimental electronic group Matmos. "It transports the listener, if they're willing, to move in that pathway back to a specific moment in time. So, it's sort of like an archive of memories, of real experiences." And Coldcut's Matt Black points out that when people sample Brown's iconic grunt, they are "sampling it because it's 'James Brown,' and you're referring to his whole canon of music and what he means to us people who love that funky music. So, a good appropriated sample has those two qualities. It has a good quality of its own, and it has a strong reference that evokes cultural resonance as well."

The classic song "Fight the Power," featured in Spike Lee's film *Do the Right Thing* (1989), exemplifies how Public Enemy mixed history and sound. "'Fight the Power' has so many different layers of sound," says Chuck D, explaining that the song is embedded with sampled loops of melodies, vocals, speeches, and other noises playing forward and backward. He characterizes "Fight the Power" as an assemblage of a quarter century of sounds that invoke the black experience. "That song contains a great deal of black music history from a twenty-five-year period," Chuck D observes. "You listen to it, and it's like [mock announcer's voice], '*This twenty-five-year period of black music is brought to you by Public Enemy.*'" From beginning to end, it is filled with musical, cultural, and political history.

Discussing another example of how sampling can reanimate our cultural history, Public Enemy's Harry Allen points to his all-time favorite song on *It Takes a Nation*—"Show 'Em Whatcha Got," which Jay-Z sampled in his hit from 2006 "Show Me What You Got." As Allen notes:

> The song is composed of the sounds of a lecture by Sister Ava Muhammad of the Nation of Islam over this incredible slowed-down drum and bass. It's this booming track, this mournful horn. By taking this speech by Sister Ava Muhammad and putting it over this music, what you get is something that has even more pathos and a kind of sadness, yet defiance, that I think was in her voice. Public Enemy found and accentuated that defiance by recontextualizing her voice by sampling it and putting it in this new work. A lot

of the sound of that album is not that of horns and drums and guitars, but the jittery staccato of digital technology. You hear Louis Farrakhan's voice, which has been digitally sampled and reedited. You have these screams and hollers and grunts and moans all brought together into this orchestra of human passion, you might say. The interesting thing is that PE used something as cold and brittle as computer chips, and samplers, to give this kind of resurrection and life to the voices of pain of black people—as uttered in song and voice.

By treating sound as both aesthetic object and historical text, sampling technologies can make the past come alive. As such, sampling is a form of aural storytelling.

For instance, we interviewed Jeff Chang in the LP-laden back room of the Atlanta record store Wax 'n' Facts. Pointing to the massive wall of LPS and CDS surrounding him, Chang noted that the store is in many ways an archive of the past. The albums are quite literally *records*, with musical history encoded into the grooves in the vinyl. The poet, musician, and filmmaker Saul Williams illustrates the historical dimension of sampling when discussing one of his favorite Public Enemy songs, "Welcome to the Terrordome," from *Fear of a Black Planet*. As Williams says, "There's this part, my favorite part of the song, where Chuck goes, 'The shooting of Huey Newton / From the hand of a nigga pulled the trigger.'" He then describes how those lyrics are punctuated by a guitar squeal that breaks through the collaged cacophony. "The thing is," Williams says, "hearing that guitar, you *know* that that guitar is a sample. You know it's not coming from someone in the studio with them now doing that. And you get the feeling that that guitar is related to the era when Huey Newton was shot."

The music historian David Sanjek maintains that sampling artists often look for sounds that offer a certain historical resonance. "I think the ways in which samples get chosen are often because there's a particular sound that people associate with an era," Sanjek says. "So I think, for example, people will hear the whacking of [Sly & the Family Stone's] Larry Graham's slap-back bass style. Probably a significant number of people won't know Larry Graham from a hole in the ground, but they'll hear that sound and it conjures up an earlier period—the sixties, the seventies." Lawrence Ferrara, a New York University musicologist and sampling expert, says that hip-hop producers "want to retain the richly analog sound that they really can't re-create unless they're going to use some kind of device that we don't use anymore in studios. So they want that particular sound."

Some critics of sampling believe that if these hip-hop producers were truly creative, they would bring in session musicians to play a guitar riff, a vocal sound bite, a flute melody, or a drum break. But that view misses the point, because many feel that there is aesthetic value and shared cultural resonance in using a particular sound recording. "What comes from a dusty old record has a different type of feel to it that allows you to create a sense of agedness," says Jeff Chang. Whether one could exactly re-create a guitar riff is a moot point for many hip-hop producers, because they want to access the sonic qualities that can only be found on a particular old album recorded in a specific time and place. They are looking for that certain kind of timbre, a certain kind of aura, that signifies, for instance, an old guitar sound taken from a funk-rock record from the 1970s. "There's something about sound popping on a record," Mr. Len says. "You can almost smell the smoke in the air and hear, like, the griminess of a great sample on an ashy-ass record." Or as DJ Abilities puts it, "The main reason I still sample is, *tonally*. I want the *sound* of it." But what if someone claims ownership of a sound?

WHEN SOUND BECOMES A COMMODITY
(AND WHEN IT SHOULDN'T)

Sometimes you can't put soul in a bottle. You can't quantify soul
with a person that just got a briefcase and sits down and thinks that
everything soulful is exclusive. There's a lot of soul that's just
not exclusive, it's just in the air.—CHUCK D

In discussions about musicians sampling the music of the past, the legal and economic issue lurking just below the surface is the question of what musical elements should be subject to property rights and what expressions should be free for the taking (and remixing). A few of our interviewees—particularly those associated with the contemporary sound-collage underground, like Vicki Bennett, the Tape-beatles, and Negativland—feel strongly that all prerecorded sounds should be up for grabs. Nevertheless, they distinguish the transformative nature of their own collages from the act of bootlegging (copying and distributing whole albums or entire musical works). Interviewees from other underground music scenes also resist a fundamentally economic and property-based view of music. For example, DJ Vadim states: "I refuse to pay for sampling. I mean, I've changed the music so I wouldn't have to pay." He alludes to the notion of transformation—which happens to be one theory of what can constitute fair use in copyright law.

At the other end of the spectrum, there are those who feel that even the smallest musical fragment should be properly licensed—a view primarily found among people employed within the mainstream music industry. As one interviewee put it: "There are rules." Most of those we interviewed, however, fell somewhere between the extremes. "Even though I respect drummers and feel like a lot of drummers are adding their own thing to a composition, by and large, I've always felt that that's the background of the music," says Eothen Alapatt of the independent label Stones Throw. Alapatt continues by stating, "It's one of those things where if you're just using a drum sound, should you be paying the publisher and the copyright owner to use that sound? I'm not really sure. I don't think so."

Protection for Rhythms?

The relationship between rhythm, sampling, and copyright law is complex. To a certain extent it underscores some of the ways that Western intellectual property law is ethnocentric. Music from Africa and the African diaspora emphasizes rhythm far more than melody, whereas the inverse is true for Western folk, pop, and classical music. Because of this history, current music-industry practices, as expressed in song publishing contracts that designate copyright owners, typically ignore the value of rhythm. "The legal definition of songwriting is really focused on melody and lyrical content," says Matmos's Drew Daniel. "It is 50 percent lyrics and 50 percent melody. What this leaves out of the equation is percussion, bass lines, noises, and the specific sounds that are used to execute the melody."

The musical fragments that tend to be sampled are often the rhythmic elements of a song. Daniel cites as examples the bongo and rhythm guitar line in Sister Sledge's "Thinking of You," which have been sampled in numerous dance records. "The samples have nothing to do with the melody of 'Thinking of You,'" Daniel points out, but their desirability as source material for sampling demonstrates the importance of rhythm. David Sanjek argues that, in practice, copyright law often ignores the fact that cultural texts are frequently produced collectively. Instead, it foregrounds the role of an original "genius" author—something that Sanjek refers to as the doctrine of original authorship.

"In many cases, the law does not acknowledge the participation and the compositional role that certain players have had in that process," Sanjek says, referring specifically to drummers. The pop provocateurs the KLF also raise this issue in their satirical book from 1988, *The Manual (How to Have a Number One Hit the Easy Way)*. In it, the KLF point out that the "copyright laws that have grown over the past one hundred years have all been developed by whites of European descent, and these laws state that fifty per cent of the copyright of any song should be for the lyrics, the other fifty per cent for the top line (sung) melody; groove doesn't even get a look in." And as they note further, "If the copyright laws had been in the hands of blacks of African descent, at least eighty per cent would have gone to the creators of the groove, the remainder split between the lyrics and the melody."[28]

Traditional Music

Another consequence of this doctrine of original authorship is that individuals and record companies can copyright elements of other cultures' traditional music. Although copyright law is complex and varies from country to country, the pioneering ethnomusicologist Charles Seeger wrote that, for the most part, "copyright laws recognize only invention or composition by an individual (or a small group). In general, they do not recognize oral traditions or folk music as copyrightable, and do not establish enduring rights to an invention or idea."[29] Much non-Western music doesn't meet the criteria for copyright protection; there must be an "original," identifiable author in order for it to be copyrightable, a requirement that puts traditional cultures at a decided disadvantage.[30] However, the person who records these sounds can "stake a claim" as Alan Lomax did, and become the de facto copyright owner. As the scholar Sherylle Mills adds, "Through the simple process of recording and transcribing, a recorder exerts enough intellectual effort to secure a copyright over field recordings. The traditional community, however, is denied ownership rights over their music if they cannot produce the requisite 'writing' and 'author.'"[31]

As Steven Feld writes in his examination of the way that these recordings have been sampled in Western pop music that circulates in the global economy: "The primary circulation of several thousand, small-scale, low-budget, and largely non-profit ethnomusicological records is now directly linked to a secondary circulation of several million dollars worth of contemporary record sales, copyrights, royalty, and ownership claims, many of them held by the largest music entertainment conglomerates in the world."[32] Feld notes that almost none of this money directly benefits the indigenous people whose music was recorded and released by outsiders.

A concrete example of this is the eponymously titled album *Deep Forest* (1992), which was created by two French producers who sampled ethnographic recordings from Ghana and the Solomon Islands.[33] Negativland's Mark Hosler describes the album as "background music" and "ear candy": "Trip Hop-y, New Age-y ambient beat stuff with pygmies from a rain forest on top of the music." The documentation for *Deep Forest*, which was released on Sony's 550 Music label, makes claims that UNESCO as well as two musicologists supported the album. One of the ethnomusicologists who made the original field recordings gave permission only after the French producers told one of them that they intended to use his recordings from the Ivory Coast for an "Earth Day" album. The musicologist was not told that the recordings from the Solomon Islands would be used for a widely disseminated commercial album. Ultimately, Sony Music garnered millions in profits from sales of the multiplatinum album and from licensing songs to Porsche, Coca-Cola, and Sony TV for use in advertising campaigns.[34]

Taking Sounds from the Bush of Ghosts

Since the late 1970s, David Byrne has drawn from non-Western music for Talking Heads as well as his solo work, and he thinks that there is certainly a difference between being influenced by certain types of music and outright theft. "Stealing is when Rod Stewart lifts the tune from a Jorge Ben tune," Byrne says, "and doesn't compensate Ben." He is referring to the fact that Rod Stewart and his co-writer on "Do Ya Think I'm Sexy" directly lifted the melody from "Taj Mahal," a song by the Brazilian music legend Jorge Ben. In response Ben sued, and Stewart agreed to donate the publishing royalties for "Do Ya Think I'm Sexy" to the United Nations Children's Fund. Providing a contrasting example, Byrne continues by noting, "If I work with, say, some Latin percussionists to lay down some grooves for a tune I've previously written, is that stealing? I don't think so. It's no more theft than playing the blues-inspired licks that have been appropriated by rock bands forever." Of course, this sidesteps the point made above about how rhythm (a central component of many non-Western musics) is left out of an authorship equation that favors words and melodies.

In 1981, Brian Eno and David Byrne released their landmark collaboration *My Life in the Bush of Ghosts*, which was one of the first records to sample from what would become known as world music. Eno and Byrne sampled several singers and orators from around the globe, including a Lebanese mountain singer, an Egyptian pop singer, firebrand preachers recorded off the radio, and several other "exotic" voices. David Byrne explains why they used so many "found" voices on the album: "I seem to recall we fell into it as a unifying thread for that record. We certainly weren't the first people to use 'found' voices in music." He continues by stating:

> I believe we did maybe one or two songs that used voices and soon realized that by using varying sources and treatments we could make that the unifying factor for the whole record. It also relieved us of the burden of dealing with who would sing any particular song, as we both sing. By avoiding that issue we created another one—as listeners often presume that whoever is singing is, if not the author, then at least the "voice" of a particular song, because the singer (or author) is conveying his or her feelings by singing. In this case, those ways of listening and of authorship were upended.

Even back in the early 1980s, Eno and Byrne chose to get permission for most everything they appropriated. However, in the case of their song "Qu'ran"—which featured Algerian Muslims chanting passages from the Koran—they ran into problems. As Byrne told the hipster music website *Pitchfork*, "Way back when the record first came out, in 1981, it might have been '82, we got a request from an Islamic organization in London, and they said, 'We consider this blasphemy that you put grooves to the chanting of the Holy Book.' And we thought, 'Okay, in deference to somebody's religion, we'll take it off.' "[35]

Byrne expands on this story in his interview with us. "This was all pre-bombings and the rise of global jihad," he says. "When a fundamentalist Islamic organization in London said they found the use of the chanting of the holy book over a music track to be offensive—prayer chanting is not considered music—we immediately replaced the track on subsequent pressings with one we had on the shelf. Maybe we could have argued the point, but we weren't out to make those kinds of points or to challenge or offend someone else's sensibilities." Not only were they being sensitive for religious and other reasons, they also didn't want to be sued. "I think we were certainly feeling very cautious about this whole thing," Byrne told Pitchfork. "We made a big effort to try and clear all the voices, and make sure everybody was okay with everything. Because we thought, 'We're going to get accused of all kinds of things, and so we want to cover our asses as best we can.' So I think in that sense we reacted maybe with more caution than we had to. But that's the way it was."[36]

There are economic issues at play when Western musicians sample traditional music, but Byrne's story shows how other issues emerge. For instance, because traditional communities frequently ascribe significant powers to music—the ability to heal, kill, create bountiful game, and so on—these cultures place an importance on the restriction and regulation of the use of music. As such, financial considerations do not factor in for them. Western law, on the other hand, places a premium on the protection of one's economic interests in property, and therefore, as Sherylle Mills argues, "Traditional music and Western law clash at the most fundamental level."[37]

Race, Ethnicity, and the Music Industry

Even though Negativland's Mark Hosler believes that "It should all be allowed" when it comes to sampling, the economics and ethics of the *Deep Forest* scenario and its ilk are unsettling for him and leave him with misgivings: "It does make me uncomfortable to see a white European person going in and taking this—in this case, indigenous people's culture—and using it in some way and making a ton of money off of it." Hosler understands how his arguments about "free culture" take on a different meaning when transposed to other contexts. "I'd say certainly, at the very least, I feel uncomfortable about it," he says.

"Personally, I wouldn't do it because I have an ethical problem with doing that." Hosler then recounts a time when he was on a panel at New York University, which included a scholar who worked with indigenous people who found his attitude toward appropriation to be "just awful." He says, "I finally I said to him, 'I think you have a very, very valid and legitimate point of view. But I'm not living in those cultures. I'm also not appropriating from them myself. I'm a white, Western man living in a white, Western, media-saturated society. I'm in America and that's what I'm dealing with.'"

It becomes difficult to argue for the free appropriation of musical elements with no restrictions at all when one considers sensitivity to cultural practices, or compensation for poor communities. Similar tensions also arise in communities within the United States and other developed nations. For instance, the blues musician Willie Dixon couldn't read or write, and by the time his daughter Shirley Dixon was eight years old, she "had filled in many copyright forms and typed his lyrics out and mailed contracts."[38] This protected him when, on the first two Led Zeppelin albums, the British megagroup used significant elements of Willie Dixon's songs by altering them slightly and then claiming ownership of the composition. Dixon eventually sued over Led Zeppelin's "Whole Lotta Love," which mined deeply from his song "You Need Love." "My daughter first brought 'Whole Lotta Love' to my attention," said Dixon. "She was all raging about it and that's what really turned me on to it. . . . We made a deal where I was satisfied and that was a very great thing as far as I was concerned because I really wasn't expecting very much."[39]

Dixon's attitude reflects the bleak resignation of many blues artists who watched whites make millions building on and taking from their music. "It may in some ways seem that there's a little bit of ugliness to that," Mark Hosler says. "Sometimes it seems a little unfair, but my God, Led Zeppelin made amazing records. They stole from the best and they took it to another place. And they did something with it that was very much uniquely their own thing." Hosler also points out a contradiction: Dixon and virtually all other early blues artists borrowed from each other, just as Zeppelin did. In fact, many of Dixon's copyrights incorporated material from the cultural commons (such as the song "My Babe," which was part of the southern country-blues tradition long before he claimed authorship).[40]

Blues musicians felt free to draw upon common musical and lyrical themes shared by others in their community. But even though blues musicians engaged in the same type of borrowing that Led Zeppelin and other rock groups did, the power dynamics in the two cases differ. Something else is going on when African Americans borrow from each other than when a white English group, backed by a powerful record label and its lawyers, does the same. Further, given that the supergroup borrowed so heavily from earlier generations of African American musicians, there is some irony in the fact that Led Zeppelin generally does not approve sample requests from hip-hop artists. "Artists have the right to be able to say no," Jeff Chang observes, "but I just find it really ironic that so many of these artists—like Led Zeppelin, who built their careers out of drawing upon a deep and broad well of musical ideas—will prevent their musical ideas from being used by a new generation of artists."

FIGHTING OVER THE SPOILS

People want to get paid, you know?—KYAMBO "HIP HOP" JOSHUA

Some musicians, like the Algerian Muslims that Brian Eno and David Byrne sampled, appear to value creative control more than money. When others sample their work without their permission, they prefer to have the sample removed from the offending track. Other musicians would rather participate economically in the sample-based tracks in which they have (involuntarily) participated musically, which can generate millions of dollars in revenue. Those situations raise the issue of fair division of the financial rewards. Who should get how much money?

Copyright holders, at least some of the time, have a legitimate interest in compensation when their songs are sampled. Some musicians count on licensing revenue to keep their careers going. The rewards of sample licensing might allow them to spend more time and effort on their compositions or recordings, and licensing can provide an additional revenue stream to augment the income musicians receive from album sales or live concerts. Moreover, licensing agreements can allow more music to enter the public sphere, as the story of "Tom's Diner" illustrates. Having Suzanne Vega and her record label organize the remixing activity around that song arguably resulted in even more re-mixes and wider distribution.

We believe that the music industry should reward creative labor. When the reward comes indirectly through a record label or publisher— filtered through a deal that might look unfair from the outside—the principle of compensating musicians for sampling might seem weak, or irrelevant. But when the label or publisher adds value and the musicians fully understand their contract when signing it, the principle can hold. But this is just a starting point. To say that copyright owners deserve compensation and that creative labor deserves reward is no answer to the complex issues posed by sampling. Musicians who sample engage in creative labor, too, which was demonstrated throughout the history of musical collage laid out in chapter 2. Thus, taking a position in favor of compensating musicians is merely to acknowledge the problem of fairly dividing the proceeds from sampling. It does not mean simply taking the side of musicians whose songs are sampled over the musicians who sample them.

Samplers and copyright owners alike have legitimate claims to the proceeds from sample-based works. Both groups contribute to the final product. This perspective suggests that a revenue split of 0/100 or 100/0 in all circumstances would be too extreme. And, in practice, neither extreme occurs very often. The music industry's business practices, with copyright law shaping them at the edges, can—under the right circumstances—strike a balance. The sample clearance system some-times splits the pie somewhere between the extremes. But the question is how often the industry succeeds at finding a convincingly fair division.

Many of our interviewees addressed the complicated relationship between musicians who get sampled and musicians doing the sampling. Some of that relationship is economic, and therefore involves rivalry. It has things in common with the relationship between any producer and supplier. The producer would like to pay less for inputs, and the supplier would like to make as much money on those inputs as possible. In addition, the relationship between sampling and sampled artists has many non-financial components—for example, a sample can pay homage to one's musical predecessors, or it can mock them. These ethical and aesthetic aspects of sampling can play into the financial issues by affecting who gets the money from sample-based music. Finding a balanced solution that adequately reflects the values of compensation and access becomes a tricky endeavor. Many interviewees had mixed feelings about the problem.

TO PAY OR NOT TO PAY, OR, TO SUE OR NOT TO SUE

There's two sides to everything. Some people like to hear
their music being sampled, some don't.—PETE ROCK

Coldcut has been around since the mid-1980s—long enough to watch the sample clearance system evolve into what it is today. "I'm sure there are a lot of excesses and horror stories around," says Matt Black, who is also co-owner of the record label Ninja Tune. "But, I also feel that copyright holders' rights should be recognized and defended to an extent, so I'm not for total anarchy in sampling." He adds, "You couldn't go and sample an entire chorus of a Beatles record and stick it on your track and go, 'Hey, I'm being totally original. I'm a collage artist, *man*, I don't owe you nothing.' It's bollocks." Those who sample—and those who have been sampled—hold varying opinions about the subject. Many samplers agree that if you take an entire hook or chorus, you should pay. But sensible people will disagree on how much you can use from a source before it's copyright infringement.

"What's clear," says Matt Black, "is that sample fees need to be more reasonable, and should reflect the proportion of what was taken." When copyright owners may demand a large percentage of the new song's royalties, it makes it difficult or impossible to legally release interesting collages. Black relates an example, using a little hyperbole: "The Rolling Stones are notorious for, 'If you sample a single smidge, you have to give 200 percent of the publishing and that will be the end of your career.'" And David Byrne tells us, "I certainly don't agree with the policies of the RIAA, but I do feel that if someone makes a commercial musical piece out of your work then you might be entitled to some percentage. The commercial part is important; I think if it's not being sold then people can sample all they want."[41]

Eothen Alapatt, who helps run the independent record company Stones Throw, experiences the complexities of sample licensing from both sides. His label releases new hip-hop records that contain samples, and it also reissues old funk and soul records that the company wants people to sample. "So, on one end you have me and people like me tracking down music because we love the way it sounded when it was sampled, and we want to see that musical culture perpetuated. We see sampling as a way of keeping that culture going," he says. "On another side, you have these musicians whose music is being sampled." Alapatt continues by adding:

> And so I'm torn between the laws that prevent people from sampling music because they can't afford to do it—because there's no set guideline to what the person who's being sampled will charge; what the publishers will demand in terms of a writer's split; down to what percentage of mechanical royalties need to be paid, right? That's on one side. And then on the other side, I represent a lot of these old musicians who are broke and need money and should be paid when their music is sampled. So I feel like there's something about sampling—which in and of itself is very beautiful and leads people like myself, and people younger than me, to get into it. But there's also the financial implications of it. And I fall into that weird gray area where I say, "Yeah, some of this stuff is fine. Sample away if you're doing it on an independent because who can afford to pay for samples on an independent level?" and part of me is like, "Well, everybody can afford to pay." It's just a matter of how much and how reasonable the person being sampled is.

In Alapatt's view, an appropriate, tailored solution depends on samplers' ability to pay as well as ethical intuitions about whether they have been reasonable. His comments, which are sensitive to many perspectives at once, suggest that striking the proper balance between competing interests requires a number of individualized considerations. There is no simple solution.

"White Lines": A Sampled Artist's Perspective

One very convoluted example of musical, cultural, and racial mixing is the case of Grandmaster Flash & the Furious Five's "White Lines," featuring Melle Mel. Tom Silverman, CEO of Tommy Boy Records, says that "White Lines" (1983) was "probably one of the biggest hip-hop records of the time, one that resonated with downtown audiences as well as the uptown audience." It was in many ways a cover version of Liquid Liquid's "Cavern"; not only does it copy the original's distinctive bass line—played by the group's bassist, Richard McGuire—but also the song's rhythmic and compositional structure. The house band hired by Sugar Hill Records essentially replayed Liquid Liquid's "Cavern," a quasi-instrumental song that was just waiting to be used as an instrumental track (the vocals of the original track rest low in the mix, ghostly and ambiguous). "With 'Cavern,'" says remix pioneer Steinski, "it was pretty funky, and the record was pretty popular, at least in downtown clubs. At the time it wasn't that much of a stretch for someone to show up in Englewood at Sugar Hill Studios with a twelve-inch of song and go, 'Yo, man. We could rap over this.'"

Liquid Liquid was an all-white musical group that emerged from a genre-mixing downtown Manhattan scene that was heavily influenced by hip-hop. As Richard McGuire tells us, "I moved to New York in the summer of 1979 and our first show was at CBGB's in the first month we were here." Liquid Liquid came to New York in part because of the post-punk "no wave" scene, but they were immediately transfixed by the music that emanated from the parks, streets, and apartment-building windows. "You start hanging out on the Lower East Side, so you would be hearing this merengue music, and you would hear this cowbell thing and you be like, 'Yeah, that's pretty good,'" McGuire says in discussing the band's shift from no wave squonk to danceable rhythms. Even though the members of Liquid Liquid were enamored with a wide range of music, hip-hop had a profound impact on the group. "It wasn't till I heard Grandmaster Flash's 'Wheels of Steel' for the first time that I thought *that was the future*," a wide-eyed McGuire says.

"It was an interesting moment in time in New York," remembers the music critic Greg Tate. "New York club culture had become very integrated—not just racially but in terms of musical styles . . . mixing up hip-hop, free jazz, punk rock. And DJs would be playing the same kind of variety of music." As Harry Allen tells us, "In the early 1980s, you had this mix of audiences around danceable music at clubs like Danceteria, Negril, and the Funhouse. You'd have high-energy Latin 'freestyle' music, as it was called back then, and hip-hop and other kinds of dance music that are kind of intermingled." Our interviewees reported to us that while working as the DJ at Funhouse, Jellybean Benitez—who would go on to produce Madonna's first songs—used Liquid Liquid's "Cavern" as the last song of the evening. This helped it gain currency among downtown clubbers and hip-hop artists. "When it turns out that Grandmaster Flash, of all people, ends up using my bass line, it was just an honor," says McGuire. "It was this amazing thing at first, and then it got complicated with all the legal stuff later."

The appropriation of Liquid Liquid's "Cavern" wasn't a sample of a sound recording. Instead, the Sugar Hill Records house band replayed the track with traditional instruments—just like they had done with a number of popular songs at the time, such as Chic's "Good Times" (replayed in "Rapper's Delight") and the Tom Tom Club's "Genius of Love" (reworked as Grandmaster Flash & the Furious Five's "It's Nasty"). As Tim Quirk, a musician who got his start in the music business in the 1980s, recalls, "Since the hook from the new tune was pretty much the hook from the Liquid Liquid song, that felt like some kind of line had been crossed. Even then, I didn't think it was illegal—just lame." This isn't to say that Grandmaster Flash didn't transform the Liquid Liquid song in some sense. But the elements (the bass line and the musical bridge) that make Flash's "White Lines" so successful come directly from "Cavern."

This prompted Liquid Liquid's record company, 99 Records, to sue Sugar Hill Records—spawning long, tangled litigation that wasn't resolved for a dozen years. As Liquid Liquid's bassist McGuire recalls:

> Shortly after I heard it, Ed, our manager, got a phone call from Sugar Hill, and it was very, very mafia-like. "We are going to pick you up in a car and drive around and talk about it," was literally what they said to him. There were rumors that there were mob connections in Sugar Hill already; that was common knowledge. So Ed went ahead with the lawsuit. . . . When the court case was going on, they allegedly hired someone with a machete to come into the store [Liquid Liquid's label, 99 Records, was also a record store], and just swing it around and scare the customers out. They were doing all these scare tactics so Ed would drop the case. . . . We won the case and then Sugar Hill filed bankruptcy. . . . [But] basically, Ed put so much money into his own lawyers it caused the demise of 99 Records.

Years later, after this protracted lawsuit, one of McGuire's DJ friends told him that Duran Duran was going to cover "White Lines" for their 1995 album *Thank You*. "I was like, 'OK, I'm going after it myself,'" McGuire says. "At that time I was a little more savvy and I had some money," he tells us. "I went after them, and we finally did an out-of-court settlement, and now the arrangement is that we get a big chunk of what anyone has on 'White Lines.'"

Enforcing its copyright has paid off for Liquid Liquid, especially because their little song has had a long afterlife in the marketplace. "It's actually amazing how many times we get sample requests all the time from all sorts of people; it's shocking to me that it still has a life," McGuire continues. "You would think that 'White Lines' was enough already, but it's still being used. And then there are some other things too—now it's like because of that, some other stuff of ours has been sampled too." Like DNA's remix of Suzanne Vega's "Tom's Diner"—which was also appropriated without permission and only settled after its commercial release—the Liquid Liquid example shows the convoluted ways that sampling can ultimately benefit the original artist who is also a rights holder. "I'm totally for sampling," McGuire says. "It's like any other art form. And I don't think it's necessarily a given that the sources are more interesting than what the end result can be with a collage." He pauses, "But at the same time, I feel both ways about it. I mean, I'm always interested in how someone can reinvent something, but there has to be some sort of structure [for compensation]."

McGuire says, "I just think that what's right is right," reflecting further on the episode. "People should get paid for what they do. But at the same time, I don't have any bad feelings about the 'Cavern' thing. I think it's helped keep our band alive. Because of this thing, the band still has this following; it has given us so much more attention, and it will have the song live on because of it." McGuire emphasizes that he is not bitter about the "White Lines" experience. "I used to say it was my cross to bear," he says, half-joking. "It's the reverse of some black musician coming up with something and being stolen by a white performer. It's like, 'Hey, maybe I'm paying for the sins of my forefathers.'"

"Planet Rock": A Sampling Artist's Perspective

When in 1982 Afrika Bambaataa crafted one of old-school hip-hop's most important songs, "Planet Rock," he essentially created a mash-up of two songs by Kraftwerk, a German electronic group. The synth pioneers were upset by Bambaataa's work—less so because they received no money than because they received no credit. "He knew perfectly well what he was doing," Kraftwerk associate Maxime Schmitt says, "He had not put the names of the authors and had not declared anything." And as the Kraftwerk member Karl Bartos adds, "It was completely the melody off 'Trans-Europe Express' and the rhythm track from 'Numbers.' So we felt pissed off. If you read a book and you copy something out of it, you do it like a scientist, you have to quote where you took it from, what is the source of it."[42]

Bartos is referring to an author's right of attribution, something that exists in some European nations such as France and Germany but receives only sporadic (some say inadequate) protection in America's copyright law.[43] Soon after the release of "Planet Rock," Kraftwerk's song publishing company sued Afrika Bambaataa, Tommy Boy Records, and Tom Silverman. It was an eye-opening experience for the budding independent-record mogul, whose label went on to release many hip-hop classics (and who had to deal with another copyright infringement lawsuit over De La Soul's *3 Feet High and Rising* a few years later). As Silverman remembers:

> I can never forget the name of the publishing company—Kraftwerk's publishing company ironically was called No Hassle Music, but it was the biggest hassle I had in my life. . . . These guys came at me like pit bulls, you know, at the throat, threatening me with everything, trying to stop the record. I had never dealt with lawyers before, or publishers—who make bankers look like sweet people. They were coming to suck blood from a guy who's just starting a little tiny record label, didn't know what he was doing, was trying his best, and I was guilty before proven innocent. There was really no law or precedent set yet in this area, so I didn't really have lawyers that knew how to defend against this. So I made a settlement, I think initially it was twenty-seven and a half cents per single, just for publishing, which is insane.

For comparison, the statutory mechanical royalty rate in 1982 was four cents per single. So Tommy Boy paid over six times as much for a sample as it would have paid for using a whole composition.[44] The litigation over the Kraftwerk sample, like that over the Liquid Liquid sample, shows that the conflict between sampler and copyright owner can be heated. Tommy Boy probably paid a higher rate because it negotiated a license only after releasing the record. The moral intuition of "taking without asking" and the legal fact of Kraftwerk's leverage over a copyright infringer changed the distribution of the rewards from Africa Bambaataa's sample-based work.

A Willingness to Pay, or Lack Thereof

De La Soul's Posdnuos states unequivocally that if someone wants to get paid for a sample, he understands that position. And Trugoy, another member of the group, says that he doesn't have a problem with the licensing system that came into being after they were sued by the Turtles. Referring to the fact that a number of early rock 'n' roll and R&B pioneers were ripped off by the music industry, Trugoy says that paying older artists for their songs that were sampled can be seen as countering "the abuse that has happened in the past." Or, as the legendary hip-hop producer Pete Rock puts it, "If someone uses a composition of someone [else], they have to pay them to use it. I can understand that." Mix Master Mike told us that if you take someone's music, especially the chorus, then the original artist should be compensated in some way. For other samplers, whether compensation is justified depends on whether the sampling work enjoys commercial success.

For some hip-hop artists—particularly those who exist at the margins of the mainstream music industry—framing "sampling" as "stealing" is a move that solidifies hip-hop's outlaw image. "Most people that sample take a loop, and they loop it, and they put some drums and a bass line," says Mr. Dibbs. "That shit's stealing. I don't really care that it's wrong. *At all.* [laughs] It's stealing. I don't care. That's the nature of hip-hop." In Mr. Dibbs's mind, it's pretty simple. "I ain't paying nobody," he says. "I ain't paying shit. I'm not paying you nothin'. Like, you can call me on the phone personally, and I'm not giving you shit because I'm not making enough money to pay eight grand for an '*uh*' from James Brown. But, if I—no, *fuck it.* I'm not paying. Ever." He adds, with the appropriate amount of bluster, "It doesn't mean it's not wrong. It means I don't give a fuck."

El-P, a hip-hop producer and owner of the independent hip-hop label Def Jux, expresses a similar view. "Hip-hop music, it's fuckin' criminal music, man. It is. Period." In the view of many hip-hop artists, theirs is a type of music that is fundamentally transgressive. It's music made by rebels, but even rebels have a sensitive side: "You know," El-P tells us, "I'm empathetic to the other argument, you know, which is, 'I don't want my music stolen or it wasn't what I intended it to be.' I understand. I care about my music just as much as anyone else." But, he adds quickly, "The only problem is that there are specific times when I've just wanted to fuckin' snatch eight bars of someone else's record and put some drums under it, 'cause that's hip-hop. That's some raw hip-hop shit right there."

Sampling without asking for permission isn't solely a transgressive decision on the part of independent artists because some artists also see it as a necessity. As Steinski puts it, "It's like painting. If painting was illegal, people would still paint; I'm still making records." For others, sampling is born out of both necessity and transgression. Mr. Len, a hip-hop producer and DJ—who performed in the underground group Company Flow with El-P—was busted for including an unlicensed sample on his solo album from 2001, *Pity the Fool* (fortunately, Mr. T didn't go after him for trademark infringement on the title as well). This dispute involved a sample taken from a piece by the avant-garde composer Philip Glass—titled "F-104: Epilogue from Sun and Steel"—which was used in the song "Taco Day," featuring the rapper Jean Grae. The legal action forced Mr. Len's label Matador Records to pull the album from retail shelves. Mr. Len acknowledges that, according to the mainstream music industry, one is supposed to clear all samples on a record. However, the hip-hop producer says that he has to consider how much the record might sell and how much money he has to pay for licensing fees before deciding whether or not to clear a sample when releasing a track.

In most cases, though, he is willing to take a chance. "I'm definitely gonna gamble, there's no question about it," he says. "And if the record blows up, then I'd much rather know that I blew a record up through all the hard work than to not take the risk at all." After getting the cease-and-desist letter from Glass and his representatives, Mr. Len proudly hung it in a special place in his studio. "I keep the letter on the wall next to where I make beats," he says. "It's my medal that makes me an official hip-hop producer. You're nobody 'til somebody wants to shut you down!" Striking a similar tone, the producer Prefuse 73 states, "Copyright laws don't stop me from doing anything I wouldn't do normally. I try not to take anything that's so obvious. You know, I got popped that one time for taking something obvious. But whatever, it's a risk you take whenever you sample."

"The thing that pisses me off," says El-P, "is that sampling still exists, it just only exists for motherfuckers who can afford it. That's the fucked up part. And I don't really know what to say about that except that it's pretty sad, you know." This is what Jeff Chang means when he says that the sample clearance system has created its own kind of digital divide separating those who can afford samples and those who can't: "You've got this huge gap now that's been created. Now, the only people that can make hip-hop throwback records—where the canon of breakbeats is being used—are the folks that are so rich that they can afford to do anything they want anyway."

Unlike a major label, an independent label cannot afford the cost of many samples. As the CEO of the independent label Def Jux, El-P expresses his frustration with this dynamic. "I have cleared samples, but attempting to do the right thing and attempting to clear samples for me always ended up with me fuckin' being even more disgusted than before." He then recounts a story about asking permission to use a bass line, to which the publisher came back with a figure that was the entire budget for the whole album. As El-P tells us, "It was like, 'Guess what asshole, fuck you. I'm not giving you any publishing. I'm not giving you any money. Fuck your sample.'"

DEALING WITH ARTISTS, PUBLISHERS, AND RECORD COMPANIES

It's interesting that when people make something,
they get really possessive about it.—TOM SILVERMAN

In late 2009, we contacted Gregg Gillis (Girl Talk)—whose previous two sample-based records had already generated a tremendous amount of attention—to confirm with him personally that he had not received any legal threats. "I've had no issues," he says. "Big Boi from Outkast came out to a show of mine in Atlanta, and he verbally confirmed that he was cool with what I was doing. Sophie B. Hawkins's manager reached out to me for a potential collabo. Thurston Moore of Sonic Youth had never heard of my stuff, but when I explained it, he was cool with it theoretically. A songwriter for Donnie Iris reached out to me to say he was into my stuff." (We checked in again with Gillis when this book was going to press in 2010, and he still did not have any problems.) However, not all artists are as open to the idea of being sampled.

"Sometimes it is the artists who won't allow their work to be sampled—not for love or money or percentages," David Byrne tells us. That kind of across-the-board recalcitrance is not uncommon. As Danny Rubin notes, "There's some publishers, and I can think of one offhand—which again, I don't want to mention—that will not ever accept submissions for samples. They'll just flatly say, 'We do not clear any samples. Please let your client know that this is flatly denied and not to sample any of our material again.'" The producer Marley Marl has said that hip-hop's graphic and confrontational reputation led some artists to deny him permission to sample their music.[45] For instance, Anita Baker will not allow any of her songs to be sampled by hip-hop artists, and James Brown forbade the sampling of his music in hip-hop songs about violence and drugs. This attitude reflected Brown's fundamental beliefs more than any bias against hip-hop. When Brown was alive, his special assistant stated that "he really doesn't want to be involved in any kind of rap that demoralizes any segment of society."[46]

As the entertainment lawyer Dina LaPolt recalls, "I had a client that sampled Steve Miller. It's brilliant. [But] he wouldn't approve it. He was clearly not interested in having his song contained in any type of rap song." For instance, when the Geto Boys attempted to rerelease their song "Gangsta of Love" through a major label distributor in the late 1980s, they had to replace the sample of the Steve Miller Band's "The Joker" that appeared on the original version. (In an intertextual domino game, the name of the Geto Boys' track derives from a line from Miller's "The Joker"—"Some people call me the space cowboy / some call me the gangster of love"—which in turn refers to Miller's song from 1969 "Gangster of Love.") After the Geto Boys got a flat "No" they switched out the Miller sample for another classic rock song they successfully cleared: Lynyrd Skynyrd's "Sweet Home Alabama." More than one interviewee told us that Steve Miller really dislikes hip-hop music, and relayed to us similar negative stories (which were told off the record).[47]

The way a sample is used can be a deciding factor for the artist whose recording or composition is being sampled. During the clearance process, Danny Rubin tells us, most licensors want to hear the song before they grant permission, because they understandably want to have some input. Hip Hop tells a story of making Jay-Z's "Streets Is Watching," which samples a song by an obscure Australian musician. It was difficult to track down the musician, and even after finding him it took months to negotiate the deal, which also carried an expensive fee. Then, after all that trouble, when negotiations came to a close the musician refused permission. "Then we had to come back and write a letter to him," Hip Hop says, "and then next thing you know he basically was like, 'Well, you can use the record but we can't have no curses on the record.'" Fortunately, it was one of the few songs that Jay-Z made without a cuss word, and so things worked out in the end.

The entertainment lawyer Shoshana Zisk experienced similar reluctance during an incident that happened when she was working at Island Records. Luke Skyywalker (real name Luther Campbell), from the foul-mouthed rap group 2 Live Crew, released a solo album on Island titled *Uncle Luke*. "He had a bunch of samples of music by Prince, like 'Darling Nikki' or different things like that," Zisk says. "Of course, Luke Skyywalker is arguably very obscene, and so Prince declined all of them. This was after the record had been mastered and delivered, and so they had to go back and rerecord the album. So I think from that point forward it was generally understood in the office that it's probably not a good idea to sample anything written by Prince." As the music manager Michael Hausman notes, "The context in which music appears is very important. . . . If the lyrics were sexist, violent, or very profane, [an artist] might not want to have anything to do with it."

Tom Silverman, however, raises several questions about how much control a copyright author or owner should have over a work once it has been widely circulated in the marketplace. "Should an artist be able to say, 'You can't take my "Stairway to Heaven" and make it "Stairway to Gilligan's Island," or anything else'? Or [say that] 'you can't use it on a hip-hop record'? You know, 'You can't take it out of context, or anything else. You can't re-contextualize what I've done. It has to stay true to the original.'" The "Stairway to Gilligan's Island" example refers to an actual dispute. The group Little Roger and the Goosebumps set the lyrics to the *Gilligan's Island* television show theme song to the music for "Stairway to Heaven" by Led Zeppelin, and in so doing essentially created a mash-up, though they performed it themselves. Recorded in 1978, it was released as a single by the independent label Splash Records, and within a month Led Zeppelin's attorneys threatened to sue the band unless all remaining copies were destroyed.

While such scenarios can be problematic—from a creative-freedom perspective—Mr. Len observes that "it all depends on what side of the fence you're sitting on. Like, if you're the one infringing someone's copyright, of course, you feel like, 'Hey man, this copyright law *sucks*.' But if it swings back around and someone samples your music for a bestiality flick," he says with a smile, "you're gonna be a little *pissed* about it, you know what I'm saying?" De La Soul's Posdnuos also sympathizes with those who are offended by the lyrical content of some hip-hop songs. "After we put together a song, it becomes very special to us. And to hear someone rhyme over it, you could be like, 'Wow, someone's rhyming over my record, or some R&B group did something over it.' I mean, like, you feel an attachment to your own creation." As he notes further, "I respect anybody who feels an attachment to a song that might be about their mother, and then N.W.A. samples it and says 'bitch' over it. It's understandable they don't want that."

When Artists Who Sample Get Sampled

Given that the Beastie Boys are widely celebrated as sampling mavericks—a reputation they earned with their *Paul's Boutique* album—they are also notoriously picky about allowing others to sample them. Mark Kates was the president of the Beastie Boys' record label, Grand Royal, and he remembers a time when a European group sampled their song "Girls" without permission. It became a huge hit, and when a friend at the United Kingdom division of Universal Records approached Kates about clearing the sample, the members of the Beastie Boys declined. His friend at the other major label told Kates, "Look, we know it was done this way, but we have a potential for a number-one single here. Is there any way you can help us?" But Kates had to tell him, "Those guys aren't into it."

Despite the fact that the group is known for sampling and even though the Beastie Boys themselves have had to scrap tracks because of uncleared samples (AC/DC and the Beatles have both denied them permission), the group sees no contradictions in the way they police their own work. Mark Kates defends their choice on aesthetic grounds: "The guys in Germany that sampled 'Girls' didn't do it in the same creative solar system that the Beastie Boys operate in. Now maybe there's a bit of hypocrisy there—in terms of the development of hip-hop and sampling and the artistic side of it—but if something sucks, it sucks."

Other artists have more open attitudes toward others sampling their work, though sometimes such attitudes stand at odds with their record labels' policies. Back when Deee-lite was making their first album in the late 1980s, Lady Miss Kier told her liaisons at Warner that she wanted to publicly declare that anyone could sample her group as many times as they wanted to do so. "And they're like, 'No, no, no. You can't do that.' I was like, 'Why? We don't think there's anything wrong with that.'" Kier says that she has been sampled in more than sixty records, but she hasn't sued anyone because they were underground dance records. She adds, however, "If it had been on a Top 10 chart, I would have went after them. And so, I don't know. I have mixed feelings about it." In an example that underscores the complex feelings that musicians have about sampling, Kier mentions a time when a dance record sampled her voice—her trademark "ooh-la-la!" But when the record was used in a car commercial, she sued. "The problem is, I don't sell cars," she says. "I turn down car endorsements. If it's an electric car, go ahead use it, you know what I mean? I live in New York. I don't drive. That's not a product I want to endorse, so I went after them."

"I have no problem with sampling," says Mark Hosler. "Negativland has no problem with it whatsoever. I don't believe that we deserve some chunk of the money from a record selling a million copies." He isn't speaking hypothetically, because Negativland has been sampled in records that have gone platinum. As an example, Hosler mentions the debut record by Marky Mark and the Funky Bunch, which sold over a million copies and featured a hit song that sampled Lou Reed's "Walk on the Wild Side." Hosler says that most of the samples on the album were cleared, "but the record starts out with about five seconds of a sample from a Negativland record. They did not clear it with us. They made no attempt to whatsoever." Even though Negativland uses a lot of found sounds on their own records, they also create their own sounds and compose songs in the studio. This was the case with the Marky Mark sample. Additionally, Hosler points out that the same snippet used by Marky Mark was sampled by the British pop reggae group UB40, and his group was also sampled on the MTV Music Video Awards.

And the Negativland member Don Joyce adds, "We approve. We absolutely approve. I mean, we do it ourselves, and we certainly can't prevent anyone else from doing it." The British sound artist Scanner (Robin Rimbaud), who has also sampled others' music, reinforced his prosampling view by choosing not to pursue a lucrative lawsuit when Bjork sampled his music on her multiplatinum record *Post*. "She used about five seconds of a track of mine," he says, "which formed the basis of her pop song. I was caught in a boiling pot of lawyers battling while I sat behind them thinking, 'What's going on?' I didn't mind that it was used for this track because I too used sounds from other places." Scanner continues by stating:

> Morally, it felt wrong to be asking for money because this sound of mine is being introduced into another work, this popular piece of music—which took it in a completely different direction. Yet somehow, my arm was being pulled behind my back to say, "No Robin, you're doing the wrong thing. All these artists are trying to do is rip you off." And it's interesting, because there was this seductive technique used by a legal firm on me, which was supposedly supporting me, but bringing me into a situation I was really unhappy with. Which was to say, "You've stolen my sample, this is completely wrong." When in fact I was sitting there thinking, "I don't really mind. I think this is great." But, what do I do? How do you stop the process once it actually starts running? And, in fact, this process ran for some months. . . .
>
> At the end of the story, I just said to Bjork's company, I said, "Look, I'm really fed up with this. I really don't have a problem with you using the piece. If you pay my legal fees, I'd be happy that the end of this story happens." My record company said, "How dare you do such a thing. I can't believe you've done it!" Dumped me off the label, and then issued my demos from my new record as my new record, but switched the name of the demos—which weren't even a finished recording—to the original name of the record that Bjork had sampled, so the marketplace would find this record thinking, "Ah, there's the record that Bjork sampled from Scanner," when in fact they were just demos that I hadn't even approved. It got to be a very messy situation.

Record labels and lawyers, who have their own interests at stake, typically mediate the relationship between artists who sample and those who get sampled. Clashing perspectives on the right licensing fee—or whether there should be any fee at all—often result. Labels, artists, and lawyers understandably feel wronged at the end of such episodes.

The hip-hop group Digital Underground had far greater commercial success than Negativland, both of which hail from the San Francisco Bay Area. Digital Underground's record *Sex Packets* (1990) spawned the hit singles "Dowhatchalike" and "The Humpty Dance," but as frontman Shock G tells us, "If it's just a little piece, a little sound bite here, and a sound bite there, use *whatchalike*. You like Humpty's voice? Funk with me. Spread it to the world, you know." The hip-hop producer Prefuse 73 says much the same thing: "If somebody's going to take something of mine, some beat of mine and use it in some different way, do something creative with it, do whatever with it, I'm not going to care."

Along this line, De La Soul's Pasemaster Mase notes, "As long as somebody really does their thing with it. I mean, there's been a few things that I've heard that I don't like—you know, 'That's wack'—but I can understand they sampled it just out of appreciation for us and all." This attitude is shared by many hip-hop pioneers, including the production mastermind for Public Enemy, Hank Shocklee. "I've always been from the school where if I'm sampling," Shocklee says, "who am I to attack somebody else from sampling from me?" We should note, however, that he did end up suing Madonna when she and Lenny Kravitz, who produced her mega-hit "Justify My Love," sampled and looped a large chunk of Public Enemy's song "Security of the First World." Musicians working in various groups and in partnership with producers face their own internal negotiations on how to handle sampling. As Chuck D puts it:

> When it comes to sonic lending, not everybody has to be on the same page. I've written songs where other songwriters say, "Well Chuck, we don't really like that you ain't trying to go after so-and-so. We co-wrote that song." So that's a time when you get into discrepancy between your beliefs and somebody else's beliefs—and they co-wrote a song with you. Just because you're like, say, "Alright I want to give my music away," they're like, "No I don't want you to give my music away, and they used a piece of my music so we gotta go after them." Even with close friends, people like DJ Premier, you know?

Attitudes toward sampling can get complicated as soon as more people enter the equation—a situation that is intensified by the fact that the music business is, well, a business. "You have to put more people around you that have some kind of business sense," Chuck D tell us. "I've sued and I've been sued. That's the nature of the business, you know, you sue and you get sued." Partly because he works with others, therefore, Chuck D's liberal attitude toward being sampled can only go so far.

Economic Relationships in Sampling

Most of the stories in this chapter focus on whether sampled artists grant permission, and on the amount of licensing fees. This economic conflict is practically inevitable: artists who sample would clearly prefer to pay less to use samples, while artists and copyright owners whose recordings or compositions are sampled would prefer to receive more revenue. Moreover, sample-based songs might cut into the market for the sampled song—say, if a song samples the hook or best part of the sampled song prominently enough to become a substitute for it. But other competing interests in the context of sampling are more subtle. Just as any record competes in the retail marketplace with other records, particular samples compete with each other in the realm of sample licensing. In the market for samples, all copyright owners could become sellers. Musicians have a finite budget to pay for sample licenses, and thus copyright owners interested in licensing are competing over scarce resources. They can compete passively, just by making their tracks available to the public. Or they can compete more actively, encouraging subsequent musicians to sample them.[48]

Those who own sampled recordings or compositions can reap considerable rewards, but only some will hit the jackpot and get sampled in a new hit song. Then again, once sampling artists become interested in certain genres of older music, many of those who are sampled can benefit. The prior works in a genre thus become complements rather than substitutes—as, for example, when funk became widely attractive to samplers. On the other side, sample-based music competes for retail sales against other sample-based music—and all music, for that matter. But musicians who sample also compete in a unique way over the inputs they use. The situation of many musicians wanting to use the same sample can drive the price of that sample upward, and owners of frequently sampled source material have been put on notice that their songs are valuable in this market. This increases the amount of policing they or their representatives might do, and it potentially increases the cost of licensing their music.

But the competition among groups within the sample clearance system should not obscure the other ways in which all musicians' interests can align. Sample-based songs might promote sales of the songs that musicians sample, and thus make their sales complements rather than substitutes. Being sampled can expose a track to a new audience, long after the track's release, and enhance the benefits of having a copyright revert back to the original composer or recording artist.[49] Once a sampler has obtained a license, interests on both sides of the transaction align. Under many licensing arrangements, sales of the sample-based track will benefit both sides, their labels, and their publishers. Licensing fees can also help recording artists recoup with respect to their record labels. As Tom Silverman, whose Tommy Boy label released "Gangsta's Paradise," points out, "There's many, many examples of an original record being outsold by the cover, or the remake that sampled part of it. Even 'Gangsta's Paradise' [by Coolio] did much more than 'Pastime Paradise' by Stevie Wonder—like *ten times more.*" Dissing his former signee, he adds, "And that was *Stevie Wonder.* Who the hell is Coolio?"

Often, both musicians who sample and the copyright owners of the sampled music have legitimate claims to shares of the proceeds from sample-based music. Many interviewees, even musicians who sample frequently, expressed sentiments in line with that premise. There are certainly particular instances of sampling that might suggest that the owners of a sampled track should receive all—or none—of the revenue from a song that samples their track. But in general, the appropriate allocation seems to lie between the extremes.

Copyright law and music-industry practices interact to set the ground rules for negotiations over samples. For each sample, however, parties on the side doing the sampling and parties on the side being sampled must ultimately answer the key question themselves: "How should the pie be split?" Whether a sample clearance system can be built that encourages parties to reach the appropriate solution all (or even most) of the time is a distinct and difficult question. Sometimes the existing system leaves all parties satisfied. Other times, the result seems unjust to one side after a licensing dispute resolves. When permission to sample is denied, there is often reason for ambivalence as one recognizes the arguments on both sides. With as many competing interests at play, some dissatisfaction becomes inevitable after a sample-licensing conflict. As the cliché goes, perhaps a fair deal means that every party walks away a little unhappy by having given something up in the compromise.

The contemporary sample clearance system, however, has not reached the desirable, moderate position one might hope that it would achieve. Some of our interviewees suggest that licensing negotiations are skewed too heavily against musicians who sample and their labels. One hypothesis is that this lopsided bargaining power results from a legal regime that provides strong property rights in samples. At the same time, we also heard that copyright owners are losing potential licensing revenue when samplers skirt the system without clearing their samples. The cumbersome nature of the licensing process that the music industry employs might explain this shortcoming. We suspect that a better licensing system—and a clarification of how exceptions to copyright protection might apply to sampling—could avoid some of the dissatisfaction that many of our interviewees have experienced. Mapping the competing positions in the controversy over sampling is a necessary first step in assessing how to improve sample licensing. In chapter 4 we explain how courts have resolved conflicts among competing interests in sampling lawsuits and how the music business has responded to key judicial decisions.

4

SAMPLING LAWSUITS

Hip-Hop Goes to Court

Formal legal disputes are woven into the history of sampling and musical collage, ranging from the 1950s "cut in" recordings to the latest lawsuit against, for instance, Lil Wayne. Filing a lawsuit is often a way to gain leverage in a licensing negotiation—an escalation of the stakes that might nudge a musician who has used an unauthorized sample toward paying a fee. Sampling litigation, like most litigation in general, often reaches a settlement before trial, or at least before a court issues an opinion. But regardless of whether a copyright owner actually sues a sampling artist, licensing negotiations always take place in the shadow of copyright law's provisions—and the ways that courts have interpreted those provisions in particular cases. Thus, even when disputes over sampling don't become lawsuits, both the federal copyright code and judicial opinions shape the sample licensing process. Before discussing sampling case law, however, we need to explain the basic framework of a copyright infringement lawsuit and what a copyright plaintiff must prove.

The strength of a copyright ultimately depends on how its owner enforces it. Sometimes business practices, customs, negotiations, or persuasion are enough to protect a copyright interest. But copyright holders must sometimes protect their rights against others through copyright infringement lawsuits, which can shape how these other solutions operate. In particular, lawsuits play a role in determining the way and the degree to which musicians can use prior works by other musicians. When a copyright owner brings a successful claim for infringement, the range of existing music to which musicians have unfettered access can shrink. On the other hand, when a musician who has sampled without permission mounts a successful defense to copyright infringement, access might be understood to expand.

To prove infringement in any area of copyright law, the plaintiff must establish two things: valid ownership of a copyright and the unauthorized exercise of an exclusive right held by the copyright holder.[1] Establishing an unauthorized exercise of a right in turn requires two steps. The plaintiff must prove, first, that the defendant engaged in copying in fact,[2] and second, that substantial similarity exists between the copyrighted work and the allegedly infringing work.[3] Plaintiffs can demonstrate that copying in fact took place by producing direct evidence of copying, direct evidence of access to the work, or by circumstantial evidence of access. George Harrison, for example, was found liable for copyright infringement based on circumstantial evidence.[4] His song "My Sweet Lord" infringed the composition "He's So Fine" (popularized by the Chiffons' hit recording) even though the court conceded that his copying was subconscious.[5] The Chiffons' song was on the radio in England in 1963, Harrison lived in England in 1963, and two themes in the songs sounded similar. Therefore, the court concluded, copying in fact must have taken place.

In a sampling case, copying in fact is not usually at the center of the dispute. A sample is a literal copy of a sound recording and often fairly simple to recognize. Moreover, if a sampler uses a sound recording, then he or she has necessarily copied the underlying musical composition as well (for purposes of the copying-in-fact part of copyright infringement, not in terms of an overall determination that infringement has occurred). For those samples that are difficult to recognize, modern forensic technologies make it increasingly easy to identify when samples have been used. For instance, in the discovery stage of a trial, a plaintiff can demand to see the original files created by music-editing software—a ProTools setup, for example—to attempt to prove that a copyrighted sound recording has been used. This serves as strong evidence of copying in fact, even if the sample has been masked, distorted, or otherwise altered in the process of remixing. For the most part, lawsuits about sampling tend not to focus on whether the sample is a "copy in fact" but rather on the next part of copyright infringement: substantial similarity.

Substantial similarity has had many interpretations over the years. One common way of evaluating substantial similarity involves asking whether a nonexpert observer who read, heard, or viewed both works would consider the allegedly infringing work and the allegedly infringed work to be similar. But how can we evaluate substantial similarity in the context of sampling in music? The sampler has used the actual sounds of the sampled source, as well as the underlying composition that structured those sounds. In this sense the similarity is exact. Yet musicians often transform and recontextualize the samples they use by putting them into complex collages that sound nothing like the sampled source material.

To address this novel legal quandary, one legal treatise on copyright has developed the concept of *fragmented literal similarity*, a method of determining whether a sample-based work is substantially similar to the source it sampled.[6] The name reflects the exactness of the similarity between the snippet of a track that is sampled and the sampled copy of that snippet. But the method also recognizes that some sample-based works are quite dissimilar from their sources. The key question thus becomes, "At what point does such fragmented similarity become substantial such that the borrowing constitutes an infringement?"[7]

According to this treatise, courts usually answer this question by looking at the plaintiff's work—in other words, the sampled artist's work, not the work of the artist who engaged in sampling.[8] Substantial similarity exists when the portion used is either large enough quantitatively or important enough qualitatively in the plaintiff's work.[9] When the amount used is tiny, on the other hand, some courts say that the sample is *de minimis*—that is, too small for the law to grant copyright protection—or that it does not meet the *de minimis* threshold. Examples include a single note or a single chord. Beyond that, there are no hard-and-fast rules along the quantitative dimension, because the qualitative dimension can always trump.

Even if a copyright plaintiff establishes copying in fact and substantial similarity, the defendant still has another legal avenue to avoid liability: fair use. The fair use doctrine is an affirmative defense to copyright infringement, meaning that a sampler who has been sued would carry the burden of establishing it as a defense. The basic premise of fair use, as we described in the introduction, is that some uses of copyrighted works by members of the public should not count as copyright infringement. Some illustrative examples are uses that are "for purposes such as criticism, comment, news reporting, teaching (including multiple copies for classroom use), scholarship, or research."[10] The list is nonexhaustive, but still suggests the rationale behind fair use. For example, uses for the sake of criticism can be fair use because copyright owners are unlikely to grant licenses to people who wish to mock them. Courts evaluate fair use on a case-by-case basis by using a four-factor balancing test, which we discuss in more detail in chapter 7.

GRAND UPRIGHT SETS THE TONE

"I bought the record, so I can do anything I want with the record, right?" Well, no, that record represents a whole set of copyrights or properties that belong to someone else and all you have bought is a license to play it in your home.—HARRY ALLEN

Legal abstractions can only provide so much guidance to the music industry. Musicians need to know how close they can come to previous songs and how much of those previous songs they can use. For a time, sampling had an ambiguous legal status, and early sampling cases generally settled out of court. The very first lawsuit involving the sample of a sound recording involved a track by the Beastie Boys. On their multiplatinum debut *Licensed to Ill*, released in 1986, the Beastie Boys sampled the phrase "Yo, Leroy!" from the funkster Jimmy Castor's record *The Return of Leroy (Part I)* (1977). Even though the Beastie Boys took less than two seconds of this vocal fragment, Castor promptly sued the group and their label, Def Jam.[11] The Beasties settled the case (just as other sampling musicians settled other lawsuits), leaving the industry without a legal judgment that provided a public precedent and had the strong, generally applicable force of law.

As the music historian and journalist Greg Tate says, "I think everybody woke up after the De La Soul's *3 Feet High and Rising* came out and they ended up losing most of their percentage of their copyrights to the Turtles." The lawsuit was prompted by the fact that a skit (not a proper song) called "Transmitting Live from Mars" contained a sample from "You Showed Me" by the Turtles. As Pasemaster Mase of De La Soul recalls, "For me, I felt like, 'Wow, we're popular now! I'm gettin' sued by somebody I don't even know!'" The case settled out of court in the Turtles' favor for a reported $1.7 million, though the group members tell us that the amount they paid out was actually far less than that.[12]

De La Soul and Tommy Boy Records each paid a share of the settlement amount to resolve the suit, but the story was widely covered and the nearly two million dollar figure scared a lot of record companies. To put this in context, the lawsuit occurred when the first wave of moral panics erupted around hip-hop. As the music writer Rob Sheffield writes, it was "around the same time that N.W.A. were getting hassled by the FBI for 'Fuck tha Police.'" He adds, "As journalist John Leland put it at the time, 'One group gets in trouble for sounding too much like the Turtles; another gets in trouble for not sounding enough like the Turtles.'"[13] Pasemaster Mase also reveals that the Turtles' management gave De La Soul the option to record a song with them—à la the collaboration between Run-DMC and Aerosmith—and if the rappers agreed to do so, the lawsuit would go away. De La Soul had no interest in collaborating, and they declined. A disgusted Pasemaster Mase shakes his head and asks, rhetorically, "It was like, where's your integrity in what you're doing, you know?"

Prior to some of these attention-getting lawsuits, sampling existed in a truly gray area legally. Harry Allen's account contradicts the notion that samplers were consciously being lawless criminals during hip-hop's "golden age." As Allen tells us, "Some of those first sampling cases, or those early records—whether it be De La Soul, Biz Markie, Public Enemy, and others—it wasn't that they were trying to be thieves or trying not to get caught. It was just like, we kind of didn't know."

In 1991, the case *Grand Upright Music v. Warner Brothers Records* effectively ended the "Wild West" period for sampling.[14] The rapper Biz Markie admitted that his song "Alone Again," from the album *I Need a Haircut*, featured a sample of the song "Alone Again (Naturally)" by Gilbert O'Sullivan. (Grand Upright Music Limited is the name of O'Sullivan's song publisher.) As Shoshana Zisk recounts, "The court's opinion began, 'Thou Shalt Not Steal.' After that, everyone in the industry said, 'Okay, we have to change the rules here.'" Judge Kevin Duffy's opinion did indeed open with the Seventh Commandment, citing the book of Exodus; however, the opinion cited *no* copyright cases. Instead, it focused heavily on whether the plaintiff truly owned the copyrights in the sampled song, and then concluded that it did.[15] Biz Markie admitted copying in fact (the sample was very obvious), but the court's opinion did not include an explicit analysis of substantial similarity.

Judge Duffy did provide a rationale, however, for his finding of copyright infringement. Biz Markie's lawyers had sought a license for using O'Sullivan's musical composition (though not the sound recording) before the release of the album with the infringing song.[16] As context, Biz Markie's lawyers had sought licenses for other samples in other songs. In a letter quoted at length in the opinion, Biz Markie's lawyers blamed Biz Markie's record label Cold Chillin' for failing to observe the usual practice and not waiting for the sample clearance to come through for "Alone Again." Thus, Judge Duffy concluded that "each defendant who testified knew that it is necessary to obtain a license—sometimes called a 'clearance'—from the holder of a valid copyright before using the copyrighted work in another piece."[17] Because he viewed the infringement as willful, he referred the case to the U.S. Attorney for the Southern District of New York for possible criminal prosecution. (We know of no evidence that any such prosecution occurred.)

Judge Duffy overstated the degree of certainty that existed in the record industry in 1991 about whether and when sample clearances were obligatory. He also erred by not conducting a substantial similarity analysis. (There is no indication that Biz Markie or his label raised a fair use defense, but if they did, Judge Duffy should have addressed that issue, too.) As the Duke law professor James Boyle quips: "When I first read the case, I seriously wondered for a moment if it were a crude parody of a legal opinion written by someone who had never been to law school."[18]

Despite these mistakes, the strong, pro-plaintiff stance of the case signaled to the music industry that samples should be cleared or infringement lawsuits would be likely. "Warner especially was particularly bitten very badly by the Biz Markie case," says Whitney Broussard, an entertainment lawyer who was working for another major label at the time. "For many years after, and I assume they still have that program going, they wouldn't let you release anything that wasn't licensed. They had a sample committee that would listen to records to see if they could find undisclosed samples. So, they take that pretty seriously."

But Biz Markie, Naturally, Was Not Alone in Getting Sued

Grand Upright was a landmark case because the court laid out at least some of the contours of how copyright law applied to sampling. It also gave copyright holders a stronger hand to play when others sampled their music. Their attempts to vindicate their copyrights would still end with out-of-court settlements in most instances. But the settlements probably involved greater amounts of money after 1991 given the unequivocal nature of Judge Duffy's decision against Biz Markie, which made the likelihood of victory in court by samplers seem small. Unfortunately, because settlement agreements are private by their nature, we lack comprehensive data on licensing fees. Thus, we cannot conduct a quantitative analysis of *Grand Upright*'s effect on settlements or the money involved in them, so we must instead rely on anecdotes and isolated reports.

The new, post–*Grand Upright* legal environment coincided with a trend of increasing commercial success for sample-based music. The music attorney Anthony Berman describes the onset of awareness around 1991: "Frankly, there was a cultural issue, you know, 'How is this going to be translated to the big record business?'" And as Matt Black of Coldcut explains, "The realization dawned on the music business that this was a new sound, and a new way of making music that could sell a lot of copies. Then naturally the lawyers moved in. There's the phrase, 'Where there's a hit there's a writ.'" Successful albums that used samples began to make more money, and (to paraphrase the late Notorious B.I.G.) more money often leads to more problems—typically in the form of increased litigation in business.

Because of this, and despite the hard line taken by *Grand Upright* and the tendency to settle, some sampling cases have continued to reach trial during the past two decades. Courts have worked out more of the detailed contours of sampling law and have filled in some of the analysis left out of Judge Duffy's opinion in *Grand Upright*. One example involved a song by c&c Music Factory that sampled a piece written by Boyd Jarvis.[19] The court considered the case as one of "fragmented literal similarity" and analyzed the musical composition (in which Jarvis owned the copyright) element by element.

In other words, the court did *not* ask whether an ordinary observer, forming an overall impression, would mistake c&c's "Get Dumb! (Free

Your Body)" for Jarvis's "The Music's Got Me." The court held that, as a factual matter, C&C Music Factory might have infringed Jarvis's composition by sampling a qualitatively important keyboard part from the work as well as an original arrangement of certain lyrical phrases.[20] This approach to the substantial similarity component of copyright infringement suggested that even sampling small portions of a work required a license.

Legal Defenses Available to Samplers

Other cases, however, pointed in the opposite direction from the expansive conception of copyright infringement represented by *Grand Upright* and *Jarvis*. In one such case, the record label Fantasy alleged that TLC's "Switch" (from their multiplatinum *CrazySexyCool*) infringed Jean Knight's recording from 1971 of "Mr. Big Stuff," in which Fantasy claimed to own the copyright.[21] La Face Records, TLC's label, won on a motion to dismiss because "Mr. Big Stuff" was recorded before the federal copyright code protected sound recordings.[22] And, as it happened, the statute of limitations for a state-law claim would have expired by the time the copyright holder sued.[23]

The highest-profile decision in a sampling case was the Supreme Court's decision in *Campbell v. Acuff-Rose Music, Inc.*, which concerned the fair use doctrine. Roy Orbison's publisher, Acuff-Rose Music, sued 2 Live Crew, with Luther Campbell (a.k.a. Luke Skyywalker) as the first named defendant. The case was based on 2 Live Crew's parody of Orbison's song "Pretty Woman." The parody borrowed from and altered the lyrics of the original composition, while also sampling the drum beat and bass line from the original sound recording.[24] But the lawsuit concerned only the musical composition copyright. As their defense, 2 Live Crew argued that their parody was a fair use.

The district (or trial-level) court and the Sixth Circuit Court of Appeals had rejected this defense, but a unanimous Supreme Court reversed those courts' decisions, holding that even commercial uses could be fair. This is because the commercial nature of a work is only one consideration under one of fair use's four factors.[25] The Court also held that parodies, in particular, have a "need for the recognizable sight or sound," thus making direct borrowing necessary in that context.[26] The end result of the case was that 2 Live Crew got an opportunity to demonstrate that their parody was fair use in the federal trial court.[27] Later in this chapter we will take up the issue of whether *Campbell v. Acuff-Rose* applies to samples in songs that are not parodies, and how fair use affects the sample clearance system.

In 2001, Marley Marl and his record company sued Snoop Dogg and his record company.[28] Snoop Dogg recorded a song, "Ghetto Symphony," which sampled from Marley Marl's song, "The Symphony." But Marley Marl's song had itself borrowed two measures from Otis Redding's musical composition "Hard to Handle," which contained the composition's signature five-note ascending pattern and five-note descending pattern. Thus, Snoop Dogg argued that Marley Marl had infringed the copyright of the earlier Otis Redding composition. If so, Marley Marl's song would be an unauthorized derivative work. And in that event, Marley Marl would not hold a valid copyright in "The Symphony," which means he could not sue Snoop Dogg for sampling his song.[29] The court denied Snoop Dogg an immediate victory on this line of defense. But it also held that the validity of Marley Marl's copyright in "The Symphony" was uncertain enough that a jury would have to decide the question.[30] This case illustrates the complexity of applying law to a chain of musical borrowing, which is an increasingly common circumstance in sample-based music.[31]

A unique and interesting case decided in 2003, *Newton v. Diamond*, arose after the Beastie Boys sampled a three-note melodic phrase—C, D-flat, and C, played on the flute over an overblown background C— from James Newton's composition "Choir."[32] (Michael Diamond, the Beastie Boys' member better known as Mike D, was the first named defendant in Newton's legal complaint.) Newton sued the Beastie Boys as well as their record label and publisher, among others. The Beastie Boys had licensed the sound recording from Newton's record label, but not the underlying composition. The Ninth Circuit Court of Appeals affirmed the federal district court's holding that the Beastie Boys' use was not copyright infringement because its similarity was below the *de minimis* threshold.

The court in *Newton v. Diamond* applied an ordinary observer interpretation in its substantial-similarity analysis.[33] The court isolated the compositional elements of Newton's song—the melody and background note, which appeared in the composition's score—from the elements of Newton's performance on the recording. In doing so, the court held that the compositional elements were "no more significant than any other section" and were instead "'a common building block tool' that 'has been used over and over again by major composers in the 20th century.'"[34] *Newton v. Diamond* thus rests on the notion that some portions of copyrighted compositions are too small and basic to protect.[35] With this decision from 2003, samplers appeared to gain some flexibility to use very small samples of the composition, although they might still have to license the sound recording (as the Beastie Boys had already done, before the lawsuit, in this instance). The issue of how small a sample of a sound recording requires a license would not be decided squarely until 2005, in *Bridgeport Music v. Dimension Films*, which we will discuss below.

The Impact of Sampling Lawsuits

Despite the victory of samplers in some key cases, the general thrust of the last two decades has been to require more licensing. Whitney Broussard addresses how this line of copyright cases has affected music industry practices this way: "I think if anything, it's become more conservative, meaning that labels are much more likely to want to get clearances for everything and be meticulous about making sure that no one's pulling the wool over their eyes as far as not disclosing samples." This risk-averse stance has come in response to the wave of sampling lawsuits. What Broussard describes is the major-label environment. When sample-based albums earn a lot of money, they also earn lots of attention from those whom they have sampled.

The musician and producer El-P describes the environment for sampling outside of the major-label context. As El-P, who owns the successful independent label Def Jux, tells us, "The problem is that everyone has existed off of this vibe, this gut feeling, you know, or this urban legend of what's OK and what's not. Everyone seems to have always had that sort of myth. No one had any facts." He continues by stating, "I was the same way for years till I started fuckin' running a record label, and then all of a sudden it started coming out of my pocket, and I was like, 'Oh, [laughs] *what?*'"

The push toward requiring licensing left something of a void. As Matt Black, in referring to Double Dee & Steinski's early records, says: "We knew that the problem there was they simply couldn't get permission to release the record that was composed entirely out of fragments of other people's recordings, and it seemed a great pity because they were fantastic pieces of work." This informed Coldcut's own approach to legal matters. "When we released our first record," Black says, "we didn't make any attempts to go through legal channels, because we knew that the legal channels did not exist." Even in the wake of *Grand Upright*, some artists found wiggle room in the legal precedents, either because some samplers had won their cases or because these artists felt they might avoid attention and litigation. But many sample-based works did get attention and sparked litigation.

Dean Garfield of the Motion Picture Association of America connected the record labels' efforts against unauthorized sample-based works to another effort to vindicate their copyrights. "There are a lot of analogies between sampling in the late 1980s and illegal downloading today," Garfield says. "In the late 1980s, it became easier for the everyday person to sample and create in ways they wanted to, and that's similar to what happened in the late 1990s with file sharing. But just because you can, or because you feel entitled, doesn't mean it's right." Beyond the fact that both are circumstances in which copyright holders asserted ownership, the sampling and file-sharing issues do have one important aspect in common: technological change. The development of the digital sampler—and its eventual decline in cost—put pressure on the law to resolve the ambiguity presented by a new flavor of alleged infringement. Similarly, the development of cheaper computers, more ubiquitous bandwidth, and networks like Napster facilitated a tidal wave of unauthorized file sharing.

Sampling and file sharing were both ambiguous but untested areas in the wake of new technologies. But the similarity ends there. Sampling, as a matter of musicians' use of existing songs rather than consumers' use, presents distinct legal issues. Cases like *Campbell v. Acuff-Rose* and *Newton v. Diamond* show that sampling is not necessarily copyright infringement—that is, it is not possible to generalize, as courts have done in the file-sharing context. Unauthorized samplers have stronger legal defenses than unauthorized file sharers.

Yet the possibility of valid legal defenses for samplers does not counterbalance the overall pro-licensing thrust of copyright law's approach to samples. Eothen Alapatt, who oversees the independent label Stones Throw, argues that the ambiguous legal environment during the "golden age" produced more creativity than the current pro-licensing environment: "The hip-hop music that most of us loved and thought was so creative existed in the late eighties and early nineties. That's when sampling was very in vogue because it was a kind of Wild, Wild West situation where no one really knew the legalities. Everyone was just doing it." Alapatt continues by noting, "I think that it would make the music much more creative again, and that's the thing that bums me out so much about the hip-hop music nowadays because people are so scared of sampling, they're going back to this synthesized music." Alapatt believes that this is the antithesis of what hip-hop is to begin with. "That might sound old-fashioned and dated," he says, "but hip-hop started with people using old records in a new way. And I hate to see it going in a different way."

Copyright law can only go so far to enforce an appropriate balance between compensation and access. Although licensing has allowed compensation to reach some musicians and copyright owners whose music has been sampled, the licensing process suffers from certain quirks, inefficiencies, and flaws (as we detail in chapter 5). By declaring that samples—even brief samples—infringe copyrights in many situations, the federal courts have banked on the music industry's ability to develop a good process for licensing samples. With its most recent high-profile sampling case, the courts put even more stock in the sample clearance system.

THE *BRIDGEPORT* RULING

I think Bridgeport basically has caused people—who in the past,
may not have gotten a license because they felt the sample was too short
—to enter into a licensing agreement.—WALTER McDONOUGH

After the *Grand Upright* case involving Biz Markie, the interpretation of copyright law by the courts and the music industry had a pro-licensing orientation. But it also allowed some wiggle room. *Newton v. Diamond*, especially, showed that some portions of a composition are just too small for the law to allow a sampling lawsuit to succeed over them. But in 2005, two years after *Newton v. Diamond* enshrined the idea that some uses of musical compositions were *de minimis*, *Bridgeport Music v. Dimension Films* held that no *de minimis* exception applied to sound recordings. This stark contrast between how small portions of sound recordings would be treated, as compared to small portions of musical compositions, represented a new development in copyright law. The decision surprised many observers.

As we discussed in chapter 1, *Bridgeport* was about N.W.A.'s song "100 Miles and Runnin'," which sampled two seconds from a guitar solo of the Funkadelic song "Get Off Your Ass and Jam." The sample consisted of three notes from a single chord played in rapid succession (or what musicians call an arpeggio). In addition, "100 Miles and Runnin'" was used in the movie *I Got the Hook-Up* without a synchronization license for the sound recording.[36] The district court actually ruled in N.W.A.'s favor, but the opinion was not without flaws. The musicologist and sample expert Lawrence Ferrara explains, in his view, where the district court's opinion went wrong:

> Now what the [district court] judge in *Dimension Films* said is to the extent that this [plays keyboard notes in the Funkadelic song] was so minimal to the original work, that therefore it represented a *de minimis* taking. In my opinion, that relied too much on the standard for the underlying composition *de minimis* test, and did not take into account sufficiently the music-technological impact of the changes. And that's why I said that while I agreed with the [district court's] decision, I didn't agree with the logic that informed the decision, and indeed it was overturned based on the logic that informed the decision by the appellate court.

The *de minimis* doctrine applies to excerpts of musical compositions that are too small to count as copyright infringement. Ferrara argues that the district court did not offer a sufficient explanation for why or how the same approach should apply to sound recordings.

The Sixth Circuit Court of Appeals reversed the district court's decision and ruled in Bridgeport Music's favor. For the Sixth Circuit, "substantial similarity [does] not enter the equation" when it comes to sampling cases. In rejecting a *de minimis* threshold for infringement of a sound recording the court drew a distinction between musical compositions, which it deemed abstract, and sound recordings, which it deemed more tangible. As the court put it, when "sounds are sampled they are taken directly from that fixed medium. It is a physical taking rather than an intellectual one."[37] Still, this distinction does not explain why a *de minimis* rule could not apply.

A key rationale for the *de minimis* rule is to avoid the administrative cost of lawsuits when takings are small. The differences between a sound recording and a musical composition do not really affect that justification. The Sixth Circuit wished to seize "a rare opportunity for a 'bright-line' rule" to avoid battles over how large a sample is too large."[38] A truly bright-line rule makes lawsuits simpler when they occur, but it does not necessarily result in fewer lawsuits. The Sixth Circuit also offered several policy arguments of an economic character to support its decision to overturn the district court.[39] The court expressed optimism that the music industry had developed a suitable licensing process; the bottom line was, as the ruling stated, "Get a license or do not sample."[40]

The court did not consider, or explicitly cast aspersions on, the possibility that N.W.A.'s sample of "Get Off Your Ass and Jam" constituted fair use.[41] But the parties settled before the district court could rule on the fair use issue. The case marked, for sound recordings, a return to the no-exceptions, no-nuance approach of *Grand Upright*, at least in the jurisdiction of the Sixth Circuit. And since most samples implicate the sound recording copyright in the song being sampled (if not always the musical composition copyright, as *Newton v. Diamond* shows), the stark rule of *Bridgeport* could profoundly affect the legal environment for sampling.

In terms of statutory legal authority, the Sixth Circuit relied on Section 114(b) of the copyright code, which explicitly excludes "entirely . . . independently created" works from the reach of the reproduction and derivative-works rights that come with sound recording copyrights.[42] To the appellate court, this implied that any work *not* entirely independently created must infringe.[43] Scholarly commentators have argued that the Sixth Circuit's reading of the statute was mistaken.[44] Thus, in future cases, the Supreme Court or courts in other judicial circuits might well adopt a different rule, or Congress could pass legislation overturning the decision. But what happens in the meantime?

The Effect of Bridgeport on Sample Licensing

The music lawyer Dina LaPolt tells us that *Bridgeport* changed the practical advice she gives her clients about sample clearance. "I would advise my clients before *Bridgeport* if they used a little snippet of a

recording that was *de minimis*, 'That's fine; we don't have to clear it,'"
LaPolt says. "Of course I'd run it by someone really smart like Nancy
Stern or Deborah Mannis-Gardner, two prominent clearance people in
the U.S., and they would say, 'You're right; don't clear it,' or they'd say it
needs to be cleared. But now I can't say that anymore." How have record
labels that put out sample-based music reacted? As Whitney Broussard
tells us, "After the *Bridgeport* case, they probably got even more conservative about clearing stuff. Basically, it said that even if you can't hear a
sample of the sound recording, you still have to clear it."

Lawrence Ferrara explains how the *Bridgeport* opinions softened
somewhat its own cut-and-dried stance. He points out that, according to the Sixth Circuit's appellate decision in *Bridgeport v. Dimension
Films*, one must acquire a license in order to sample a sound recording. "Take a one-second wood block sound—if you sample it, pay for
it," Lawrence Ferrara says, by way of example. "That was basically the
message. There was such an outcry of the low threshold for having to
sample that they sent in an amended decision, which basically said, 'But
there could always be some factors that might suggest otherwise.'"

Bridgeport only changes copyright law for the samples that last between zero seconds and whatever tiny amount (two seconds?) was
previously thought by some in the industry to be *de minimis*. Perhaps
those samples are tiny enough to avoid detection, but digital technology for identifying samples has improved considerably. A setup involving a copyright regime that protects such tiny fragments seems absurd,
both legally and practically. Public Enemy's Hank Shocklee feels that
the decision has led to even more confusion. "If I sampled a kick drum
from someone, or I sampled a snare from someone, now you're saying
that I have to get clearances for those tiny fragments?"

In the end, musicians have been left with a number of questions,
partly because *Bridgeport*, by the Sixth Circuit's own admission, represented a change in the law. The decision contradicted many people's
previous understanding of copyright law, and as suggested by the following questions that Shocklee raises, changes in the law can have unfair effects. "Should you be allowed to go backwards and basically sue
people retroactively for something that they've done in the past when
it was legal?" Shocklee asks. "That would be like if all of a sudden we
decided that there's a ticket for going through a yellow light. Well, now,
does everybody that's gone through a yellow light before get a ticket

now? Because that's the equivalent to what's happening in sampling right now."

The Sixth Circuit in *Bridgeport* openly acknowledged that it was "announcing a new rule."[45] Taking advantage of the retroactive nature of this rule, Armen Boladian of the plaintiff companies Bridgeport Music and Westbound Records has continued to bring lawsuits. Recent cases have targeted songs by Notorious B.I.G. and Public Announcement.[46]

The Broader Effects of Bridgeport on Creativity

Mia Garlick of Creative Commons puts *Bridgeport* into the context of the music industry's approach to technological change: "The law has perceived digital technologies to be a threat and has imposed more blockades against the use of media by consumers," Garlick says. "Courts have been very insistent about clearance, particularly with [*Bridgeport*]." This feeling, that *Bridgeport* represented attempts at stronger copyright enforcement, led to an online civil-disobedience demonstration by the digital activist group Downhill Battle. They encouraged the public to create songs made solely from the three-note sample from "Get Off Your Ass and Jam," which they then collected and made available online.[47]

Lawrence Ferrara describes the effect of *Bridgeport* on sample-based music as follows: "I believe that this decision in the Sixth Circuit has been extraordinarily chilling, because it basically says that whatever you sample has to be licensed, in its most extreme interpretation." Even if the case might leave room for limitations or exceptions to copyright (such as fair use), the baseline assumption has changed. As Ferrara says, "As a result, particularly for the students in my department, for high school kids who are using various kinds of software packages and creating samples and songs in their rooms, it's chilling because how do they ever release any of that?" Dina LaPolt concurs with this somber view of the case: "I think it's terrible. I think it's absolutely terrible, and literally the day it came out I cried. I swear I cried." Others see *Bridgeport* in less dire terms, noting that judicial opinions with unexpected or unpopular results can be catalysts for legislative (or other forms of) change.

Whitney Broussard discussed with us the decision's ripple effects on other genres of music that involve less-direct forms of musical borrowing. "It's fed back now into this system of jazz and blues where now a lot of that stuff is getting cleared because people are sensitized to the issue." Even though *Bridgeport* prohibited only the application of the *de minimis* rule to sound recordings, cautious people in the music industry might decide to clear uses of small portions of musical compositions just to be safe. As Broussard says, "I've seen situations with our clients where, for instance, a jazz player now has to go clear a replay of something when they probably wouldn't have had to do that twenty years ago."

Overall, we heard from many interviewees that the balance between compensation and access had been upset. Hank Shocklee's and Lawrence Ferrara's comments suggest that tiny snippets of sound recordings may not deserve copyright protection. As the law professor Leslie Kurtz writes:

> The court [in *Bridgeport*] also said that minimal takings from a sound recording should be treated differently from minimal takings from a musical composition, because sampling even a small part of a sound recording takes something of value, and because the taking is a physical rather than an intellectual one. But the taking is no more physical than printing a book, a music score, or a work of art. All involve some form of copying. Nor is it clear that there is some particular artistic value in a small portion of a sound recording, compared to [the value of] a small portion of some other work.[48]

The lack of parallelism in the treatment of musical compositions and sound recordings may cause problems for musicians, as Whitney Broussard's anecdote about jazz and blues attests. Siva Vaidhyanathan puts it this way: "This shows you how difficult things can be in the compositional process. When you mix law and creativity, you get some wacky results."

Defenses to Copyright Infringement after Bridgeport

Might copyright law still allow musicians some wiggle room? As we stated in chapter 3 and reiterated at the beginning of this chapter, copyright law contains several limitations and exceptions. The Harvard law professor Terry Fisher describes how *Bridgeport* might admit these limitations and exceptions, even though it laid down a clear baseline that all sound recording samples now had copyright protection:

What makes the law in this area very murky is the possible availability to the samplers of two legal defenses. One of them is the fair use doctrine, which gives some latitude for modifications, transformative uses of other people's copyrighted materials, even if otherwise they would constitute copyright infringements. And the second defense arguably available when the sample slice is small is the principle of no liability for *de minimis* takings. And there's been a great deal of controversy among courts shared by lots of cacophonous disagreement among scholars concerning the applicability of those two defenses. Some courts have gone very far in rejecting the defenses. The most famous of those decisions is the *Bridgeport Music* case. . . . Others are significantly more generous. So the bottom line is the law is unstable in this area. And its murkiness contributes to the confused business practices in which some samplers routinely do seek licenses. Others don't at all.

The Columbia law professor Jane Ginsburg explains that fair use is moot when a sample falls below the *de minimis* threshold. She adds that samples may be non-infringing because the sample is not substantially similar to the song sampled:

You don't even get to fair use if there's just too little there in what you sample. Even though I think that the Ninth Circuit may have been wrong in saying there was too little there [in *Newton v. Diamond*], it's still support for the proposition that there will be circumstances in which the sample is too trivial to rise to the level of even being a "prima facie copyright infringement," which would then trigger the fair use defense. You don't have to defend if it's not copyright infringement in the first place.

Consider the visual context—a collage. It might be that a small amount of somebody's photograph or other work of visual art, painting or drawing, is copied and is potentially recognizable on its own, but then after it's been collaged and laid over and all these other things done to it in the visual format, it's barely recognizable. The first argument would be that too little was taken to count in the first place. The second argument would be that even if the amount taken was not trivial, the work incorporating the copied material is not "substantially similar" to the copied work because the copied material has been so altered. If the copied work is not substantially similar, it's not infringing. Either way, there is no infringement up front, so we don't even get to fair use. Applying that reasoning to sound recordings or to samplings, I guess the question would be what happens to those sounds?

Are they so substantially remixed and combined with other things that you wouldn't recognize them anyway?

Ginsburg's comments explain how the defenses of *de minimis* use or lack of substantial similarity are a denial that copyright infringement occurred in the first place. Where successful, these two defenses mean that copyright does not protect the portions of the sampled tracks at issue.

Fair use is subtly different because it is an affirmative defense. When a particular sample is fair use the sampler is not liable for copyright infringement, but the sampled portion of the work is still deemed to be protected by copyright. Another sampler using the same portion in a different way or in a different context may not succeed with his or her fair use defense. Again, *Bridgeport* did not speak to the fair use defense but rather only addressed the *de minimis* doctrine. The Sixth Circuit actually amended its opinion to state that it had not considered fair use, but did not mean to suggest anything one way or the other about whether N.W.A.'s use of the sample might be fair. So what, if anything, does *Bridgeport* tell us about fair use?

Lawrence Ferrara explains his view that *Bridgeport* implicitly casts aspersions on the availability of fair use. "If you were to read that, what you'd basically say is there is no fair use. What that court said is, 'If you sample it, pay for it. If you sample it, license it,' period, which suggested that there is no fair use." While the court did not actually reach a decision on the fair use issue, Ferrara's comments highlight why— practically speaking—fair use may have taken a hit in *Bridgeport*. To fully vindicate a sample as fair use against a claim of copyright infringement, a sampler has to deal with defending himself or herself from a lawsuit. The legal process is both expensive and uncertain.

Moreover, defending a lawsuit under United States law means offering several different (and possibly conflicting) defenses simultaneously. When the *de minimis* defense disappears for samples of sound recordings, samplers would have to rely on fair use even more heavily. Therefore, each prospective lawsuit is even more difficult, with one of the sampling artist's small array of defenses taken away. After *Bridgeport*, with the strong copyright baseline it sets up, more samples must rely on a fair use defense to be considered non-infringing. Samplers may not like their reduced odds.

There are others, however, who do not read *Bridgeport* as a discouragement to fair use claims. Among the members of this group is the American University law professor Peter Jaszi, who has a more optimistic view of how fair use might be useful in the context of sampling. "[Fair use] has the potential to solve parts of the problem and not other parts of the problem," he says. "It has the potential of getting sample uses distributed into two classes: (1) those that need to be compensated, and (2) those that don't need to be compensated. I think it would turn out that, as the law developed, there would be significant pieces in each set." Perhaps the Sixth Circuit's stark view on the *de minimis* threshold will spur the music industry to begin establishing clearer, broadly accepted norms about what uses are fair.

Thus, views differ about what *Bridgeport* means for the fair use doctrine. Lawrence Ferrara's comments emphasize the difficulty and expense of vindicating one's fair use rights in court, which strengthen the business imperative to seek licenses. He reads *Bridgeport* as having the practical effect of commanding musicians to license every sample— regardless of the opinion's neutrality, on its face, regarding fair use. Peter Jaszi's comments emphasize the possibility of reaching a consensus on a definition of samples that the music industry will deem fair, thus making licenses unnecessary, both legally and practically, for such samples. He is loath to let *Bridgeport* cast aspersions on an important public right, and we will discuss Jaszi's ideas further in chapter 7.

As we have discussed above, *Bridgeport* has shifted copyright law to the benefit of copyright owners by eliminating the *de minimis* defense for samples of sound recordings. No one knows for sure whether the decision will damage creativity in ways that some fear it will. Either way, the Sixth Circuit fell short of its stated goal of increasing certainty about the legal status of samples. Its decision has been questioned as a matter of both law and policy, thus making it uncertain whether it will survive future litigation or legislation. Meanwhile, given the difficulties of licensing, fair use—a notoriously unpredictable doctrine—could play an increasing role in sampling. Gregg Gillis's aggressive stance on fair use, described in the introduction, suggests this might be happening already. Despite its practical flaws, fair use could carve out room for more unlicensed but legal samples in the marketplace—a situation that would provide a safety valve that can release some of the pressure built up in the sample clearance system.

5

THE SAMPLE CLEARANCE SYSTEM

How It Works (and How It Breaks Down)

Copyright law—the federal statute and the judicial opinions interpreting it—applies directly when parties are litigating a particular case. More often, however, copyright law matters indirectly as a foundation or a background upon which negotiations over licenses take place. In the second instance, the music industry's business practices are what matters most to the negotiations between artists who sample and those who are sampled (and their representatives). Thus, our interviews for this book focused most intently on the workings of the sample clearance system. We asked detailed questions about the mechanics of obtaining sample licenses, which we have included in appendix 2. In asking these questions, we observed that the current system greatly benefits certain musicians, record labels, and publishers. On the other hand, we also discovered that the sample clearance system has several significant flaws that affect those in the industry as well as the music-listening public.

THE BUSINESS OF CLEARING SAMPLES

I mean, as the music itself changed, the use
of the sample became increasingly prevalent. It became
something that just was cleared as a regular course.
—ANDREW BART

During the 1990s, as a generation of sampling artists matured and as digital technology made both sampling and the policing of sampling easier, the modern sample clearance system developed. This system converted sampling—at least, most major-label sampling—from an underground relationship between musicians and the records they sampled to an above-ground relationship between licensees and licensors. Revenue began to flow through the sample clearance system, to the benefit of at least some parties. As Matt Black of Coldcut says, "I'm glad that a legal framework has developed . . . because it means that actually people can release records with samples in them now. They can actually be released and everyone can benefit from it."

The music attorney Shoshana Zisk explains one of the most fundamental facts of this new business of licensing samples: "All sample clearances are handled on a case-by-case basis and they all have to be negotiated." Because each sample clearance is unique, the individual characteristics of the new track that uses a sample, the sampled source, the musicians involved, the copyright owners, and their representatives will shape how a negotiation proceeds. This is where lawyers and sample clearance houses enter the picture, though sometimes record labels have their own in-house expertise. As Dina LaPolt explains, "You have the major labels—like specifically J Records and Arista—they have in-house sample clearance people in their company, which is amazing." But other labels outsource to specialized sample clearance houses some of the tasks involved in licensing samples.

Sample clearance houses offer expertise in handling the licenses that generate the complicated revenue flow we described in chapter 3. As the sample clearance professional Danny Rubin says, "I would say maybe between three sample clearance houses we probably do about 90 percent of the sample clearances for the major record companies. As for smaller labels, sometimes they'll do it in-house—or use agencies that we've never heard of—or use their attorneys." With that amount of business at the major-label level, the sample clearance houses are able to develop relationships with many sampled artists and the associated copyright holders for their works. They also offer a less-expensive solution to the problem of all the transaction costs that can pile up while trying to track down multiple copyright holders. "I have several sample clearance people that I use frequently," Dina LaPolt says. "Where they might charge a flat free to clear a use, some of them charge an hourly rate that might be 50 bucks an hour, which is nothing compared to what a lawyer would charge."

Danny Rubin described for us the perspective of the sample clearance house on the process of licensing a sample. He says that what his firm would do for a sampling client is to track down the owners of the copyrights to a particular source. "With a sample, you need clearance on two copyrights—the owner of the master recording and the owner of the musical composition or publishing," Rubin says. "And what we do is we do research and track down the owners, and then we contact them on your behalf and then negotiate a rate, which could be a royalty or it could be a one-time payment. And we take care of all the formal contracts and get the samples cleared for you."

Researching and tracking down the copyright owners can be a time-consuming part of clearing a sample. This is especially so with samples of older records, when the original publisher or record label no longer exists, companies have merged or gone bankrupt, or copyrights have been sold to an aggregator like Bridgeport Music. Or *all* of those things may have occurred, in a long and confusing chain of events. Still, negotiating a rate can be even more difficult than locating owners. Sample clearance houses have developed relationships with many musicians and their representatives, thereby facilitating negotiations that would be difficult or impossible otherwise. The direct fees for licensing a sample are generally borne by the recording artist and the songwriter—and sometimes the producer—not their record label or publisher. But, partly because of the potential liability for copyright infringement, the sampling musician's record label will often pay the clearance fees to make sure the sample clearance happens, and then charge the costs against the artist's account to be recouped.

Opening Negotiations

Licensing talks start in two ways: the sampling artist proactively seeks a license, or the owner of a copyright in the sampled source (perhaps the sampled artist) objects to the use of their work and seeks out the sampling artist. How negotiations start can greatly affect the ultimate outcome. Some sampling artists do not proactively seek a license. In our interviews we found that some artists didn't know enough about the system, while others didn't think anyone would notice. Sometimes this license avoidance works in an artist's favor, but in other cases it can hamstring a career or lead to significant legal costs.

Paul Miller, a.k.a. DJ Spooky, explains the perspective he took early in his career: "My first couple albums were meant to be provocations, so I never really felt that it was going to be above the threshold [of detection]." He continues, "So that was when I was much younger and I felt like, 'Okay, well, I just kind of want to throw this out there as a message in a bottle about sampling.' It's a mistake many young producers and artists make, but it's also where you find some of the richest material." The likelihood that musicians will seek clearances for the sources they use increases as their careers progress and as their sales increase. The musician and independent label owner Tim Love describes these changing incentives over the course of his career: "My first album is completely uncleared 'cause at the time I didn't really know anything about it. We never got called. I mean, we only sold a few thousand copies and, you know, never got on the charts or anything like that. So we were always under the radar."

Tim Love further observes that as he learned more about the industry it became obvious that in not clearing samples he was limiting his opportunities. He discovered that sample clearance is necessary to having his own music licensed to appear in television, films, and advertisements—or even getting his music licensed to larger record companies. The owner of the Def Jux record label, El-P, came to a similar realization. "I just started the label because I'm an artist and I wanted to put music out," he says. "Eventually I realized that not only am I in danger here, I'm limiting myself because of the current quagmire. One of the ways we make money is if a car company wants to use a portion of the music we make. We can't do that if it's laden with other people's music. We just can't do it."

Jeff Chang, who co-founded Soulsides, an important independent label that operated during the 1990s, tells a story that nicely illustrates many of the complexities of sampling in the modern marketplace:

> I had a friend who had put out a record that used a sample and suddenly it got picked up for a TV commercial. So, now it's running on TV coast to coast and around the world in all of these big sporting events. The original artists who recorded the song were very, very obscure. They had been sort of lost through the sands of time. They were a small group from a distant

era that made a couple of underground records and never really broke big. But they're listening to the TV out of the back of their ear one day, and they hear their song coming on. They get mad, and they find a lawyer. The lawyer steps up to my friend, the artist, and says, "That's our sample. Let's negotiate on this." The owner of the sample in this particular instance has my friend over a barrel because the song has gotten so big they think there's a lot of money being generated out of this.

So, my friend—the artist—had to figure out a way to fairly compensate the artist, because he wants to. It's a recognition of the debt they owe to the artist. It's not like people that are sampling are all heartless thieves. [My friend] says, "I want to be able to give them some money," but at the same time, the people that are making the claim upon my friend are asking for ridiculous amounts. They're asking for 200 percent of the composition. They're asking for all these back royalties that have supposedly been paid to my friend, the artist. At some point my friend had to say, "Look, if you do this, you're going to run me out of business. I'm just going to have to stop licensing this record to be used in commercials or in shows or that kind of thing. We'll pay you what's fair, but you can't run me out of business on this. I'm going to have to declare bankruptcy on this." The other side said, "Okay, we understand," because they don't want to see that line of money dry up. They don't want to kill the golden goose. So, they came to some sort of an agreement, and now they've got an agreement that allows everybody to be properly compensated.

For musicians trying to assess the likelihood of being pursued by the owners of the uncleared samples they have used, what matters is how the samples are used and whether the copyright holders are likely to identify any samples. As DJ Spooky says, in the context of the improved technological tools for identifying samples and of more zealous policing by copyright owners, "I really am very cautious these days about recognizability, because of, you know, the fact these days a lot of record labels have whole departments with people just sitting there listening to records all day."

The Structure and Terms of Sample Licenses

Sample licenses take different forms. In a seminal essay on licensing, the music lawyer Whitney Broussard summarizes the different types:

"There are five basic classes of deals that are used to grant consent for the use of a sample: gratis; buyouts; royalties; co-ownership; and an assignment of the copyright."[1] Sound recording licenses usually involve a buyout (a lump-sum payment) or, if the sampling track has large expected commercial potential, a royalty.[2] Buyouts today typically range from $500 to $15,000 per sample, but in special cases they can cost as much as $50,000 (or even $100,000 in some very special cases). Royalties range from $0.01 per record to as much as $0.15 per record.

Because royalties impose the need for continued administrative and transaction costs, buyouts are the most common arrangement when the licensing revenue is small. Copyright holders may also offer licenses for no charge, or merely in return for attribution. The electronic artist Scanner relates some examples of buyouts versus gratis licenses: "I've been sampled on a couple of people's records, and they've come to me and said, 'We gave Stevie Wonder $500, we gave Nirvana $1,000. What do you want?' What does one say in these situations? You know, for one of them, I said, I'd like my name on the record. I'd like it to say sampled from this Scanner record. They said, no, we won't do that, we'd rather just pay you the $500 so we don't have to put this credit on there—which is quite an interesting situation."

Musical composition licenses typically involve a royalty or co-ownership of the new song's musical composition copyright. Either arrangement results in a percentage of the proceeds going to the sampled songwriter and publisher. In the case of a royalty, the percentage ranges from 10 to 50 percent; with a co-ownership deal, the range is 25 to 50 percent. As Shoshana Zisk tells us, "When I was working in copyright at Motown, you'd get one song and there'd be fourteen people that you had to get permission from. And each one of them is like, 'I own 6.2 per cent, I own 8.9 percent.' There's a pie graph of a song and everyone has a slice." The exact percentage depends on various factors including, for example, how much of the composition is sampled, whether the sample includes the whole melody or just an incidental snippet, how the sample is used in the new song, and who the sampling artist is.[3] More rarely, the sampled songwriter and publisher will demand full assignment of the sampling work's copyright.[4]

In practice, many factors influence the buyout fee or the royalty rate in a sample license.[5] These factors apply to both sound recordings and musical compositions. To some extent, the list contains some factors that would be considered in a copyright infringement lawsuit. In this sense, parties negotiate sample licenses in the shadow of the law. But other factors come from industry practices and the demands of copyright owners. We can split the list of factors into two.

First, some factors that influence the licensing fee (whether a buyout or a royalty rate) pertain to the song that is sampled and characteristics of the sampled musician:

—Quantitative portion of the recording or composition used
—Qualitative importance of the portion used
—Whether the sample comes from the chorus, the melody, or the background
—Whether the sample comes from the vocal portion or the instrumental portion
—Recognizability of the portion sampled
—Whether the sampled musician had a major label or distributor
—Popularity of the sampled recording or composition
—Level of the sampled musician's commercial success and fame

Second, other factors pertain to the new song seeking to use the sample and the characteristics of the sampling musician:

—Number of times the sample is repeated
—Quantitative portion that the sample represents with respect to the new song
—Qualitative prominence and importance of the sample in the new song
—Perceived aesthetic qualities of the new song, such as genre or quality
—Whether the new song is of a violent or pornographic nature, or is otherwise objectionable
—Level of commercial potential for the new song
—Whether the sampling musician has a major label or distributor
—Level of the sampling musician's commercial success, fame, and ability to pay

In addition to these substantive factors, the process followed by a musician seeking licenses can influence whether licenses are achieved as well as the eventual licensing fees. For instance, it matters whether the sampling musician's representatives contact the copyright holders of the sampled track in advance of releasing the song. Buyouts, royalties, and co-ownership percentages are generally lower when the sampler's side initiates licensing discussions before release.[6] As DJ Spooky told us, he prefers to clear samples at "the very beginning . . . I'd much rather just get it sorted out in advance." Clearing samples earlier not only reduces licensing fees but also minimizes the chance for holdups or extra hassle in getting sample-based tracks released. As noted by Kanye West's co-manager, Kyambo "Hip Hop" Joshua, "You really take care of samples beforehand. If it's after, you're gonna be paying more. You know, like if they hear the record in the market before you reach them, they'll come and get you."

Musicians' understandings of sample licenses—and assessments of their fairness—reflect a distinction between sampling a large part of a song versus sampling a small amount. As Matt Black told us, "You can't just take big slices of someone else's work. If so, you should pay. However, if you sample one snare drum off a Rolling Stones record and add 99 percent of the song yourself, you shouldn't pay the Rolling Stones 100 percent of the royalties."[7] The musician Mr. Len states further, "Some artists will feel, you know, 'I made your record, you know, so I want all of it. I want 100 percent publishing.' Or 'I want a 90 10 split on your royalties or your sales,' so it really all depends." And Pete Rock echoes these sentiments by noting: "Sometimes people want, you know, 70 percent of your song, you know. And what can you say to that?"

Navigating the System

A lesson emerges from the complex institutions, processes, and terms involved in sample licensing: having a detailed knowledge of the system is essential. This is especially true when dealing with samples of musicians who recorded or published within the major-label system. Sample clearance often requires an understanding of copyright law; familiarity with record contracts, publishing contracts, and sample-licensing agreements; knowledge of music-industry institutions and relationships with particular individuals within those institutions; and, perhaps most important, common sense about how to conduct licensing negotiations. Without these skills, musicians who sample face a hurdle to creativity—or at least to marketing and distributing the fruits of creativity. Similarly, without these skills, musicians whose songs are sampled may not collect any licensing revenue.

Musicians often must employ an experienced music manager or music lawyer to surmount the system's hurdles. Some musicians grumble about the role of lawyers in sample clearance, as we saw in chapter 3, perhaps shifting their resentment from copyright holders to the lawyers representing those musicians or companies. It can be frustrating to be in a system where licensing negotiations only rarely involve musician-to-musician talks because intermediaries are the norm. Even independent musicians without any business relationships will encounter the world of record labels and publishers once they sample major-label music. In that event, negotiations are more likely to succeed with the benefit of a manager's or attorney's input.

Musicians who discover that their songs have been sampled without their permission can also benefit from representation, even if they operate independently from the major-label world. Recall Jeff Chang's story related above about the obscure group that sought to collect licensing revenue from his friend's group after their song was featured in a TV ad. Although the obscure group's lawyers overreached at first (a strategy that could have originated with their clients rather than them), they eventually negotiated a deal that benefited all parties. Navigating the sample clearance system calls for several kinds of legal and business experience that most musicians lack, especially at the beginning of their careers.

It is not that musicians lack the aptitude for understanding sample clearance; in fact, spreading knowledge of the system to them is one reason we wrote this book. Musicians can and do learn how sample clearance works—eventually—but a number of our interviewees describe learning those lessons the hard way. This state of affairs may seem out of line with larger trends in the music industry, such as the decline of the major labels in terms of sales revenue and the advent of direct online sales by musicians who forgo signing with a label. But even in a hypothetical world without record labels (which isn't here yet and might never arrive), songs that are sampled would still have copyright owners, and managers and lawyers would still play a role in licensing.

The Benefits of Licensing

Licensing fees, along with the transaction costs of obtaining licenses, can act as a deterrent to making sample-based music. But bringing sampling into a licensing framework can also benefit both sampling and sampled artists and lead to interesting artistic opportunities. Despite their initial reluctance, most major record companies—which often own the copyright to sound recordings, or "the masters"—have realized that they are sitting on potential treasure troves. Rather than suing remixers, they are increasingly commissioning works and giving sampling artists access to record company vaults. "I'm now in the position of reconstructing other people's back catalogs," says the British sound artist Scanner. "At the present moment in time, I'm reconstructing the back catalog of Warner Classics, a classical music label that releases Vivaldi, Mozart, Erik Satie, all kinds of artists. I've got complete freedom to sample what I like from their back catalog to make a new record." Scanner has also had the opportunity to take the roughly twenty-five albums of work by the American noise-rock pioneers Swans and remix it into one album. As Scanner says, "For me, it's quite extraordinary to be making these works, which would generally be deemed bootlegs, but with full approval of the labels and the artists."

Similarly, back in 1993 the classic jazz label Blue Note commissioned the album *Hand on the Torch* by US3, a group of British producers led by Geoff Wilkinson. Just as Deee-lite built their hit "Groove Is in the Heart" on a sample from Herbie Hancock's "Bring Down the Birds," the US3 track "Cantaloop (Flip Fantasia)" drew from Hancock's "Cantaloop Island." *Hand on the Torch* became the Blue Note label's first platinum-selling album, fueled by the success of "Cantaloop" as a single. The song originally began as an unauthorized bootleg, but Blue Note chose not to sue out of the realization that there was money to be made. "I worked on that one," says the entertainment lawyer Whitney Broussard, who was employed by Capitol Records, the jazz label's parent company. "Capitol was in a unique position to do that because it controlled those masters and it also had contracts with those artists that didn't generally require them getting permission from the original artists."

This kind of archive-mining collaboration can benefit the record companies and the sampled artists themselves—both dead and alive. Tupac Shakur's estate has licensed several of the late rapper's copyrighted songs, which has helped to bring in a significant amount of revenue after his death. (He has earned more money in royalties in the afterlife than during his time here on Earth.) As Dina LaPolt, who oversees the estate's legal affairs, says, "Let me give you a great real-life example." She then cites Jay-Z and Beyoncé's "'03 Bonnie & Clyde," which as one of the biggest-selling singles of 2003 received a great amount of radio play and won several awards. "We own 37½ percent of that song," says LaPolt. "That was great for us—it was great money. Not only was that great, when Jay-Z won his award, we won awards too because we are a songwriter. . . . So when he won his BMI awards and all these other things, we won those awards, too. When he was making public performance monies because his song was on the radio 24/7, we were making public performance monies, too. It was great."

The potential benefits from licensing, then, are relatively easy to see. Each side in the transaction can reap financial gains, awards, and publicity. Royalty and co-ownership agreements can create common interests for musicians who sample and copyright owners (including, perhaps, the sampled musicians). And licenses can allow artists who sample to proceed without fear of potential copyright infringement litigation. But the modern sample clearance system also creates difficulties. We have put the problems with licensing into four categories—expense, relationships, bureaucracy, and timing—each of which impacts how sampling artists, and their record labels, can legally release their music.

THE ISSUE OF EXPENSE IN SAMPLE CLEARANCE

I say there's two types of samples: the really fucking expensive type, and the really, *really* fucking expensive type.—DINA LAPOLT

Sample licenses are expensive, in part because each sample typically requires two licenses: one for the sound recording, or master, and one for the musical composition. (In the case of Jay-Z's "Hard Knock Life," a third license—a performance rights license—was required to release the song legally, because the sample came from a theatrical production of *Annie*.) But the two (or more) sides are not necessarily equally expensive, as El-P explains. "The master side is the one that you almost always get hit hard for," he says, "because that's the side that's controlled by the record label. And anyone who's really litigious or gives a fuck about sample clearance—usually that's a major label." We asked our interviewees about how sample clearance has changed over the past two decades. In response, the clearance professional Danny Rubin said that he believes that sampling has become more expensive. Pat Shanahan, another sample clearance expert, agrees, saying, "I've noticed there is very little sampling going on anymore because it has now become so exorbitantly expensive to do so."

"It's tough to do," says De La Soul's Trugoy, echoing the others: "It gets expensive." He says that a lot of people assume that sampling artists have plenty of money to pay for the samples they want to use, but in actuality, he says, "We don't make as much money as people may think." Trugoy emphasizes that his group definitely wants to make a living off their music, but he acknowledges that this can be hard in light of "what we have to give up—financially—just to make these creative records." The payment options all have down sides. Flat-fee advances make sample licensing expensive up front, while royalty payments cut into future profits on an ongoing basis. The attorney Andrew Bart explains it this way: "The cost of [licensing] is so high when you pay off all of the owners of the different samples that there's probably very little left for the compiler to receive his profit once all of the money is split among the various sample owners. So I would think that at some level, there's going to be an economic limit to how much you want to use a sample. Because it cuts into the profitability of the song."

"With every project I've done over the years," Shanahan says, "the publishers and labels want more and more money. It has literally knocked the smaller artists out of the game altogether. Only the ones who are very, very well off can afford to sample anymore." Because many sample licenses require an advance—instead of, or even in addition to, a royalty payment—only larger organizations with more cash on hand can afford them. As Shoshana Zisk relates, "I remember when I was working at Polygram, which is now Universal, seeing some of the sample clearance spreadsheets coming across my desk and sometimes people were paying up to maybe $25,000 per sample. I think if somebody was putting out an indie record and they received a quote of 'yes, you can sample this, but it's going to cost you $25,000,' they would probably just go into another line of work." Tom Silverman voiced a similar concern: "I would like to see a level playing field where the smallest guy working in his home studio in the Bronx, or anywhere in the world, could come up with something without censoring himself because he's afraid of being sued."

Mark Kates is a former label executive (including a stint as president of the Beastie Boys' Grand Royal Records) as well as a DJ himself. As he tells us, "You generally start at paying $5,000 to even have a conversation. They won't even really consider it for less than that." But the ultimate price for the sample license can go much higher. The CEO of Tommy Boy Records, Tom Silverman, says, "I've seen samples that cost $50,000, easily. If I go to somebody and I want to sample a Marvin Gaye lick, I might have to pay Marvin Gaye's estate, like Erick Sermon did, $100,000 for one sample. An advance!" Danny Rubin describes the more common price ranges for both master use licenses and publishing licenses. He tells us that in today's market an advance will usually cost—depending on the length of the sample and who the original artist is—somewhere between $5,000 to $15,000 (though there are always the outliers, like Silverman's example of $100,000 to sample Marvin Gaye or the reported $100,000 that 2 Live Crew had to pay to sample dialogue from Stanley Kubrick's *Full Metal Jacket*).[8]

"The royalty is usually going to fall anywhere from a penny per unit to as high as 12 or 15 cents per unit," Rubin says. "Then you have a cost on the publishing side. Similarly, they're going to ask for an advance. Usually on the publishing side, the advance will be a little lower, probably average somewhere around $4,000 or $5,000, and you'll have to assign a percentage of your new copyright to the publishing company of the song that you sampled." Advances can be quite imposing, even for a major-label recording artist. But smaller figures can still discourage independent musicians.

If the typical prices charged for sample licenses are justified—in the sense of being reasonable, economically efficient, or both—then this isn't a problem. In that case, samples would be a cost of making music that not every musician can afford, just like many other things that not every consumer or small business can afford. But in a relatively small market like the market for samples, prices might not be reasonable or economically efficient.[9] It's possible that distortions, such as the concentration of record-label ownership, allow copyright owners to overcharge for samples. Many of the musicians we interviewed expressed dismay at some of the prices they had been quoted.

As Pasemaster Mase of De La Soul states, "If you're sampling anything from Slick Rick and Doug E. Fresh's 'The Show' and 'La Di Da Di'—that was like a six grand, six thousand dollar figure to start with, just to even sample the words, 'Hit it!'" And El-P offers a caricature of a licensing negotiation: " 'Hey, can we use this bass line? [laughs] *Please*?'

And they're like, 'Yeah, sure, give me all your publishing revenues and give me ten thousand dollars.' You can be completely blindsided by some gigantic, outrageous price." For instance, when De La Soul made the mistake of trying to sample Paul McCartney, they grew frustrated and ultimately gave up and dropped the sample from the record. "We reached out to his people," group member Trugoy says. "He loved the song, was with it, but was like, 'You can use it, but I need all the publishing. All of it.' It was just crazy."

Two effects of the sample clearance system have come to fruition. First, fewer musicians working within mainstream distribution systems engage in sampling. Second, the musicians who do sample extensively have had to abandon the traditional commercial-recording model. Even though sample licenses typically count as recording costs that artists are required to recoup before they receive any royalties, record labels usually provide the money up front. So the size of the label determines whether a musician can afford sample clearances. Pat Shanahan—who has had extensive experience licensing samples for music publishers—told us that the artists on most independent labels can't afford to sample: "There's no way they can afford to. So what they do, I don't know. I don't know if they remove their samples. I assume that's what they do . . . because it has literally become unaffordable unless they have a major, major budget to work with." But Eothen Alapatt told us that his small label, Stones Throw, bears the expense: "It's painful for a small company with very tight cash flow to pay out for samples, but we *do* do it."

When using a sample is very important to a musician, sometimes they will reluctantly pay the quoted price because they see no other choice. De La Soul's Trugoy relates the following story about a sample from the group's third album. "It was *Buhloone Mindstate*, we had recorded a song we wanted, it sounded great, and was the intro to the album," he says. "We found out that they wanted like maybe fifteen grand and a crazy amount of percentage of the song. And we were like 'Nah, we can't do this, this is ridiculous, this isn't even worth it.' We went back and found new music for the intro, but it kind of totally spoiled the feel of the album. So we actually went back and paid the amount, shared the splits the way they wanted it."

Here's where the complexity of the competing interests between musicians who sample and copyright owners becomes significant.

Copyright owners want as high a price as they can get. But if they demand overly high prices, they can price themselves out of the market for samples, harming themselves along with the sampling musicians. An example of the musician's perspective was provided to us by El-P: "So if there was a give and take, publishers could make money, and we could actually pay for it without feeling like we're getting ripped off. But they're too fuckin' greedy, so they're gonna force us all to not sample anymore." The entertainment lawyer Anthony Berman describes one of the major ways in which the prices for individual samples have created obstacles for any new musical work that wants to use two or more samples: "Sometimes, if you sample three records, you might get all three copyright holders demanding to own 100 percent of your new sampled composition. Three times 100 percent is 300 percent, but you only have 100 percent to give." In our interviews, we heard about many manifestations of this fundamental "royalty stacking" problem, which we mentioned in the introduction.

Jeff Chang, who has worked with many artists over the years, offers an eye-opening example of what a well-known artist did when he encountered this impossible scenario. (We won't reveal the identity of this artist, because there would be obvious legal consequences.) The artist had previously released a classic, critically adored, sample-based record on an independent label, but when the same record was rereleased on a major label, Chang relates, the artist "was shocked to hear back from [the label's] lawyers that he needed to turn in a sample clearance sheet." There was no room in the budget to clear all of the samples, especially because some of the songs contained upward of forty to fifty samples from different sound sources. "So he took a very interesting approach," Chang says. "He kind of looked at it from the point of view of, 'Okay, well, if somebody's gonna get my money for this, who deserves to get it the most?' You know? [laughter] And he went in and kind of selectively gave [the label] a list of samples that they should go ahead and get cleared."

As the music manager Michael Hausman told us, "You can get some pretty outrageous quotes, and that hasn't helped creativity very much. There has to be some kind of reasonable price." A more flexible pricing system might benefit everyone. The pricing of sample licenses, especially when it renders songs containing multiple samples impossible to release legally without losing money on each copy, is a kind of economic inefficiency.[10] It represents a failure of many individual copyright holders to act collectively for the sake of all copyright holders.

Individual licensors—for example, the owners of copyrights in musical compositions—are frequently demanding a large share—say, 50 percent—of songs that sample their compositions. They do this out of their own self-interest. But by acting this way, the licensors are forcing musicians to endure potential losses whenever they sample more than one source per track. As a result, musicians wishing to create collages from samples must either refrain from creating them in the first place, decline to release them, give them away for free, or sell them illegally in the underground economy. Whichever course of action the would-be collagists choose, the individual self-interest of the potential licensors has carried them to the collectively undesirable outcome of receiving no revenue at all.

THE IMPORTANCE OF RELATIONSHIPS IN SAMPLE CLEARANCE

I think that in some instances, people would be more willing to license to a major than an independent simply because there's a possibility that they would sell more records, given the distribution.
—WALTER MCDONOUGH

Previous or continuing business relationships can grease the wheels of sample licensing. Discussing the popularity of mash-ups and the new class of creators, Dina LaPolt states: "[If] one of my clients mashed up something that I thought was brilliant, I would do whatever it takes to get it cleared." Despite her positive attitude, most independent creators do not have access to LaPolt's industry expertise, which a musician would need to successfully license a mash-up of famous songs. Bill Stafford tells us that licensing—for independent artists, including those without a label at all—is "very, very difficult. Without someone there to help them along, it's the bottom of the pile."

Many musicians would lack the necessary familiarity with both copyright law and the music industry without legal representation or without affiliating with a label and publisher. LaPolt illustrates the value of having expert representation with strong business relationships: "So, if one of the quotes came in and my client co-wrote that song, then I'll call the music publishers of that sample and I'll try to get it down. . . .

I'll say, 'Hey, I know you quoted 60 percent. Can you come down?' And you get it down as low as possible so your songwriter gets to keep more of the copyright." Business relationships represent the connections between parties to a licensing negotiation. More than that, relationships involve stored knowledge about customary licensing practices, such as what type of royalty to ask for and which offers might be negotiable.

Pat Shanahan, who has worked at a variety of music publishing firms, elaborates on the difficulties for independent musicians seeking sample licenses on their own: "Basically if they try to do it themselves, they usually become quite frustrated because everyone is very busy at these companies, unless you know people and have relationships." In prospective sample-licensing negotiations, musicians need representatives with strong business networks. For instance, when Big Daddy Kane tried to sample "I'll Take You There" by the classic gospel-soul group the Staple Singers, he ran into problems clearing the sample. "We wrote the rhymes and made the track," Kane says, "but apparently Prince owned the rights to all the Staple Singers songs and wasn't tryin' to let no rappers use them." Kane was still signed to an independent label at the time, and so his song, also titled "I'll Take You There," went unreleased. Things turned around when Kane and Prince became labelmates. "When I signed with Warner Bros., that was the same label Prince was on, so then Prince was cool about it."[11]

Relationships within the industry can be a way of making it quicker (and cheaper) to figure out whom you need to license from and how to contact them. It also matters which sort of record label and publisher a musician affiliates with. Major labels have more resources and strong continuing business relationships with each other. As Deee-lite's Lady Miss Kier tells us, "The good thing about being on a major label is they [Warner] had a great legal department that made sure we had to clear all samples—which we wouldn't have known anything about." Danny Rubin explains the importance of a label or publisher's size, as follows: "It's a business about making money, and if an artist is going to come out and sell 250 copies of a record from the trunk of his car, and only going to be able to pay the publisher or a record company an advance of $1,000, it's really not in the company's best interests to spend time working out a license for that. In the long run, the costs of the transaction are going to outweigh the benefit or the profits or the revenue from the transaction."

"Everything's about relationships," says Dina LaPolt. "If I like you, I'll help you. If I don't like you, it's going to be difficult and expensive. That's just the way of the world." The transaction costs of obtaining licenses reinforce the importance of relationships, and the complicated nature of sample licensing makes it impractical for musicians to do without experienced lawyers or professionals. Affiliating with a major label, with the attendant increase in potential sales, makes sample clearance feasible. Sampling musicians seeking licenses essentially *must* establish relationships with music lawyers, sample clearance professionals, major labels, and large publishers—partly to take advantage of *their* business relationships.

THE SAMPLE CLEARANCE BUREAUCRACY

I think increasingly, because [sample clearance] is difficult,
expensive, and time consuming, people that are talented enough
are trying to avoid dealing with it.—MARK KATES

Transaction costs are all the ancillary costs that accompany the act of buying things. For instance, when you need groceries, the time and energy spent driving to the store and getting cash from an ATM might be your transaction costs. Sample clearance—that is, buying licenses or otherwise obtaining permission—involves many transaction costs. Some of these costs are typical for the music industry, while some are idiosyncratic to the sampling context. For the musicians who can employ them, sample clearance houses can reduce the costs of having representation, tracking down the relevant copyright holders, and reaching deals. Danny Rubin explains that the "other fee that you're gonna have to pay is either a lawyer or a sample clearance agency to clear the songs, which is how I make my money, and we do it based on a per-clearance flat fee. For me, it's usually $500 per clearance." He's talking about $500 per negotiation with the owners of both the sound recording and the musical composition. This pushes the clearance costs even higher, because most samples will involve at least two negotiations—if not more because one or both copyrights are split among multiple owners. Also, $500 per clearance is the cost of a smooth transaction; a difficult negotiation can cost thousands.

Despite the availability of clearance professionals for some musicians, transaction costs remain a headache. Songs containing multiple samples face particular problems. The licensing fees themselves are a large expense. But the associated transaction costs of negotiating two types of licenses (publishing and master use) per sampled source—and then accounting to all the stakeholders after the record is released—also result in considerable costs. "It's a lot of accounting work," Tom Silverman says, speaking of the early albums by De La Soul that his company Tommy Boy released. "You have to pay out on 60 different people on one album. It's quite a nightmare actually." The total transaction costs per album balloon as the number of samples used increases, even if the costs per transaction hold steady. Again, as stated above, a typical sample implicates two copyrights, for a sound recording and a musical composition, and each copyright may have been divided up among multiple owners. Moreover, copyrights last longer than they used to, making licensing necessary even for very old works. Thus, the number of necessary negotiations can become quite large.

As the music attorney Whitney Broussard states, "I think that when you're dealing with rights holders trying to get a sample cleared, it's really not a priority for them. . . . In publisher's cases, they're trying to issue mechanical licenses and get synch[ronization] uses and things that are sort of the normal bread and butter of a company." Broussard continues by noting that

> [these companies] are dealing with a million other issues and they sort of have to get to it. So I think that's a structural problem and that's very problematic. And the other side of that, or sort of the corollary to that, comes when you look at a fairly typical rap album with, say, fourteen, fifteen, sixteen songs on it, or sometimes maybe considerably more, and maybe two or three samples on each song. Now you have a problem—that's like forty-five sample clearances that you need to get done. Or even twenty is an unmanageable number, very difficult to manage. So now you're faced with just the sheer magnitude of the friction in the system, which just slows the whole process down to almost a crawl.

Friction is a great metaphor for transaction costs. Despite the theoretical benefits of licensing, which offers the promise of mutually beneficial exchange, some energy is lost as the necessary motion occurs to get a license done.

The pricing of sample licenses is not transparent; there is no menu.

Hank Shocklee asks in frustration, "If I'm sampling, let's say, forty seconds of a song and that becomes my entire song, well, do I pay the same amount if I sampled one second of it? . . . Who determines these prices? Who determines the rates and all that stuff?" Although negotiations start with an idea of typical price ranges (for the advance, buyout, royalty rate, or share), each negotiation is idiosyncratic. Musicians can only know exactly how much the specific samples they have used will cost once negotiations have progressed. This makes licensing transactions more time consuming and costly than, say, simple purchases at Wal-Mart that are based on advertised, clearly marked prices.

It takes time, effort, and money to learn or even get a sense of how much a given sample will cost, or whether it can be cleared at all. For instance, Mark Kates told us about trying to clear a sample on Beck's biggest album, *Odelay*, before it was released. The song "Jackass," one of the album's hits, contained a sample from "It's All Over Now, Baby Blue"—a Bob Dylan song as recorded by Them, whose lead singer was Van Morrison. Not only did Beck have to acquire a license from Bob Dylan's publishing company, they had to get permission to use Them's sound recording. "It was a really, really difficult sample to clear on that record," says Kates. "I mean, we literally were dealing with like the upper echelon of the Irish music business, and it finally got done, but it wasn't easy."

Licensing fees can surprise less-experienced musicians, who compose and record unaware of the potential cost of the sample licenses they will need. Even veteran musicians who sample face uncertainty over what they might owe for sample licenses—or even if it is possible to clear a sample. One type of transaction cost is known as search cost, meaning the expense of discovering and locating the copyright owners of the sampled sources. "In some cases, it's not even the original artist," observes Eothen Alapatt of Stones Throw Records. "It's three other different people that represent their publishing or had the publishing on that record thirty years ago, and they give you a quote that you can't deal with. We've had to pull tracks off of records because of that."

Alapatt provides a specific example of the difficulties generated from copyrights changing hands over the years:

> If we're talking about, for instance, Ethiopian records—even if you went and found the division of Universal Records that supposedly purchased the

Phillips Ethiopia catalog, the chances of Phillips Ethiopia having contracts that survived the regime changes in Ethiopia or any proof that they own the music is so far-fetched. You might get to a person at the company who would just take the blanket stance that they own it—regardless of whether it was proven or not—because they were Phillips Ethiopia, bought by Polygram, bought by blah blah blah, bought by Universal. And they could actually stop you from putting the record out even though they don't have proof that they actually own the material. . . . If I found that an artist of ours used a track that was released on Phillips Ethiopia in 1974, I would say there's no way in hell we're gonna try to clear this sample. We're just gonna put this out.

Smaller labels or musicians would have a hard time bearing the search costs of tracing the ownership of copyrights in such a situation as Alapatt describes. As he suggests, they would also have trouble disputing a major label's claim of ownership because they lack the resources to litigate against a global conglomerate to challenge the validity of their claimed copyrights.

"The question is, who do you contact? You have to find the writers on the record," says Hank Shocklee. "Then when you go and look and find the writers of the record, you try to find the publishing company that was associated with those writers. Well, when this thing starts getting transferred and people start signing their rights over to the next third party and the fourth party and fifth parties and things of that nature, well, we're not privy to that information." Speaking to Shocklee's frustrations, the artist manager Hip Hop bemoans the current confusing state of sample licensing.

> KEMBREW: Do you think the licensing system is efficient or inefficient?
> HIP HOP: I didn't even know it was a *system*.
> KEMBREW: There's no system? It's just free-for-all, is that what you mean?
> HIP HOP: Yeah.

Interestingly, there literally was no system back in 1981 when David Byrne and Brian Eno released *My Life in the Bush of Ghosts*. As Byrne recounts: "Yes, there were no sample clearance agencies to help clear stuff back then. We delayed the record release by about a year (it was more or less finished before *Remain in Light* came out) to try and contact as many of the sources as possible. Lots of detective work." He continues by saying:

We knew that if we didn't, it might not reflect well on us later. Luckily no one could quite figure out what we were doing—and it certainly didn't seem like a project that would generate oodles of cash for us—so pretty much everyone said OK when we finally found them. . . . The big exception was that the original vocal on "The Jezebel Spirit" was the late radio evangelist Katherine Kuhlman. She's pretty well known in certain circles, so apparently on her death bed Oral Roberts, another radio evangelist, had her sign over the rights to her recorded programs. Or so we heard. He absolutely refused to grant us the right to use her voice—so we reworked the track with the radio exorcist—which worked out maybe even better.

Byrne's story brings up another type of transaction costs, known as hold-up costs. Suppose that a certain track includes five samples, and that all licenses for four of the samples have been negotiated. What if one of the copyright holders for the last sample cannot be found? What if they decide to "hold you up" for a higher buyout or royalty, perhaps knowing that they are the last necessary licensor? The costs involved in breaking such an impasse are a key part of the costs of negotiating licenses. And some copyright holders may refuse to license samples at all. In this situation, if other licenses for a track have already been negotiated, the transaction costs spent to that point—not to mention the effort in creating that particular mix of the track—have been wasted. And there are other expenses related to hold-up costs. If one has to go back in the studio to rework a track (or, even worse, remaster a whole record), it can get very expensive in requiring artists or labels to spend money they don't actually have.

TIMING DIFFICULTIES IN SAMPLE CLEARANCE

This process can take anywhere from two to twenty weeks.
I mean it's very, very long.—BILL STAFFORD

As illustrated in some of the stories in chapter 3 and elsewhere, it matters whether samples are cleared before or after the record's release. When copyright owners detect unauthorized sampling, they may demand larger buyouts and greater royalty rates. After the record has been released, they may have some notion of the sampling record's success, and thus the sampling artist's ability to pay. Acrimony can pervade the negotiation, and the copyright owner can threaten an infringe-ment lawsuit. Because of the possible penalties for not clearing samples beforehand—in terms of higher prices or, worse, a lawsuit—most la-bels seek to have all samples cleared as soon as possible. As Eothen Alapatt says of his label, "We've actually become more proactive in the last couple of years at talking with our artists before the music is fin-ished or because the record is turned in, and finding out what they've used so we can kind of assess what we're gonna have to pay and how the budget might be affected as a result."

Beginning the sample clearance process earlier in a record's produc-tion cycle helps reduce the risk of penalties. It also assists with finan-cial planning for the label. As Danny Rubin explains, "Usually there's a deadline that the record company has to get all samples cleared by a certain date, and usually that date is only a few months away. So I would say if I haven't found something within a few weeks or a month it's usually too late." Such frustration can extend beyond the level of mere annoyance, as the following example from Michael Hausman in-dicates: "I did have this one issue with [the now-defunct record com-pany] Imago with Aimee Mann where the issue of samples became a problem—it delayed the record. . . . And you know, the idea that you might have to go back and un-record things, erase things or change ar-rangements. I mean, I think those are real costs not only in studio time but also in the momentum of a project."

Pat Shanahan tells us that some companies are very good at respond-ing fairly quickly with price quotes, but other companies are very slow to respond. It can take months to hear from them, he says, though he points out that a lot of times it is not their fault. It depends on whether or not the request is high on the company's list of priorities. Chris Lighty, a hip-hop management company executive, states that "it's very hard to find these [copyright owners] and very expensive. You can spend be-tween $5,000 and $10,000 just trying to obtain a license and still come up dry."[12] As for examples of coming up dry, Lighty discusses a case in which a production team assumed that the licensing of a sample was imminent. They completed and mastered the album, only to find that the license was rejected. The production team had to go back to the studio to remaster the album—deleting the song with the unauthorized sample in the process. As Lighty puts it, "We decided it was expensive to remaster, but not as expensive as getting sued."[13]

The rapper and producer Kanye West—whose innovative production work on Jay-Z's records has been heard by millions—learned this licensing lesson when making his debut in 2004, *The College Dropout*. He is on a label, Jay-Z's Roc-A-Fella Records, that can afford the ridiculously high prices that companies charge. But West still had problems clearing the samples for the single "All Falls Down." As he told *Entertainment* Weekly, he wanted to include a sample of one sung line taken from Lauryn Hill's *MTV Unplugged* album from 2002, but "the problem was, it had to get cleared through MTV and also through Sony" (the network that originally broadcast Hill's performance and the record company that owns her master tapes). "The sample was going to end up costing like around $150,000."[14] This is an extremely large amount of money, especially when it is added to the cost of recording, promotion, music videos, and the like.

Even though West and his record company were willing to pay for this brief fragment of a sound recording, the bureaucratic wheels turned so slowly that negotiating would have significantly delayed the release of this long-anticipated debut. Not only did the label need permission from Lauryn Hill's record label, it also had to get permission from Hill herself, for contractual reasons. As Kanye's manager Hip Hop remembers, "She was like, 'I like it, but don't use my voice.'" He explains that she felt that because she wasn't making any records at the time, she didn't want her voice to be used on a new record that would likely be popular—and it did become a hit. As a solution, West employed the services of the R&B songstress Syleena Johnson to sing Hill's part, thus legally bypassing the need to negotiate a master use license for the *MTV Unplugged* album.[15]

Whitney Broussard agrees that the implications of a delayed record-release date can be far-reaching for artists, and he states that delay can "drastically affect an artist's career. If tensions flare up, a label can cool on an artist. . . . And if you miss one Tuesday [release date], you can't necessarily go to the next." Broussard also notes that a delayed record release can affect the financial reporting for the label: "It can skew the earnings for a record . . . so that they fall over two quarters instead of one." To satisfy investors, the major record labels generally want to show as much earnings as soon as possible. For big-name artists, delays from sample clearance can affect their apparent financial performance.

Smaller labels face more grave problems with timing, as they have a smaller roster of artists and a much smaller number of releases per year to spread out financially. As Eothen Alapatt explains:

> Sometimes you're in the position where you have the record in production, and you have to halt production of it because you can't find the answer that you need. As much as we believe in this creatively, we all have to stay in business, so we can't take risks. . . . If you have a record that's done, and let's just say it was done a month ago in July. That means a record company would be putting it into production and it would be set to release in September or October, probably late September. Well, if you're an independent, you don't have the luxury of pushing it back to November because you can't afford the retail programs necessary to market the record between October and December. It's exorbitant. It's the way the music industry works, because the retailer is trying to sell shelf space to major labels. So you have to start in the end of January when the cycle begins anew for independent companies; we can start affording to buy shelf space. So you might be with an artist who has a hot single on the radio, or, nowadays, a hot single on the Internet, and you want to get that record into production immediately, but you can't clear a sample. Well, you could lose four months at the drop of a hat, as well as a lot of money.

The seasonal cycles of promotion in the record business make it especially costly to miss a record-release date, magnifying the overall cost of any inefficiencies in the sample clearance system. Because the sample clearance bureaucracy takes time to navigate in general, sample-heavy records can translate into financial difficulties for labels. Even the tiniest problems can have large effects. For instance, if one owner of a song sampled on a key track on a sampling artist's record is especially difficult to reach by phone, the costs can multiply—with a sort of butterfly effect—into a damaged career for the artist and missed Wall Street expectations for the artist's label.

However, not everyone involved in the system agrees that the system is broken. As Dina LaPolt states: "Those people that are actually doing the deals and being in the industry don't have time to sit around and talk for nine hours about how we can streamline and do all this stuff, because we're all doing it. I don't have a problem with it and I don't think a lot of my colleagues have a problem with it. It always seems to be the people that are the least successful or not even in my music industry who are the ones that have a problem with how the music industry goes." Still, commercial success has become a threshold for being able to clear samples. Without commercial success, it is quite difficult to have money and the relationships to afford the transaction costs of licensing. This is especially true of the tens of thousands of amateur mash-up artists who have absolutely no relationship with the music industry except for being consumers of its products.

THE LICENSING SYSTEM AND MASH-UPS

It just went to a level that shocked even me. I'm like, "Oh, my God.
These are just kids just having fun dragging tracks on top of each other."
They're not trying to make any comment at all. They're not coming from
some arty, lefty, progressive, intellectual background or anything. . . .
It was just, you know, the ultimate in punk rock.—MARK HOSLER

Mash-ups, which involve artists layering a vocal melody line from one song on top of an instrumental melody from another song, present unique licensing problems. The mash-up technique is a musical tradition that actually goes back many decades. One of the earliest examples is Alan Copeland's *"Mission: Impossible* Theme/Norwegian Wood" from 1968. Copeland started out in the late 1940s as a member of the vocal group The Modernaires. He then became an arranger for Ella Fitzgerald, Frank Sinatra, and others, and later did work as a TV-theme composer. Just what gave him the idea to plop the vocal melody of the Beatles' "Norwegian Wood" (originally in a 3/4 waltz time signature) on top of the *Mission: Impossible* theme song (in jazzy 5/4 time) is a complete mystery. Even more remarkably, it won a Grammy for best contemporary pop performance by a chorus, though Copeland's song can't be said to have launched a mash-up trend in the late 1960s.[16] Indeed, that wouldn't happen for another thirty years.

The origins of the modern mash-up can also be heard in the medleys found on disco twelve-inch singles, where a mixer would seamlessly segue from one song to the other. Sometimes these were unlikely medleys, like Donna Summer's 18-minute dance megamix that effortlessly fused her versions of "Heaven Knows," "One of a Kind," and "MacArthur Park." Even closer to the potpourri spirit of mash-ups, the postmodern Euro-disco duo the Pet Shop Boys masterfully blended the high-minded "Where the Streets Have No Name" by U2 with the 1960s schlock of "Can't Take My Eyes Off You," made popular by Engelbert Humperdinck and others. In the case of the Pet Shop Boys, the group rerecorded these songs themselves, whereas twelve-inch megamixes were usually drawn from the original recordings. But in both instances, they were medleys—rather than laying vocals from one song atop a different song's instrumental.

"What people call the 'mash-up technique' has been basically an evolution from sampling and DJ-ing," says Coldcut's Matt Black, speaking of the mash-up's origins in dance-music culture, beginning with disco. "It's the idea that you can mix two different things together, particularly two well-known things that people actually recognize." Hip-hop used many of the mixing methods employed by disco producers and DJs, which help us to draw a direct line from disco to hip-hop to the mash-up. In hip-hop's earlier, more experimental form, DJs threw virtually everything but the kitchen sink into the mix. "My audience was the most progressive of all," Afrika Bambaataa said about hip-hop in the 1970s, "because they knew I was playing all types of weird records for them. I even played commercials that I taped off the television shows, from *Andy Griffith* to the *Pink Panther*, and people looked at me like I was crazy."[17]

Following in that spirit, one of the first collages to mix the instrumentation from one sound recording with the vocals from another was a seven-inch single from 1996 by the Evolution Control Committee (the songs originally appeared on a 1994 cassette). Each side of the single uses a Herb Alpert instrumental as the backing track for a rap from a Public Enemy song: "Rebel without a Pause" on the A-side and "By the Time I Get to Arizona" on the B-side.[18] TradeMark Gunderson of the Evolution Control Committee was able to get his hands on Chuck D's vocals because most hip-hop singles are released with an a capella track included—for the express purpose of mixing it with another instrumental track. Chuck D is well-known for his liberal attitude on the sampling of his own music. When we asked him how he felt about the Evolution Control Committee's mash-ups, which comically paired his vocals with the brassy, easy-listening sounds of Herb Alpert, he replied, "I think my feelings are obvious. I think it's great."

The practice of releasing a capella vocals on hip-hop singles played a direct role in the emergence of the mash-up as we know it. As Pam the Funkstress of The Coup explains, "The a capella is the DJ's best friend.

When twelve-inch singles come out these days, they have an a capella version, which makes it easier for us to put the vocals over a different beat—drop that beat out and scratch something in and make that a capella just sound totally different." And as Matmos's Drew Daniel tells us, "What's so great about hip-hop and R&B is that every single comes with an a cappella on the flip side. It's like being given some sort of naked photograph of a celebrity."

One of the very first collaged compositions to be labeled as a mash-up was Freelance Hellraiser's recording from 2001 of "A Stroke of Genie-us"—a composition that places the pop diva Christina Aguilera's a capella vocals atop the indie-rock music of the Strokes. Another song that helped establish the mash-up as a popular musical genre was Soulwax's "Smells Like Teen Booty," a track that fuses the hard-rocking instrumentation of Nirvana's "Smells Like Teen Spirit" with the R&B vocals from "Bootylicious" by Destiny's Child. "That song is fucking amazing," says Negativland's Mark Hosler. "The combination, when you hear it, it works so great and it has a completely different groove. And I remember hearing that and thinking, 'Wow. This could have been a hit. Like, this totally isn't kind of quirky and funny—it rocks.'"

Drew Daniel believes that mash-ups can be interesting, but are not always so. "I think that it can reach a banal 'stealth oldies' level, where it's just sort of oldies by another means," he says. "Like, 'Oh it's Wham! and Van Halen.' It's not actually interesting. It's like, 'Wow, you've made another jalapeno-mint sandwich!' And no one wants to eat it." Vicki Bennett agrees with this assessment. She believes that the mash-up movement had pretty much played itself out almost as soon as it had started. But she also believes there is still an upside, in terms of the bigger picture. "Now that most people in the Western world can somehow get their hands on either a computer or some means of duplicating and arranging," Bennett says, "it means that people are far more equal in the creation of art. It isn't so much an elite thing. It means that there's going to be a lot more bad art made, but I think that it's good that even bad art is made than no art at all."

The Internet's digital distribution power makes it possible for mash-ups to circulate, while the billions of MP3s available online provide the grist for new compositions. "There's a phenomenal availability of material," says Ian Edgar, a member of the London-based group Eclectic Method. "What we do would be absolutely impossible, because it would cost too much. You can't buy all of these tunes you're going to DJ, and you can't buy all of these videos. They're transmitted on TV, someone encodes them, they go out on KaZaa, and it's rich pickings." And as Negativland's Don Joyce observes, "The Internet's like a big flea market. There's everything out there."

The contemporary mash-up phenomena also couldn't have happened without the recently developed computer programs that allow amateur bedroom composers to juxtapose two or more songs in interesting ways. "Today, algorithms have been written within the computer that actually will do things like time-stretch it perfectly for you," the sound artist Scanner says, "or you can change the pitch in real time. So, you can take a Christina Aguilera track with a Nirvana track and actually pitch it so it fits perfectly." What is also interesting about mash-ups is that—with a few notable exceptions—their creators have not incurred the legal wrath of copyright owners. They are largely tolerated or ignored by the mainstream music industry, and since the turn of the millennium thousands of individuals have posted and shared their mash-ups without consequence.

The Grey Album

Because of copyright and licensing issues, few mash-ups stand a chance to receive a legitimate commercial release, including *The Grey Album*. In early 2004, a then-underground hip-hop producer named Danger Mouse spent over one hundred hours chopping up instrumental fragments from the Beatles' self-titled release from 1968, known as *The White Album*, and adorning them with vocals from Jay-Z's recently released *The Black Album*—all without asking permission. (Jay-Z had given tacit approval to samplers when he reportedly said of his album, "remix the shit out of it.") Danger Mouse—who was not signed to either a major label or an independent one at the time—manufactured only a few thousand CD copies, but *The Grey Album* spread on file-sharing networks, and it received coverage and praise from the *New Yorker*, the *New York Times*, and *Rolling Stone*. Even Dean Garfield, who led the MPAA's worldwide anti-piracy initiative, liked Danger Mouse's illegitimate pop confection. "I actually have listened to *The Grey Album* a number of times," he says, "and there's a lot I found to be enjoyable about it. I thought the mixture of music was creative, mixing the genres."

"It was so popular," Dina LaPolt says, speaking about *The Grey Album*. "It was played all over the radio. Cease-and-desist letters every which way but loose, kids downloading at college, it was huge. It was on everybody's iPod. It was fantastic. You go to a spin class at a gym, they're playing it. Everybody has it." That the record label EMI sent out cease-and-desist letters was ironic, given that *The White Album* features "Revolution 9," a *musique concrète* sound collage that draws from a variety of found sounds, musical recordings, and radio broadcasts. "When DJ Danger Mouse did *The Grey Album*," LaPolt says, "everybody flipped out. No one would clear it and you know what? He put it out. Was that right? No, but what he did is he made a statement." Negativland's Mark Hosler takes a somewhat different view: "What's interesting about *The Grey Album* is the artist himself didn't seem to have any interest in trying to protest this or see it a point to struggle and resist. It was really fans of the work and people who cared about this issue—they took the work and posted it online."

Chuck D observes that the brouhaha surrounding *The Grey Album* "is a culmination of a lot of people just being mad that everything is now equal and that people now can jump to high heights from low places." Chuck D and others argue that companies like EMI are reacting to the fact that digital technologies help level the playing field between individual artists and the culture industry machine. "What's happening today is the artist is becoming more of a curator, in some ways," says Scanner. "I wonder today if that's what lots of musicians are becoming. They're becoming curators, in a sense. They are collaging these elements together and curating this new world. But it's happened at such an accelerated speed that the lawyers are still caught in laws that were built and written many, many years ago that could not take into context these kinds of radical shifts in perception of how one creates work."

With regard to EMI's legal strategy, Dean Garfield explains that for various reasons the Beatles don't want their works distributed in ways in which they don't have the final say. He emphasizes, furthermore, that this is fully within their right. Even though Garfield admits to liking *The Grey Album*, he points out that "there's a lot in life, generally, that is enjoyable that we're not allowed to do. And though I would groove to *The Grey Album* if I were in my own home, I understand why that's not the way to go about it." Indeed, Garfield says that the proper way to go about it would have been to try to negotiate a license with EMI. And Michael Hausman states, along the same lines: "I personally like Brian [Burton, a.k.a. Danger Mouse], and I like *The Grey Album*, but it brings up a lot of ethical issues. I think people have the right to complain about it, you know?"

Three years later, mash-ups were being discussed in Congress. "Mr. Chairman, I want to tell you a story of a local guy done good," said Congressman Mike Doyle (D-Pennsylvania), addressing the House Telecommunication and Internet Subcommittee in early 2007. "His name is Gregg Gillis and by day he is a biomedical engineer in Pittsburgh. At night, he DJs under the name Girl Talk. His latest mash-up record made the top 2006 albums list from *Rolling Stone*, *Pitchfork*, and *Spin* magazine, among others," said Doyle. "In one example, Mr. Chairman, he blended Elton John, Notorious B.I.G., and Destiny's Child all in the span of thirty seconds."[19] It was certainly one of the more unusual speeches that have reverberated through the halls of Congress, and it was likely the first time a congressman (or anyone else) uttered "Elton John" and "Notorious B.I.G." in the same sentence.

TRYING TO MAKE (BUSINESS) SENSE OF MASH-UPS

You put a cappella vocals out there and you become
fifty-fifty partners with somebody else who might have come up with
an incredible piece of work. It is like a universal network of studios
where technology allows people to have studios in bedrooms,
instead of big expensive studios.—CHUCK D

"I think the record industry is a lot cooler about mash-ups at the moment," Scanner says, "because things are so bad for them. The major companies are already scared. How do they sell their product?" Some record companies are appropriating the appropriations—as opposed to tracking down the anonymous creators and trying to sue them. We have seen the rise of what the mash-up artist Freelance Hellraiser calls a "Lawyer's Mix," in which two songs are legitimately licensed and then mashed up by a third-party record company. For instance, the Sugarbabes got a number-one hit in the United Kingdom when they sang the vocals from Adina Howard's "Freak Like Me" over an instrumental by the 1980s electro-pop artist Gary Numan—with approval from all the rights owners. In a somewhat humorous turn of events, Freelance Hellraiser bitterly wrote on his website that these mash-ups are being done "without giving credit to the people who came up with the original idea."[20]

In Freelance Hellraiser's case, his popular Aguilera/Strokes mash-up was released two years later as a legitimate single. But Freelance Hellraiser wasn't paid. Even though his gripe boils down to complaining about someone ripping off his own unauthorized borrowings, it nevertheless underscores some troubling labor politics at work. As Scanner observes, "What could be better than getting a kid who does it for free in their bedroom? They don't have to pay anything." What sort of protection or compensation should he or she have, if any? Scanner continues by stating, "Instead of saying to this kid at some point, 'We know who you are, we're taking you to court,' they say, 'Actually, we want to release this as a record.' The kid's very happy, because he or she gets their product out on the street, and probably paid next to nothing for it." He also points out that the old pop star who was sampled gets another hit, and the sound recording and musical composition copyright owners rake in the money.

Speaking about mash-ups, the MPAA's Dean Garfield believes that the market will sort out the issue of mash-ups: musicians whose songs get mashed up will offer the public their own mash-ups. "Not long after *The Grey Album*," Garfield tells us, "Universal Records put out a mash-up collaboration of their own, and not long after that Jay-Z did his collaboration with Linkin Park, which was also quite popular." Discussing the impact of *The Grey Album*, Dina LaPolt says that "everybody flipped out, heads spun three degrees south, changed everything. Now mash-ups are huge. People are saying, 'Let's make this work.'" But how? Dean Garfield emphasizes that music companies and motion picture studios are interested in selling music and entertaining people, and so they will go where the market leads them. "So if people like mash-ups," Garfield says, "they'll produce them."

Licensing The Grey Album *(Hypothetically)*

Legitimate mash-ups have reached the marketplace, but they might not substitute for unique, organic, and popular mash-ups. Even though many people liked Danger Mouse's collage, the market did not magi-

TABLE 1. *The Grey Album* by the numbers: Hypothetical sales of a licensed version

Actual sales and downloads of *The Grey Album*	
Original production run of CDs	3,000
Copies downloaded on "Grey Tuesday" (Feb. 24, 2004)	100,000
Danger Mouse's sales record	
Sales and chart position of Gorillaz' *Demon Days* (2005)	2,000,000+
	(no. 6)
Sales and chart position of DANGERDOOM's *The Mouse and the Mask* (2005)	<500,000
	(no. 41)
Sales and chart position of Gnarls Barkley's *St. Elsewhere* (2006)	1,000,000+
	(no. 4)
Related sales records for comparison	
Sales of the Beatles' *The White Album* (1968)	19,000,000+
Estimated bootleg copies of Prince's *The Black Album* (1987)	500,000
Sales of Jay-Z's *The Black Album* (2003)	3,000,000+
Hypothetical sales of *The Grey Album*	1,000,000

cally adjust EMI's policy of banning Beatles samples. Instead, *The Grey Album* was downloaded millions of times, no one was compensated, and EMI ended up sending out hundreds of cease-and-desist letters to individuals and websites that hosted the album. Table 1 suggests what revenue *The Grey Album* might have earned if the copyright owners of the Beatles' music and that of Jay-Z had licensed it.[21]

Suppose, as we do in Table 1, that 1,000,000 people would have bought a licensed version of *The Grey Album*. The artist's share of the sales revenue would have been approximately $1,990,000 (see the figures for the distribution of CD revenue cited at the beginning of chapter 3). Now imagine a hypothetical licensing deal that would have allowed legitimate sales of the album. Suppose the Beatles and Jay-Z agreed to receive equal shares of the revenue, in which each sampled copyright owner made $950,000 per million sold. That would still leave $90,000 per million sold for Danger Mouse, so everyone could have benefited. As it happened, the Beatles and Jay-Z did not license *The Grey Album* (and might have been unwilling to agree to equal shares, even if they did license it), so the album generated almost no revenue whatsoever.

Millions downloaded *The Grey Album*, and yet no one earned money from those downloads. If the album was so popular and critically acclaimed, why couldn't a powerful record label make it work? Whitney

Broussard answers by saying that major labels are not in business for the sake of art. "They're in it to make money," he says. "And so anything that they can't really make money on, they're not gonna work with." Broussard is sure that a record company would have released *The Grey Album* if it were feasible, but the Beatles' public stance against being sampled was a clear deterrent that prevented the album from being released legitimately. As Siva Vaidhyanathan observes, "Another one of the absurdities of the music industry is nobody made a dime for one of the year's most successful albums. . . . And it didn't have to be that way. If we had a more rational system to deal with samples, more people could make money from this phenomenon." He then waxes philosophical: "But at least we got to dance to it, and that was good."

The Bleak Prospects for Licensing Mash-Ups

It is unlikely, we believe, that an amateur mash-up maker will have sufficient resources and contacts to secure licenses that will allow him or her to release a collage legitimately. It is also unclear whether the music industry will sort out another problem we discussed earlier in this chapter: royalty splits. The owners of the composition copyrights to "Smells Like Teen Spirit" by Nirvana and "Bootylicious" by Destiny's Child, for example, would each likely demand 100 percent ownership of the new composition. In other words, each would view the mash-up as a cover version—merely a new rendition—of their composition. But mash-ups are, for obvious reasons, quite different from covers, and the end result of this supposedly rational and responsible business behavior is a situation where at least 200 percent is demanded, but only 100 percent exists to give away.

A far more daunting prospect—one that might give an entertainment lawyer a stroke—would be trying to clear Girl Talk's album *Night Ripper* (2006), which sampled at least 150 songs, or the follow up album *Feed the Animals* (2008), which doubled that number. Assuming that Gregg Gillis or his record label could figure out who owns the copyrights and get all the necessary permissions, the problem doesn't end there. It's not even as simple as "just" acquiring and paying for 150 or 300 licenses for *Night Ripper* and *Feed the Animals*, respectively, because some of the songs that Gillis samples already contain multiple samples themselves. For instance, one of the songs used on *Night Ripper*—the Pharcyde's hip-hop hit "Passing Me By" (1992)—was composed from samples of "Summer in the City" by Quincy Jones, "Are You Experienced?" by Jimi Hendrix, and four other songs from lesser-known artists. Another song sampled on *Night Ripper*—P.M. Dawn's "Set Adrift on Memory Bliss"— not only contains an instantly recognizable sample from Spandau Ballet's "True," which provides the song's hook, but also a horn and drum sample from the Soul Searchers' "Ashley's Roachclip" and another drum sample from Bob James's "Take Me to Mardi Gras."

A final example comes from *Feed the Animals*, on which Gillis used a two-second clip from Deee-lite's "Groove Is in the Heart," which itself samples Vernon Burch's "Get Up" and the bass line from Herbie Hancock's "Bring Down the Birds." "Groove Is in the Heart" also features two spoken-word samples. One comes from a belly dancing instructional record by Bel-Sha-Zaar with Tommy Genapopolulis and the Grecian Knights—which provides the "We're going to dance and have some fun!" spoken-word introduction to the song. The other is a one-second speaking-in-tongues-like vocal outburst from Sweet Pussy Pauline's "Hateful Head Helen." Gillis only samples the "one, two, three, *bluhlbluhlbluhlbluhl*" part of "Groove Is in the Heart," which takes two seconds. But if one counts the songs within songs embedded in the full sound recording of the Deee-lite song—as the current licensing system requires one to do—the already-absurd number of licenses that Gillis and his label have to acquire would multiply further beyond reason.

What makes this maddening for a sample-based artist who wants to go legit is the fact that each stakeholder has veto power—and can also make any sort of monetary demands it pleases. Even if Gillis tried to get permission to release his records, it would be virtually impossible to clear the many copyrighted song fragments embedded in his records. "It's just not reasonable to go that route," Gillis says. "If we went through the clearance process, it'd probably take our entire lifetime to try to clear the album." Whitney Broussard agrees: "I think that most major record companies would just throw up their hands and say, 'We're not going to do it,' because it's just too much work. Each license can be a few thousand dollars, just in transaction costs—plus a few thousand dollars in license fees. And when you add that up over 150 samples, if you license everything, most companies probably wouldn't do it. As major labels, they understand that they're relatively big targets. They don't want to release things that haven't been cleared."

Gatekeepers and Distributors: Another Obstacle

For a time, listeners could purchase Girl Talk's *Night Ripper* from iTunes, but the online music store has since pulled the album—apparently because of concerns related to sample clearance. Other online retailers have, on and off, offered the album for sale. The disruption of the album's availability highlights a larger problem of the information age. Popular media or information tools like the iTunes store, a built-in feature of the widely used iTunes software, can act as a de facto gatekeeper. Sure, there are millions of places to get music on the Internet. But a large percentage of consumers use a small number of outlets to buy or listen to music, and as information gatekeepers these outlets must make decisions about how to patrol their borders. For instance, they have to decide whether to respect a fair use defense for sampling or whether to enforce the claims of copyright holders who would deny that defense. It is not an easy decision because both sides often have legitimate claims.

Even when artists simply want to manufacture a CD with samples, gatekeepers (in this instance, pressing plants) can stand in the way. "The problem now is, of course, we are trying to get them manufactured," says Mark Hosler. "Back in the 1980s and early 1990s when we were doing recordings that had all sorts of stuff on them, nothing happened. The pressing plants weren't concerned. The pressing plant that pressed the *U2* CD and LP never said a darn thing." In 1998, when Negativland submitted their CD *Over the Edge Volume 3* to the CD pressing plant they had used for years, the plant would not press their CD—a decision based on then-recent guidelines from the Recording Industry Association of America (RIAA). The guidelines, which the RIAA maintained were aimed at curbing piracy, emphasized the fact that pressing plants are liable for infringing material, which at the time could result in a fine of up to $100,000 per uncleared sample infraction.[22]

For a while, it looked as though Negativland would not be able to manufacture the CD, or any of their CDs. But after they submitted their master tape anonymously to a smaller (unidentified) pressing plant that was initially reluctant, their record was released.[23] Negativland responded to the RIAA's new guidelines with a terse press release and an organized email campaign that aimed to persuade the RIAA that their guidelines were too limiting. In a press release that addressed this campaign and Negativland's complaints, the RIAA president and CEO Hilary Rosen denied that her organization's guidelines had anything to do with Negativland's activities. In a letter written to Rosen, Negativland called her denial "sadly disingenuous," and they pointed out that they never had a problem pressing their CDs until the RIAA issued new guidelines. And, as the group stated further: "Our records contain plenty of samples and free appropriation for which we claim 'fair use.' We do not counterfeit, pirate, or bootleg anything."[24]

In a surprising turn of events, after a month-long letter-writing campaign organized by Negativland, the RIAA revised its guidelines. This was an impressive victory considering the David-and-Goliath scenario pitting a band whose recent releases have sold fewer than ten thousand copies against the organization that represents every major record company. The amended guidelines state the following: "Some recordings presented for manufacture may contain—as part of an artist's work—identifiable 'samples or small pieces of other artists' well-known songs. In some instances this sampling may qualify as 'fair use' under copyright law, and in other instances it may constitute infringement. There are no hard and fast rules in this area and judgments on both 'fair use' and indemnification must be made on a case-by-case basis."[25]

In an RIAA press release, Rosen made it clear that the amended guidelines were written as a response to Negativland's grassroots campaign when she stated, "Hopefully, this step will give bands like Negativland the fair shake they deserve with CD pressing plants."[26] The new guidelines were "a very positive and extraordinary concession on the part of the RIAA," said Negativland, cautiously adding, "though it remains to be seen as to how this will play itself out in the real world and how much this will actually help." Nevertheless, Negativland stated, "On the plus side, this is the first time EVER that an organization who represents the interests of the mainstream corporate music world . . . has actually acknowledged that a gray area exists in copyright law and that collage is a legitimate and valid form of music."[27]

Unfortunately, since this incident, and in spite of the amended guidelines from the RIAA, Negativland and other artists have still had trouble pressing CDs.

The overarching problem is that the decisions of iTunes, CD pressing plants, and other parts of the supply chain for digital music carry a lot of weight. A small number of corporations end up making the decision for all of society—without checks and balances and without informed public debate. Newly emerging technologies like audio fingerprinting, which attempts to aurally identify copyrighted material online, are providing previously unimaginable opportunities for surveillance and control. Then again, the media gatekeepers do not have complete control. Technological restrictions on information and entertainment have often been defeated in the past. Still, the media gatekeepers of the future might use audio fingerprinting to help copyright holders sniff out samples in songs and enforce their copyrights, perhaps too aggressively. New technology and fear of litigation could combine to lead music distributors to require the licensing of *all* samples—regardless of fair use, the *de minimis* doctrine, and other legal limits on copyrights. This would exacerbate the current inefficiencies of the sample clearance system.

Although individual licensing negotiations sometimes lead to reasonable agreements, the sample clearance system as a whole has many flaws. It is difficult to get a sense of the relative frequency of good and bad outcomes. No data set surveys a random sample of musicians who might wish to sample and then follows their path toward either sampling without permission, obtaining a license, or having permission denied. It is hard to imagine collecting such a data set properly. The lack of data makes the music industry's process for licensing samples hard to evaluate, and it also thwarts any systematic, quantitative assessment of changes to that system—not to mention the effect of landmark decisions like the *Bridgeport* case.

In the absence of quantitative measures, our interviews provide a rich source of qualitative information. The collective experience of our interviewees raises issues and suggests ways in which the sample clearance system performs poorly. The problems we heard about include arguably excessive licensing fees; difficulties in clearing songs that contain multiple samples (made worse by high clearance fees); multiple kinds of transaction costs; outright refusals to license; barriers to licensing for independent musicians who lack business relationships with record labels, publishers, or sample clearance houses; the royalty stacking problem that occurs when a song contains multiple samples; and the failure of the industry and mash-up artists to develop an approach to licensing mash-ups.

Many of these criticisms are debatable in terms of both their validity and their importance. For instance, those who believe copyright owners should control the contexts in which fragments of their music appear may favor a system that allows for denials of permission to sample. And it is true that some mash-ups have been licensed, which suggests that the problem might not be so dire. Yet other criticisms have undeniable salience—such as the royalty stacking problem (which we address in more detail in chapter 6). Perspectives differ widely on the sample clearance system's performance. Some of the many competing interest groups might benefit from certain changes, but others might lose out. Changes to copyright law might have complex or unintended consequences. Different licensing practices could be more expensive for the industry to employ, and the transitions to new practices could have their own costs. Even with these caveats, however, feasible alternatives to the current sample clearance system may exist that would remedy some of the inefficiencies we have described so far—an issue that we will cover in chapter 7.

6

CONSEQUENCES FOR CREATIVITY

An Assessment of the Sample Clearance System

Clearing a sample does not always go smoothly, and for that matter sometimes clearance is impossible. In this chapter, we examine the effect of the sample clearance system on musicians' creative endeavors. We have already discussed some of the more extreme responses made by musicians to sample clearance problems: namely, some may drop a given sample from a song, or decline to sample at all; alternatively, others may use whatever they want by forgoing a license and hoping to escape detection and a potential copyright infringement lawsuit. But between those two extremes, a more varied array of creative and business responses are available to musicians. This chapter addresses the options musicians have for mitigating the potential harm that licensing difficulties can cause to their creative projects, and how that harm should factor into assessments of the sample clearance system.

In chapter 5 we isolated the most important frustrations and inefficiencies of the sample clearance system: expense, relationships, bureaucracy, and timing. A worrying picture emerges from those details. The music industry—including everyone from record labels and publishers to managers and musicians—has fostered a very rigid "clearance culture" in which it is assumed that every audio quote should be licensed. The phrase captures an environment in which licensing, however inefficient at times, has become the enforced norm, even when it is not necessarily required by copyright law. In this chapter, our interviewees share their impressions about the effects of the clearance culture on creativity.

"Historically, I think we are at a time where we're sampling less, and certainly copyright law had a major part in that," explains the musicologist and copyright expert Lawrence Ferrara. And as the MC and producer Aesop Rock states, "A lot of mainstream stuff now is just avoiding sampling completely, which can be done well or really badly." He points to the superproducer Timbaland as someone who doesn't sample much and builds most of his compositions using "original" sounds. Danny Rubin mentions other producers, such as The Neptunes, who typically avoid using samples, in part because they want to retain as much of their copyrights as possible. "The fewer samples that they use, the more money they can make because they keep more of the copyrights for themselves instead of having to share copyrights with sample publishers and pay royalties to sample record companies," says Rubin. "They keep it all to themselves."

Musicians sometimes enjoy flexibility when they face difficulties in licensing samples, but other times they do not. The songs in which musicians want to sample multiple sources present systematically insurmountable licensing challenges. To illustrate this problem, we estimated the hypothetical licensing costs of two prominent sample-based albums from the late 1980s and early 1990s (from which many samples were probably not cleared). Our analysis, which we present later in this chapter, suggests that musical collage—that is, releasing songs that sample several sources—is effectively impossible in today's commercial music industry.

This state of affairs pushes the most complex and musically interesting sample-based works into either the noncommercial sector, the underground economy, or nonexistence. The impediments to licensing and commercially releasing musical collages represent a significant cost of the current sample clearance system. But do the system's attributes outweigh that cost? We conclude this chapter by considering how to assess the system as whole. We do not aim to reach a grand, definitive conclusion, but rather to guide our discussion about the possible policy solutions we suggest in chapter 7.

REPLAYS: WHEN SAMPLE CLEARANCE FAILS

We wouldn't sample, but we would take a snitch of a song and replay it.
—PAM THE FUNKSTRESS

Replays (or interpolations) involve recording a new version of the musical composition underlying the sample in order to avoid obtaining a master use license for the sound recording. As Dina LaPolt explains, "If I'm representing an artist who samples something, I encourage them to replay it because that way they only have to pay for the music publishing royalty as opposed to the master use royalty—*in addition to* the music publishing royalty" (emphasis added). If the copyright holder of the sound recording is holding up negotiations, a replay allows a musician to circumvent the holdup. Replays are a way to keep the sample in some sense while avoiding the cost of a master use license.

Regarding the musical value of replays, Lawrence Ferrara says that he tells his music technology students the following: "If there's a sound that you like, then isolate it. Try to re-create it on regular synthesis instruments—the sounds of which nobody owns and then manipulate it whatever way you want. But in that final mix, that original sample must not be there." Ferrara continues by noting, "It's perfectly okay to sample anything and to listen to it, to dissect it. There's no copyright law that prohibits you from isolating any section of any song and sampling it, and listening to it. The key is once you've studied it and figured out what you like about it, then re-create it and make sure that that sample doesn't end up in the final product. Then you're absolutely in the clear." In this way, artists can avoid paying for either master use or even publishing licenses by using an in-studio band to replay and transform a melody or rhythm from a previously existing song. Take, for instance, this exchange with one of Kanye West's managers, Kyambo "Hip Hop" Joshua:

KEMBREW: So basically if you replay it, you don't have to get permission from the record company for the sound recording master, is that what you're saying?

HIP HOP: For the master, and sometimes if we change it enough we won't need clearance from the publishing, neither.

KEMBREW: Oh, really? So basically if you transform the original beat or melody, you don't even have to ask permission?

HIP HOP: Yeah, sometimes. Like we have to do that with people like Anita Baker, who don't clear nothing.

KEMBREW: Oh yeah, I've heard that over and over again.

HIP HOP: Yeah. We had a song, it was a real hard street record, and I didn't even know it was an Anita Baker sample until the guy sent me the information. I'm like, "Oh, God." That was [the hip-hop artist] Memphis Bleek, and we just, you know, we played that song over. It turned out good. It was like it still had the same feel, but it just wasn't an Anita Baker sample. But, hey, that's money we didn't have to pay.

Recall from chapter 5 the disscusion of Kanye West's "All Falls Down," which contained a Lauryn Hill sample that could not be cleared. Because West and his record company had permission from the song publisher but not the sound recording copyright holder, the production team had to bring in a singer to replay, or re-sing, Hill's vocal hook. What impact did that decision have on the aesthetics of the song? Did doing a replay rather than using the original sound recording make it better or worse? As Hip Hop says, "They're both similar, but I think I like the newer one better because he was able to do more with the vocals." Indeed, the people involved in making "All Falls Down" ended up preferring the replayed, nonsampled version they created in order to release the album on time.

No such serendipity occurred for the Beastie Boys on their *Check Your Head* album, in which the opening track, "Jimmy James," initially contained a Jimi Hendrix sample. The album version of that song "isn't the one we had originally wanted to put on there," the group member MCA said, explaining that the sample clearance was refused by the Hendrix estate at the time. In order to release the album on schedule, the Beastie Boys had to replace the Hendrix sample with instrumentation that the group played. "I like the original version best," says MCA, "that's the way the song was supposed to be heard."[1]

We asked Danny Rubin whether, in his experience while working at major labels, an artist has ever dropped a sample from a song because of clearance difficulties: "Yes, on many occasions that's happened," he says. "I would say it's pretty common to go and try to negotiate a license for a sample and to go back to the client and for them to say, 'Wow, that's way too high. We've got to take this out.' And oftentimes, they'll either replay it or rework the song so that you can't hear the sample or something like that." Referring to the copyright clampdown of the early 1990s, Joe Schloss, the author of *Making Beats*, says: "People moved away from sampling, and either used it in a much subtler way, a much more disguised way, or didn't use it at all."

The Beastie Boys albums that followed *Paul's Boutique*—specifically *Check Your Head* and *Ill Communication*, released around the same time as Dr. Dre's *The Chronic* (1992)—primarily used live instrumentation and contained far fewer samples. Speaking to this trend, the Beastie Boys' Adam Yauch says, "I guess the hectic sampling laws are a bit of a deterrent from sampling, so sometimes it's easier to just make up something new." Some musicians, however, feel that using a replay in certain situations negatively alters the sound or the feel of the final track. As De La Soul's Trugoy says, "I think for me personally hip-hop lost a little bit of its feel because of it. You know, when you can't sample, I think it definitely loses a big part of what hip-hop is."

Although copyright law can take a toll on creativity, musicians are not helpless—that is, they do have some ability to adjust. One of the first and most notable artists to do this was Dr. Dre on *The Chronic*. As Ferrara explains, "Dre will be on a drum machine creating the actual beats, and in many cases will have a live keyboard player, a live guitarist, and a live bass player even." In those instances, they are mostly creating the sounds themselves, with little if any sampling occurring. And as Chuck D notes further, "He was one of the smart guys—he was very clever with using musicians." He pauses, adding, "Still, there was something lacking. He couldn't use a lot of vocal samples, he would have to go in the studio and reproduce the sounds on the original recording."

"I'm still sampling," says El-P, a hip-hop producer and independent record company owner, "but not for the same reasons I used to." He approaches sampling differently today. "Now I'm sampling because I like the way something sounds and I'm going to take that piece and I'm going to run it through about thirty different experiments to see what comes out of it, and usually what comes out of it is completely different than what I liked the initial sample for." Some have argued that the changes in the sample clearance system have forced hip-hop artists to learn to play other instruments besides a sampler or turntable, or has encouraged them to pursue other creative directions. While this is certainly true, hip-hop probably would have evolved in this way without legal restrictions.

Just because licensing requirements spurred creative workarounds doesn't necessarily mean that limiting creative options was a good or a necessary thing. It just means that hip-hop survived in one form or another. Making the effort to hide samples or steering away from sampling toward other techniques may have either negative creative effects or serendipitous ones—it's hard to generalize. But dropping a sample entirely from a finished song has an obvious cost in terms of musical creativity. The goals of compensating copyright owners and granting sampled musicians the right to deny permission may be worth it, but those goals may thwart other musicians' artistry.

Mimicking the Sound of Sampling

Many have argued that the problems posed by sample licensing have opened up new opportunities for more sophisticated musicianship. When the Atlanta-based production crew Organized Noize—which went on to make hits for R&B and hip-hop artists like TLC and Outkast—started out, they were discouraged by industry executives from using samples. One of those people was Pebbles at LaFace Records—the company that the production team was affiliated with. As the music journalist Roni Sarig quotes Ray Murray of Organized Noize, "Pebbles told us we couldn't sample, period, [saying] 'Don't bring me no music with samples in it, I'm not clearing no samples.'" Sarig himself explains that "Pebbles' request was likely motivated by the cost of samples, but it presented an opportunity: a chance for Organized Noize to find its own voice."[2]

Organized Noize took inspiration from Dr. Dre's *The Chronic* in that they chose to avoid samples by using session musicians. But unlike Dr. Dre they avoided musical interpolations altogether, creating a distinctive, "organic" sound that nevertheless invoked the feel of a sample-based track. We should also note that the TLC song "Switch"—the subject of the lawsuit mentioned in chapter 4—did not involve Organized Noize, which produced the majority of the *CrazySexyCool* album from which the song came. Instead, it was the fellow Atlanta-based artist Jermaine Dupri who produced the track that contained the offending sample.

"People have been forced to get extremely creative," says Saul Williams, who points to recordings made in the mid-1990s by Tricky,

Portishead, and Bjork. On Portishead's second album, for instance, some of the sounds went through multiple generations. The group would play a guitar riff, press it onto vinyl, and then sample their original guitar riff—"just to have the effect of it being sampled," Williams says. Here's the way it worked: Portishead's Adrian Utley would record his guitar and then press it up on a dub plate—a term derived from the Jamaican music industry to describe a specially made piece of vinyl, often produced in a limited edition of one. Barrow would then cut up and scratch those guitar sounds to create Portishead's instrumental backing tracks, which would be mixed into the group's compositions.[3]

Indie rock groups were also influenced by the hip-hop aesthetic in the late 1980s and early 1990s. The band My Bloody Valentine, for example, used digital samplers to record, layer, and cut up their own instrumentation. In interviews conducted in the late 1980s, the group's mastermind, Kevin Shields, professed his love for Public Enemy's Bomb Squad production team, which he saw as an exemplar of sampling as art. On their classic from 1991, *Loveless*, My Bloody Valentine delivered a similarly dense squall, though in this case the samples consisted of sounds they made themselves. Shields says that most of the songs on that album have samples, and he singles out the track "Only Shallow" as a composition that features several samples layered on top of each other—in this case, of Shields's guitars. He explains that "it was the usual rock and roll bending the strings type of thing, but I had two amps facing each other, with two different tremolos on them. And I sampled it and put it an octave higher on the sampler." He adds that "in those days we didn't have a keyboard so we played it all by pressing the button on the sampler."[4]

When the San Francisco Bay–area group The Coup began recording in the 1990s, they decided to use live musicians rather than rely primarily on samples to drive the group's music. "I guess it was a conscious decision for us not to sample," says Pam the Funkstress, a DJ and an original member of The Coup. "In the early 1990s, that's when people were just taking someone's song and rapping over the whole song. Same beat, same everything—they just took a sample, add a little high kick, a little high hat and drum and take the whole song. You have no creativity in it at all." Boots Riley, the group's MC and musical mastermind, says that when composing a new Coup song he might start off with a sample and build rhythms around that sample. But by the end of the recording process he takes that sample out of the mix while keeping the traditional instrumentation he built up around it. As Pam the Funkstress explains in more detail, "Boots, he's into sounds, he likes the Moog instruments, you know, the heavy deep bass, weird guitars. So he listens for certain things in a song, and he will ask one of our musicians to play that for him and then he will re-create the whole thing. Boots will start off and say, 'Listen to this.' And you hear it, and about two days later it's something totally different."

As these anecdotes have illustrated, musicians have found a number of creative responses to the current sample clearance system—many of which have produced exciting new music. "I definitely think that it lost something, but I don't think it's for better—or for worse," says the artist manager Hip Hop. "I think it's just something that kind of naturally happens in all types of music. I think that copyright law kind of made it happen quicker, where certain people had to subject themselves to only using one sample and clearing it, or subject themselves to playing something over. That's how you got the sound from the West Coast—you know, like when Dre did *The Chronic*."

This doesn't mean that all hip-hop artists have totally given up on sampling, because there are popular artists out there, such as Ghostface Killah, who still uphold the tradition of building their music from samples. Many of our interviewees—including Hip Hop, Eyedea & Abilities, and De La Soul—singled out this member of the Wu-Tang Clan as a case in point. "Ghostface samples all the time," says Hip Hop. "He had a great line on his new album [*More Fish*] where he says, 'It costs a lot to make my records, but it means a lot to me,' You know what I mean?"

TRANSFORMING AND DISGUISING SAMPLES

If you can catch me then I didn't do my job.
Straight up, it's my fault.—EL-P

Sampling always involves a transformation of one kind or another. "When you hear something you recognize that's been sampled," the music historian and critic Greg Tate tells us, "you realize that something's happened in the translation. You know, something got compressed in a certain kind of way. Something got sweetened or roughed up, and the recontextualization has altered the sonic properties of the thing." Musicians transform sampled sounds for compositional or tonal reasons. But the pressures of licensing have added another motivation alongside the creative impulse: some musicians disguise samples to evade detection. "People started to get pretty savvy about what they were sampling, and how they would mask it," says Tate. Depending on the artist and the situation, musicians will have different motivations or inspirations, perhaps trying to avoid paying licensing fees, or to pursue a creative vision, or both.

"Think of sampling as being represented by two different painters," says DJ Vadim, offering an analogy. "One guy makes a photocopy of the Mona Lisa—that's P. Diddy, who just samples the choruses of songs. The other guy takes the same painting, chops it up, and it doesn't even look like the Mona Lisa anymore. He's made it into a cow, or a spaceship. That's what sampling can be like." Drawing from his own experience, DJ Vadim claims that on an average track he creates, there could be upward of one hundred samples collaged together. However, he transforms them enough that he says that it would be impossible for someone to figure out where they came from.

As Mix Master Mike, in discussing how sampling artists got better at disguising sounds through technological means, explains: "I could take something and I could spin it backwards, or I could take a loop and kind of chop it up into sixteen pieces." Aesop Rock adds to this list of transformative techniques by emphasizing the importance of layering sounds. "I have some synthesizers and some other noisemaking gear and I layer it," he says, "which helps to camouflage the samples as well as put some creativity into it as opposed to just straight thievery." DJ Abilities—of the hip-hop group Eyedea & Abilities—points to El-P, who makes his music almost entirely out of samples but does so in a way that is nearly impossible to detect. "El-P, he's really creative," MC Eyedea tells us. "Probably the most creative sampler out there to me, because he just takes each sound and he plays it out on a keyboard. He's basically playing it out, he just happens to sample."

"You're running through effects, chopping shit up, and placing it and rearranging it so that it just is not recognizable," El-P says as he gives us a demonstration in his studio. "Okay, here's the most obvious, this is the most rudimentary 'Sound Changing 101.'" He then rotates his chair and turns to his keyboard, saying, "You sample a sound, this is the root key [hits a key to the far right of the keyboard], and then you play it down here [lower on the keyboard scale], hence, slowing the sound down, distorting the sound, and making it unrecognizable." As El-P continues in telling us how he uses digital technologies to create new compositions: "I use fragments, fragments of music. Things that I can bend and twist at will, things that I can shape and connect into my own forms and pieces, that, frankly, are just unrecognizable. . . . If you are using a horn to distort and play as a bass line, you know, and then EQ-ing it so that it has bass and it just has a different sound to it—you know, how is anyone going to be able to recognize that? How is anyone going to be able to come after you for that?" During a discussion with El-P, the jazz musician and music educator T. S. Monk notes that "young men like El-P here understand how you can take a sound, and turn it sideways and press it down and stretch it out and move it—to actually take that raw material and create something new. I understand that creative process completely." As El-P's music exemplifies, one positive effect of the clearance culture has been to push sampling even farther into more complex transformations and collages.

Flying Below the Radar

Creative choices like disguising samples have a business aspect, too. Hiding samples saves money; licensing samples increases the cost of expression.[5] Musicians considering whether to use a sample have three options: sample the song and obtain a license; sample the song but don't obtain a license; or don't sample the song at all. Musicians who sample must balance the economic benefits of licensing (that is, avoiding uncertainty and possible litigation, encouraging future artists to license their works, and so on) against the costs of licensing: the licensing fees paid to various copyright holders and the transaction costs involved in obtaining licenses. At some level, regardless of whether these considerations are completely conscious, musicians face these tradeoffs when considering whether to sample.

Of course, musicians also bring non-financial considerations into their decisions. Imagine a situation in which a musician wants to sample a particular song. Suppose that a license would be prohibitively expensive, and that the expected harm from infringement litigation would be very great.[6] A musician in such a situation might be so committed to the sample artistically that they decide to go ahead and sample without a license, running the risk of litigation even though the expected costs outweigh the benefits. The cost-benefit analysis is a factor in or a constraint on the musician's decision, but it is not necessarily decisive in whether the sample gets used or licensed.

Another wrinkle is accounting for the various business contexts in which musicians choose to operate. Decisions about sampling and licensing can depend on more than the decisions made by musicians. Indeed, other entities—record labels and publishers, especially—can have a large role. Moreover, licensing costs affect not only the decisions about individual samples but also the choices about how to release entire albums. Speaking broadly, licensing costs can affect how and whether musicians choose to participate in the commercial music industry. At the same time, the range of options in terms of business models means that the impact of requiring licensing is not straightforward.

For example, take a particular copyright owner who increases the licensing fee for sampling a particular song or flat out denies permission. The would-be sampling musician has additional options besides paying more or abandoning the sample. In particular, the musician could adopt a different approach to releasing his or her music that avoids the need for licensing, or perhaps the sampler will dare the copyright owner to enforce the law. Musicians have four major categories of business models that they can pursue, and the parameters of their sampling and licensing decisions differ from category to category:

—Commercial recording: By this, we mean any model in which a musician signs contracts with a record label (major or independent) and a publisher. In this model, any samples used must be licensed, as most major labels require artists to list all samples used on a "clear sheet," and many indie labels require clearance as well. The biggest tradeoff for sampling artists using this model is weighing the increased revenue from participating in the traditional music industry (CD retail, label support for radio play, sponsored tours, uses in commercials, and so on) against the increased expense of paying for any samples they use.

—Noncommercial recording: Some musicians might record new songs, but release them noncommercially by offering them as free Internet downloads or at free live performances.[7] These musicians do not pay to license any samples, either because they make a strong fair use argument as to the noncommercial nature of their recordings, or just figure that the risk of litigation is quite low. (Nevertheless, even the noncommercial duplication of copyrighted material can infringe a copyright.)

—Underground recording: In this model, musicians sell their recordings through retail and Internet channels (mostly lower-profile outlets), and decline to license the samples in the hopes of avoiding detection. They might alter their samples considerably or use very small snippets. Danger Mouse's *The Grey Album* provides a good example of an underground record, in that the album was originally made available in independent record stores and online retailers before EMI sent Danger Mouse a cease-and-desist letter. After the letter, fans of the album distributed the album on the Internet through noncommercial channels (which makes it a kind of hybrid underground-noncommercial album). While this distribution generated no royalties for Danger Mouse, the album did provide exposure for him, which has helped him build a profile as a producer as well as sell his subsequent releases with Gnarls Barkley and other projects.

—Live performance only (no recording): Finally, musicians can simply decline to make new recordings and instead seek to earn revenue through live performances and sales of merchandise (like T-shirts). In this manner, the earning potential may be enhanced by the value, in terms of audience enjoyment, that samples add to the songs. But charging ticket prices and selling merchandise means that obtaining licenses might be necessary, though there is no case law that has clarified this situation.[8] The licenses needed for this model, however, might cost less than licenses for manufacturing and distributing copies of CDs and digital downloads. Live performance is a growing way that music fans can hear sample-based music—such as when thousands attend shows by Girl Talk or by Eclectic Method.[9]

Each of these four business models involves tradeoffs for musicians who sample. The primary tradeoff is between the revenue from selling recordings and the cost of licensing samples. Musicians who decide to sample choose between not recording at all and, on the other hand, making recordings and dealing with copyright issues in some way— whether by licensing, distributing recordings for free, or attempting to fly below the radar. A related tradeoff is that musicians participating in the commercial-recording model generally have the ability to earn more revenue from touring; merchandising; licensing their recordings for commercials, films, and television; and so on. Musicians employing the other models can to try to participate in these ancillary revenue streams, which flow from recordings or performances. But the consolidated structures of the media and entertainment industries limit the potential revenue for musicians who do not partner with a record label and a publisher.

Musicians may choose to combine different business models, or employ different models at different stages of their careers. For example, Danger Mouse shifted from an underground-recording model to a commercial-recording model after the release of *The Grey Album*. An even more high-profile example of someone who mixes business models is Lil Wayne, who was well-known in the late 2000s for the prolific mix tapes that he released noncommercially on various websites and file transfer services. He followed up three year's worth of free releases with *Tha Carter III*, the biggest-selling record of 2008, which serves as another example of how an artist can parlay his or her noncommercial recordings into income.

Within each model, musicians still have a range of creative options for dealing with individual samples, such as hiring musicians, recording a replay, or abandoning a sample. In and of itself the situation of having these options complicates the picture. Moreover, because creative decisions can be made sample by sample, the models are not mutually exclusive. As musicians make decisions about individual samples, they may choose to license some samples and not others. (That approach, in our terminology, would be a hybrid of the commercial-recording and underground-recording models.) Still, we think the four business models work as archetypes that illustrate the basic tradeoffs that sample licensing poses for musicians.

Because musicians have choices about how to borrow from previous works and choices about how to try to make a living in the music industry, changes in copyright law or the music industry's policies on sample clearance will have complicated effects. Over the longer term, making sampling more costly might alter the course of some musicians' careers or change the way they make music. Making sampling more difficult or more expensive could prevent some songs from being created as well as keep some songs that are created from ever reaching the public. But it might also just lead musicians to release the music in a different way, perhaps on a smaller scale or on a noncommercial basis.

Marketing Responses to Sample Clearance Difficulties

During our talk with Dina LaPolt, she gave us the music business perspective on the financial advantages of employing samples on fewer tracks: "I'd say to a client, 'You're going to have fifteen songs on your record. Well, if you sample on every single song, you're going to pay a ton of money and hardly get any money for yourself. So why don't you do ten songs without samples and three songs with samples and the songs that you're using samples on, get the record promotion people involved, and ask them what they think. Play it for some program directors. If they think they're hits, then that's what you do.'" Rather than changing the way they use samples, of course, musicians could change the way they bring their music to market. As Danny Rubin says, "Plenty of times an artist will sample something, and we'll come back with a quote that's too high or an outright 'No,' and the artist will be forced to shelve that song and not release it on the album." He also notes that "a lot of times these songs pop up either on mix tapes or on the Internet in certain hip-hop circles. They appear on some of these sites that you can download unreleased material."

Selling mix tapes exemplifies the underground-recording model that we described above. In such a model, musicians run a much greater risk of copyright infringement litigation. Free distribution over the Internet, on the other hand, represents the noncommercial-recording model. (One risk involved is that a noncommercial sampler's Internet service provider will respond to a copyright owner's request to take down the material.[10]) Rubin's quote about shelved songs getting Internet distribution shows that artists do respond to the increased cost of sampling and of sample clearance by adjusting their business models. On the other hand, as the arrest in 2007 of DJ Drama illustrates, underground channels like the market for mix tapes may be disappearing, leaving fewer places for uncleared songs to go.[11]

Avoiding the mainstream distribution system gives musicians who sample more freedom in a creative sense, but they also have a ceiling in terms of sales and career opportunities. "I think there are limitations in how many CDs we can sell," Gregg Gillis of Girl Talk says, "because it's so difficult to access the album." He sees pluses and minuses to the underground approach. "I think there's a roof as far as CD sales. It is a concern, but not as far as where the music can spread," Gillis says. "It's funny, because a lot of kids come out for my show, and I might have some CDs for sale, and people didn't even realize that *Night Ripper* [Girl Talk's album from 2006] was out on CD. They thought it was just a download phenomenon that their friends passed to them—which is cool to me. I mean, I just like the music to be distributed any way possible, and that's what has amazed me." Over the course of writing this book, Girl Talk's albums have appeared on all the major online music stores—iTunes, Amazon, eMusic, and Rhapsody—only to be removed and then offered again several times. At the time of this writing, only iTunes does not carry albums by Girl Talk.

Sampling artists respond in multiple ways to expanded copyright protection for samples and more aggressive policing of samples. The musicians can, for example, use fewer samples, smaller samples, or sample more sparingly; use substitutes for expensive or difficult-to-clear samples; use replays; sample but try to evade enforcement; change business models, perhaps to a noncommercial or underground model; or simply stop sampling. But for all musicians who sample, the changing legal and business environment has altered the creative process and the constraints on that process.

ALBUMS YOU CAN'T (OR DON'T) MAKE ANYMORE

An album like De La Soul's *3 Feet High and Rising*, or Public Enemy's *Fear of a Black Planet*, it's difficult to make it today. It couldn't come out today unless you've got a lot, lot, lot of money to spend on clearing the samples.—RAQUEL CEPEDA

In looking at what happened after hip-hop's golden age, one great point of comparison we can turn to is "Incident at 66.6 FM" and "66.6 Strikes Again" from Public Enemy's album *Fear of a Black Planet* (1990) and their *New Whirl Odor* (2005), respectively. As Chuck D explains: "'Incident at 66.6 FM' was actually [made from] a live radio interview that I did at WNBC in New York before a show we did with Run-DMC at Nassau Coliseum. The host of the show was Alan Colmes [the former co-host of Fox News Channel's *Hannity & Colmes*]. Alan said he tried his best to sue us back then, but NBC, who owned the broadcast, felt it would be a waste of time." The track cuts up the interview, and although it is an interstitial piece it is one of the album's highlights because it showcases the ingenious ways that Public Enemy remixed the media in order to comment on it. It has a strong case for fair use, but when they went back to the original source material for the track from 2005, the clearance culture got to Chuck D. "This time we got permission from Alan and gave him song credits."[12]

And there are also many instances when ideas for sampling never leave the drawing board. As Tom Silverman says, "We had great ideas about doing songs that never even went to completion because we knew we wouldn't be able to clear the samples." As we quoted Posdnuos saying in chapter 1, Silverman's Tommy Boy Records gave De La Soul "a list of people *not to touch*." The problems for De La Soul's music went beyond a mere list of forbidden samples. Danny Rubin used the group as an example of one whose method of music making is now impractical. "I mean, the one thing that comes to my head is that De La Soul used, like, sometimes ten or twenty samples in a song," Rubin says, alluding to the problem of royalty stacking. "Today it's cost-prohibitive to put even two—or more than two—samples in a song."

We discussed earlier how Public Enemy's original approach to crafting their tracks has also become impractical, and we now want to return to this assertion and back it up with numbers. As DJ Spooky tells us, "What happened to Public Enemy in the late eighties and early nineties is they had to change their composition strategy, mainly because of the impact their records had on the music industry itself." As the hip-hop scholar Joe Schloss elaborates, "Public Enemy's album had tons of samples on it. They were done at a time where people didn't know about sample laws, but it seems to me that, legally, you couldn't make Public Enemy's *It Takes A Nation of Millions To Hold Us Back* now, because the sample clearances would cost so much more than you could ever hope to make on any album."

Some in the music industry, however, deny this oft-repeated assertion. One skeptic is Dean Garfield from the MPAA (formerly of the RIAA), whose doubts we quoted in chapter 1. The debate over whether we have "lost" certain albums because of the sample clearance system partly turns on how much alteration one believes that a musician's work can or should withstand. With options like replays or substitute samples available, sampling musicians have some flexibility in their compositional or recording choices. But given today's relative dearth of some types of collage-based music in the mainstream market, perhaps that flexibility is not always sufficient, at least not for a certain type of creativity.

One of our aims in our work was to evaluate the pervasive claim that certain sample-heavy hip-hop albums from the late 1980s and early 1990s have become impractical to make, or at least impractical to release commercially. To do this, we decided to take two prominent examples—Public Enemy's *Fear of a Black Planet* (1990) and the Beastie Boys' *Paul's Boutique* (1989)—and calculate the hypothetical cost of licensing those albums under the sample clearance regime of today. Our basic method was to collect a list of the samples used in those two albums, estimate how much it would cost to license both the sound recording and the musical composition in each of the samples, and then add up the totals to get a ballpark figure of the hypothetical licensing cost.

Data Collected on Samples Used

We collected a list of identifiable samples used in each song for each of the two hip-hop records we studied. To accomplish this, we used for both albums an Internet database for samples called the "The Breaks," the albums' Wikipedia entries, our interviews with artists, and our own musical knowledge.[13] With *Paul's Boutique*, we had the additional benefit of a website solely devoted to identifying samples and lyrical references in that album.[14] In most cases, all of the sources either confirmed or supplemented the other ones. In just a few cases (fewer than five), we had to resolve conflicts between sources. In general, we gave credence to the specialized *Paul's Boutique* website over "The Breaks," and to "The Breaks" over Wikipedia.

For each sample, we obtained the sampled artist, the sampled song, and the record label of original release. We conducted additional research to determine whether a record label was a major one or an independent. When we lacked information about the publishers of the musical compositions in the sampled songs, we made an assumption that the publisher had a similar stature to the record label in order to place it on the scale from major to independent. We also had some information about how much or what part of the sampled song was used. For the songs on *Paul's Boutique*, we had accounts of how prominently or how often the sample figured into the sampling work—thanks to the specialized website devoted to that album. We had less information about how the songs on *Fear of a Black Planet* used particular samples, partly due to the Bomb Squad's unique wall-of-sound production method that often masked the original source material.

Estimating Licensing Costs

As we discussed in chapter 5, a long list of factors determines the eventual licensing fee that the sampling side and the sampled side negotiate. The list has two parts: factors pertaining to the sampled song and the sampled musician's characteristics, and factors pertaining to the sampling song and the sampling musician's characteristics. The music lawyer Whitney Broussard summarizes the role of these factors into a two-dimensional table (see table 2), which we have updated with his generous assistance and also expanded slightly. Creating the table requires summarizing a host of complex qualitative and subjective factors into a scale from low to high.

The rows in the table reflect how the sampled song was used and the sampled musician's attributes, ranging from a "low" profile to a "high" one. We added the categories "famous" and "superstar" to reflect the great expense of sampling the works of musicians like the Beatles or Led Zeppelin. The columns in the table reflect the way that the sample is used in the new song and the sampling musician's attributes, ranging from "small" to "moderate" and finally to "extensive."

Using the data we collected from the websites described above, we classified each sample along the two scales used in the table.[15] First, we put each sampled song into one of the five categories from "low" to "superstar," as reflected in the rows of the table. We usually focused on a subset of the factors that would be considered in a real-world negotiation (making an admittedly imperfect assessment of those factors). We focused most on the length of the sample, the qualitative importance of the sampled portion in the sampled song, whether the sampled musician was on a major label as opposed to an independent one, and the sampled musician's level of fame. An example would be our categorization of the Beastie Boys' sample of Curtis Mayfield's "Superfly" in the song "Eggman" on *Paul's Boutique*. Mayfield's song is a well-known popular track, but it was released on his own independent record label, Curtom Records.[16] On balance, we placed this song in the "high" row of the table.

TABLE 2. The cost matrix for sample licenses

		Use in the sampling work		
		Small	Moderate	Extensive
Profile of the sampled work	Low	SR: $0 to $500 MC: Not infringement	SR: $2,500 or $0.01/copy MC: $4,000 or 10%	SR: $5,000 or $0.025/copy MC: 25%
	Medium	SR: $2,500 or $0.01/copy MC: $4,000 or 10%	SR: $5,000 or $0.025/copy MC: 25%	SR: $15,000 or $0.05/ copy MC: 40%
	High	SR: $5,000 or $0.025/copy MC: 25%	SR: $15,000 or $0.05/copy MC: 40%	SR: $25,000 or $0.10/copy MC: 50% or co-ownership
	Famous	SR: $50,000 or $0.12/copy MC: 100% (assignment)		
	Superstar	SR: $100,000 or $0.15/copy MC: 100% (assignment)		

Note: "SR" denotes the sound recording copyright in the sampled song; "MC" denotes the musical composition copyright in the sampled song.

Second, we put each sample into one of the three categories from "small" to "extensive," as reflected in the table's columns. Again, our data were not rich enough to consider all the factors listed in chapter 5, which include the subjective perceptions of sampled musicians about how the sample from their song is used in the new sample-based song. We focused most on the approximate length and prominence of the sample in the sampling song. For example, because the Curtis Mayfield sample provides the bass line for "Eggman"—an important part of the song but not the lead melody or vocal—we placed it in the "moderate" column of the table.

For samples that went into the "famous" or "superstar" row, how the sample is used is irrelevant. That is, for samples of prominent artists, the column classification does not matter because the sampler will pay the same licensing fee either way. Because we had less information about how the samples were used in *Fear of a Black Planet* than we had for *Paul's Boutique*, we picked the "moderate" column as a default for all samples on that album. Because Public Enemy was on a major label (Def Jam/Columbia), the "potential commercial success" and "major versus independent" factors would have meant higher licensing fees and thus worked against them. But the group's tendency to use many small fragments of songs would have resulted in lower fees and thus worked in their favor. To reflect these countervailing factors, we chose to make the across-the-board assignment of "moderate."

Putting each unique sample into one of five sampled-song categories (the rows of table 2) and one of three sampling-song categories (the columns) requires a rough, subjective judgment. We reduced a complicated set of factors—which would sometimes require protracted and detailed negotiations in the real world—into a multiple-choice question with subjective answers. For this reason, we do not purport to describe this quantitative exercise as an exact science. Rather, it is meant to provide an estimate of the scale of the impediments to licensing sample-based works in the collage style (with multiple samples per track).

After deciding the row and column to which each sample belonged, we could assign a licensing fee. We used the numbers in table 2, which reflect the licensing fee that a sampler would pay at the time of this writing. We did this to simulate how the contemporary music industry would handle these two albums from sampling's golden age of the late 1980s and early 1990s. We assumed that licenses in every box took the form of a royalty rate (for the sound recording copyright) or a percentage share (for the musical composition copyright). For example, we categorized the Beastie Boys' sample of Curtis Mayfield's "Superfly" in the "high" row and the "moderate" column. Thus, looking to table 2, we estimated that licensing the sound recording would require paying a royalty rate of $0.05 per copy to the copyright owner and that licensing the musical composition would require giving the copyright owner a 40 percent share.

For samples in the "low" row and the "small" column, we assumed a licensing fee of zero. This corresponds to a copyright owner granting permission without charge. It would also represent situations in which use of the sample did not infringe either of the copyrights in the sampled song (e.g., because the use was *de minimis* or constituted fair use). Once we had assigned a licensing fee to each sample contained in *Fear of a Black Planet* and *Paul's Boutique*, we added up the licensing fees by track. We added the royalty rates paid to sound recording copyright holders separately from the percentages paid to musical composition copyright holders, since the two types of music copyrights have separate revenue streams associated with them. Table 3 displays the results for *Fear of a Black Planet* and table 4 displays the results for *Paul's Boutique*.

TABLE 3. Applying the cost matrix to *Fear of a Black Planet*

Track no.	Track name	Time	Identifiable samples	Sound recording royalty ($)*	Musical composition share (%)
1	Contract on the World Love Jam	1:44	5	0.20	170
2	Brothers Gonna Work It Out	5:07	8	0.46	365
3	911 Is a Joke	3:17	7	0.32	250
4	Incident at 66.6 FM	1:37	0	0.00	0
5	Welcome to the Terrordome	5:25	9	0.52	435
6	Meet the G That Killed Me	0:44	0	0.00	0
7	Pollywanacraka	3:52	5	0.15	125
8	Anti-Nigger Machine	3:17	12	0.50	435
9	Burn Hollywood Burn	2:47	2	0.13	110
10	Power to the People	3:50	2	0.08	65
11	Who Stole the Soul?	3:49	6	0.48	375
12	Fear of a Black Planet	3:45	4	0.10	85
13	Revolutionary Generation	5:43	6	0.15	135
14	Can't Do Nuttin for Ya Man	2:46	2	0.04	35
15	Reggie Jax	1:35	0	0.00	0
16	Leave This Off Your Fuckin' Charts	2:31	1	0.03	25
17	B Side Wins Again	3:45	1	0.03	25
18	War at 33 1/3	2:07	0	0.00	0
19	Final Count of the Collision Between Us and the Damned	0:48	0	0.00	0
20	Fight the Power	4:42	11	0.60	485
	TOTAL		81	3.73	3120

Retail price of a CD	$18.98
Public Enemy's share of revenue per CD	
Recording artist's royalty	$1.19
Musical composer's royalty	$0.91
Sample licensing fees per CD	
Royalties due to SR copyright holders	−$3.73
Royalties due to MC copyright holders (3120% share x $0.091)	−$2.84
Net loss per CD (Revenue minus licensing fees)	−$4.47
Estimated transaction costs ($500 per clearance x 162 clearances; i.e., two per sample for 81 samples)	$81,000
Estimated sales of *Fear of a Black Planet*	$1,500,000
Artist's estimated total losses from releasing record	−$6,786,000

Note: Figures in the table have been rounded to the nearest cent. Exact figures were used to calculate the totals in the bottom row.

TABLE 4. Applying the cost matrix to *Paul's Boutique*

Track no.	Track name	Time	Identifiable samples	Costs Sound recording royalty ($)	Costs Musical composition share (%)
1	To All the Girls	1:29	1	0.03	25
2	Shake Your Rump	3:19	15	0.68	555
3	Johnny Ryall	3:00	8	0.46	340
4	Eggman	2:57	12	0.40	345
5	High Plains Drifter	4:13	6	0.39	275
6	Sounds of Science	3:11	9	0.93	650
7	3-Minute Rule	3:39	4	0.25	205
8	Hey Ladies	3:47	19	0.54	470
9	5-Piece Chicken Dinner	0:23	1	0.10	50
10	Looking Down the Barrel of a Gun	3:28	4	0.24	175
11	Car Thief	3:39	6	0.31	240
12	What Comes Around	3:07	4	0.29	185
13	Shadrach	4:07	9	0.29	215
14	Ask for Janice	0:11	0	0.00	0
15	B-Boy Bouillabaisse	12:33	–	–	–
15-a	a. 59 Chrystie Street	–	8	0.33	255
15-b	b. Get on the Mic	–	1	0.03	25
15-c	c. Stop That Train	–	2	0.03	25
15-d	d. Year and a Day	–	4	0.20	145
15-e	e. Hello Brooklyn	–	1	0.12	100
15-f	f. Dropping Names	–	5	0.14	125
15-g	g. Lay It on Me	–	1	0.05	40
15-h	h. Mike on the Mic	–	2	0.04	35
15-i	i. A.W.O.L.	–	3	0.14	85
		TOTAL	125	5.92	4565

Retail price of a CD	$18.98
Beastie Boys' share of revenue per CD	
Recording artist's royalty	$1.19
Musical composer's royalty	$0.91
Sample licensing fees per CD	
Royalties due to SR copyright holders	−$5.92
Royalties due to MCcopyright holders (4565% share x $0.091)	−$4.15
Net loss per CD (revenue minus licensing fees)	−$7.87
Estimated transaction costs ($500 per clearance x 250 clearances; i.e., two per sample for 125 samples)	$125,000
Estimated sales of *Paul's Boutique*	2.5 million
Artist's estimated total losses from releasing record	−$19,800,000

Note: Figures in the table have been rounded to the nearest cent. Exact figures were used to calculate the totals in the bottom row.

Next, we added up the licensing fees across all tracks. This gives us the per-copy licensing costs. To turn the royalty share for musical composition copyrights into dollars, we multiplied by the statutory rate of $0.091—that is, the current rate for mechanical royalties set by the federal government.[17] This rate effectively determines the maximum that record labels will pay out to license the musical composition(s) used in one song.[18]

Finally, we used the number of copies sold of each album to estimate the total licensing fees that would be paid today. We also estimate the transaction costs by multiplying $500 (which is the usual fee charged by the sample clearance professional Danny Rubin) by the minimum number of clearances that would be necessary—two clearances per sample, one for the composition and one for the recording. This is a conservative estimate because it assumes that all negotiations go smoothly and that no copyrights have been divided in a way that requires negotiating with multiple owners for a single clearance. A more complete account of the transaction costs would include monetary amounts representing time spent, delays in the release of the albums, and so on, but we sought only a rough estimate. Adding the total estimated licensing fees and the estimated transaction costs gives us an estimate of the total licensing cost per each copy sold. This calculation represents our attempt to estimate what these albums would cost to license today.

Revenue from Album Sales

Public Enemy and the Beastie Boys would each—in our hypothetical exercise—sell their albums for a typical retail price of $18.98. We estimate that as the recording artists they would receive a royalty of $1.19 on each copy sold. This represents approximately 6 percent of the retail price. It is an approximation based on what the groups would receive from their record labels after paying their producers, accounting for the various deductions in major-label contracts, and so on.

In addition, because Public Enemy and the Beastie Boys wrote or co-wrote some of the songs, the label would pay the statutory rate of $0.091 per composition used—up to a limit. Recording contracts limit how much record labels will pay for the musical composition copyrights implicated by the albums they sell. Record labels will only pay mechanical royalties on a fixed number of compositions—usually ten to twelve—no matter how many tracks are on the album. For example, even if an album includes fifteen songs, the record label would pay a maximum of the statutory rate of $0.091 multiplied by ten compositions, for a total of $0.91. Under this clause, the artist is held responsible for any excess money owed to the copyright owners of compositions that the artist has covered or sampled.

Thus, record-label contracts exacerbate the problem of paying the musical composition royalty shares on songs that sample multiple existing songs. Artists who give up percentages of publishing as a condition of receiving licenses must pay all those committed amounts on every copy sold out of their own diminished royalties. We assumed that each group had a clause limiting the record labels to paying for ten compositions per album. Public Enemy had twenty tracks on *Fear of a Black Planet,* and the Beastie Boys had fifteen tracks on *Paul's Boutique.*[19] Both albums hit the limit of $0.91, regardless of whether we take into account further recording-contract complications like controlled composition clauses.[20] This further limits the licensing revenue available to pay musical composition copyright holders.

Results, Caveats, and Conclusions

In the case of the two records examined here, the artists pay out more than they receive. Neither album would be commercially practical to release. Each artist, having licensed away more royalties and more publishing than the amount that they would receive on each track of the album, *would go further into debt with every copy sold to the public.* The prices for all of the samples—multiple samples on each track—simply exceed the artist's piece of the recording-revenue pie. Public Enemy would lose an estimated $4.47 per copy sold. The Beastie Boys would lose an estimated $7.87 per copy sold. The total amount of debt incurred for releasing these albums, according to our estimates, would be almost $6.8 million for Public Enemy and would be $19.8 million for the Beastie Boys.

Our estimates of the licensing costs may be lower than what they probably would have been in reality, for three main reasons. First, we have only used easily identifiable samples—those named by devoted fans who contribute to Internet sites, or those identified by the authors of *Creative License.* However, especially on the Public Enemy album, it is possible that dozens more tiny samples were used that we could not identify. (Public Enemy members told us that, for instance, there are definitely more than eleven samples in their song "Fight the Power.") Second, we have assumed that all sampled artists were contacted *before* the album's release to achieve the lowest fee possible. (In other words, the licensing fees in table 2 are based on licensing that occurs before the sample-based record hits retail stores.) Third, we have assumed a minimum of transaction costs by simply applying a $500 fee per license as might be charged by a sample clearance house rather than factoring in all the costs incurred when copyright holders are difficult to find, when they "hold out," and so on. All of these factors tend to push our estimates of the licensing cost for these two albums lower than the actual clearance costs would be today.

Some upward biases exist, too. Although we assumed that samples in the "low" row and "small" column of table 2 would carry no licensing fee, we also assumed that every other sample would require a license that carried a fee. Yet some of the artists who sample might have granted permission without a fee. Next, we assumed that licensing fees were rigid, regardless of how many other samples were being used in the same Public Enemy or Beastie Boys song. Some copyright owners might agree to a lower-than-usual fee. Finally, we assumed ongoing royalties would be paid, not one-time buyouts.

Other limitations of our methodology could push our estimates upward or downward. We assumed that the groups would be selling CDs rather than downloads, which would alter both the retail price and the groups' share of the sales revenue. As we mentioned above, putting each sample into one of the eleven boxes in table 2 is not an exact science. We have oversimplified a complex negotiating process, which could make estimates inaccurate in either direction—that is, our method renders our estimates imprecise. In addition, the hypothetical exercise left out the issue of refusals to grant permission or a license. Many of the samples involved in these two albums might never be cleared: the Beatles, Led Zeppelin, Pink Floyd, the Eagles, and Prince might all have said "no"—as they typically do. In that case, Public Enemy or the Beastie Boys would either have to drop the samples in question, alter the song, or risk litigation. Dropping a sample saves money on licensing fees, but altering a song can be expensive (studio time, remastering costs, and other such things). Differences in various tracks could reduce the value of the album to consumers or reduce the aesthetic value of the work. On the whole, it is difficult to say whether refusals to license would increase the cost of attempting to release these two albums commercially today.

Our approach does not achieve a perfect simulation, but it does give us a sense of the scale of the licensing costs for *Fear of a Black Planet* and *Paul's Boutique* if they were released, as is, today. Despite all of our caveats, tables 3 and 4 provide some concrete information. The sheer number of samples alone would make licensing these albums very difficult, to put it mildly. We do not pretend to have hit upon the exact licensing costs; instead, we hope to bring the challenge of licensing collage-style sample-based works into higher relief. Today, releasing such albums commercially would probably result in losing money with every copy. Even if our estimates for *Fear of a Black Planet* are twice as high as the real licensing costs, and even if our estimates for *Paul's Boutique* are three times too high, the groups would fall further into debt every time they sold an album. (And remember, there are good reasons to think our estimates are too low.) From this analysis, we conclude that various aspects of the licensing system—law, business practices, costs—have made at least some forms of musical collage totally impractical.

ASSESSING THE SAMPLE CLEARANCE SYSTEM

> There is no reason why it has to be like that for artists to get paid.
> We ought to be focusing on ways to assure creativity while also making
> sure artists get paid for their work.—LAWRENCE LESSIG

How do our interviewees evaluate whether sample licensing works as well as it should? Some focus on the efficiency of the system—whether every licensing negotiation that should happen (that is, those that would benefit copyright holders, would-be licensees, and the public) does happen. This perspective focuses on the friction in the system—namely, transaction costs. "My criticism, I guess, comes with the process," says Bill Stafford. "I think that there should be some way of streamlining it. It shouldn't take eight months to clear something. I think that there needs to be something better." Our findings in chapter 5 describe how a sample licensing negotiation can cost dearly, experience delays, or break down completely. The sample clearance system imposes many transaction costs that gum up the machinery. No system is perfect, but improvements seem possible.

Other interviewees assess the sample clearance system based on the works that aren't made because of the system's constraints. Tom Silverman thinks of the scenario "when you have some kid in the Bronx with two turntables, and he could be a musical Einstein. He could have the idea for a record that could sell fifty million copies and change the world, but he can't do it." The estimated cost of licensing albums that feature multiple samples per track like *Paul's Boutique* and *Fear of a Black Planet* shows that such albums would be practically impossible to license today. This partially explains why the reissue in 2009 of *Paul's Boutique* contained no bonus tracks or any other material from that era; otherwise, new licenses for those recordings would need to be secured. This explanation echoes what Chuck D told us when discussing the long-planned reissues of Public Enemy's *It Takes a Nation of Millions to Hold Us Back* and *Fear of a Black Planet.* He said that they are sitting on the record company's shelf because they couldn't successfully get all the permissions they needed for the expanded deluxe editions—which count as a "new release."

To release those albums today, either the samples originally desired would have to change, or the work could not be distributed commercially. This stifles a certain form of creativity by limiting the possibilities musicians can explore when they seek to borrow from existing works. As Harry Allen puts it, "I'm talking about the failure of music business's imagination. It's almost like the business forced an evolutionary dead end in the case of an album like [*Fear of a Black Planet*]." Critiques based on transaction costs and the royalty stacking problem both boil down to economic inefficiency. But the two issues are distinct problems. Even in the absence of transaction costs—in an imaginary, frictionless system—the current process for sample licensing can seldom handle the licensing of new tracks that sample multiple existing tracks. As we have described, each copyright holder expects too great a royalty, regardless of the expense of the transaction itself. While they are distinct issues, high transaction costs and royalty stacking reinforce the inefficiency of the sample clearance system.

A third economic problem, implicit in our interviewees' description of the sample licensing process, stems from the sequential nature of musical production. Obviously, source music must be created before another track can sample it; indeed, the source might predate the sampling track by four decades or more. Furthermore, musicians who sample almost always create their sample-based music before they begin seeking the licenses. Until they have constructed their collages, musicians don't know what combination of samples will achieve the desired sound. And it would often be wasteful to incur search costs, transaction costs, and licensing fees before knowing for certain which samples are needed. For all of these reasons, a licensor and licensee do not typically meet in advance of recording to split up their revenue and production costs. (Economists have dubbed this the "division of profit" problem.[21]) Unfortunately, this leaves only after-the-fact licensing negotiations, which can fail—even when it would be beneficial to society to ensure the creation of both a sampled source and a new track that samples it.[22]

Transaction costs, royalty stacking, and the division-of-profit problem in sequential creation suggest that copyright law and the sample clearance system ought to be redesigned. The current system for sample licensing won't always produce the desired result. But we must temper or at least complicate the story of these three failures of the market. When thwarted by licensing requirements, musicians can adjust by using replays, substituting other samples, or taking other actions (such as releasing their work noncommercially). The MPAA's Dean Garfield (formerly of the RIAA) argues along these lines by saying, "I can suggest an alternative for people who feel stifled by the costs of sampling, which is—be creative. There's nothing that compels you to sample someone's work. You can just listen to it and vibe off it and create something new."

As we have explained in several sections of this chapter, sampling musicians can sometimes mitigate the costs of an inefficient licensing system. But other interviewees describe sample licensing's constraints on musical practice as a threat to creativity. Even if musicians can work around the constraints—and sometimes produce great work in doing so—should they have to? Rather than evaluating the system economically, these commentators take a view rooted more in ideas about freedom of expression. For example, consider the outlook of the musician Sage Francis:

When I first started putting out music, it was to other people's beats that they sampled from somebody else that they didn't get permission for. I mean, that slows down the process of creativity, when you're so consumed with legalities of your art, you know, that's no place for an artist to be in. And it will never happen; it will never take precedence over what people do to create. I never write a song and fear that someone's going to steal it, or I need to hurry up and copyright this stuff. You get over that after a while, you know? I have a well of information, I have a well of ideas and I dip into it and I pull stuff up out of the mug. Not all this stuff is mine. I mean it almost feels like, to a degree, that it's public property. I mean, I get these ideas from other places, I get these words from books, you know, and I put them in my own little special way, and if people enjoy it enough that they want more from me, they'll support me, and I give them more, and I'm given the opportunity to do that. And I never ever fretted about copyrights.

Here Sage Francis describes a mismatch between how creativity works and how copyright law and the sample clearance system works. Under the copyright statute and cases from *Grand Upright* to *Bridgeport*, sampling musicians must not only pay copyright owners but also obtain permission. In a system that requires permission to sample in the absence of fair use,[23] self-censorship can become a problem. As M. C. Schmidt of Matmos puts it, "Another danger inherent in all this is the cop in your own head. One of the worst casualties of all this lawyerly stuff is people not doing things because they are afraid maybe someone will sue them in the future." Thus, viewed from an expressive, non-economic perspective, the economic inefficiencies of the sample clearance system are ultimately a free speech problem.

Despite the three types of economic inefficiencies we have illustrated and discussed, musicians and businesses in the music industry sometimes have enough agency to work around the inefficiencies. And despite the potential chilling effect of an expensive and bureaucratic licensing system, avenues like noncommercial Internet distribution arguably provide an outlet for musical collage. Further, we cannot resolve the debates between the economic and cultural perspectives: we think both perspectives explain part of the problem with sample licensing, and neither perspective is complete without the other.

We think the evidence suggests that the sample clearance system has not achieved a balance between compensation and access, or between expression and control. The information we have collected from our interviewees suggests that any reform that could "grease the wheels"—or make licensing transactions easier and less expensive—would be highly desirable to most stakeholders in the music industry. We also think that our findings about the royalty stacking problem for tracks with multiple samples, along with our rough estimates of modern licensing costs applied to albums from sampling's golden age, demonstrate a serious problem for that subset of sample-based music. For both economic and cultural reasons, we think legal and business reforms to the sample clearance system are desperately needed. In the next chapter we examine several of these proposals.

7

PROPOSALS FOR REFORM

No single reform can fix the deficiencies in sample licensing. Only a set of complementary reforms that change both copyright law and business practices can address all of the system's shortcomings. The royalty stacking problem for sample-heavy musical collages, for example, may require more fundamental reform than the inefficiency that sometimes hinders clearances for major-label artists. A multifaceted approach also fits with the wide variety of scenarios in which one musician samples another. Sampling occurs across generations and across genres, on major labels and independents, and in the background or foreground of sample-based music. Government policies and business practices should reflect this fact.

Practically speaking, the best solutions are systems that artists and other music-industry interest groups would voluntarily embrace. Incremental change may be preferable to sweeping legislative change, and some parts of the current sample clearance system may already reflect a reasonable balancing of the competing interests involved in sampling. Moreover, Congress—which would need to instigate any changes in copyright law—probably lacks the capacity, time, and expertise to get all aspects of the balancing act just right. Instead, it seems wisest to look for opportunities for other institutions—whether the federal courts, record labels, or artistic communities—to make specific changes that improve the sample clearance system. The ideal reforms will alleviate the current system's restraints on artistic freedom while upholding, when appropriate, the rights of musicians or copyright holders to compensation and control. Enhancing the sample clearance system's efficiency brings with it the prospect of increasing the music industry's revenue. This could provide a strong incentive for artists and labels to embrace some structural changes that promote openness and transparency. In this chapter, we examine four categories of policy changes that have been articulated: enhanced property rights, compulsory licenses, non-infringing uses, and innovations in voluntary licensing.

ENHANCED PROPERTY RIGHTS

[A] private property system . . . reduces the cost of contracting and raises the cost of free-loading while, at the same time, it provides incentives and guidance for investment in producing information [goods such as music].
—HAROLD DEMSETZ, "Information and Efficiency"

Copyright law is the foundation of sample licensing. If compositions and recordings—or more specifically, portions of them—did not receive government protection through copyright law, licensing would be unnecessary, unless private techniques could somehow prevent unauthorized copying of musical works. In theory, the exclusive rights that copyright holders enjoy provide incentives to create or finance creativity, to distribute works publicly, and to manage works as resources—investing in works and licensing their use only when appropriate, so as not to diminish their value.[1] If copyright law succeeds in these goals, then making copyrights even stronger could—theoretically, at least—solve the problems of the sample clearance system.

Scholars of law and economics might describe this approach as aiming to enhance—meaning to clarify, expand, and better enforce—copyright holders' property rights in samples. Property rights are a requisite feature, perhaps the central feature, of market transactions. If property rights are well defined and reliably enforced, the theory goes, then individuals can more confidently exchange money for goods and services. Clear definitions of property are important for effective valuation of the property and for avoiding misunderstandings and later disputes. Reliable enforcement helps maintain the value of property, making it more worthwhile to purchase.

Suppose a buyer wants to purchase half of a large estate of farmland. To make an offer, the buyer will need to know which half of the lot she is getting. Perhaps one half has rich soil and the other half has poor soil. Or maybe the public has the right to use a particular road or path that crosses part of the land. The buyer will also want to know that the seller truly owns the land in the first place. She is far less likely to agree to the transaction if the land's ownership is under dispute with a third party claiming rights to a portion of it. Suppose the seller could take the buyer's money, take back the half he just sold, and no sheriff would come to kick the seller off the buyer's rightful parcel. Neither the buyer nor anyone else would be very eager to purchase the land if the property rights they attempt to purchase wouldn't be enforced. Defining and enforcing property rights are essential to a market for land.

What does all this have to do with sampling? Some scholars of law and economics since at least the 1960s have advocated treating all property—including "intellectual property" such as music—in the same way. The economist Harold Demsetz puts it this way in the context of patenting inventions: "Appropriability is largely a matter of legal arrangements and the enforcement of these arrangements by private or public means. The degree to which knowledge is privately appropriable can be increased by raising the penalties for patent violations and by increasing resources for policing patent violations."[2] In other words, just because information isn't tangible like land doesn't mean the government can't enforce and assign property-like rights in information.

Defining intellectual property rights successfully means achieving clarity in what rights copyright holders have and what rights users have. For samples, the law must decide to whom it will assign this "property" right: the copyright holder, other musicians, or the public. In part, this means specifying what size of sample must be licensed.[3] Five seconds? One second? One-tenth of a second? Five notes? Three notes? Do samples of just the drumbeat have to be licensed? What about the bass line, or drum pattern? Clarity also requires defining the business contexts in which sampling requires a license. If you sample a song and sell a million copies, have you infringed the copyrights in the song? What if you sample something but never sell it or distribute it? Enhancing property rights for samples means enforcing whatever clear rules the copyright law sets up by putting penalties in place and making sure courts enforce them. Clear rules have some benefits, like certainty for parties. But adopting rules forgoes the benefits that come from flexibility—the ability to tailor the law to unique situations.[4]

The Policy Behind Bridgeport

The *Bridgeport* decision, discussed in chapter 4, emphatically makes the argument for the perspective of strong property rights. By eliminating the *de minimis* threshold for sound recordings, the court expanded copyright holders' property rights in samples to include any portion of a sound recording (no matter how small), which was beyond what had been widely understood. The court discusses at length the benefits of better defining property rights in samples. Writing for a unanimous three-judge panel of the U.S. Court of Appeals for the Sixth Circuit, Judge Ralph B. Guy Jr. opens his policy argument as follows:

> To begin with, there is ease of enforcement. *Get a license or do not sample.* We do not see this as stifling creativity in any significant way. It must be remembered that if an artist wants to incorporate a "riff" from another work in his or her recording, he is free to duplicate the sound of that "riff" in the studio. Second, *the market will control the license price* and keep it within bounds. The sound recording copyright holder cannot exact a license fee greater than what it would cost the person seeking the license to just duplicate the sample in the course of making the new recording" (emphasis added).[5]

With the first highlighted phrase, echoing the *Grand Upright* decision from 1991, Judge Guy explains that samples will be treated as commodities subject to well-defined property rights: sampling any amount of a sound recording constitutes infringement.[6] From there, the economic benefits of property rights that we described earlier will flow naturally—at least in theory.

In the second highlighted phrase, Judge Guy anticipates a criticism of the court's decision. If samples become commodities and all samples must be licensed regardless of length, the price of samples could become exorbitant. Judge Guy assures the reader that the price of licensing a sample could not increase without restraint. The market will, in his view, discipline copyright owners, who will not charge too high a price for licenses out of fear that they will lose the sale to other copyright owners who would undercut their price.[7] Furthermore, musicians who sample will always have an alternative production technology that they can use to make music. Judge Guy argues that no musician will pay more for a sample than it costs to create a replay by hiring other musicians.[8] (This argument assumes that a replay is a close enough substitute for a sample of the original source. To the extent that replays fall short of being close substitutes, they would do less to limit sample prices.)

The court argues that the possibility of using a replay shows that sampling ought to be viewed as copyright infringement. If replays involve some cost to make, and if many artists choose to sample instead, then samples must be cheaper than replays. Therefore, Judge Guy argues, musicians reap an economic savings from sampling: "When you sample a sound recording you know you are taking another's work product. . . . [E]ven when a small part of a sound recording is sampled, the part taken is something of value. No further proof of that is necessary than the fact that the producer of the record or the artist on the record intentionally sampled because it would (1) save costs, or (2) add something to the new recording, or (3) both."[9] Failing to compensate copyright owners for the things of value they make, such as recorded material, might undermine their incentive to produce such goods. But, more than this economic argument, the court mainly appeals to moral sensibilities. As the law professor Tracy Reilly puts it, *Bridgeport* relies on "the common economic theme that, like it or not, has applied to American jurisprudence since the inception of our Constitution: if you want to 'borrow' or, more accurately, take something of value that belongs to somebody else, you had better obtain their permission and negotiate a fee for such use."[10]

This argument has some ethical appeal. But it begs the question to whom the law will assign the property rights in samples. Copyright law sometimes gives rights to owners, but other times it gives rights to the public (including musicians who sample) through doctrines like fair use. In all cases, the listener (or sampling musician) is taking something of value. Pointing out that sampling musicians take something of value doesn't prove anything about whether a particular instance of sampling is copyright infringement.

The *Bridgeport* court stands on firmer logical ground when it points out the complexity and expense of copyright litigation:

> This case also illustrates the kind of mental, musicological, and technological gymnastics that would have to be employed if one were to adopt a *de minimis* or substantial similarity analysis. . . . When one considers that

[the trial-level judge in *Bridgeport*] has hundreds of other cases all involving different samples from different songs, *the value of a principled bright-line rule becomes apparent*. We would want to emphasize, however, that considerations of judicial economy are not what drives this opinion. If any consideration of economy is involved it is that of the music industry. As this case and other companion cases make clear, it would appear to be cheaper to license than to litigate.[11]

The Sixth Circuit wants to define property rights clearly to avoid lawsuits and instead promote voluntary, well-informed transactions within the music industry. With clearly defined property rights, musicians who sample would know ahead of time that they must pay and copyright owners can anticipate receiving licensing revenue.

To the extent that *Bridgeport* expands property rights beyond previous understandings, the court's decision makes sampling more expensive. Judge Guy, to conclude his policy justification of the court's ruling, addresses the ruling's potential creative impact:

[T]o pursue further the subject of stifling creativity, many artists and record companies have sought licenses as a matter of course. Since there is no record of those instances of sampling that either go unnoticed or are ignored, one cannot come up with precise figures, but it is clear that a significant number of persons and companies have elected to go the licensing route. Also there is a large body of pre-1972 sound recordings that is not subject to federal copyright protection. Additionally, just as many artists and companies choose to sample and take their chances, it is likely that will continue to be the case.[12]

The argument here is threefold (which we will not discuss in order). First, not every sample has copyright protection—some sound recordings are in the public domain.[13] Second, every property-rights regime has leaks. Some people violate property law all the time, perhaps in small ways like trespassing on a lawn to cut a corner. Musicians can still choose to risk copyright-infringement litigation if they expect their benefits to outweigh their costs.

Finally, Judge Guy points out that some licensing was already happening before *Bridgeport*. Many copyright owners had already asserted, and many sampling musicians had already acknowledged, a property right in samples. The court adds that "the record industry, including the recording artists, has the ability and know-how to work out guidelines, including a fixed schedule of license fees, if they so choose."[14] So if the music industry wants to improve the sample clearance system through private, business means, they have the freedom to do so. Clear, well-enforced property rights might help them in that effort.

Will Enhanced Property Rights Work?

In a market that is functioning well, supported by strong property rights for samples, both copyright owners and musicians who sample should be able to earn revenue from sample-based works. Clear property rights facilitate the licensing transactions that get compensation flowing to those who are sampled while allowing samplers to distribute their works without uncertainty about copyright-infringement litigation. The music historian David Sanjek, writing in 1992, articulated this optimistic view:

> Samplers should apply for the appropriate licenses, respect the rights of copyright holders, and be respected in turn as equal creators. Responsibility for obtaining clearance should fall to either the artist, the label, or both. Samplers realize that in the litigious environment of the United States, there is nothing to be gained and much money potentially to be lost by being a renegade. Surely some obscure materials will be sampled and overlooked, but the process should proceed devoid of recrimination and with the opportunity for money to be made by both the sampler and those whom he samples.[15]

The approach of enhanced property rights tries to maximize the size of the pie. It aims for efficiency in the clearance system, which ideally generates value for all parties, including a flow of compensation to copyright holders. If it seems worth paying a licensing fee to create a sample-based song, then the sampling musician can pay and both sides of the transaction will benefit.

Bridgeport has many critics. Some commentators find the decision lacking as a legal matter by arguing that the court got its interpretation of copyright law wrong (as we discussed in chapter 4). Other critics focus on the consequences of expanding property rights, and they worry that the decision will stifle creativity. Tracy Reilly derides these critics by describing their concerns as "mere conjecture that because musicians will not have enough money to purchase licenses legally and hire competent counsel to negotiate such licenses on their behalf, they will stop making music altogether."[16]

In working with the interviews done for this book, we have attempted to go beyond conjecture to describe the sample clearance system in terms of actual music-industry practice. The success stories we have related throughout show that licensing can work, but only in certain contexts. Other times—for example, when the excessive transaction costs of tracking down copyright owners deter a potentially beneficial licensing deal—the licensing system cannot handle what an approach of expanded property rights would ask of it. In those situations, listeners lose a valuable piece of music, copyright owners lose licensing revenue, and musicians who sample do appear to have their creativity stifled.

Our research shows that the Sixth Circuit did in fact rely on "mere conjecture" in *Bridgeport*. The economic theory of property rights makes logical sense, in the abstract, but it also requires a leap of faith to believe that the theory will bear out in practice. Judge Guy expressed confidence that the music industry could apply its "know-how" to improve sample licensing once the court ruled that all samples required a license or permission from the sound recording copyright holder. But so far—six years after the decision—the music industry has not reformed the sample clearance system, and it doesn't look like it will in the near future. The royalty stacking problem, for instance, has received little attention and has inspired no private-sector solution. Leaving aside the difficult question of the fairness of expanding property rights for copyright holders, the evidence we have collected in this book significantly contradicts the *Bridgeport* court's economic presumptions.

COMPULSORY LICENSES

Compare compulsory licensing for compositions, which works
so well when people make covers of people's songs, to what happens in
sampling. Why is it easier to use three minutes of someone's song than
[it is to sample] three seconds of someone's song? That doesn't
make any sense.—SIVA VAIDHYANATHAN

Another option to address the problems with sample licensing is to *weaken* copyright owners' property rights. Scholars of law and economics distinguish between two ways to protect an interest in property: with a property rule or a liability rule.[17] Property rules are the more familiar idea: they mean you can't take someone's farmland or use someone's car without that person's say-so. With property-rule protection, the owner has the right to name her price or deny permission outright—as well as call the police to prevent theft or trespass or to restore her property to her after an unauthorized taking. A liability rule, on the other hand, requires prospective users only to pay a government-determined amount of compensation to the property owners, and liability rules do not require users to obtain the owners' permission. With liability-rule protection, the law does not force a user to return the property unless she neglected to pay the necessary compensation.

Thus, a common way to weaken copyright holders' property rights is to give them liability-rule protection for some uses instead of property-rule protection. In copyright, the usual form of liability-rule protection is a compulsory license, under which the copyright holder loses the right to deny permission for certain specified uses. Congress fixes the level of compensation that copyright owners receive when others engage in those specified uses (that level is often called the "statutory rate"). Compulsory licenses may be justified when copyright owners are too reluctant, or the transaction costs of voluntary licensing are too high, to expect licensing to happen without government intervention.

Music copyright contains a handful of compulsory licenses already. For example, once a musical composition has been recorded and distributed with the permission of the composition's copyright holder, it is subject to the mechanical license of section 115 (described in chapter 3). As the entertainment lawyer Shoshana Zisk explains, "Instead of having to do an individual negotiation with the copyright owner, they can get a compulsory license and pay the going rate that Congress sets. There's a certain kind of freedom in that. However, a compulsory license doesn't apply to sampling." The copyright code specifies that cover versions have to be sufficiently faithful to the original, but the code states that if you change the "basic melody or fundamental character" of the covered song or composition—like what happens in sampling—then you cannot use the compulsory license.[18]

Thus, faithful cover versions receive privileged treatment in copyright law as compared to sample-based musical collages, which are treated as infringing derivative works and require permission or a license. Siva Vaidhyanathan decries this distinction:

> Think about Aretha Franklin's version of "Respect." What a lot of people don't realize is Aretha covered Otis Redding's composition "Respect." Now, think about how this worked: Otis Redding's version of "Respect" is actually kind of sexist. Aretha Franklin's version of "Respect" is a powerful feminist anthem. It is a new version, a very new version of an existing composition. . . . The reason we have both of those versions of "Respect" is that there is compulsory licensing. Aretha Franklin's "Respect" was a huge hit. Otis Redding's "Respect" was a minor hit. But Otis Redding got paid twice for coming up with this arrangement, this composition. And Aretha Franklin got what she deserved for building on Otis Redding's work. The system worked out beautifully. As a result, the world has both songs and we're better off for it.

Vaidhyanathan convincingly argues that the mechanical license, as applied to cover versions, has created a cultural and financial windfall for the music industry and for the listening public. But the owners of musical composition copyrights doubtless disagree.

Eliminating the copyright holder's right to deny permission has many economic implications. The price that copyright owners receive under the mechanical license is probably lower than what they could have charged otherwise. More cover versions occur, partly because they are cheaper and partly because owners cannot deny permission. And some kinds of transaction costs will decline, since there is no need for negotiation and no possibility of delay from holdouts.[19] Andrew Bart puts it nicely: "It's either a regulated economy or it's a free market economy, and we have models of both of them within the music industry. For an example, think of licenses as a pure free market economy while mechanical licenses are a regulated economy."

The Case for Compulsory Licensing

Compulsory licenses are an appealing solution to some who think the current sample clearance system deters sampling. Throughout the history of the music industry, compulsory licenses have been one plausible legislative remedy when the licensing environment for a new or less-traditional use of music becomes a sludgy morass. As Tom Silverman tells us, "There's a whole school of fantastic created music that could arise if the copyright laws were different. If there was a compulsory license on a percentage basis for sampling, like there is for covering of songs, it would allow so much creative freedom. . . . The original creators should be compensated, but they shouldn't be able to block some visionary from using it in a new way." Bill Stafford says that "there would be more" sampling activity under a compulsory license. He continues by stating, "Just by the sheer physics of it, you wouldn't have people stopping projects, or waiting, or delaying."

Andrew Bart thinks sampling activity would probably increase, but he is more tentative: "If there was the equivalent of a mechanical license for sampling where it was non-negotiated but you had an automatic right to do it. . . . Then it really would depend on what the rate was, but I think even there it probably would increase the usage to some degree. Although that's a little bit more speculative." Siva Vaidhyanathan emphasizes another benefit of setting the rates by statute, explaining that one would know the costs up front: "You know that there is a very good chance that if you do things the right way and in good faith, you're going to be able to make the work that you want to build."

"I think it would be great if there was a compulsory license similar to recording a cover song," says Philo Farnsworth, whose Illegal Art record label releases Girl Talk's records. "That would at least give artists more options. They could create and obtain a license for all the samples for a reasonable fee—though it would have to be nuanced to not punish artists who use more than one sample per track. Artists could still claim fair use, but that would at least provide safer avenues since fair use is a very grey area."

But how should the rates be set? Tom Silverman advocates a quantitative approach: "Anybody should be able to sample any music for x amount based on certain criteria—one of them being how much of the song is used, what percentage of the original melody is used." Eothen Alapatt outlines a different approach with an invariable rate per sample. "I really do feel like there should be some kind of a set guideline for the usage of samples like we have with cover songs," he says. "And you pay a certain amount per unit sold to the person whose music is sampled, regardless of whether you use a whole bunch of that song or a little bit. . . . I've always thought that there should be something along the lines of a penny rate per sample per unit sold."

Many versions of a compulsory license for samples would be more complicated than the mechanical license. Setting prices based on "the percentage of the melody taken" would be problematic. Which melodies would count—vocals? On just the chorus, or on the verse, too? A guitar melody? Bass? Keyboards? Any melody in the song? Charging a fixed rate for any sample would address those quandaries and make for a much cleaner provision in the copyright code. But a fixed rate per sample violates certain expectations within the current system. Licensing fees for samples currently depend on both quantitative and qualitative factors, which reflects a deeply held belief that each sample ought to be evaluated individually.[20] In light of this, many of our interviewees who are part of the mainstream music industry voiced opposition to the idea of a compulsory license for samples.

The Case against Compulsory Licensing

Establishing a compulsory license for samples would likely increase the number of sample-based works and would reduce the transaction costs of negotiating (though not necessarily administrative costs, since a compulsory license still requires paperwork, documentation, accounting, and verification). "There is the view that maybe we should alleviate that process or streamline it by having a statutory license," says the entertainment attorney Anthony Berman, though he adds that there is a lot of resistance to this idea. "First, unlike a mechanical license in the traditional sense, which is pretty much a very straightforward use of a song, there's a lot of mystery to sampling, there's a lot of nuances. Obviously, the publishers are very resistant to that. They don't like it because they feel that the negotiation process is very beneficial to them, because they can make more money."

Andrew Bart further explains this resistance on the part of many powerful industry players. He concedes that the policy behind a compulsory license leads to more efficiency because the use cannot be vetoed and a price cap has been set. "Sample licensing doesn't have that right now, and so there's inefficiency," he says. But he also notes that "efficiency, to a certain degree, reduces discretion." Copyright holders lose discretion—the right to deny permission—under a compulsory license. Permission has an economic dimension; it facilitates a higher price for licensors. As Dina LaPolt says, "If I'm an artist that gets sampled a lot, I want to get as much money out of you as I can. Don't take away my negotiation right. If you want to sample Tupac, you better have some money. That's just how it has to work. The bigger the artist, the more money that they can make for themselves."

Of compulsory licenses, the sample clearance professional Danny Rubin states that "in theory, it sounds great. It's great for artists that are going to sample and artists who want to use samples. However, it's impractical, because the owners of the existing copyrights will never agree to something like that." The precedent of carving into the exclusive rights granted by copyright law would not sit well with copyright holders. The MPAA attorney Dean Garfield agrees with Rubin's assessment of the political viability of this proposal. "A compulsory license for sampling just wouldn't work, period. It forces authors to give up control of their work," Garfield says, arguing that he doesn't think that a compulsory license would help in promoting creativity. If licensing prices decreased, record labels and publishers would lose revenue, thus reducing their ability to invest in promoting new artists. Even Matt Black of Coldcut, who has long used samples in his music, states: "I'm not sure that that would be practical. I think it's up to each rights holder to negotiate what they feel their sample is worth. They should not necessarily be forced to comply with an external system of valuation."

In addition to its economic implications, discretion also has a moral dimension, which many interviewees emphasized. "Artists really like the idea of having control of their work," Bill Stafford emphasizes. "They're certainly dependent on it for income, and then there are certain other things that they might be more concerned about." When asked about a compulsory licensing scheme for samples, the artist manager Michael Hausman replies, "I'm not in favor of that. I think that the artist needs to be able to say no. As much as that goes against how much I love sampling, I still feel like the artist needs to be able to say no." With strong property rights, artists have discretion to control how their work is used—say, to avoid being sampled in what they consider an offensive context. Compulsory licenses would eliminate this discretion by taking away a right that many musicians hold dear.

Alternative Compensation Systems

Because a compulsory licensing scheme would be difficult to design, some commentators have sought a big-picture solution. While reforming the copyright code in controversial ways, why not think big? Whitney Broussard suggests that maybe musicians could pay into a fund that would grant them a "blanket license" allowing the freedom to sample whatever they want in exchange for a fee. Terry Fisher, of Harvard University and the Berkman Center for Internet and Society, has developed a similar proposal to what Broussard describes. In his book *Promises to Keep* (2004), Fisher argues that "We should consider a fundamental change in approach." He proposes that we "replace major portions of the copyright and encryption-reinforcement models" with monetary payments after the fact, like prizes, for invention and creation—what Fisher calls "a governmentally-administered reward system."[21] His proposal would scrap large parts of the current copyright code.

Here is Fisher's alternative compensation system in a nutshell: Creators register with a one-page form submitted to the Copyright Office, which would use unique identification numbers to track digital distributions of the work. The government would raise taxes, and the Copyright Office would divide and pay out the revenue to registrants based on some formula that reflects the frequency that those copyrighted works were heard or viewed. Fisher's proposal handles the issue of sequential musical creation with a compulsory license of his own design:

> What about recordings that incorporate portions of other recordings—rap songs that contain "samples" of other copyrighted recordings, movies that contain excerpts of other movies, and so on? To gather the information necessary to compensate fairly both the creator of the incorporated work and the creator of the incorporating work, the form would require each registrant to indicate how much of the material contained in the submitted recording had been taken from other registered recordings. A precise accounting would be unnecessary. Rather, the registrant would pick among five ways of characterizing the proportion of the recording that had been taken from others—none; a small amount (less than 5 percent); some (5 to 50 percent); most (50 to 95 percent); all or almost all (95 to 100 percent)—and then list the registration numbers of the works incorporated in whole or in part.[22]

Fisher anticipates and addresses a potential problem with honesty in registration, in which some might choose to underreport how much of someone else's work was used. As Fisher writes, "To deter such behavior (and to encourage others to detect and challenge it), we might provide that proof of underreporting would result in all of the revenue that the registrant would have earned through the system being diverted to the registrant of the recording from which the underreported material was taken."[23] He does not go through the details of the revenue-distribution formula, which would likely involve statistical techniques like those of BMI and ASCAP, or like those of the radio-ratings company Arbitron or the record-sales company SoundScan. In the end, Fisher notes, "How exactly the division should be made should be left to the Copyright Office."[24]

An important economic feature that Fisher's proposal shares with compulsory licenses is that samplers would not have to pay up front. Instead, payment for any samples that a musician uses would be taken out of his or her revenue distributions from the Copyright Office. This eliminates the requirement of coming up with a large amount of financing to clear the samples on an album in advance. Where Fisher's proposal differs from other compulsory licenses is in his quantitative approach—that is, in using the portion of the sampled work used to determine the price of sampling. The proposal sidesteps the kind of arguments we see in sampling case law and in sample-license negotiations about qualitative importance, melody versus drum part, and so on. As he writes, "Because these figures would be determined quantitatively (by dividing the duration of the incorporated material by the duration of the composite recording) rather than qualitatively (assessing how important to the final product was the incorporated material), they would be relatively easy to determine."[25]

With this quantitative approach, Fisher aims to balance ease of administration against the need to tailor the compulsory license based on the particular sample in question. On the negative side, many of the critiques we heard regarding compulsory licenses would also apply to Fisher's proposal. Turning all of copyright into a tax-and-distribute system and changing sample clearance into a compulsory license would face strong political opposition. Discretion has a particular economic and moral value to creators, their affiliates, and their copyright assignees. Losing that discretion is a major cost. Nonetheless, Fisher's book outlines the benefits of a free-flowing system that also provides compensation to copyright holders: "The set of artists who made their creations available to the world at large . . . would increase. . . . [And] both consumers and artists would enjoy greater freedom to modify and redistribute audio and video recordings."[26]

Despite the hurdles and drawbacks of a compulsory license, the potential benefits that Fisher describes should not be dismissed out of hand. The key roadblock to establishing a compulsory license for samples is that many of the competing interests in the music industry—labels, publishers, and musicians—do not see it as advantageous. A compulsory license would reduce the licensing fees that labels and publishers obtain. It would also limit discretion, a prerogative that musicians who own their copyrights or who have reserved the right to approve samples in their contracts especially enjoy. Because we see the music industry's opposition as such a high hurdle, we do not see compulsory licensing as a realistic option in the near term.

NON-INFRINGING USES

I understand fair use as having fairly strict criteria.
Are you ripping people off? Are people buying your music instead
of someone else's? Or is your music becoming something new and not
negatively impacting the original artist? If so, then you can potentially
use it without asking for permission.—GREGG GILLIS (Girl Talk)

Another way to resolve some of the inefficiencies of the sample clearance system is to expand, codify, or otherwise clarify the set of non-infringing uses. These carve out a space for musicians who sample to use existing works without obtaining permission or paying a fee. For the uses that remain infringing, copyright holders' property rights are sharpened—thus generating some of the benefits described above. The benefits of clear legal rules can accrue, in other words, even when those who sample, rather than those who have been sampled, have an entitlement to use certain samples. The two main ways to delimit non-infringing uses are to set a *de minimis* threshold for copyright infringement and to classify some samples as fair use.

A de Minimis *Threshold for Sound Recordings*

As described in chapter 4, the *de minimis* threshold in copyright law refers to the level below which courts deem the amount a musician takes from a copyrighted work too small to consider copyright infringement. (The Latin phrase *de minimis non curat lex* means "the law does not concern itself with trifles.") Part of the motivation for the *de minimis* threshold is administrative—the costs of litigation are too great to fight over tiny violations. But the *de minimis* threshold allows musicians a certain freedom to borrow small building blocks, like the three notes used by the Beastie Boys at issue in *Newton v. Diamond*. Limiting copyright protection to samples that reach a certain size helps prevent copyright from extending to ideas or concepts like a single note or a short phrase, when it is supposed to apply only to particular expressions of ideas.[27]

Decisions like *Newton v. Diamond* recognize a *de minimis* threshold for musical compositions. But *Bridgeport's* reading of section 114(b) of the copyright code foreclosed the possibility of applying a *de minimis* threshold to the infringement of sound recordings, at least in the Sixth Circuit. The *Bridgeport* court read the section as an extension of the rights of the sound recording copyright holders to everything not explicitly reserved to the public. Yet section 114(b) is better understood as a limitation on rights with respect to sound recordings.[28]

Congress could revise section 114(b) to clarify its meaning. One approach would involve setting a quantitative threshold for *de minimis* use, such as one second of the sampled recording or 1 percent of its length. Another approach is to allow the federal courts to determine the *de minimis* threshold on a case-by-case basis. Outside of the Sixth Circuit, courts need not follow the holding of *Bridgeport* and could apply a more defensible interpretation of section 114(b). The problem is that most cases never reach a judicial opinion; instead, parties tend to settle beforehand—largely because of the high cost of litigation. It is also an open question how much a future judicial opinion (say, one that runs counter to *Bridgeport*) can affect licensing practices. Whether courts have traction in that regard would determine the relative appeal of focusing on them in any reform efforts. Another alternative is to require some *de minimis* threshold, but allow the music industry to determine the specifics.

The absence of a *de minimis* rule for sound recordings has broad consequences. Without it, the *de minimis* rule for musical compositions becomes less meaningful for samplers, because most samples infringe both the sound recording and the musical composition copyrights in the sampled song. However implemented, a *de minimis* threshold should apply to the infringement of sound recordings to provide leeway in copyright law's balancing act between those who sample and those who have been sampled.

Defining Fair Use

An important set of non-infringing uses falls under the fair use doctrine. Fair use is designed to protect freedom of expression, and has an analogue in the "fair dealing" body of law in Canada, Britain, and many other Commonwealth countries. As Terry Fisher says, "The fair use doctrine, as its name suggests, is designed in the first instance to allow people to engage in activities [that] though on their face would violate the copyright law, nevertheless seem on balance, fair." Courts recognized fair use in the nineteenth century. The fair use statute was written into the U.S. Copyright Act of 1976 to allow unauthorized uses of a copyrighted work for the purposes of education, criticism, and parody, among other things. As Dean Garfield elaborates, "There are certain exceptions to the concept of exclusivity, which is the predominant concept; there are [opposing] concepts like fair use, which allow someone else to use a copyrighted work, as long as the use is *fair*."

"And 'fair' is really an equitable and balanced term," Garfield continues. "If you are taking something that someone worked on and are transforming it in some significant way or if you are using it for educational purposes, then the lines that are drawn on the exclusive use of the copyright end there." The deeply rooted fair use legal tradition in the United States is, however, relatively unique in the world, which means that its effectiveness is quite limited by geography (the fair dealing statutes in other countries arguably do not allow as many freedoms as fair use in the United States). Quite aptly, the legal scholar Rosemary Coombe reminds us that fair use is "a local ordinance in a global information economy." We take this caveat seriously, although there's also no reason why fair use can't be exported—just as we can look to other kinds of exceptions to copyright protection from foreign jurisdictions that could be imported.

Campbell v. Acuff-Rose, the lawsuit pitting 2 Live Crew against Roy Orbison over the rap group's parody of "Pretty Woman" (as described in chapter 4), set a very important precedent regarding fair use. As the

Columbia law professor Jane Ginsburg explains, "In that parody case, the Supreme Court held—not as a descriptive matter, but as a normative matter—that there was no market for parody." She explains that a licensing market for parodies "does seem sort of counterintuitive. You don't really want the copyright owner to be able to control what people say about their work and whether people make fun of the work, including by copying some parts of the work in order to make fun of it."

Nearly ten years after that Supreme Court decision, the Wu-Tang Clan member Ghostface Killah successfully claimed fair use for his marijuana-drenched parody of "What a Wonderful World," popularized by Louis Armstrong. "I see buds that are green / red roses too / I see the blunts for me and you," rapped Ghostface. Although the language is not subtle, Mr. Armstrong probably would have thought the parody was funny—he was a notoriously heavy smoker of marijuana.[29] In any event, such examples show that it is well established that parody is within the core of fair use.

Although there is no hard-and-fast rule that allows us to instantly assess whether something is a fair use, the statute provides four factors to help us determine the legality of our borrowing. According to section 107 of the Copyright Act, these factors include: "(1) the purpose and character of the use, including whether such use is of a commercial nature or is for nonprofit educational purposes; (2) the nature of the copyrighted work; (3) the amount and substantiality of the portion used in relation to the copyrighted work as a whole; (4) the effect of the use upon the potential market for or value of the copyrighted work."[30] In the 2 Live Crew case, a unanimous Supreme Court stated that these four factors should not be seen as a rigid checklist, where if the allegedly infringing work fails one of the four tests—a yes/no binary—then the borrowing is illegal. Instead, the Court explained the four factors as existing on a continuum in which an overall balance of fairness is struck between the old work and new work. In other words, the high court held that just because something is for profit doesn't disqualify it as fair use.[31]

Campbell also explained that the first factor asks "whether and to what extent the new work is 'transformative'" and that parody "has an obvious claim to transformative value."[32] What *Campbell* suggested but did not resolve is how courts should decide which uses other than parody also qualify as "transformative." As Jane Ginsburg explains:

Courts have elaborated on that first factor to inquire if the use is "transformative." So in other words, are you just copying from the prior work so that you recycle it for pretty much the same thing as where you started, or are you doing something really creative, productive, giving new interpretation and so forth to what you've copied? In [the sampling] context, it's probably a good argument that the use is transformative—although that might depend on the nature of the sample, I don't know. And if, for example, I sample the bass guitar because I don't have a bass guitarist, and somehow this substitutes for a musician, that doesn't sound so transformative. But if I'm sampling because I'm weaving it in with other stuff or something like the *Grey Album*, there, I think you could make an argument that that's transformative.

The law professor Peter Jaszi suggests that the first of the factors for fair use may favor a musician who sampled where "the sample was substantially transformed. This would not be the drumbeat, necessarily, but it might be the vocal selection that was tweaked and modified and then inserted in a context different from the one in which it was originally used." The notion of transformative use probably offers the most promising avenue for a significant number of samples to be considered fair use. Jaszi tells us that the concept of transformative use was not very well developed when sampling was emerging in the 1980s, but today it is more established and better understood.

The second factor for fair use—the nature of the copyrighted work—seldom plays a role in sampling cases, but the third and fourth factors often do. The third factor asks courts to determine how much the sampling musician has taken, both quantitatively and qualitatively. Jane Ginsburg offers an illustration of this issue:

The Grey Album I think is an interesting example because it doesn't take too long before you get the joke, but it just keeps going and going and going—"As My Guitar Gently Weeps" is the one I was thinking of [a sample taken from the Beatles' *The White Album*]. And, of course, this is somewhat of a delicate operation because it is putting the court in the position of making what some might say is an artistic judgment. Who is the judge to decide whether you took more than you needed to take for your expressive purpose? But if the alternative is, "I'm the artist, I'm the creator, and I decide how much I can take," then all bets are off. That's completely self-serving, so you need some sort of standard. And so courts do tend to look fairly carefully at whether they think that the defendant has been gilding the lily.

In this way, the third factor injects much of the case-by-case subjectivity and unpredictability that characterizes fair use analysis. The fourth factor, harm to the copyright holder's market, can loom large in the fair use analysis. With this factor, it matters to courts whether copyright holders are trying to license uses like the one in question—that is, whether they are seeking the potential licensing revenue from samples. If so, then the fair use claim might be weaker; if not, the fair use claim seems much stronger. Jane Ginsburg argues that because a market for sound recording sample licensing has already developed, this can cut against the fair use arguments of musicians who sample.

Commenting on the World

Fair use has an important role in preventing copyright from limiting freedom of speech. As Terry Fisher explains, "The premier example here would probably be the dispute over *The Wind Done Gone*, which is a novel that, among other things, critically comments upon *Gone with the Wind*. In particular, it attacks its arguably racist dimensions." He explains that after a good deal of litigation in that case, the Court of Appeals excused *The Wind Done Gone* from copyright infringement "primarily on the ground that we want to afford room in modern culture for critical commentary." Although this is a literary example, the same overall logic holds true for the sampling of, for instance, political speeches or news broadcasts for the purpose of parody or criticism. The entertainment attorney Whitney Broussard argues that once public figures, entertainers, or politicians insert themselves into the popular culture—and put energy into being part of the public discourse—they are fair game for commentary.

One person who has engaged in just this sort of sampling is Matt Black of Coldcut. "I think that our politicians are employed by the public and are fair game," he says, discussing Tony Blair and George W. Bush. "Let's take Tony Blair, who said, 'The lunatics have taken over the asylum.' He's a public figure; he's making that statement as a public figure in a public place, and I think that statement and that material is public property. I would argue that we are allowed to use that one to broadly fair use." Black explains that collage can be a useful tool for political commentary because it enables one to take a mass mediated message and, as he puts it, "freeze it, analyze it, and build it back up again. We often say, the truth is in there, so if you actually take Bush's words and you rearrange them, then you can actually find out what he's really saying."

Similarly, Public Enemy sampled the speeches of public figures. "When we recorded *It Takes a Nation* and *Fear of a Black Planet*," Chuck D tells us, "we used vocal samples from all over the place. We might use different TV samples and vocal samples from radio, or political speeches." Hank Shocklee, a founding member of Public Enemy, affirms this when he says, "Public Enemy was not just a group that made hip-hop records that people can just dance to. It was also a source of information." The golden-age records released by Public Enemy evoked and invoked— through the sampling of certain sounds, voices, and news broadcasts— the black power era of the late 1960s and early 1970s, all the while staying firmly rooted in the contemporary moment. "What we wanted to create was kind of like a 'reality record,'" Shocklee explains. "You hear it out there on the streets, and now what you heard in the streets is now back in the record again."

For instance, *Fear of a Black Planet* contained numerous samples of radio and television broadcasts *about* the group (and sometimes, as is the case with their song "Incident at 66.6 FM," you hear Flavor Flav interrupting a call-in radio show that was critical of the group). "We got so far into sampling, we even sampled ourselves, media coverage of ourselves. Our whole reason for doing music in the first place is because we wanted to sample from culture and put it back out there in the world," Shocklee says. In response to this view, Whitney Broussard states: "I think that that kind of cultural back and forth is what culture's about—and the law should be very cautious about limiting that in any way, because you want that discourse." And the musician Tim Quirk further adds, "It's absolutely a free speech issue. And when the copyright law clashes with First Amendment law, First Amendment law has to win."

Fair Use in the Music Industry

In the United States music industry, fair use exists more in theory than in practice. "Fair use is a misnomer," says Dina LaPolt. "People start screaming, 'Fair use, fair use, fair use,' but it's just a defense, which means you have to defend it." Tim Quirk points out that you will get a different opinion about what fair use is depending on whom you ask. "If you ask a lawyer for a record company, which I have done—if you ask Cary Sherman, head of the RIAA [Recording Industry Association of America]—he will look you in the eye and say, 'There is no such thing as fair use.' He will actually say that. And he will say, 'It is nothing but a negative defense to a copyright infringement claim. It doesn't exist absent a claim that you have done something wrong.'" Many of those whom we interviewed between 2005 and 2008 exhibited ignorance or indifference toward this legal doctrine. Take the following exchange, for instance:

KEMBREW: "Are you familiar with the legal doctrine of fair use?"
EOTHEN ALAPATT: "No."

And another example:

KEMBREW: "Have you ever worked with an artist who sampled without permission under the belief that they were making fair use of a copyrighted material?"
WALTER McDONOUGH: "No."

Dina LaPolt points to the example of Weird Al Yankovic, who people mistakenly assume invokes the fair use doctrine in his song parodies of Nirvana, Madonna, and others: "I asked him myself. 'Weird Al, do you get permission?' He says, 'Always, always,' because he doesn't want to pay for defending his actions. He's got five kids. He doesn't want to pay some copyright lawyer a hundred grand to defend his fair use claim." Bill Stafford used to license Weird Al's parodies when they were both employed by Arista Records. "All of his items were indeed parody," Stafford says. "And they would probably pass that [fair use] test. But no one wanted to find out. No one wanted to go down that road." Whitney Broussard explains this cautious impulse, which leads to record companies and artists ignoring the possibilities that fair use allows. "You know, fair use is a noble concept, but as a business strategy it's really, really weak," says Broussard. "You really can't rely on that for business purposes. You really can't say, 'Well, I'm going to jump into the gray area, here, and hope this works out okay.' Some companies do that, but for larger companies that are big targets for lawsuits, it's rare that they would do that."

Dina LaPolt summed up this perspective about fair use as follows:

"It's a useless part of the Copyright Act. It should be just deleted. No one gets it." Some of these dismissive attitudes stem from the fact that very few fair use cases involving music have ever been decided by a court, in part because of the cost of litigating a copyright infringement lawsuit. As Andrew Bart says, "The odds are astronomical that [a fair use] case will settle at some point before it goes to trial. That's why there are so few reported decisions. There's very little reason to be going all the way through the trial with all of the legal expense that it entails. As opposed to just trying to cut some sort of settlement." Put bluntly, asserting fair use is a problematic business strategy. Copyright infringement suits could follow—a situation that limits distribution opportunities while presenting potentially devastating costs (a quarter million dollars or much, much more) just to defend oneself.

The Future of Fair Use: Proposals and Opinions

Bridgeport not only created a bright line on the licensing front, but it also may have weakened fair use—despite the fact that the court made no explicit ruling on fair use in that case. Copyright infringement defendants, like any others, have to marshal all the legal defenses they can. Without a *de minimis* threshold for sound recordings, sampler defendants have to rely more heavily on fair use as an affirmative defense. But fair use, with its case-by-case, unpredictable nature, makes a better backstop than a baseball bat. Peter Jaszi emphasizes, however, that it is important not to give up on fair use, even in the nebulous world of digital sampling. He tells us that when the sampling system was forming twenty years ago, "the two paths that were taken were the path of comprehensive licensing on the one hand—especially for artists with major label contracts—and the path of transgression on the other. The middle road, the road that considers the possibility that much of the sampling practice may in fact be perfectly okay under fair use, was not explored."

Jaszi suggests that the music community could now develop a "best practices" statement that defines the kinds of sampling it considers to be a fair use, which would necessarily involve a series of conversations among sampling artists. As he explains:

Recent scholarship has established beyond doubt that courts—and other decision makers who care and who have roles in determining what is or isn't fair use—are influenced by the expressed consensus of various practice communities as to what is considered within those communities to be honest and reasonable dealing. So if a court wants to know if a given bit of quotation in a trade book is or isn't fair use, they look in other places for the standards and practices of the publishing community. And if the court wants to know whether a particular clip in a broadcast program is or isn't fair use, they look to the standards and practices of the broadcast community. This is an opportunity for artistic communities, should they choose to take it, to get involved—not only in responding to what lawyers may say about fair use, but to having a role in shaping the doctrine itself.

Commenting on the idea of a best practices statement involving sampling, Whitney Broussard observes, "Personally, I think that it would be a better system and you'd see more interesting art if the boundaries of fair use were (a) broadened and (b) clarified so that you could go into the studio and know that this is going to be fair use." Despite the fact that someone like the hip-hop producer El-P would like to see fair use expanded to embrace sampling and musical collage, he remains skeptical. Responding to Peter Jaszi's call for a music community-defined statement of best practices for sampling, El-P tells us: "I do want to point out that it is *not going to happen* because the musicians cannot talk to each other directly because we don't even own what we make. I've been in situations where I not only had permission to use something, but I became their friend and they were excited about the music, and I couldn't do it. I was going to put money in their pocket because I respected them. I went out of my way to contact them, to have a real conversation between two creative people. . . . The reason why none of this will ever happen is because the people who ultimately control it aren't really artists. It's the companies."

Jaszi responds by emphasizing that even though artists don't own much of the music they create—at least on the sound recording front, where record companies insist on ownership—this fact is still not a reason for musicians to avoid taking charge of shaping the development of fair use. As he argues, "You don't have to be a copyright owner in order to have strong aesthetic and ethical preferences for what is good and bad practice in sampling." After the music community establishes which sampled uses would be fair and which would not, the next step would be to see how courts respond to the question of whether digital sampling could be considered a fair use. Of course, this could very well happen *before* such a document is drafted.

Philo Farnsworth—who operates the Illegal Art label, which releases Girl Talk's albums—seems to be an obvious candidate for a lawsuit. To the surprise of many who have been following Girl Talk's brief career, there have been no lawsuits—despite the existence of hundreds of potential infringements of famous songs on each of the project's recent albums. Why no lawsuits? "One reason may be that the mainstream music industry does not want to see a test case go to court," Farnsworth tells us. "No one knows which side might win. As it now stands, only a small number of artists will dare to release an album with uncleared samples. If a case weighed in our favor, it would open the door for a multitude of artists to feel more comfortable about sampling without permission." When asked if being sued would be a good thing for the art and law of sampling, Farnsworth responds, dryly, "It would be good if we were able to win in court. It would be counterproductive if we lost."

One recent judicial opinion deemed a visual-art collage to be transformative and thus fair use. In 2006, the U.S. Court of Appeals of the Second Circuit ruled on a case involving the appropriation artist Jeff Koons and the photographer Andrea Blanch. In *Blanch v. Koons*, Blanch's copyrighted image, which featured a woman's feet and legs, was incorporated into one of Koons's collages, titled *Niagara*. In creating this collage, Koons integrated, and altered, Blanch's work by taking her image and changing the colors, medium, size, details, and background on which it was presented. The court ruled in Koons's favor by stating that its transformative nature made it a fair use. "I think that the Jeff Koons *Niagara* case could be used as a model for non-parody appropriation in music," says Farnsworth. "It seems that one of the key things courts look at in a fair use case is the fourth factor of fair use. That seems to weigh in our favor, as it would be ridiculous to suggest that anyone was buying a Girl Talk album in place of buying one of the original sources he is sampling."

"Even though fair use doesn't achieve the result of getting everyone paid all the time," Peter Jaszi says, "it may achieve the result of making it possible for artists to do the work they want to do." Fair use can also reduce the kinds of economic inefficiencies that occur when new technologies emerge, which often complicate existing distribution or broadcast contracts, for instance. "Fair use, where it applies, is independent of contracts," Jaszi points out. "It overrides many, although not all, contracts. Fair use, where it applies, is independent of platforms. It applies throughout the distribution system, without regard to the mode and nature of the distribution."

In terms of legislative intervention, Congress could reduce the uncertainty surrounding fair use. For instance, it could amend section 107 of the federal copyright code, which codifies the fair use doctrine, to clarify whether a sample-based song that is not a parody can qualify as a transformative use in at least some cases. Such a signal might spur various stakeholders in the music industry to work out a set of guidelines about which uses count as fair. The federal courts could also implement a clearer way to address fair use in sampling cases, perhaps by including a workable definition of transformative uses for cases that don't involve parodies. Realistically, though, it is unlikely that Congress would be motivated to alter the copyright code for the benefit of such a small class of constituents—remixers—and there is no guarantee that legislators would get it right. In fact, it's quite possible that Congress could make things worse by retooling the federal copyright code, especially given the lobbying power and influence of the entertainment industries that have Congress's ear.

INNOVATIONS IN VOLUNTARY LICENSING

The better question is, "Is it possible for the sample clearance process to become more efficient?" And I don't know. That's a more difficult question to answer because you'd need the cooperation from record companies, publishers, lawyers, and artists, and it might be a tough undertaking.—DANNY RUBIN

Reforms to the music industry's business practices can take many shapes. They can originate in the non-profit sector or at a single record label. They might span the entire music industry or just one artist's catalogue. Some require no government intervention, while others would benefit from government subsidy or persuasion. What these innovations have in common is their focus on promoting voluntary, mutually beneficial sample-licensing transactions.

Creative Commons Licenses

Being granted strong property rights (like those the *Bridgeport* court bestowed upon sound recording copyright holders) does not require copyright holders to exert their property rights to the fullest in every situation. Some potential licensors might want to render negotiations moot by declaring to potential samplers: "In certain situations that I specify, you can just use a sample without asking me." Why would copyright owners do this? They could have economic reasons; being sampled might raise awareness of their commercial work. Or the reasons might not be economic; for example, in letting samplers use their work without a costly discussion about permission.

This approach to sharing has been facilitated by Creative Commons, a non-profit organization founded in 2002 that provides creators with free legal tools that clearly mark what a downstream creator can do with a particular work. As Mia Garlick, a former general counsel for Creative Commons, explains, "Creative Commons has arisen as a solution to a problem that arose because of digital technology. You had this huge culture conflict between people who wanted to preserve an all-rights domain and those people who wanted to move for a no-rights-reserved domain." Mark Hosler of Negativland elaborates by saying, "The idea of Creative Commons was, 'Hey, we're not trying to change the laws, we're going to try and just make up our own set of agreements over here, kind of make up our own sandbox to play in that has the type of copyright relationships and agreements that we'd like to have.'" The organization argues that too often the debates over the impact of copyright on creativity are polarized, leading to two extreme positions: "all rights reserved" or "no right respected." As Hosler puts it, Creative Commons "expresses a gray area. Copyright is not just this binary, either/or—it's either total complete ownership and control or none. There's somewhere in the middle.

The website for Creative Commons describes the licenses developed by the organization as offering a middle ground: "some rights reserved." As Garlick explains: "What the Creative Commons license is doing is they clearly say to people, 'You know what, I'm happy for you to quote me, I'm happy for you to sample me, I'm happy for you to remix me,' and that way people can engage in creative expression and creative reuse much more readily and without any fear that they're going to have an army of lawyers outside their door." To that end, in 2005 Creative Commons debuted three versions of a "Sampling License," with the following announcement:

> Creative Commons first considered offering a Sampling License at the suggestion of collagist People Like Us (a.k.a. Vicki Bennett) and Negativland, the appropriationist art collective that has since served as the public discussion lead during the license drafting process. During this process, and thanks to FGV [Fundação Getulio Vargas] Law School, we learned that Gilberto Gil, Brazil's Minister of Culture had long been thinking along similar lines. We combined these independent inspirations and, before long, had new licenses to offer to the public. The Sampling licenses let artists and authors invite other people to use a part of their work and make it new. For example:
>
> —To take a sample from one musician's song and include it in a new one.
> —To use a clip from a film and mix it into your own video creation.
> —To take a piece of a photograph and put it into a new collage.

On certain conditions, that is. Creative Commons initially offered three versions of the Sampling license. Each reflects a slightly different creative style:

> —Sampling: People can take and transform pieces of your work for any purpose other than advertising, which is prohibited. Copying and distribution of the entire work is also prohibited.
> —Sampling Plus: People can take and transform pieces of your work for any purpose other than advertising, which is prohibited. Noncommercial copying and distribution (like file-sharing) of the entire work are also allowed. Hence, "plus."
> —Noncommercial Sampling Plus: People can take and transform pieces of your work for noncommercial purposes only. Noncommercial copying and distribution (like file-sharing) of the entire work are also allowed.[33]

Creative Commons actually retired the three sampling-specific licenses in 2007, citing a lack of demand and the undesirability of limiting sharing in the basic "Sampling" license. But musicians who wish to allow sampling can still use some of the general-purpose Creative Commons licenses. In addition, the CC-Mixter website—developed by Creative Commons and now administered by ArtisTech Media—remains fully active. CC-Mixter offers a database, searchable using

Google, that is full of Creative Commons-licensed works for the purpose of sampling.[34] "I think Creative Commons is a great concept," says the MPAA attorney Dean Garfield. "Anything that allows authors to disaggregate the bundle of rights that they have is a very good thing. It gives more control to authors and it gives it to them in a way that is very efficient." And as the musicologist Lawrence Ferrara adds, "Creative Commons gives you an enormous database of sounds that enables you to sample, and to contract with that artist through Creative Commons."

On the other side, however, Creative Commons does have its critics. For example, a French copyright holders' association, writing in the *Columbia Journal of Law and the Arts*, issued this warning to creators who might use Creative Commons licenses: "(1) You will not be paid. . . . (2) You cannot both make exclusive deals and grant Creative Commons licenses. . . . (3) You cannot change your mind. . . . (4) You will not receive any help from Creative Commons if the rights you retained are violated."[35] In another article from a law review, Zachary Katz argues that some of the Creative Commons licenses conflict with each other, which raises problems for the creation of derivative works like mash-ups.[36] Other critics maintain that Creative Commons licenses diminish the value of copyrights, or at least fail to empower creators to determine how their music will be used.

For Bill Stafford, it's an economic issue. "I think that it's a good tool for exposure," he says. "I don't think it's a tool by which these writers are going to make a career on, because they're not going to get any money. So for junior artists, baby acts, whatever, I think it's fine. But after a point, I think they need to graduate upward." On a similar note, Peter Jaszi adds: "I don't think any of the existing CC licenses would work very well because they don't involve money, and if what artists want is to get money, and if what other artists want to do is to pay fair money, then it would have to be some different kind of license and not one of the off-the-shelf Creative Commons licenses." Another limitation of Creative Commons as a solution to the problems surrounding sampling is that, as a relatively new organization, Creative Commons is not widely known in the music industry. With few exceptions, most of the music industry representatives and many of the artists we spoke with were unfamiliar with Creative Commons.

For example, when Danny Rubin was asked if he was familiar with licenses offered by the Creative Commons, his response was, simply,

"No." And Michael Hausman—the manager of Aimee Mann, Suzanne Vega, and others—says, "I wish I knew more about them. It seems to me like it's only as good as the music that gets put in there." Some of our interviewees also pointed out that most of the music that is being licensed under a Creative Commons scheme is relatively new. "If you want James Brown," Rubin says, "it's not available through a Creative Commons license, so it doesn't actually solve the problem." And Shoshana Zisk adds, "I think that maybe younger artists right now probably know more about it than the people who are like in their fifties and sixties who don't know how to use the computer and all that."

Regardless of these limitations, Creative Commons can work in harmony with the other policy solutions we have discussed. Strong property rights give copyright holders the power to call the shots—including using a Creative Commons license. And a transaction-facilitating institution like a central clearinghouse (discussed below) could disseminate information about which musical works are subject to which specific version of a Creative Commons license. Thus, Creative Commons licenses can complement other solutions to address any inefficiencies in the sample clearance system, and they can do so without requiring Congress or the courts to change anything. But, even as representatives of Creative Commons acknowledge, it is not a total solution to the problems that plague the sample licensing system.

Negotiation-Free Transactions

Ultimately the sample clearance system is a creature of private industry. Although it operates in the shadow of the federal copyright code as enacted by Congress and the case law on sampling as decided by the federal courts, it is a collection of business transactions. The best policy solution may be an incremental one that accepts a need for licensing samples but makes the process for doing so more efficient. Private-sector solutions might involve record labels offering easy-to-use web interfaces for licensing or copyright holders forming a collective-rights organization to handle sample-licensing transactions as a one-stop shop for samplers. Such developments may hold more promise than statutory or judicial approaches.

There are some promising examples of new business models that license music without negotiations. For example, the online label Magnatune offers its artists' works for many types of licenses, including use in films, ads, TV, and even mash-ups.[37] Other, similar services exist, such as Rumblefish and Pump Audio, recently purchased by Getty Archives. The potential user simply selects criteria from a menu, stating territory, music length, and duration of use, and then clicks a "calculate" button to automatically show the price. This is an efficient system that could generate more licensing through its ease of use and automatic pricing.

But owners' power of negotiation is lost in the process. The power to deny permission has both economic and non-economic benefits: it allows licensors to hold out for the best price and it allows artists to decide how their work will be used. Still, some artists might view the tradeoff of more licenses for less discretion as acceptable and opt in to this type of voluntary system. Or perhaps record labels or publishers can develop a way to limit the samples licensed via the web to uses that were not morally offensive to the artist or the copyright holder. Either way, if it seemed that increased licensing volume would offset the potentially lower, automatic prices for licenses, then record labels might see enough potential profits to adopt such systems.

Transaction-Facilitating Institutions

Despite the theoretical benefits of well-defined property rights, markets are not perfect in practice. Laws, regulations, private entities, customs, and habits have to work together in any market to allow buyers and sellers to confidently engage in exchange. But this can be a messier process than that described by economic theory, and these institutions are not designed perfectly. Confidence in market transactions may break down, transaction costs may thwart some licenses, and accurate information might not reach those who would benefit from market exchanges. These limitations of all markets apply to the market for sample licenses as well.

Throughout this book, we have discussed the difficulties with high fees, burdensome transaction costs, and relationships with industry insiders. These are not the characteristics of a smooth, frictionless market. Even the *Bridgeport* opinion suggested that parties in the music industry may need to come together to set licensing guidelines and standardize prices (within the limits of antitrust law, one assumes).[38] In light of the limitations of markets, scholars of law and economics have celebrated what might be called transaction-facilitating institutions. These are institutions, often private businesses, that grease the wheels of exchange by reducing the transaction costs of each individual licensing deal. The music industry features some of the primary examples that scholars cite: the performance rights organizations (PROS) such as BMI, ASCAP, and SESAC; and the mechanical rights organization set up by the National Music Publishers' Association, the Harry Fox Agency.[39] As the law professor and intellectual property scholar Robert Merges states:

> The history of collective rights organizations such as ASCAP supports the main theoretical point raised earlier: that a property rule for IPRS [intellectual property rights] can be transformed into a voluntary liability rule, in the form of an effective institution to carry out IPR transactions. ASCAP acts as a central depository for members' rights to control public performances of their works. It issues "blanket licenses" covering the relevant copyrights of all members of the society to radio and television stations and other entertainment outlets. It then monitors the songs played and divides up the total receipts among all members on the basis of a complex pro rata formula. Broadcast Music Incorporated (BMI) is a rival organization, founded expressly to compete with ASCAP, which operates similarly. These are only two of the seventy-two music-related collective rights organizations that operate in some 182 countries. Each, to a varying degree, regularizes transactions among holders of strong "property rule" entitlements. In many cases these organizations also establish compensation schemes that operate according to agreed-upon formulas, such as the broadcast-monitoring based system run by ASCAP. These pre-agreed compensation formulae are akin in many ways to statutory compulsory licensing formulae, which is why I call the institutions that administer them instances of a voluntary, or contractual, liability rule.[40]

Merges's point is that some transaction-facilitating institutions take a large group of strong property rights (that have property-rule protection, under copyright law) and require only a single license. Once a user purchases that one group license, each property right effectively becomes subject to liability-rule protection—but voluntarily so, not by government fiat. Skipping the step of permission can, in theory, reduce transaction costs and allow more licenses more easily. Should a PRO-like organization exist to handle sample licenses?[41]

Gummed-Up Transactions

A transaction-facilitating clearinghouse would address specific transaction costs such as how and where to contact copyright holders. Regarding the idea of a hypothetical central clearinghouse, Matt Black states: "I think that could well be a good initiative. Actually contacting rights holders can be very difficult and time consuming and I think anything which would make that easier would probably be a good thing." And Shoshana Zisk tells us, "I think that there are difficult situations where you just can't find who owns the sample and just trying to do that investigative work sometimes makes it difficult—a little bit more inefficient also." Whitney Broussard agrees, saying, "I think that it's a real problem, in a general matter, not just for sampling but for other uses of copyrighted works, that you don't always know who owns stuff."

These comments were in line with the experiences of music librarians, including some at the Library of Congress itself. It has been impossible, difficult, or prohibitively expensive to find the copyright owners of, for example, Mexican folk recordings, old music scores, and rare 78-rpm ethnomusicological recordings.[42] Any institution that provided an up-to-date database of copyrighted works and their various associated copyright holders would improve matters. Inadequate information about who owns what costs everybody money. Pat Shanahan describes a situation in which "extensive searching was done to try to find the current owner. Everything documented and they just disappeared or couldn't find them. The hope would be that especially someone that elusive would be happy to have a windfall at the end of the day rather than just lose out on it completely."

Just as the blanket licenses used by ASCAP and BMI make licensing quicker and easier for radio stations than securing hundreds of individual licenses each day, perhaps some institution could simplify the mechanism for samples. The sheer paperwork involved in clearing multiple samples may be discouraging some transactions. Bill Stafford describes the often-cumbersome nature of the clearance process by explaining that there is a lot of back and forth between all the parties— and a lot of distrust. "People won't even send partially executed licenses now," he says, speaking to this distrust. "They'll send one, one way. And it goes back. Then it gets signed. And it goes back again. And granted, we scan. And we have fax. But it's still just a tremendous amount of back and forth." He says that he would like to see a more streamlined electronic way of attaining licenses.

Another inefficiency in the current system we heard about in our interviews was a lack of published, transparent pricing. Whitney Broussard explains the problem as well as the benefits of a clear menu of sample-license prices:

> It would be ideal if there were some sort of rate sheets or whatever, like in the same sense that if you were going to go in the studio and you were going to record a record and you were going to use a bunch of session musicians. . . . When you're trying to create a business it's very, very important to have a pretty good idea of what your costs are going to be. If you have no idea what your costs are going to be or your costs are unascertainable then you're in for some real problems. You might get lucky and you might not get lucky, but you could end up in a very bad situation.

A transaction-facilitating institution might simplify pricing or at least gather and disseminate prices, thereby providing musicians who sample with more certainty. This might also change copyright holders' attitudes. As Danny Rubin tells us, "Other inefficiencies that trouble me are—and this is just from a personal standpoint—publishers that outright deny uses of their samples, without even consulting their artists, because that's their policy. Where, in certain situations, their artists or their writers could be benefiting from the income of licensing these samples." Transparent pricing in sample licensing would alert some copyright owners to the money they have forgone, perhaps prodding them to license more samples.

How a Central Sample Clearinghouse Might Work

There are many possible roles for a central sample clearinghouse. As Lawrence Ferrara says, "I think there should be a central clearinghouse. . . . A clearinghouse might, on one end of the spectrum, simply disseminate information. On the other hand, at the other end, there might indeed be a clearinghouse that is an adjudicator, an assessor of samples." Thus, as Ferrara notes, not all transaction-facilitating institutions are the same. Some could be as simple as a database of copyright holder's contact information: we call this version an authentication database. Establishing such an institution would represent a small, but perhaps useful, step away from the current system. A much larger change would involve creating an institution for samples that would be similar to BMI or ASCAP. Such an institution would serve as a meeting place for potential sample licensors to set up an electronic commerce platform for licensing or even to work out a standardized pricing structure.[43]

The high cost of setting up a clearinghouse makes some people think that the government would have to mandate the creation of a copyright database, or at least put pressure on private institutions to develop one.[44] Others believe that private institutions can do the job best, or at least develop the appropriate technology. To flesh out some of the details of a hypothetical clearinghouse for samples, Terry Fisher makes an analogy to a recent initiative of a private business, as follows:

> CCC, the Copyright Clearance Center, released a very impressive piece of software and associated deep database that consists of an application—a piece of software that people in businesses or academic communities load onto their computers that enables them whenever they come upon a piece of text, a document they're interested in using in some way, say for example, reproducing and sharing with their colleagues, to very quickly ascertain, with a few clicks of a mouse, its copyright status and more specifically what kinds of uses the copyright owners are going to permit upon what terms. So suppose I come across an article discussing a scientific or artistic or legal topic I'm interested in and I want to share it with my class or send it to a colleague. I click on a button in this application and it connects to a database under the control of the CCC and it tells me, "Sure, you can do the following things for free or you can do the following things by paying this amount of money, which the copyright owner has selected."

What about a more comprehensive model, where the clearinghouse actually gets involved in the licensing transaction? Hank Shocklee sketches out how a system for samples based on the PRO model might work:

> I think that people really want to clear these things, but once again who do you go to? I think if there was a better system in place, [you would know] who the contact people were and if this system was 100 percent foolproof, almost like a BMI. You know that when you fill out a BMI form, whenever your record is played there's people that just send money to BMI. So there

could be just an arbitrary figure, just because I'm playing records, that I'm going to spend $2.00 per record, whatever the case may be, for clearances. Well, that situation, even if it was something like that, the money will go into a pot and it will be doled out to the original writers. That would be a better, at least an attempt at a better system than what we have today. Because right now it's a go for yourself, anything goes, wild, wild west kind of a situation when it comes to sampling.

This kind of clearinghouse would do more than provide information; it would handle the flow of money between samplers and copyright owners. It would therefore require a formula for how the money would be distributed to the copyright holders. It might also develop standards for which samples could be used without charge. Lawrence Ferrara explains how this might work in practice:

> You [would] need to basically have musicologists work with music technologists in figuring out what a standard would be for *de minimis*, based on the technology and the musicology. I think that what needs to be done, in terms of sampling and copyright law, is that musicologists who are analysts—music theorists in particular, as a subcategory of musicology—need to get together with the music technologists, and they need to set standards and basically say, "Three notes," or, "This particular kind of sound," and so forth, a wood block sound for a second, that's simply a *de minimis* taking, if you will. . . . There's never going to be, by the way, a bright line. There isn't a bright line in terms of underlying composition either.

In the end, some of the logistical hurdles with a central sample clearinghouse might persist. But a transaction-facilitating institution might provide samplers with information about who to call. It might create an easier path to negotiate licenses—or at least let sampling musicians know quickly that permission will be denied.

Attributes and Critiques of Transaction-Facilitating Institutions

The music manager Michael Hausman sees the authentication database as the most appealing version of the transaction-facilitating institution: "That seems like a good idea. I wouldn't necessarily see it as an agency that would actually do the clearing but that it could sort of act like a master database of recorded music so you would know who the rights owners are and you would know where to go to get the clearance. There might also be information on there about whether it's clearable at all. Whether it's ever been cleared. Whether they're interested in being sampled. And maybe you could have some information about what types of samples might be allowable. I think that's a great idea." Hausman's comments suggest that an authentication database could level the playing field. With access to such information, it would matter less whether an artist was affiliated with a major label or an independent one. Musicians would have a better chance to find out who was interested in being sampled and who was not, with fewer unfortunate surprises after recording.

Andrew Bart, on the other hand, advocates an institution that operates more like a PRO: "The only way that it would make sense to have a central clearinghouse, if you believe in this value system, is to act in the—basically in the role of a Harry Fox Agency and to clear samples the way that they clear mechanical licenses." But Danny Rubin questions this PRO-style approach: "How would the one, central clearinghouse have access to all of the information on all the different songs and the artists and writers? I think there has to be competition in order for these clearinghouses to be able to put forth the effort and the resources to find this material. If there was only one central clearinghouse, there would be really no incentive to find all this stuff. . . . Let's say I was the only clearinghouse out there. What would motivate me to work harder to get your clearances faster and at a lower rate if I had no competition?" Dina LaPolt expresses related doubts about a clearinghouse that functions like a PRO. "Who's going to fund that?" she asks. "Every record company and publisher has millions of copyrights. What are we going to have one central database where everybody reports to? We can't even do that for public performance. It's a pipe dream, but it would be nice." Competition among the PROS was one positive attribute described in the essay by Robert Merges cited above. Radio stations have to acquire three blanket licenses, not just one, to get permission to play most songs on the air.[45] So there is a tradeoff between the convenience of one-stop shopping and the dynamic benefits of competition among clearinghouses.

Espousing a different concern about a central clearinghouse for samples, Peter Jaszi explains the pitfalls for sampling musicians of abandoning fair use and relying on licensing alone:

I have one concern about both collective and compulsory licensing solutions, and it is that they extinguish the use rights that now exist under fair use. In other words, the surest way to make certain that the fair use doctrine is not going to evolve in this context as it has in so many others would be to create a comprehensive system for either voluntary collective or compulsory licensing. And this is a dilemma that comes up in many different areas. For instance, in the area of education, clearly, educators have fair use rights. Clearly, the fair use rights of educators are pretty substantial, and clearly, educators are uncertain about the contours of those rights. And what content owners through their organizations are basically saying to educators is, "Look, why worry? Why fuss with the question of whether you're entitled to do something? Just pay us, or have your institution pay us so much a year, and you can use all the content you want." Well, it's a very attractive solution—blanket licensing by institutions to cover educational use. Is it a healthy solution? I'm not so sure. So, I have a philosophical concern.

Despite being an affirmative defense, fair use represents a right of the public and of musicians who wish to sample. Giving up on that right because licensing is more practical in the short term could cost sampling musicians more licensing-fee money than they need to pay under the law while undermining the possibility of making fair use more practical in the long term.

The clearinghouse solution, especially the PRO-style version, faces many practical barriers. To the extent that an institution like a PRO for samples became involved in setting prices and adjudicating disputes over prices, it might represent too great a sacrifice of copyright holders' current discretion over their compositions and sound recordings. Under some of the stronger versions of this idea, copyright holders would be giving up their ability to deny permission, name their own price, and make decisions about each potential licensee individually. Many copyright holders, including some we interviewed, would hesitate to give up control. This may explain why no PRO-style clearinghouse for samples exists already.

Other practical problems involve funding and logistics. One proposal to fund a clearinghouse would be to charge a certain fraction of every licensing fee—but this would get the clearinghouse involved in each license (rather than just maintaining a database). But funding isn't the only administrative hurdle. Some copyrights would be difficult even for the copyright holders to verify. And since many samples infringe both the sound recording copyright and the musical composition copyright, every record label and every publisher would have to participate in this one organization—an unprecedented level of coordination in the music industry.

An Authentication Database:
Facilitating Transactions, but Modestly

Both the preceding critiques and the practical difficulties make an institution that functions like a PRO seem controversial, unlikely, and—for a number of stakeholders—undesirable. An authentication database, on the other hand, seems quite appealing. An authentication database would have fewer potential benefits than a PRO-style institution but would also carry fewer costs. A centralized, searchable database, managed by a disinterested party, would contain the names and current contact information of the musical composition and sound recording copyright holders in as many songs as possible. We think an authentication database would greatly reduce inefficiencies in tracking down and seeking permission. The existence of collaborative online software and open-source database technologies could propel this notion forward in the future. Finding a way to finance the authentication database presents an obstacle, but not an insurmountable one. User fees and value-added features could generate revenue to cover the costs.

The benefits of such a database could extend beyond sampling, after all, to other uses made possible by new technologies, such as ringtones for cell phones. The database need only provide information to would-be samplers about who they must request a license from. This approach would leave untouched the issue of copyright holders' control over their songs. Perhaps that is a downside for those who dislike the status quo on that front. But it is an upside for those who value the benefits of that control; and, if successful, the database could mature into a more active transaction-facilitating institution. An augmented form of an authentication database might offer copyright holders the option to publish prices (perhaps a menu of prices that vary based on what's sampled) or some indicator of their willingness to license. But this further push, encouraging copyright holders to license, need not be part of the concept at the beginning, or at all.

In short, an authentication database may provide the best hope among solutions that seek to facilitate transactions. It could grease the wheels of the sample clearance system, but it would not reallocate the basic rights that various music-industry stakeholders currently have. It could generate licensing revenue, increase the amount of music released, and respect the interests of copyright holders. While laborious to set up, the expense is not overly burdensome and could be financed through per-transaction fees on the sampler side.

As we stated at the outset of this chapter, many of the reforms we have discussed are not mutually exclusive. Different reforms will target distinct aspects of the problems in the sample clearance system. Musicians seeking to use multiple samples per track would benefit from both a *de minimis* threshold for sound recordings and a more established notion of transformative use under the fair use doctrine. An authentication database could coexist with an expansion or clarification of non-infringing uses, which would open up sample licensing to more musicians on independent labels. Because the music industry is a creature of both copyright law and private industry, the best approach to the sample clearance system's shortcomings is a set of legal and business reforms that will complement each other. Again, we recognize that this is no easy task.

CONCLUSION

It's no longer just about music sampling. It's about movie clips,
it's about YouTube, and it's about all of these new vehicles that we have.
I mean, I've got stuff on my phone that's unbelievable.
—T. S. MONK

In many cases, sound collage creates something new and interesting from its constituent parts. At the same time, the original composition was written by someone other than the collage artist, and yet another person may have created the sampled sound recording—such as the Isley Brothers covering a Lennon and McCartney song, or the Beatles performing the Isleys' "Twist and Shout" on one of the Fab Four's early albums. All of these stakeholders brought something of value into the world, and—from a creative perspective, at least—the more art in existence, the better (even if not all of it is brilliant). However, artists who have been sampled might think differently about this proposition, especially if they hear their musical work in a context that disturbs them.

How can these conflicts be resolved? And, from a legal perspective, which of the competing claims is likely to succeed? Because the sampled musicians' creations came first, it would seem that copyright law would dictate that their interests trump those of the sampling musician. Unless a limitation, exception, or defense applies, the rights they enjoy in the composition and sound recording will also apply to a sample of that composition and sound recording. If they wish to license the sample, they can name their price (as high as they want) and they may also deny permission entirely. But wait—what if a limitation, exception, or defense *does* apply? After all, nothing in copyright law says that these factors apply only in limited situations; indeed, they might apply frequently. At this point, we hand off the sampling quandary to the music business, with its informal and formal practices that guide its decisions. From our research, we know what their answer will be regarding copyright limitations: the default setting is total protection for samples.

As we have demonstrated, individuals and organizations within the mainstream music industry typically ignore the existence of fair use, the *de minimis* threshold, and other exceptions to copyright protection. So, in order to participate in the commercial system, they contend, sampling musicians must license everything. This book makes clear the harmful consequences that can result: exorbitant licensing fees, recalcitrant copyright holders, high transaction costs, royalty stacking that makes tracks with multiple samples nearly impossible to release, and so on. We have also discussed a number of proposals for reform, many of them fairly incremental and modest. Some of the more sweeping proposals we discussed (such as a government-mandated compulsory license for samples) are not realistic, politically or practically, at the moment. But that doesn't mean we should simply embrace the status quo and give up with a complacent shrug.

A THOUGHT EXPERIMENT

Some roadblocks caused by copyright law seem to call for stronger medicine and require us to ignore conventional thinking in order to find ways out of the impasse. For example, take Ezra Pound's complaints about copyright during the early twentieth century. The law professor Robert Spoo documents that, toward the end of the First World War, this influential modernist poet and literary editor decried the protectionism of United States copyright law, which disadvantaged foreign authors at the hands of copycat publishers. Instead of copyright terms for a limited amount of time—subject to various formalities— Pound favored a strong copyright of perpetual duration and few formalities, which authors could claim regardless of national origin. In one important way, it seems counterintuitive that Pound wanted to use copyright to perpetually lock up culture from the past. After all, he had a significant hand in editing T. S. Eliot's *The Waste Land*—a poem that appropriated heavily from earlier literary texts that had passed into the public domain or were written before copyright law existed.

However, Pound's maximalist proposal included three major limitations—in the form of compulsory licenses. First, an author's heirs need to keep the book in print; if they don't respond to requests for licenses within a reasonable time, they forfeit their rights. Second, foreign authors must publish in a country within a reasonable amount of time or they forfeit their copyright in that jurisdiction. Third, once a book makes it big, rival publishers can offer an inexpensive version for the masses in return for a fixed royalty paid to the author.[1] "Pound passionately believed that communication should not be hampered by the monopoly power that copyrights confer," Spoo writes. "Yet he did not feel that the work of dissemination could be left to an unfettered public domain, because he believed that authors and their heirs were entitled to remuneration for as long as works remained of interest to the public, and he worried that the expiration of copyrights created unequal competition between past and present writers."[2] This position was likely influenced by the fact that Pound saw his modernist peers—already commercially hampered by their challenging ideas and writing styles—struggling to compete with the older, cheaper, and therefore more accessible books that had fallen into the public domain.

Pound was also concerned with the way that copyright law can be used to block access to the past. For instance, copyright holders often do let books go out of print when they are still under copyright, and it is not unusual for publishers (then and now) to deny permission to those who want to give an orphan work a new home—at a press that wants to publish that work. Copyright law gives publishers the power to squash translations, even if no other translations exist in a domestic marketplace. Pound felt these denials made it harder to commune with the past while also preventing intercultural exchanges that flow between languages and nations. "It is not hard to see that what Pound initially characterizes as perpetual protection for authors' intellectual labor is essentially a scheme for maximizing the availability of works and translations," Spoo writes. "In the end, Pound seems more interested in supplying the market with affordable books than with increasing protections for authors. His is a rare kind of copyright proposal: a consumer-side scheme couched in a plea for creators' rights."[3] Implicit in Pound's proposal for copyright reform is a theory of communication that values the free transmission of culture across national boundaries and across time.

We see little merit in the idea of perpetual copyright, and we actually favor putting some burdens on copyright holders in terms of formal requirements like requiring registration.[4] But we find Pound's proposal illustrative for two key reasons. First, it underscores the importance of the creative community having a say in copyright policy by advocating for their own interests. This echoes what the law professor and fair use expert Peter Jazsi says when advocating for the kind of community-created best practices in fair use that he has helped facilitate. "Fair use is far too important to be left to the lawyers," he tells us. "These days, one practice community after another is coming together to define their own best practices around the issues that concern them most." The hip-hop producer El-P agrees by emphasizing, "To me, it's in the hands of the musicians. Resolving these issues is not going to be done with the lawyers. . . . It's going to have to involve the musicians."

Second, Pound's proposal reminds us that copyright, at a fundamental level, is designed; there is nothing inherently natural or essential about how copyright law currently regulates culture. We make choices about the architecture of copyright law that influence how the music business engages in commerce. Conversely, business practices profoundly affect the how the law is written, especially in an age when industry lobbies have a strong hand in drafting legislation put forward by Congress. In this way, copyright law is socially constructed and also powerfully shaped by political and economic interests. With this in mind, what if we thought differently about samples (and artistic appropriation, more generally) in a way that allowed us to redesign copyright's rules?

From there, we can proceed with our thought experiment, which contains a proposal that is probably more radical than modest. Recall from chapter 7 the discussion about property rules and liability rules, which are different methods used to protect copyright holders' interests in samples. Copyright usually involves property-rule protection, in which the owner has the right to name a selling price or deny a use (which is currently the rule for musical samples). But copyright law also includes some liability rules—namely in the form of compulsory licenses, like the mechanical license that facilitates the recording of cover versions. With this very important liability rule, musicians who want to reinterpret someone else's song neither have to obtain permission from the rights holder nor negotiate a fee because the government sets an affordable rate.

Without this compulsory license, the robust tradition of cover songs that has been sustained for over a century surely wouldn't have flowered, perhaps for similar reasons that ended sampling's golden age. Today we use email and fax machines to negotiate deals, transmit paperwork, and sign contracts. These changes, however, still haven't significantly reduced the friction caused by haggling over the right to sample parts of individual songs. In the absence of these communication technologies, and without a compulsory license, imagine how difficult it would have been for Ella Fitzgerald or her record company to secure the rights to record, say, a Cole Porter song (especially if every cover song required an individual negotiation). Because much of the recording industry was built on the distribution of cover songs, it may never have grown to be the juggernaut it is today if Congress had not changed the copyright statute in 1909. Substantial financial rewards can come from giving up some control, in the form of liability rules. This is a lesson the music industry might want to contemplate as it struggles to adjust to new technologies.

The choice between property rules and liability rules is one way to describe familiar debates about how to design copyright protection. But there is another dimension to copyright law's design—who gets the entitlement to sample in the first place? Who will start out with the right to do what they want: the copyright owner whose work has been sampled and who wants to deny permission or demand a fee, or the artist who did the sampling? Copyright law makes a choice about who has what rights as a default and then leaves people to reach private agreements (or not) based on the rights the law has assigned them.

The choice over two possible recipients of the entitlement to do as they wish (the owner of the sampled work and the sampler) and two possible ways to protect that entitlement (property rule and liability rule) generates four options.[5] First, we have property-rule protection for sampled musicians, the current regime. Second, we have liability-rule protection for sampled musicians—that is, a compulsory license for samples similar to that for cover versions. Third, we have property-rule protection for sampling musicians, which amounts to saying that all samples fall below the *de minimis* threshold and thus do not constitute infringement. (Such a rule would require a definition of "sample" to avoid undermining copyright in whole compositions and whole sound recordings entirely.) Fourth, we have the "reverse liability rule," which is the most counterintuitive option because it has no analogue in copyright law. Under this rule, musicians are entitled to sample as a default, but this entitlement is subject to the right of the sampled copyright holders to stop them in return for a statutory fee.

An illustration might help explain the reverse liability rule and how it differs from the other three rules. Imagine a conflict between a factory that releases pollution into the air and a nearby town whose inhabitants desire to breathe clean air. The law could give the townspeople the right to clean air (rule 1); give the townspeople the right to clean air, but allow the factory to pollute so long as it pays a government-specified fee akin to a civil fine (rule 2); grant the factory the right to pollute as much as it wants (rule 3); or—and this is rule 4, the reverse liability rule—the law could give the factory only liability-rule protection over the right to pollute. Under this rule, so long as the townspeople paid whatever fee the government specified, they could have clean air. The factory would have no say-so. But the townspeople would compensate the factory for shutting down its harmful activities.

Many of us might prefer rule 1—the right to clean air. Rule 4 is unfamiliar but you might imagine how it could work in certain contexts—for example, a community would raise money to stop or reduce pollution by the local factory. Imagine the United States before environmental regulation; citizens at that time usually lived under rule 3. Thus, either rule 2 or rule 4 would be preferable from the perspective of townspeople living next to factories. Any rule has advantages and drawbacks and affects parties differently. The key is to make explicit the fact that the law chooses who has the entitlement to use the air and how that entitlement will be protected.

Returning to our thought experiment for the music industry, artists who sample are in the position of the factory, and the copyright owners whose works are sampled are like the townspeople. Instead of preventing pollution in the air, owners may want to keep certain sample-based works off the air. We do not mean this analogy as a commentary on the morality of artists who sample; indeed, throughout this book we have emphasized the legitimate interests on both sides of sampling controversies. Our point is that—although it is unfamiliar—we can imagine a world in which the law gives artists who sample an entitlement to sample what they wish, yet be subject to the right of copyright owners to pay them a government-specified fee to stop them.

The aspiration of a reverse liability rule would be to flip the default assumption about the way samples are subject to copyright protection. Copyright law would deem musical collage valuable and signal that musicians should expect others to remix their work. This seems like a realistic perspective, given that once a creative work enters the public sphere, the original author cannot realistically control most of what people will do with it. (French literary theorists such as Roland Barthes settled that question decades before kids began mashing things up on YouTube.) Under a reverse liability rule, if copyright owners were content to allow a sample, nothing would happen. But if it were economically, ethically, or aesthetically important to a composition or sound recording copyright holder to stop another artist from sampling his or her work, then he or she could pay a modest fee to prevent the sample. Copyright owners' blocking rights would be subject to fair use, however, in order to protect parodies and other transformative uses.

For example, if the copyright owners of the Turtles' compositions or sound recordings wanted to stop De La Soul from sampling a Turtles song, then the copyright owners could pay to block De La Soul's use. Perhaps that price would be worth it to the Turtles in order to protect the market value of their hit songs from the sixties or to express their disdain for hip-hop. If the owners sought to exercise that option, De La Soul could either claim fair use or try to negotiate a voluntary license in return for the owners forgoing their blocking rights. Thus, the legal default would not change to such an extreme that all sampling would be free. Some samples could be blocked, for a price. But the baseline understanding of copyright *would* change in a way favorable to sampling.

The reverse liability rule could be placed within a larger scheme, applying only to samples of a certain length. There could be a sliding scale of how strongly the law protected samples of copyrighted compositions and sound recordings: brief samples would get no protection, medium-length samples would get the protection of reverse liability rule, and longer samples would get the strong protection of a property rule. Thus, the liability rule and reverse liability rule choice might apply only to samples above a *de minimis* threshold (measured quantitatively, say, at one second) and below some upper threshold (say, three or four seconds) that represented the boundary for samples long enough to still require a negotiated license. Artists making sound collages using brief or medium-length samples, as in Public Enemy's work from the late 1980s, could benefit greatly from this change. But the licensing system would stay the same for artists using large, prominent samples that are unlikely to constitute fair use. For example, the long sample of the Police's "Every Breath You Take" used in P. Diddy's song "I'll Be Missing You" would probably still require a voluntary, negotiated license.

In light of the inefficiencies of the current sample clearance system, property-rule protection for sampled musicians has obvious flaws. Assume for the moment that society was prepared to move away from that approach. What options are left? Liability-rule protection for sampled musicians—a compulsory license—takes away their control, that is, their right to deny permission to sample. We learned from our interviewees that discretion can be worth as much or more than licensing revenue. Property-rule protection for sampling musicians would leave the sampled musicians with nothing—neither control nor compensation.

So why not give copyright owners a choice? When a particular work is first released, the copyright owner could choose between a compulsory license (rule 2) and a reverse liability rule (rule 4).[6] With a compulsory license, copyright holders would receive an entitlement in samples and the right to get paid, but no authority to block samples. With the reverse liability rule, the copyright owner would let other musicians have the default entitlement to sample them while retaining the right to pay a fee to squelch tracks that sample their works.[7] Copyright owners would still enjoy two kinds of autonomy under this plan: the right to choose which rule they want and, under the reverse liability rule, the right to control the context in which their music is sampled. Although many musicians do not retain the copyrights in their work, this autonomy would still benefit those who had negotiated for control over this choice in their recording and publishing contracts.

To avoid unfairness and the potential for abuse, we envision the fee under the reverse liability rule being paid to the government rather than to the sampler. This would deter those who would sample a famous musician for an easy payday. The fee of the reverse liability rule could be relatively affordable (maybe $200). The total amount payable each year would have a cap (say, $1,000), at which point copyright owners could block any further samples for free for the rest of the year. Perhaps the government could use the revenue to fund the authentication database. Or perhaps the revenue should fund the National Endowment for the Arts, on the rationale that blocking one work of art — a musical collage — calls for compensation to the public in the form of supporting some other work of art. Alternatively, instead of cash the copyright holder could give up other rights. For instance, obtaining the right to block samples might require accepting a reduction in the copyright term. Under this approach, if Prince (for example) wished to prevent sampling of his music of which he owns the copyrights, he would have to accept that his copyrights would expire after, say, twenty-eight years, instead of lasting until seventy years after his death.

Our suggestions recognize a simple social fact: people like to quote, remix, and play with words, ideas, sounds, and images, and this has been true in one way or another throughout human history. Sampling software tools merely extend this impulse into other media, and numerous websites now allow people to share their remixes with ease. This desire to borrow and share is not going away, and the technologies that enable this practice are becoming more robust and more widely available on a daily basis. Forcing the law to acknowledge these cultural, technological, and historical realities would cultivate a set of rules that make more sense for the majority of amateur creators, and for a growing number of professional ones. As we suggested earlier, a fair deal means that everyone walks away a little unsatisfied, but the alternative would be to further criminalize these increasingly commonplace activities.

We have concluded with this discussion not for the sake of advocating it as a particular plan—for it is far from perfect—but rather as a reminder that we as a society *design* copyright law. Choices about copyright law can shape or feed into business and creative practices, as we have demonstrated in this book. Just the same, copyright law responds (or should respond) to business and social realities. The process for sample licensing that has developed over the past two decades has led to an ad hoc system. The modern system is unable to handle tracks featuring multiple samples like the dense collages of sampling's golden age. Even though the sample clearance system protects copyright owners, it can be so complicated, inefficient, and unpredictable that it inhibits the circulation and creation of new sample-based music (even if the artists who originally composed and recorded a song have no problem with someone else remixing it).

The sample clearance system is a microcosm of not just the music industry but also the various entertainment industries that dominate today's media landscape. George Clinton, when discussing the fact that many producers sampled from his Parliament-Funkadelic records, told us that "funk is the DNA of hip-hop." One can say that sampled musical phrases are a type of genetic material woven into a lot of new music. And just as samples are the DNA of collaged compositions, songs are among the most ubiquitous elements found in television shows, movies, videogames, user-generated online content, and practically any other kind of media currently being produced. This is why we think everyone should care about the particular case of sampling, because the same dynamics that create problems for musical remixers reverberate throughout all culture industries.

The disputes that have arisen over sampling implicate many issues of broad importance, such as achieving creativity within economic and legal constraints; artistic control and moral rights; appropriation and sequential innovation; fair compensation for intellectual property; and freedom of expression. It would be tragic if some of the best-loved types of music remain impossible to release widely, and it would be equally tragic if the only solution to this problem were to further remove control from artists. Throughout the history of the recording industry, musicians have traditionally been powerless to enforce or benefit from their rights without first signing away full rights or percentages of revenue in recording contracts. We understand that controlling one's copyright can be an important labor issue for artists, and it shouldn't be taken lightly.

In this book we have taken an approach to the problems of sample licensing that follows the Nobel Prize–winning economist Ronald Coase's call for interdisciplinary collaboration. These complex issues call for approaches that pay close attention to history, culture, technology, media, law, and economy. Also required is empirical research that involves talking to people who have a direct stake in these matters. As pressure grows on the existing system, we urge policy makers, the creative community, and the public to consider reforms both incremental and daring. We need a combination of initiatives to confront the ways that the law has not yet caught up with contemporary creative practices — or, for that matter, very old creative practices. Sampling is but one incarnation of the sorts of social exchanges that are defining the experience of being human in the twenty-first century. If we don't address the impasse between samplers and samplees, it will be to everyone's detriment that the law and the practice of everyday life will increasingly diverge.

APPENDIX I

Interviewee List

The following is a list of interviewees we spoke with who were either directly quoted in this book, or whose insights helped shape our analysis. The interviewees appear in alphabetical order by last name, except for artists who are obviously using a pseudonym; in those cases we alphabetized the names by the first letter.

ARTISTS

Steve Albini, recording engineer
   and musician
Aesop Rock
Big Gipp, Goodie Mob
Craig Baldwin, collage filmmaker
Vicki Bennett, People Like Us
Matt Black, Coldcut
David Byrne
Cappadonna, Wu-Tang Clan
Cee-Lo, Gnarls Barkley and Goodie
   Mob
George Clinton, Parliament-
   Funkadelic
Chuck D, Public Enemy
Wayne Coyne, Flaming Lips

Drew Daniel, Matmos
DJ Abilities, Eyedea & Abilities
DJ Kool Herc
DJ Muggs, Cypress Hill
DJ Qbert, Invisibl Skratch Piklz
DJ Premier, Gang Starr
DJ Vadim
Lloyd Dunn, the Tape-beatles
Ian Edgar, Eclectic Method
El-P
Flaggs, Land of Da Lost
Geoff Gamlen, Eclectic Method
Bobbito Garcia
Gregg Gillis, a.k.a. Girl Talk
Guru, Gang Starr

Miho Hatori, Cibo Matto
John Heck, the Tape-beatles
Hell Razah, Sunz of Man
Mark Hosler, Negativland
Wyclef Jean, The Fugees
Don Joyce, Negativland
Kid 606
Killah Priest, Wu-Tang Clan
Kool Keith
Lady Miss Kier, Deee-lite
Tim Love
MC Eiht
MC Eyedea, Eyedea & Abilities
MC Lyte
Richard McGuire, Liquid Liquid
Meen Green
Method Man, Wu-Tang Clan
Paul Miller, a.k.a. DJ Spooky
Mix Master Mike, Invisibl Skratch Piklz and the Beastie Boys
T. S. Monk
Thurston Moore, Sonic Youth
Mr. Dibbs
Mr. Len
Mr. Lif
Lou Nutt, Land of Da Lost
Yoko Ono
Pam the Funkstress, The Coup
Pasemaster Mase, De La Soul

Pete Rock
Posdnuos, De La Soul
Pras, The Fugees
Prefuse 73
Tim Quirk, Wonderlick and Too Much Joy
Lee Ranaldo, Sonic Youth
Ras Kass
Redman
Boots Riley, The Coup
RJD2
RZA, Wu-Tang Clan
Sage Francis
Scanner
M. C. Schmidt, Matmos
Shock G, Digital Underground
Hank Shocklee, Public Enemy
Steinski, Double Dee & Steinski
Clyde Stubblefield, The James Brown Band
T La Rock
TradeMark Gunderson, Evolution Control Committee
Trugoy, De La Soul
Twick, graffiti artist
Voodoo
Saul Williams
Jonny Wilson, Eclectic Method
Wobbly

ENTERTAINMENT LAWYERS AND RECORDING INDUSTRY EXECUTIVES

Eothen Alapatt, Stones Throw Records
Andrew Bart, entertainment lawyer
Anthony Berman, music lawyer
Whitney Broussard, music lawyer
Philo Farnsworth, Illegal Art label founder
Ken Freundlich, music lawyer

Dean Garfield, vice president of anti-piracy, Motion Picture Association of America

Mia Garlick, former general counsel of Creative Commons

Michael Hausman, music manager (Suzanne Vega, Aimee Mann)

Kyambo "Hip Hop" Joshua, member of Kanye West management team

Mark Kates, formerly of Grand Royal Records

Dina LaPolt, music lawyer (clients include Tupac's estate)

Walter McDonough, music lawyer, Future of Music Coalition cofounder and general counsel

Neeru Paharia, Creative Commons

Rick Prelinger, Prelinger Archives

Danny Rubin, sample clearance expert

Pat Shanahan, sample clearance expert

Tom Silverman, CEO of Tommy Boy Records

Bill Stafford, publisher-side clearance expert

Brian Zisk, entrepreneur, Future of Music Coalition cofounder and technology director

Shoshana Zisk, music lawyer

SCHOLARS AND JOURNALISTS

Harry Allen, hip-hop activist and media assassin

Raquel Cepeda, journalist and hip-hop historian

Jeff Chang, journalist and hip-hop historian

Joanna Demers, musicologist at the University of Southern California

Lawrence Ferrara, musicologist at New York University and sampling expert witness

William W. "Terry" Fisher, Professor of Law, Harvard University

Jane Ginsburg, Professor of Law, Columbia University

Peter Jaszi, Professor of Law, Washington College of Law, American University

Lawrence Lessig, Professor of Law, Harvard University

Carrie McLaren, *Stay Free!* Magazine editor and Illegal Art Show curator

David Sanjek, director of the Popular Music Research Centre, University of Salford

Joe Schloss, ethnomusicologist at New York University

Greg Tate, journalist and music historian

Siva Vaidhyanathan, media studies scholar at the University of Virginia

APPENDIX 2

Interview Questions

QUESTIONS FOR LAWYERS, RECORD EXECUTIVES, AND OTHER PEOPLE WHO WEAR SUITS

General Matters

(1) In your experience in the music industry, in what ways have you encountered the sample clearance process? Which end of the licensing process have you been on?

Licensing Samples and the Sample Clearinghouses

(2) Can you briefly walk me through how musicians obtain clearance to use samples?

    Probe: (2A) How has the process changed over time, specifically in response to court decisions like *Grand Upright* back in 1991 or *Bridgeport* in 2005?

(3) Who decides, and how is it decided, what samples to clear and what samples to take a chance on getting through undetected?

    Probes: (3A) Does sample clearance usually happen before composing? Before recording? Before releasing the record?

    (3B) How often have you seen samples get cleared after the record is released, and what problems did it cause?

(4) How does the process of licensing a sample differ between a major-label artist obtaining a clearance versus an independent artist?

(5) Many samples require at least two clearances—from the sound recording copyright holder and the musical composition copyright holder. How does the sample clearance process differ between these two types of copyrights?

> *Probe*: (5A) How often are each of those copyrights themselves divided among multiple parties? In other words, how often are *more* than two clearances necessary for one sample?

(6) Under what circumstances would a sample clearinghouse be used?

Creative Issues

(7) Do you believe that the establishment of the sample licensing process has affected the way artists and producers use samples, especially when you compare it to the late 1980s?

> *Probe*: (7A) Have those changes been positive, negative, some of both, or neutral, in your view, with respect to the quality or integrity of the music?

(8) Has an artist you've worked with ever substituted one sample for another—or changed a composition or recording in another way—because of the expense or difficulty of licensing a sample?

(9) Do you think tighter restrictions on sampling ever led an artist you've worked with to: (i) hire session musicians to do "replays," (ii) make different kinds of works, perhaps different styles or genres, (iii) not release certain songs or albums, (iv) release certain songs or albums noncommercially, e.g. for free Internet download or file sharing, (v) refocus his or her activities away from composing and recording toward touring or other things?

Business Issues

(10) What costs are involved with the current sample clearance system?

> *Probes*: (10A) What types of transaction costs are involved, such as sample clearance fees, lawyers' or record executives' time?
>
> (10B) What business costs are associated with sample clearance, such as those associated with increased studio time or delaying the release of an album while waiting for a clearance to come through?
>
> (10C) What percentage of the album budget would you estimate goes to sample licensing costs?

(11) Do the licensing fees from samples provide meaningful income to record companies and publishers?

> *Probe*: (11A) If not, what do record companies and publishers gain from the current sample clearance system?

Copyright Law

(12) With respect to samples, does copyright law strike the right balance between circulation and compensation?

(13) What about the role of fair use?
  Probes: (13A) Have you ever worked with an artist who sampled without permission under the belief that they were making fair use of copyrighted material?
  (13B) Should more artists take advantage of fair use?
  (13C) Example?

(14) If sampling were made automatically permissible, without the need to acquire a license, do you think artists would sample more, less, or just as often as they do now?
  Probe: (14A) Do you think the fact that sampling without permission is illegal, and therefore transgressive, makes it more attractive to musicians?

(15) There are two extreme myths about how sampling fees impact the sampled artists. Some people have said George Clinton received more money in the 1990s from licensing than any other period in his career, and others say that artists almost never see money because of bad record contracts. Where does the truth lie between these two myths?
  Probe:(15A) Can you think of any examples?

(16) Originally, copyright protected entire works, and the protection for pieces of those works was more ambiguous. Now, Congress and the courts have made it clear that samples are protected. What is the rationale for putting samples under copyright?
  Probes: (16A) Do you think protecting samples under copyright is justified or necessary?
  (16B) Does copyright protect samples from a musician's work to protect a meaningful income stream from licensing fees? Is that a good reason?
  (16C) Or does copyright protect samples because musicians have a right to protect the integrity of their work—to prevent it from being altered or put in a context they don't approve of? Is that a good reason?

Litigation

(17) Sometimes, during litigation, ProTools or other similar software files are subpoenaed. If someone took a sample and their ProTools files were opened, would it be possible to prove that the sample was taken from a particular record?

Probe: (17A) What technology is available to compare samples to the original recording where they might have come from?

Policy Solutions

(18) Does the sample clearance system need to become more efficient?
  Probes: (18A) What inefficiencies in the system are most troubling to you?
  (18B) What perpetuates these inefficiencies?

(19) Are you familiar with the licenses offered by Creative Commons? [If yes, the probes]
  Probes: (19A) Do those licenses present a viable alternative for commercial musicians who are releasing music?
  (19B) Do you think the artists you've worked with could create sample-based music by using only material released under a Creative Commons license?

(20) How would you improve the sample clearance system?
  Probes: (20A) Should there be just one central clearinghouse for samples, so that information about the owners of copyrights and their stance on sampling were easier to obtain?
  (20B) What if artists were presented with a "menu" of sampling options, with different prices for different kinds of samples, so that prices could be more standardized and known ahead of time?
  (20C) Would you be interested in a "compulsory licensing" system in which, for instance, you would fill out a simple one-page form indicating the recordings you sampled, and a portion of the proceeds would be distributed to the copyright holders for those sampled recordings?

Thanks. [*end interview*]

QUESTIONS FOR ARTISTS AND PRODUCERS

The Art and History

(1) Do you use samples in your work? [If yes, proceed to question (2). If no, skip to question (4)]

(2) When was the first time you remember hearing a sample from one song in another song?
  Probes: (2A) Can you give an example of an excellent use of a sample in someone else's record?
  (2B) What is special about how that sample is used?

(3) What are your favorite examples of ways you've included samples in your work?

(4) Have other artists sampled your work?

(5) Do you approve or disapprove of how other artists have used your work in samples or quotations?

(6) Can you explain what makes one use of a sample creative and interesting to you, and another use of a sample uncreative?

(7) Why has sampling been so important to hip-hop?
    Probe: (7A) Do you have any favorite artists who sample or a favorite time
      period for sample-based music?

Technical Questions

[If respondent answered yes to question (1), proceed to question (8). If no, skip to question (11)]

(8) What is the equipment you use and what steps do you have to go through to go from sampling an LP or CD to placing a fragment into a new song?

(9) Can you explain some techniques producers use to transform samples and make them unrecognizable?
    Probes: (9A) What's the point of making a sample unrecognizable?
    (9B) What do you gain by transforming a sample so much?
    (9C) Do you lose anything by making a sample unrecognizable?

(10) How have your equipment and sampling technology changed over the years?
    Probes: (10A) Have you encountered any technical difficulties when sampling
      from digital files?
    (10B) Has digital rights management, or DRM, such as the DRM on iTunes
      files, ever prevented you from experimenting with samples from a piece
      of music?

(11) When you select a portion of a sound recording that you want to sample, what software programs and hardware are available that enable you to isolate one sound from the other sounds going on at the same time on that sound recording, so you can get a clean sample?

(12) Have you ever replayed records, or hired musicians to replay records? Why did you choose to do so, as opposed to sampling the sound recording?

(13) Have you ever used samples of public-domain works or samples of freely available works (like CDs of royalty-free samples) in your music?

The Law

(14) Do artists always need to get a license when they sample another artist's sound recording, or are there exceptions?

> *Probes*: (14A) Are there exceptions like a "safe harbor" if you sample less than five seconds?
>
> (14B) Where do you think the line is between fair use and copyright infringement for samples?

(15) What about the underlying songs, as opposed to sound recordings—are the rules different? Do artists always need to get a license when they quote another artist's song or composition without sampling the sound recording, or are there exceptions?

> *Probe*: (15A) Are there exceptions like a "safe harbor" if you only borrow three notes from a song?

(16) Do you know any artists who have been sued for copyright infringement because of samples they did not license?

> *Probe*: (16A) Do you *know of* artists who have been sued for sampling?

Licensing

(17) Do you typically obtain a license when you sample a sound recording? [If yes to question (17), proceed to question (18). If no, skip to question (19)]

(18) Do you obtain licenses for *all* the samples you use?

> *Probes*: (17A) How do you decide which samples to clear? Does it rely on the sample's length, context, who you're sampling, or what other factors?
>
> (17B) When do you clear the sample: (i) when composing, (ii) before recording, or (iii) before releasing the record?

[Skip to question (20)]

(19) Why do you choose not to license the samples you use?

> *Probes*: (19A) Is licensing too expensive?
>
> (19B) Do you feel you can rely on the doctrine of fair use in using samples, perhaps because your uses are transformative?
>
> (19C) Do you feel you can "fly below the radar" because your recordings sell a relatively limited number of copies?

(20) Do you think the current sample licensing system encourages creativity?

> *Probe*: (20A) Is licensing very difficult or complicated?

(21) Do you expect other artists to seek your permission or obtain a license if they want to sample your work?

Probes: (21A) Are there certain artists who you would deny the right to sample your songs? Why?

(21B) Are there certain musical or lyrical contexts in which you wouldn't want your music sampled? Why?

(22) Should artists receive compensation when their work is sampled?

Probe: (22A) Does it make a difference if it was the hook of the song as opposed to something unintelligible or heavily altered?

Chilling Effects

[If respondent answered yes to question (1), proceed to question (23). [If respondent answered no, skip to question (25)]

(23) Does the need to license samples increase your time spent in the studio?

Probe: (23A) In what other ways does clearing samples take up your time [respondent should answer yes to all that apply]: (i) meeting with lawyers, (ii) meeting with record label, (iii) delaying the release date of recordings, or (iv) other time-consuming activities?

(24) Are there any artists you don't sample because it would either cost too much to clear or they won't give permission?

Probe: (24A) Do you or other artists you know have stories about samples that were impossible or difficult to clear?

(25) How do copyright law and the need to acquire licenses for samples affect how you make music?

Probes: (25A) Do you ever substitute one sample for another because of the expense or difficulty of licensing a sample?

(25B) Have you changed the genre or style of your work?

(26) How do copyright law and the need to acquire licenses for samples affect the way you participate in the music business?

Probe: (26A) Have you ever had to shelve or rerecord a track because of copyright clearance problems?

(26B) Have you released music noncommercially, e.g. for free Internet download?

(26C) Have you shifted time from composing and recording to touring?

(27) Has copyright law affected how you make music in any way, such as the choice of what genres you participate in, the songs you allude to or borrow from, or your decision not to make sample-based music?

Thanks. [*end interview*]

The Art and History of Sampling

(1) How has sampling been so central to hip-hop music?
  Probe: (1A) Do you have any favorite artists who sample or a favorite time period for sample-based music?

(2) Can you explain what makes one use of a sample creative and interesting to you, and another use of a sample uncreative?

(3) Can you talk about an artist or artists who are notable for their use of sampling, or is there a notable time period for sample-based music?

(4) How is sampling different in the last few years compared to sampling in the mid to late 1980s?

Technical Questions

(5) Can you explain some techniques producers use to transform samples and make them unrecognizable?
  Probes: (6A) What is the point of making a sample unrecognizable?
  (6B) What do you gain by transforming a sample so much?
  (6C) Do you lose anything by making a sample unrecognizable?

(6) Have you heard about artists "replaying" samples with live musicians, and can you explain why they do it?

(7) How has sampling technology changed over the years?

The Law

(8) Do artists always need to get a license when they sample another artist's sound recording, or are there exceptions?
  Probe: (8A) Where do you think the line is between fair use and copyright infringement for samples?

(9) Is there a difference in the way samples are cleared (or not cleared) by artists on major labels, independent labels, or artists who self-release their music?

(10) Do you *know of* artists who have been sued for sampling because of samples they did not license?

Chilling Effects

(11) Do you think the current sample licensing system encourages creativity?

    Probe: (11A) Is licensing very difficult or complicated?

(12) Does the need to license samples increase time spent in the studio for artists?

    Probe: (12A) In what other ways does clearing samples take up time [respondent should answer yes to all that apply]: (i) meeting with lawyers, (ii) meeting with record label, (iii) delaying the release date of recordings, or (iv) other time-consuming activities?

(13) Are there any musicians that producers don't try to sample because it would either cost too much to clear or they won't give permission?

    Probes: (13A) Do you know of any stories about samples that were impossible or difficult to clear?

    (13B) Do you think the rise in the use of synthesizers is at all connected to the difficulty and expense of clearing samples?

(14) Are there any examples you can think of where copyright law and the need to acquire licenses for samples affects the way sampling artists make their music?

    Probes: (14A) Do artists ever substitute one sample for another because of the expense or difficulty of licensing a sample?

    (14B) Has the licensing system changed the ways artists use samples?

(15) Do you believe that the establishment of the sample licensing process has affected the way artists and producers use samples, especially when you compare it to the late 1980s?

    Probe: (15A) Have those changes been positive, negative, some of both, or neutral, in your view, with respect to the quality or integrity of the music?

(16) Do you think tighter restrictions on sampling ever led sampling artists to: (i) hire session musicians to do "replays," (ii) make different kinds of works, perhaps different styles or genres, (iii) not release certain songs or albums, (iv) release certain songs or albums noncommercially, e.g. for free Internet download or file sharing?

(17) How would you improve the sample clearance system?

    Probe: (17A) Should there be just one central clearinghouse for samples, so that information about the owners of copyrights and their stance on sampling were easier to obtain?

    (17B) What if artists were presented with a "menu" of sampling options, with different prices for different kinds of samples, so that prices could be more standardized and known ahead of time?

(17c) Would you be interested in a "compulsory licensing" system in which, for instance, you would fill out a simple one-page form indicating the recordings you sampled, and a portion of the proceeds would be distributed to the copyright holders for those sampled recordings?

Thanks. [*end interview*]

NOTES

INTRODUCTION

1. Mark Katz, *Capturing Sound: How Technology Has Changed Music* (Los Angeles: University of California Press, 2004), 138.

2. All quotations contained in this volume that are not cited were drawn from our interviews (see appendix 1). Note that on occasion parts of the quoted interviews were lightly edited for the purposes of clarity and readability.

3. *U.S. Code* 17 (2006), § 107.

4. *Campbell v. Acuff-Rose Music, Inc.*, 510 U.S. 569, 579 (1994).

5. Robert Levine, "Steal This Hook? D.J. Skirts Copyright Law," *New York Times*, August 6, 2008, http://www.nytimes.com/.

6. U.S. Constitution, art. I, § 8, cl. 8.

7. Joanna Demers, *Steal This Music: How Intellectual Property Law Affects Musical Creativity* (Athens: University of Georgia Press, 2006), 9.

8. For an exhaustive song-by-song examination of musical borrowing in popular music, see Timothy English's *Sounds Like Teen Spirit: Stolen Melodies, Ripped-Off Riffs, and the Secret History of Rock and Roll.*

9. "In no case does copyright protection for an original work of authorship extend to any idea, procedure, process, system, method of operation, concept, principle, or discovery, regardless of the form in which it is described, explained, illustrated, or embodied in such work." *U.S. Code* 17 (2006), § 102(b).

10. Harold Demsetz, "Information and Efficiency: Another Viewpoint," *Journal of Law and Economics* 12, no. 1 (1969): 1–22. Demsetz and the property-rights theorists who have followed him argue that copyrights organize investment in creativity. Granting someone a copyright arguably gives him or her

greater incentive to tend to the value of that work. To continue with the Arcade Fire example, the band invested time and money for music equipment and their unique recording space (a former church in Farnham, Quebec). See Darcy Frey, "One Very, Very Indie Band," *New York Times Magazine*, March 4, 2007, 31. Moreover, both Merge Records and the band itself spent time and money to promote *Neon Bible*. The more purchasers and listeners, the greater the social benefits from the Arcade Fire's work. Therefore, the argument goes, centralizing control over *Neon Bible*, even after its creation, by granting a copyright is socially beneficial.

11. Ronald H. Coase, "Why Economics Will Change" (lecture presented at the University of Missouri, Columbia, April 4, 2002), http://www.coase.org/.

12. See, for example, Arnold Plant, "The Economic Aspects of Copyright in Books," *Economica* 1, no. 2 (May 1934): 167–95; and Stephen Breyer, "The Uneasy Case for Copyright: A Study of Copyright in Books, Photocopies, and Computer Programs," *Harvard Law Review* 84, no. 2 (1970): 281–355.

13. William M. Landes and Richard A. Posner, *The Economic Structure of Intellectual Property Law* (Cambridge, Mass.: Belknap Press, 2003), 52–53.

14. Some samples do not constitute copyright infringement because of a limitation or exception enshrined in the law. We discuss such provisions in more detail below.

15. We provide a lengthier discussion of the two kinds of music copyright— musical compositions and sound recordings—in chapter 3. We often use the more colloquial terms "song," "track," or "source" as umbrella terms to refer simultaneously to both the musical composition and the sound recording. That is, we use these nonlegal terms to represent the unified whole as experienced by listeners to a piece of music. We thus restrict our usage of "musical composition" and "sound recording" to technical, legal contexts.

16. Michael Heller, *The Gridlock Economy: How Too Much Ownership Wrecks Markets, Stops Innovation, and Costs Lives* (New York: Basic Books, 2008), xiii.

17. *Sony Corp. of America v. Universal City Studios, Inc.*, 464 U.S. 417 (1984).

18. Audio Home Recording Act of 1992, Public Law No. 102–563, U.S. Statutes at Large 106 (1992): 4237, codified at *U.S. Code* 17 (2006), §§ 1001–1010.

19. The rewards and losses may not correlate with the copyright owners' stance in the dispute. In the case of the VCR, the movie industry increased its revenues for years (thanks to movie rentals) despite losing its battle to squelch the new technology.

20. See, for example, *Newton v. Diamond*, 388 F.3d 1189 (9th Cir. 2003).

21. *U.S. Code* 17 (2006), § 115(a)(2).

22. Neil Weinstock Netanel, *Copyright's Paradox* (Oxford: Oxford University Press, 2008).

CHAPTER 1. THE GOLDEN AGE OF SAMPLING

1. Brian Coleman, *Check the Technique: Liner Notes for Hip-Hop Junkies* (New York: Villard Books, 2007), 87.

2. Ibid., 152.

3. Ibid., 151.

4. Dan LeRoy, *Paul's Boutique* (New York: Continuum, 2006).

5. Simpson quoted in Angus Batey, *Rhyming and Stealing: A History of the Beastie Boys* (New York: Omnibus Press, 1998), 104.

6. LeRoy, *Paul's Boutique*, 36–37.

7. Coleman, *Check the Technique*, 353.

8. Chuck D, *Lyrics of a Rap Revolutionary: Times, Rhymes and Mind of Chuck D* (Beverly Hills, Calif.: Off Da Books, 2006), 105.

9. Coleman, *Check the Technique*, 192.

10. Ibid., 17.

11. Matt Diehl, "The Making of *Paul's Boutique*," *Rolling Stone*, December 11, 2003, 138.

12. Coleman, *Check the Technique*, 400.

13. See, for example, Melville Nimmer and David Nimmer, *Nimmer on Copyright*, rev. ed., vol. 4, § 13.05[G] (New Providence, N.J.: Matthew Bender, 2009), which discusses the Ninth Circuit and Seventh Circuit's endorsement of the view that downloading and uploading online constitute copyright infringement.

14. See *MGM Studios, Inc. v. Grokster, Ltd.*, 545 U.S. 913 (2005).

CHAPTER 2. LEGAL AND CULTURAL HISTORY OF SOUND COLLAGE

1. Chris Cutler, "Plunderphonics," in *Sounding Off! Music as Subversion/ Resistance/Revolution*, ed. Ron Sakolsky and Fred Wei-Han Ho, 67–86 (Brooklyn, N.Y.: Autonomedia, 1995); Austin Clarkson, *Stefan Wolpe: A Brief Catalogue of Published Works* (Islington, U.K.: Sound Way Press, 1991).

2. Herbert Russcol, *The Liberation of Sound: An Introduction to Electronic Music* (Englewood Cliffs, N.J.: Prentice-Hall, 1972).

3. Cage quoted in Frances Dyson, "The Ear That Would Hear Sounds in Themselves: John Cage, 1935–1965," in *Wireless Imagination: Sound, Radio, and the Avant-Garde*, ed. Douglas Kahn and Gregory Whitehead (Cambridge, Mass.: MIT Press, 1994), 379.

4. David Revill, *The Roaring Silence: John Cage—A Life* (New York: Arcade, 1992), 43; Glenn Watkins, *Pyramids at the Louvre: Music, Culture, and Col-

lage from Stravinsky to the Postmodernists (Cambridge, Mass.: Belknap Press, 1994).

5. Joshua Kun, "A Select History of Found Sound," *Option,* March-April 1997, 65–68; David Ewen, *Composers of Tomorrow's Music: A Non-Technical Introduction to the Musical Avant-Garde Movement* (New York: Dodd, Mead and Company, 1971).

6. Russcol, *The Liberation of Sound.*

7. Watkins, *Pyramids at the Louvre,* 406.

8. Ibid.

9. Larry Polansky, "The Early Works of James Tenney," in *The Music of James Tenney,* ed. Peter Garland, 119–294 (Santa Fe, N.M.: Soundings Press, 1984).

10. Greg Prato, "Dickie Goodman: Biography," *AllMusicGuide.com,* http://www.allmusicguide.com/; Chuck Miller, liner notes to *Dickie Goodman & Friends, The King of Novelty: Greatest Fables,* vol. 2, Luniverse B000Y5D5YE C D, 1998.

11. Miles, *Paul McCartney,* 484.

12. Edwin Pouncey, "Rock Concrete: Counterculture Plugs into the Academy," in *Undercurrents: The Hidden Wiring of Modern Music,* ed. Rob Young, 153–62 (London: Continuum, 2002).

13. Russcol, *The Liberation of Sound.*

14. The Tape-beatles, "The Tape-beatles Undergo Severe Trauma, Depression," *RetroFuturism,* no. 13 (July 1990): 1596–97.

15. John Oswald, "Creatigality," in *Sounding Off! Music as Subversion/Resistance/Revolution,* ed. Ron Sakolsky and Fred Wei-Han Ho, 87–90 (Brooklyn, N.Y.: Autonomedia, 1995).

16. Phil England, "That's Irritainment," *Wire,* June 2008, 22.

17. David Toop, *Ocean of Sound: Aether Talk, Ambient Sound and Imaginary Worlds* (New York: Serpent's Tail, 1995).

18. Norman Lebrecht, "Echoes Strike a Chord," *Daily Telegraph,* May 11, 1996, 7; Lewis Lockwood, *Beethoven: The Music and Life* (New York: Norton, 2003), 438.

19. Watkins, *Pyramids at the Louvre.*

20. Ibid., 400.

21. Ibid., 342.

22. Ibid., 343.

23. Malcolm MacDonald, *Brahms* (New York: Oxford University Press, 2001), 152–53.

24. Walter Ong, *Orality and Literacy* (New York: Routledge, 1982), 133.

25. Joe Klein, *Woody Guthrie: A Life* (New York: Delta Trade Paperbacks, 1980), 120.

26. Michael Chanan, *Musica Practica: The Social Practice of Western Music from Gregorian Chant to Postmodernism* (New York: Verso, 1994).

27. Joshua Kun, *Audiotopia: Music, Race, and America* (Berkeley: University of California Press, 2005), 49.

28. Ibid., 54.

29. Ibid., 55.

30. Cheryl L. Keyes, *Rap Music and Street Consciousness* (Urbana: University of Illinois Press, 2002), 21.

31. LeRoi Jones, *Blues People: Negro Music in White America* (New York: HarperCollins, 1963).

32. Mark D. Moss, "Who Owns the Songs the Whole World Sings?" *Sing Out! Folk Song Magazine* 42, no. 1 (spring 1998): 3.

33. Roger Catlin, "Blues Greats Guilty of 'Borrowing,' Too," *Chicago Sun-Times,* July 29, 1992, B41.

34. Willie Dixon, *I Am the Blues: The Willie Dixon Story*, with Don Snowden (New York: Da Capo, 1989), 90.

35. David Ritz, *The Adventures of Grandmaster Flash: My Life, My Beats* (New York: Broadway Books, 2008), 80.

36. Christopher Dunn, *Brutality Garden: Tropicália and the Emergence of a Brazilian Counterculture* (Chapel Hill: University of North Carolina Press, 2001), 178.

37. Ibid., 6.

38. Ibid., 93–94.

39. Alexander G. Weheliye, *Phonographies: Grooves in Sonic Afro-Modernity* (Durham, N.C.: Duke University Press, 2005), 21.

40. Michael E. Veal, *Dub: Soundscapes and Shattered Songs in Jamaican Reggae* (Middletown, Conn.: Wesleyan University Press, 2007), 66.

41. Ibid., 193.

42. Tricia Rose, *Black Noise: Hip-Hop Music and Black Culture in Contemporary America* (Hanover, N.H.: Wesleyan University Press, 1994).

43. Nelson George, *Hip-Hop America* (New York: Viking, 1998).

44. Ritz, *Adventures of Grandmaster Flash*, 54.

45. Steven Hager, *Hip Hop: The Illustrated History of Break Dancing, Rap Music, and Graffiti* (New York: St. Martin's Press, 1984), 36.

46. Ritz, *Adventures of Grandmaster Flash*, 66.

47. Ibid.

48. Ibid., 100.

49. Imani Perry, *Prophets of the Hood: Politics and Poetics in Hip Hop* (Durham, N.C.: Duke University Press, 2004), 71.

50. Ritz, *Adventures of Grandmaster Flash*, 74.

51. Kurt B. Reighley, *Looking for the Perfect Beat: The Art and Culture of the DJ* (New York: Pocket Books, 2000).

52. Tim Lawrence, *Love Saves the Day: A History of American Dance Music Culture, 1970–1979* (Durham, N.C.: Duke University Press, 2003).

53. Peter Shapiro, *Turn the Beat Around: The Secret History of Disco* (New York: Faber and Faber, 2005).

54. Bill Brewster and Frank Broughton, *Last Night a DJ Saved My Life: The History of the Disc Jockey* (New York: Grove Press, 2000).

55. Lawrence, *Love Saves the Day.*

56. Brewster and Broughton, *Last Night a DJ Saved My Life.*

57. Ibid.

58. Reighley, *Looking for the Perfect Beat*, 32.

59. "I was told a story by Rick Rubin of how he went on to produce the first song on Def Jam, T La Rock's 'It's Yours,'" says Saul Williams, referring to the cofounder of the seminal hip-hop label Def Jam which he started in 1984. It was the first song Rubin produced before he went on to work with Run-DMC, LL Cool J, and the Beastie Boys—not to mention later efforts with Johnny Cash, Tom Petty, Metallica, and the Red Hot Chili Peppers. "What happened," Williams tells us, "was he would go to clubs in New York in the late seventies and early eighties, and he'd hear DJs spinning breakbeats and people rhyming over them. And then he'd run out and buy the latest Sugar Hill or Enjoy record label twelve-inch, and it would be the same rapper, but he'd be rapping over a bass line or some disco line, and he would always be disappointed." Rubin was used to hearing hip-hop music in the clubs and in parks, and he was annoyed because the recorded versions only featured the rappers atop rerecorded disco tracks.

60. David Toop, *Rap Attack 2: African Hip-Hop to Global Hip-Hop* (London: Serpent's Tail, 1991).

61. Harry Allen, "Hip-Hop Hi-Tech," in *Step into a World: A Global Anthology of the New Black Literature*, ed. Kevin Powell, 91–95 (New York: Wiley and Sons, 2000).

62. RZA [Robert Diggs], *The Wu-Tang Manual*, with Chris Norris (New York: Riverhead, 2005), 195.

63. Ibid.

64. Charles Aaron, "?uestlove: The *SPIN* Interview," *SPIN*, June 2008, 84.

65. Allen, "Hip-Hop Hi-Tech," 91.

66. RZA, *Wu-Tang Manual*, 193.

67. Ritz, *Adventures of Grandmaster Flash*, 25.

68. Allen, "Hip-Hop Hi-Tech," 95.

69. John Henken, "Sounding Off by the Numbers: Making Music the MIDI Way," *Los Angeles Times*, October 16, 1988, Calendar, 66.

70. David Goldberg and Robert J. Bernstein, "Reflections on Sampling: A Sampler of Issues," *New York Law Journal* (January 15, 1993): 3.

71. Stan Soocher, "License to Sample," *National Law Journal* (February 13, 1989): 1–5; Richard Harrington, "The Groove Robbers' Judgment: Order on 'Sampling' Songs May Be Rap Landmark," *Washington Post*, December 25, 1991, D1.

72. Steve Hochman, "Judge Raps Practice of 'Sampling,'" *Los Angeles Times*, December 18, 1991, F1.

73. Shawn Taylor, *People's Instinctive Travels and the Paths of Rhythm* (New York: Continuum, 2007), 102.

74. George, *Hip-Hop America*, 89.

75. Rose, *Black Noise*, 79.

76. Silverman's explanation covers only what the *radio stations* did; their blanket licenses from the copyright holders of the sampled compositions (through the performance rights organizations ASCAP and BMI) arguably covered broadcast performances of a sample-based track like "Lesson 1." On the other hand. what Double Dee, Steinski, and Tommy Boy did—fixing the track to vinyl and making copies of it—risked infringing the reproduction and derivative-works rights of both the composition and sound recording copyright holders in the sampled sources. That said, the artists and the label could argue for various defenses to infringement, such as fair use.

77. Bob Gourley, "Pop Will Eat Itself," *Chaos Control Digizine*, 1994, http://www.chaoscontrol.com/.

78. Paul Simpson, *The Rough Guide to Cult Pop* (London: Rough Guides, 2003), 199.

79. Mark Rose, *Authors and Owners: The Invention of Copyright* (Cambridge, Mass.: Harvard University Press, 1993), 39.

80. Simon Frith, *Music and Copyright* (Edinburgh, U.K.: Edinburgh University Press, 1993), 5.

CHAPTER 3. THE COMPETING INTERESTS IN SAMPLE LICENSING

1. Sometimes the musical composition copyright is known as the © ("circle-c") copyright, while the sound recording copyright is known as the ℗ ("circle-p") copyright.

2. We say "two *potential* copyrights" to cover situations such as the following: a contemporary artist recording a version of a composition dating from before 1923 and thus having an expired copyright; a sound recording from before 1972—meaning it predates federal protection for sound recordings—that also lacks state-law protection.

3. *U.S. Code* 17 (2006), § 106. The exclusive rights that accompany sound recordings and musical compositions differ. For example, sound recording copyright holders have only a limited performance right (applying only to some "digital audio transmissions") and have no display right. See Digital Performance Right in Sound Recordings Act of 1995, Public Law No. 104–39, U.S. Statutes at Large 109 (1995): 336, codified at *U.S. Code* 17 (2006), §§ 106, 114, 115.

4. Of course, the owner of the sound recording copyright and the musical composition copyright can be one and the same, as when an artist records renditions of their own songs or compositions and retains both copyrights. But the two types of copyrights remain distinct. For instance, the artist can still license the sound recording to a record label and license the musical composition to a publisher.

5. Jeffry Scott, "Will Federal Pact Slash CD Costs?" *Atlanta Journal and Constitution*, May 12, 2000, 1G; Todd Brabec and Jeff Brabec, "CD, Tapes, and Record Sales," American Society of Composers, Authors and Publishers [ASCAP], http://www.ascap.com/.

6. See, for example, Lee & Thompson, "Royalties: Other Uses," in *Guide to Music Industry Agreements*, § 3.10, http://www.leeandthompson.com/. Synchronization licenses for film fall under the same broad category of master-recording licenses that do not involve sales of the artist's own recordings by the record label. Donald S. Passman, *All You Need to Know about the Music Business*, 4th ed. (New York: Simon and Schuster, 2000), 401–2.

7. In some sampling cases, it appears that tiny enough samples could be deemed *de minimis* by a court and thus not constitute infringement. But in *Bridgeport Music, Inc. v. Dimension Films*, 410 F.3d 792 (6th Cir. 2005), the U.S. Court of Appeals for the Sixth Circuit held that any amount taken from a sound recording constituted infringement. We discuss the possibility of sampling as fair use in more detail below.

8. In a standard recording contract, recording artists' royalties from record sales and from other uses are recouped against advances, recording costs, video production costs, and other costs. If a recording artist has not yet earned enough royalties to pay the record label back for these recoupable expenditures, we say that they are not recouped. Until the recording artist is recouped, any royalties they earn act as a credit in a sort of negative-balance account with the record label. This "account" is cumulative across albums and sometimes across contracts (a phenomenon called "cross-collateralization," meaning that if one album by a recording artist fails commercially, they may never see positive income beyond their advances). See Passman, *All You Need to Know about the Music Business*, 100–104.

9. As Cary Sherman of the Recording Industry Association of America has stated, "Record companies try to make a profit and they know that 90 percent

of their artists will not succeed. They pay vast amounts on advances, promotional and marketing costs for these artists and rely on the handful of artists who succeed to recover their losses and make a profit." Quoted in Eric de Fontenay, "Should Artists Pay for Labels' Mistakes?" *Musicdish.com*, September 6, 2001, http://www.musicdish.com/.

10. Exactly who counts as a "featured artist" depends on contractual agreements between the record label and the named recording artist and contractual (or sometimes informal) agreements between the named recording artist and the session musicians.

11. "In situations where the artist gets a percentage of the [record] company's net receipts . . . where the artist gets 50% of the fee paid . . . the producer gets a pro-rata share of the artist's earnings, based on the ratio that the producer's royalty bears to the [artist's] all-in rate." Passman, *All You Need to Know about the Music Business*, 137. "All-in rate" simply refers to the fact that the producer's share is taken out of the artist's royalties.

12. Ibid., 133–35.

13. *U.S. Code* 17 (2006), § 115(a). To take advantage of the compulsory license, one must meet certain administrative requirements in the statute. Oftentimes, the parties (i.e., the record label and the musical composition copyright holder) opt out of the statutory scheme but pay the statutory rate or somewhat less.

14. U.S. Copyright Office, "Mechanical License Royalty Rates," U.S. Copyright Office, http://www.copyright.gov/.

15. The music lawyer Whitney Broussard explained to us that "75 percent [is] more common in modern contracts, 50 percent more common in older contracts." Sheet music is handled differently. See Passman, *All You Need to Know about the Music Business*, 260.

16. See the discussion of *Newton v. Diamond* in chapter 4.

17. Tim Wu, "Jay-Z versus the Sample Troll," *Slate.com*, November 16, 2006, http://www.slate.com/.

18. Steve Morse, "Setting the New Market in Sampling," *Boston Globe*, March 3, 2002, L1.

19. For more background on "Tom's Diner," see Suzanne Vega, "Tom's Essay," *NYTimes.com*, September 23, 2008, http://measureformeasure.blogs.nytimes.com/.

20. Stetsasonic, *In Full Gear*, Tommy Boy Music TBCD 1017, 1988.

21. Ritz, *Adventures of Grandmaster Flash*, 68.

22. Jeff Leeds, "Dispute over Sampling Fees Has George Clinton in a Legal Funk," *Los Angeles Times*, May 20, 2001, C-1.

23. Eric Schumacher-Rasmussen, "Owners of P-Funk Catalog Sue over 500 Samples," *MTV.com*, June 11, 2001, http://www.mtv.com/.

24. Coleman, *Check the Technique*, 401.

25. Oscar Brand, *The Ballad Mongers: Rise of the Modern Folk Song* (New York: Funk and Wagnalls, 1962).

26. Georgina Boyes, *The Imagined Village: Culture, Ideology and the English Folk Revival* (New York: Manchester University Press, 1993), 224.

27. Because the Lomax song credit appears in the liner notes of KRS-ONE's album that contains "Sound of Da Police," we are assuming he must have at least paid a song publishing royalty for his sampled use. KRS-ONE, *Return of the Boom Bap*, Jive 01241–41517–2, 1993.

28. Bill Drummond and James Cauty, *The Manual (How to Have a Number One the Easy Way)* (London: KLF Publications, 1989), 60.

29. Anthony Seeger, "Ethnomusicologists, Archives, Professional Organizations, and the Shifting Ethics of Intellectual Property," *Yearbook for Traditional Music* 28 (1996): 87–105.

30. Sherylle Mills, "Indigenous Music and the Law: An Analysis of National and International Legislation," *Yearbook for Traditional Music* 28 (1996): 60.

31. Ibid., 67.

32. Steven Feld, "Pygmy Pop: A Genealogy of Schizophonic Mimesis," *Yearbook for Traditional Music* 28 (1996): 1–35.

33. Mills, "Indigenous Music and the Law."

34. Ibid., 59.

35. Chris Dahlen, "David Byrne," *Pitchfork.com*, July 17, 2006, http://pitch fork.com/.

36. Ibid.

37. Mills, "Indigenous Music and the Law," 57.

38. Steve Hochman, "Willie Dixon's Daughter Makes Sure Legacy Lives On," *Los Angeles Times*, October 8, 1994, F10.

39. Dixon, *I Am the Blues*, 222.

40. Ibid.

41. The RIAA has insisted on samples being licensed in some contexts, but its view is not necessarily extreme. Three major labels—Sony BMG, Universal Music Group, and Warner Music Group—actually supported the defendants in a recent high-profile sampling case. See Brief of Amici Curiae Sony BMG Music Entertainment, UMG Recordings, Inc. & Warner Music Inc., June 17, 2005, filed in *Bridgeport Music, Inc. v. Dimension Films*, 410 F.3d 792 (6th Cir. 2005).

42. Pascal Bussy, *Kraftwerk: Man, Machine and Music* (London: SAF Publishing, 2001).

43. See Roberta Rosenthal Kwall, "The Attribution Right in the United States: Caught in the Crossfire Between Copyright and Section 43(a)," *Washington Law Review* 77 (2002): 985–1033.

44. U.S. Copyright Office, "Mechanical License Royalty Rates."

45. Jube Shiver Jr., "Digital Double Trouble: From Rap Music to Medical

Formulas, Little Seems Safe from Duplication," *Los Angeles Times*, April 11, 1994, A1.

46. Charisse Jones, "Haven't I Heard that 'Whoop' (or 'Hoop') Somewhere Before?" *New York Times*, December 22, 1996, B44.

47. Attempts to reach Steve Miller to confirm these accounts were unsuccessful.

48. As we quoted the music lawyer Dina LaPolt in the previous section: "I think a lot of rap artists that get sampled, I mean they know how much money it generates. So they encourage other artists to sample their materials as well."

49. For copyrights transferred on or after January 1, 1978, the original owner can terminate a transfer of rights after thirty-five years under certain conditions. *U.S. Code* 17 (2006), § 203.

CHAPTER 4. SAMPLING LAWSUITS

1. *U.S. Code* 17 (2006), § 501.

2. Julie Cohen, Lydia Pallas Loren, Ruth Gana Okediji, and Maureen A. O'Rourke, *Copyright in a Global Information Economy* (New York: Aspen Law and Business, 2002), 319.

3. Ibid., 354.

4. *Bright Tunes Music Corp. v. Harrisongs Music, Ltd.*, 420 F. Supp. 177 (S.D.N.Y. 1976).

5. "It is apparent . . . that neither Harrison nor Preston [an organist in Harrison's band] were conscious of the fact that they were utilizing the He's So Fine theme. However, they in fact were, for it is perfectly obvious to the listener that in musical terms, the two songs are virtually identical except for one phrase." Ibid., 180.

6. Nimmer and Nimmer, *Nimmer on Copyright*, vol. 4, § 13.03[A][2].

7. Ibid.

8. "The quantitative component [of substantial similarity analysis] generally concerns the amount of the *copyrighted work* that is copied, a consideration that is especially pertinent to exact copying." *Ringgold v. Black Entertainment Television, Inc.*, 126 F.3d 70 (2d Cir. 1997). The music lawyer Whitney Broussard observes that this differs from the usual approach to substantial-similarity that applies in cases that do not involve sampling.

9. Nimmer and Nimmer, *Nimmer on Copyright*, vol. 4, § 13.03[A][2].

10. *U.S. Code* 17 (2006) § 107.

11. Don Snowden, "Sampling: A Creative Tool or License to Steal?" *Los Angeles Times*, August 6, 1989, Calendar, 61.

12. Siva Vaidhyanathan, *Copyrights and Copywrongs: The Rise of Intellectual Property and How It Threatens Creativity* (New York: Fast Track, 2001), 141.

13. Rob Sheffield, "Beat Pirates," *Blender,* April 2009, 40–41.

14. As Passman notes in *All You Need to Know about the Music Business*: "[The record industry's] 'catch me if you can' attitude came to an abrupt halt" (307).

15. "The only issue, therefore, seems to be who owns the copyright to the song 'Alone Again (Naturally)' and the master recording thereof made by Gilbert O'Sullivan." *Grand Upright Music Ltd. v. Warner Brothers Records, Inc.,* 780 F. Supp. 182 (S.D.N.Y. 1991), 183.

16. In the proceedings, one of Biz Markie's attorneys is quoted as follows: "Biz Markie would like to obtain your consent to the use of the 'Original Composition.'" Quoted in ibid., 184.

17. Ibid., 184–85. The reasoning that seeking a license is evidence of infringement proved faulty as a general proposition because the defendant can still invoke fair use. As the Supreme Court would hold three years later, "[T]he offer [to license] may simply have been made in a good faith effort to avoid this litigation . . . [B]eing denied permission to use a work does not weigh against a finding of fair use." *Campbell v. Acuff-Rose Music,* 585 n.18.

18. James Boyle, *The Public Domain: Enclosing the Commons of the Mind* (New Haven, Conn.: Yale University Press, 2008), 147–48.

19. *Jarvis v. A&M Records,* 827 F. Supp. 282 (D.N.J. 1993).

20. Ibid., 291–92.

21. *Fantasy, Inc. v. La Face Records,* No. C 96–4384 SC ENE, 1997 U.S. Dist. LEXIS 9068 (N.D. Cal. June 24, 1997).

22. Ibid., *4–*5.

23. Ibid., *7–*8.

24. Joan Biskupic, "Court Hands Parody Writers an Oh, So Pretty Ruling," *Washington Post,* March 8, 1994, A1.

25. *Campbell v. Acuff-Rose Music,* 584.

26. Ibid., 588.

27. Ibid., 594.

28. *Williams v. Broadus,* 99 Civ. 10957 (MBM), 2001 U.S. Dist. LEXIS 12894 (S.D.N.Y. August 27, 2001).

29. Remember from the previous section that copyright infringement has two parts: (1) showing that the plaintiff owns a valid copyright, and (2) showing that the defendant has exercised an exclusive right of the copyright holder without authorization. The second part itself has two parts: (2)(a) copying in fact, and (2)(b) substantial similarity. So the court is talking about step (2)(b) in its analysis of whether Marley Marl infringed Otis Redding, which feeds into step (1) of the analysis of whether Snoop Dogg infringed Marley Marl.

30. Ibid., *15.

31. Wayne Marshall, "'Mad Mad' Migration: Caribbean Circulation and the

Movement of Jamaican Rhythm," paper presented at the Caribbean Soundscapes conference, March 11, 2004, http://www.wayneandwax.com/.

32. *Newton v. Diamond*, 1191.

33. "To say that a use is de minimis because no audience would recognize the appropriation is thus to say that the use is not sufficiently significant." Ibid., 1193.

34. In the passage, the court is quoting the testimony of the defendants' expert, Lawrence Ferrara. Ibid., 1196.

35. A case that does not involve sampling—*Jean v. Bug Music, Inc.*, 00 Civ. 4022 (DC), 2002 U.S. Dist. LEXIS 3176 (S.D.N.Y. Feb. 27, 2002)—corroborates this by holding in a declaratory judgment for the plaintiffs that a later composition with three identical words and three identical notes to a prior composition did not infringe.

36. The musical composition had received a synchronization license. Ibid., 796.

37. Ibid., 802.

38. Ibid., 804.

39. See chapter 7 for a detailed exposition of *Bridgeport*'s economic rationale.

40. Ibid., 801.

41. Ibid., 805.

42. *U.S. Code* 17 (2006), § 114(b).

43. *Bridgeport Music v. Dimension Films*, 800.

44. See, for example, Leslie A. Kurtz, "Digital Actors and Copyright—From *The Polar Express* to *Simone*," *Santa Clara Computer and High Technology Law Journal* 21 (May 2005): 793–95.

45. *Bridgeport Music v. Dimension Films*, 804.

46. For the case involving Notorious B.I.G., see Jonathan V. Last, "The Samples: A Tale of Morality, Technology, Biggie, and the Law," *Weekly Standard*, March 31, 2006, http://weeklystandard.com/. For Public Announcement's case, see Susan Butler, "Bridgeport Wins Verdict against UMG," *Billboard.biz*, February 13, 2007, http://www.billboardbulletin.com/.

47. Katie Dean, "Remixing to Protest Sample Ruling," *Wired.com*, September 22, 2004, http://www.wired.com/.

48. Kurtz, "Digital Actors and Copyright," 795.

CHAPTER 5. THE SAMPLE CLEARANCE SYSTEM

1. Whitney C. Broussard, "Current and Suggested Business Practices for the Licensing of Digital Samples," *Loyola Entertainment Law Journal* 11 (1991): 479–503.

2. Donald Passman, in *All You Need to Know about the Music Business* (307–8), notes that record labels often want an advance on their royalty payments.

3. See Broussard, "Current and Suggested Business Practices for the Licensing of Digital Samples," 496–500; Passman, *All You Need to Know about the Music Business*, 308.

4. See Broussard, "Current and Suggested Business Practices for the Licensing of Digital Samples," 500.

5. Ibid., 496–98.

6. Ibid., 498.

7. "The Verve were forced to pay 100 per cent of their royalties from 'Bittersweet Symphony' to Rolling Stones' lawyer Allen Klein. Now their million-selling album, *Urban Hymns*, could be removed from sale because former Stones manager Andrew Loog Oldham feels he is entitled to a share of the profits, too." Sam Taylor, "Top Ten Lawsuits," *Observer*, Jan. 31, 1999, 14.

8. David Browne, "Settling the Bill: Digital Sampling in the Music Industry," *Entertainment Weekly*, January 24, 1992, 54.

9. The market for samples is "small" (or "thin") in the sense that a typical track is only likely to be licensed for sampling once or twice per year, if at all. In such an infrequent market, prices are highly unlikely to become public and an efficient meeting of supply and demand seems less likely. This argument depends on the uniqueness of each sampled track. On the other hand, most licensing fees have a common structure and fall within a standard range of buyout levels or royalty percentages. In that case, one might aggregate all samples into one market, which would not be small.

10. For the classic reference on inefficiency resulting from the failure of collective action, see Garrett Hardin, "The Tragedy of the Commons," *Science* 162, no. 3859 (December 13, 1968): 1243–48. The particular problem of overlapping intellectual property rights has been dubbed "the tragedy of the anticommons," since it results from too many owners of a resource, not a lack of private ownership. For more information on this idea, see Heller, *The Gridlock Economy*.

11. Coleman, *Check the Technique*, 42.

12. Deborah Russell, "Judge Clips Biz Markie on Sampling Issue," *Billboard*, January 4, 1992, 1.

13. Ibid.

14. Neil Drumming, "How Kanye Got 'Down' without Lauryn," *Entertainment Weekly*, April 16, 2004, 78.

15. Ibid.

16. Irwin Chusid, liner notes to *Golden Throats 4: Celebrities Butcher Songs of the Beatles*, Rhino/Wea B0000033XB CD, 1997.

17. Jim Fricke and Charlie Ahearn, *Yes Yes Y'all: The Experience Music Project Oral History of Hip-Hop's First Decade* (New York: Da Capo, 2002).

18. The Evolution Control Committee, "Past Releases: The Whipped Cream Mixes," The Evolution Control Committee, http://evolution-control.com/.

19. House Committee on Energy and Commerce, Subcommittee on Telecommunications and the Internet, *The Digital Future of the United States: Part II, the Future of Radio*, 110th Cong., 1st session, 2007, statement of Representative Mike Doyle of Pennsylvania.

20. Kembrew McLeod, *Freedom of Expression: Resistance and Repression in the Age of Intellectual Property* (Minneapolis: University of Minnesota Press, 2007), 163.

21. Wikipedia, "Danger Mouse," "The Grey Album," http://en.wikipedia.org/ (accessed March 2, 2007); Recording Industry Association of America (RIAA), "Gold and Platinum: Searchable Database," RIAA.com, http://www.riaa.com/ (accessed December 17, 2009). Note that because these are interactive sites with user-generated content, it is possible that the data on them have changed since the accessed dates stated.

22. Various documents relating to the exchange between Negativland and the RIAA are available at Negativland, "Negativland and the RIAA," NegativWordWideWebLand, http://www.negativland.com/.

23. Mark Jenkins, "In Negativland's Plus Column," *Washington Post*, September 20, 1998, G4.

24. Negativland, "Negativland and the RIAA."

25. Ibid.

26. Ibid.

27. Ibid.

CHAPTER 6. CONSEQUENCES FOR CREATIVITY

1. Coleman, *Check the Technique*, 27.

2. Roni Sarig, *Third Coast: OutKast, Timbaland, and How Hip-Hop Became a Southern Thing* (New York: Da Capo, 2007), 124.

3. David Sheppard, "What Kept You?" *MOJO Magazine*, May 2008, 62–67.

4. Mike McGonigal, *Loveless* (New York: Continuum, 2007), 55–56.

5. Landes and Posner, *The Economic Structure of Intellectual Property Law*, 52–53.

6. By "expected harm" we mean the probability of being sued multiplied by the following tripartite sum: (1) the probability of losing a lawsuit (if sued) times the amount of damages and the amount of legal fees in the instance of losing, plus (2) the probability of winning a lawsuit (if sued) times the amount of legal fees in the instance of winning, plus (3) the probability of settling a lawsuit (if sued) times the amount of the settlement and the amount of legal fees in the instance of settling.

7. Whether musicians employing the noncommercial-recording model could lawfully engage in *paid* live performances of their sample-based works is a more complicated issue. See the discussion below of the model of live performance only.

8. Creating a sample-based work live in concert (i.e., mixing the music live, in real time) without sample licenses implicates two of the exclusive rights of copyright owners. First, live performances infringe the public performance right in the musical composition copyrights in sampled songs. Sound recording copyrights have a public performance right, but it is limited to online performances. *U.S. Code* 17 (2006), § 106(6). The blanket licenses that concert venues purchase to cover live performances of entire songs may not apply to samples; whether they do depends on the specific terms of those licenses. Second, sample-based works performed live could implicate the derivative-works right in both the sound recording copyright and the musical composition copyright. The sample-based works would certainly infringe as unauthorized derivative works if they were captured and fixed as they were performed. But there is some controversy over whether fixation is required to infringe the derivative works right. See Tamara C. Peters, "Infringement of the Adaptation Right: A Derivative Work Need Not Be 'Fixed' for the Law to Be Broken," *Journal of the Copyright Society of the U.S.A.* 53 (2006): 401–46. Fair use could still succeed as a defense to infringement of either the performance right or the derivative works right. But any fair use defense would be weakened (though not foreclosed, as the Supreme Court held in *Campbell v. Acuff-Rose Music*) by the commercial nature of the live performance.

9. A concert promoter who booked a Girl Talk show told us that he had assumed that the blanket license that allows for bands to play covers—or DJs to spin whole songs—also allowed mash-ups to be performed at the venue. Whether the promoter's assumption was correct depends on the specific terms of his venue's licenses.

10. *U.S. Code* 17 (2006) § 512(c)(3)(A).

11. Samantha M. Shapiro, "Hip-Hop Outlaw (Industry Version)," *New York Times Magazine,* February 18, 2007, 29.

12. Chuck D, *Lyrics of a Rap Revolutionary,* 107.

13. Xombi, The-Breaks.com, http://the-breaks.com/index.php; Wikipedia, "Fear of a Black Planet: Partial List of Samples," "Paul's Boutique: Samples List," http://en.wikipedia.org/. The data from these sites were originally collected in December 2006. Note that because these are interactive sites with user-generated content, it is possible that the data on them have changed since the accessed dates stated.

14. Brad Benjamin, Paul's Boutique Samples and References List, http://paulsboutique.info/.

15. The values contained in table 2 are based primarily on Whitney Broussard, "Current and Suggested Business Practices for the Licensing of Digital Samples," 503, as well as on our discussion with him in 2006 to update some of the figures. We are grateful for Broussard's assistance with this project. We also relied on Passman, *All You Need to Know about the Music Business*, 306–8, and various project interviews, especially the comments of Danny Rubin, to estimate license fees for usage of samples.

16. See Union Square Music, "The Story of Curtom," Union Square Music, http://www.unionsquaremusic.co.uk/.

17. U.S. Copyright Office, "Mechanical License Royalty Rates."

18. Many authorities say that the statutory rate of section 115(a) acts as a ceiling—it is the most that record labels will pay. See, for example, Passman, *All You Need to Know about Music Business*. Other commentators we spoke with noted that the statutory rate need not be a ceiling—if composers had more bargaining power they could demand slightly more than the statutory rate, and the record label might pay it to avoid the cost of complying with the statute's administrative procedures. But practitioners maintain that the rate functions as a ceiling.

19. The fifteenth track on *Paul's Boutique*, "B-Boy Bouillabaisse," is actually a medley of nine songs. We treated it as just one track for the purposes of estimating the impact of the controlled composition clause and the excess mechanical royalties clause. But we do break down the licensing fees by each of the nine songs within the medley in table 4.

20. A controlled composition clause is a standard part of most major label contracts with recording artists. Many recording artists record their own songs. When that occurs, record labels seek to pay less than the statutory rate (just because they can). A controlled composition clause typically limits those recording artists who are also composers to receiving only 75 percent of the statutory rate, or $0.06825, on compositions in which they own the copyright. We allowed for the potential impact of this clause, but with or without the controlled composition clause each album bumps up against the excess mechanical royalties limit of $0.91.

21. Jerry R. Green and Suzanne Scotchmer, "On the Division of Profit in Sequential Innovation," RAND *Journal of Economics* 26, no. 1 (1995): 20–33.

22. For a fuller discussion of this economic model, see Peter DiCola, "Sequential Musical Innovation and Sample Licensing," in "Essays on Regulation of Media, Entertainment, and Telecommunications" (Ph.D. diss., University of Michigan, 2009), 76–112.

23. We address fair use in much more depth in chapter 7.

1. Landes and Posner, *The Economic Structure of Intellectual Property Law*.

2. Demsetz, "Information and Efficiency," 10.

3. "The smooth functioning of copyright law depends upon an implicit 'minimum size' principle." Justin Hughes, "Market Regulation and Innovation: Size Matters (or Should) in Copyright Law," *Fordham Law Review* 74 (2005): 578.

4. See, for example, Louis Kaplow, "Rules versus Standards: An Economic Analysis," *Duke Law Journal* 42 (1992): 557–629.

5. *Bridgeport Music v. Dimension Films*, 801. Emphasis added.

6. As discussed elsewhere, this does not preclude an affirmative defense of fair use.

7. Even though one sample is not a perfect substitute for another, perhaps samples can substitute for each other *to some degree*. If so, then a high enough price for one sample will lead licensees toward another, substitute, sample. In this way, the market discipline on prices that Judge Guy contemplates could still hold true.

8. See the discussion of replays in chapter 6.

9. *Bridgeport Music v. Dimension Films*, 801–2.

10. Tracy L. Reilly, "Debunking the Top Three Myths of Digital Sampling: An Endorsement of the *Bridgeport Music* Court's Attempt to Afford 'Sound' Copyright Protection to Sound Recordings," *Columbia Journal of Law and the Arts* 31 (2008): 401.

11. *Bridgeport Music v. Dimension Films*, 802. Emphasis added.

12. Ibid., 804.

13. The court's argument here isn't as strong as it could be with respect to the availability of sound recordings made before 1972. Even though these do not have federal copyright protection, many of them have copyright protection under state law.

14. *Bridgeport Music v. Dimension Films*, 804. The court did not discuss whether an industry-wide "fixed schedule of fees" would comply with antitrust law.

15. David Sanjek, "Don't Have to DJ No More: Sampling and the 'Autonomous' Creator," *Cardozo Arts and Entertainment Law Journal* 10 (1992): 621.

16. Reilly, "Debunking the Top Three Myths of Digital Sampling," 398.

17. Guido Calabresi and A. Douglas Melamed, "Property Rules, Liability Rules, and Inalienability: One View of the Cathedral," *Harvard Law Review* 85 (1972): 1089–1128.

18. *U.S. Code* 17 (2006), § 115(a)(2).

19. Ibid. In general, it is said that the compulsory license is never actually invoked; rather, it merely spurs a standard negotiation and pegs the rate of compensation. Passman, *All You Need to Know about the Music Business*, 210–13.

20. See chapter 5 for details, including the lists of the factors that parties consider when negotiating the price of a sample license.

21. William W. Fisher III, *Promises to Keep: Technology, Law, and the Future of Entertainment* (Stanford, Calif.: Stanford University Press, 2004), 202.

22. Ibid., 235.

23. Ibid.

24. Ibid., 234.

25. Ibid.

26. Ibid., 203.

27. Copyright does not protect ideas. *U.S. Code* 17 (2006), § 102(b). See also Hughes, "Market Regulation and Innovation," 617–18.

28. "The exclusive right of the owner of copyright in a sound recording under clause (2) of section 106 is limited to the right to prepare a derivative work in which the actual sounds fixed in the sound recording are rearranged, remixed, or otherwise altered in sequence or quality." *U.S. Code* 17 (2006), § 114(b).

29. Robert, "Ghostface Killah Wins Copyright Infringement Case," *Rap News Network*, October 27, 2003, http://www.rapnews.net/.

30. *U.S. Code* 17 (2006), § 107.

31. *Campbell v. Acuff-Rose Music*, 584–85.

32. Ibid., 579.

33. Creative Commons, About the Sampling Licenses, http://creativecommons.org/.

34. Creative Commons, CC-Mixter, http://ccmixter.org.

35. Association Littéraire et Artistique Internationale [ALAI], "Memorandum on Creative Commons Licenses," *Columbia Journal of Law and the Arts* 29 (2006): 262–63.

36. Zachary Katz, "Pitfalls of Open Licensing: An Analysis of Creative Commons Licensing," *IDEA: The Intellectual Property Law Review* 46 (2006): 391–413.

37. Magnatune, "Music Licensing at Magnatune," Magnatune, http://magnatune.com/.

38. *Bridgeport Music v. Dimension Films*, 804.

39. Mechanicals are defined in chapter 3. As Donald Passman explains in *All You Need to Know about the Music Business* (222), the Harry Fox Agency "act[s] as a publisher's agent for mechanicals. They issue mechanical licenses for the publisher, police them (i.e., make sure the users pay), and account to the publisher." In return, they receive a percentage of what they collect.

40. Robert P. Merges, "Of Property Rules, Coase, and Intellectual Property," *Columbia Law Review* 94 (1994): 2669–70.

41. We emphasize that such an institution would have to comply with federal antitrust law or obtain some kind of exemption.

42. Library Copyright Alliance, letter to Jule L. Sigall, Associate Register

for Policy and International Affairs, March 25, 2005, http://www.copyright
.gov/, 5–6.

43. If sample licensors got together to set specific prices, they would have to
deal with the federal antitrust authorities, the Department of Justice, and the
Federal Trade Commission. Note that ASCAP and BMI operate under consent
decrees from the Department of Justice that constrain their operations; those
consent decrees might serve as a model.

44. Interestingly, ASCAP's modern form was strongly affected by antitrust
lawsuits and investigation by the Department of Justice. The blanket licenses
offered by ASCAP and BMI are each subject to a consent decree monitored by
a federal judge. Sanjek and Sanjek, *Pennies from Heaven*, 184–211.

45. A small fraction of songwriters and composers in the United States are
represented by a third PRO, the Society of European Stage Authors and Composers (SESAC). In addition to SESAC's original client base of European artists,
it has expanded to include United States artists in multiple genres.

CONCLUSION

1. Robert E. Spoo, "Ezra Pound's Copyright Statute: Perpetual Rights and the
Problem of Heirs," *UCLA Law Review* 56 (2009): 1775–1834.

2. Ibid., 1832.

3. Ibid., 1797.

4. See Christopher Sprigman, "Reform(aliz)ing Copyright," *Stanford Law
Review* 57 (2004): 485–568.

5. See Calabresi and Melamed, "Property Rules, Liability Rules."

6. Perhaps copyright owners could switch rules at a later date, after the initial
publication of their work. But they would have to provide notice of the opera-
tive rule in some sort of registry. Moreover, all samplers who took advantage
of the previous rule would be grandfathered in for sample-based works created
at an earlier time.

7. Since each sample implicates two copyrights, a composition and a sound
recording, copyright law would have to devise rules to handle situations in
which the copyright holders in sampled sources did not agree.

BIBLIOGRAPHY

DISCOGRAPHY

Beastie Boys. *Paul's Boutique,* Capitol CDP 7 91743 2 CD, 1989.
KRS-ONE. *Return of the Boom Bap.* Jive 01241–41517–2, 1993.
Public Enemy. *Fear of a Black Planet.* Def Jam 314 523 446–2 CD, 1990.
Stetsasonic. *In Full Gear.* Tommy Boy Music TBCD 1017, 1988.

LEGAL CASES

Bridgeport Music, Inc. v. Dimension Films. 410 F.3d 792 (6th Cir. 2005).
Bright Tunes Music Corp. v. Harrisongs Music, Ltd. 420 F. Supp. 177 (S.D.N.Y. 1976).
Campbell v. Acuff-Rose Music, Inc. 510 U.S. 569 (1994).
Fantasy, Inc. v. La Face Records. No. C 96–4384 SC ENE, 1997 U.S. Dist. LEXIS 9068 (N.D. Cal. June 24, 1997).
Grand Upright Music Ltd. v. Warner Brothers Records, Inc. 780 F. Supp. 182 (S.D.N.Y. 1991).
Jarvis v. A&M Records. 827 F. Supp. 282 (D.N.J. 1993).
Jean v. Bug Music, Inc. 00 Civ. 4022 (DC), 2002 U.S. Dist. LEXIS 3176 (S.D.N.Y. Feb. 27, 2002).
MGM Studios, Inc. v. Grokster, Ltd. 545 U.S. 913 (2005).
Newton v. Diamond. 388 F.3d 1189 (9th Cir. 2003).
Ringgold v. Black Entertainment Television, Inc. 126 F.3d 70 (2d Cir. 1997).
Sony Corp. of America v. Universal City Studios, Inc. 464 U.S. 417 (1984).
Twentieth Century Music Corp. v. Aiken. 422 U.S. 151 (1975).

Williams v. Broadus. 99 Civ. 10957 (MBM), 2001 U.S. Dist. LEXIS 12894 (S.D.N.Y. August 27, 2001).

WORKS CITED

Aaron, Charles. "?uestlove: The *SPIN* Interview." *SPIN*, June 2008, 84.

Allen, Harry. "Hip-Hop Hi-Tech." In *Step into a World: A Global Anthology of the New Black Literature,* edited by Kevin Powell, 91–95. New York: Wiley and Sons, 2000.

Association Littéraire et Artistique Internationale [ALAI]. "Memorandum on Creative Commons Licenses." *Columbia Journal of Law and the Arts* 29 (2006): 261–69.

Audio Home Recording Act of 1992. Public Law No. 102–563, U.S. Statutes at Large 106 (1992): 4237. Codified at *U.S. Code* 17 (2006), §§ 1001–1010.

Batey, Angus. *Rhyming and Stealing: A History of the Beastie Boys.* New York: Omnibus Press, 1998.

Benjamin, Brad. Paul's Boutique Samples and References List, http://paulsboutique.info/.

Biskupic, Joan. "Court Hands Parody Writers an Oh, So Pretty Ruling." *Washington Post,* March 8, 1994, A1.

Boyes, Georgina. *The Imagined Village: Culture, Ideology and the English Folk Revival.* New York: Manchester University Press, 1993.

Boyle, James. *The Public Domain: Enclosing the Commons of the Mind.* New Haven, Conn.: Yale University Press, 2008.

Brabec, Todd, and Jeff Brabec. "CD, Tapes, and Record Sales." American Society of Composers, Authors and Publishers [ASCAP], http://www.ascap.com/.

Brand, Oscar. *The Ballad Mongers: Rise of the Modern Folk Song.* New York: Funk and Wagnalls, 1962.

Brewster, Bill, and Frank Broughton. *Last Night a DJ Saved My Life: The History of the Disc Jockey.* New York: Grove Press, 2000.

Breyer, Stephen. "The Uneasy Case for Copyright: A Study of Copyright in Books, Photocopies, and Computer Programs." *Harvard Law Review* 84, no. 2 (1970): 281–355.

Brief of Amici Curiae Sony BMG Music Entertainment, UMG Recordings, Inc. and Warner Music Inc., June 17, 2005. Filed in *Bridgeport Music, Inc. v. Dimension Films,* 410 F.3d 792 (6th Cir. 2005).

Broussard, Whitney C. "Current and Suggested Business Practices for the Licensing of Digital Samples." *Loyola Entertainment Law Journal* 11 (1991): 479–503.

Browne, David. "Settling the Bill: Digital Sampling in the Music Industry." *Entertainment Weekly*, January 24, 1992, 54.

Bussy, Pascal. *Kraftwerk: Man, Machine and Music*. London: SAF Publishing, 2001.

Butler, Susan. "Bridgeport Wins Verdict against UMG." *Billboard.biz*, February 13, 2007, http://www.billboardbulletin.com/.

Calabresi, Guido, and A. Douglas Melamed. "Property Rules, Liability Rules, and Inalienability: One View of the Cathedral." *Harvard Law Review* 85 (1972): 1089–1128.

Catlin, Roger. "Blues Greats Guilty of 'Borrowing,' Too." *Chicago Sun-Times*, July 29, 1992, B41.

Chanan, Michael. *Musica Practica: The Social Practice of Western Music from Gregorian Chant to Postmodernism*. New York: Verso, 1994.

Chuck D. *Lyrics of a Rap Revolutionary: Times, Rhymes and Mind of Chuck D.* Beverly Hills, Calif.: Off Da Books, 2006.

Chusid, Irwin. Liner notes to *Golden Throats 4: Celebrities Butcher Songs of the Beatles*, Rhino/Wea B0000033XB CD, 1997.

Clarkson, Austin. *Stefan Wolpe: A Brief Catalogue of Published Works*. Islington, U.K.: Sound Way Press, 1991.

Coase, Ronald H. "Why Economics Will Change." Lecture presented at the University of Missouri, Columbia, April 4, 2002, The Ronald Coase Institute, http://www.coase.org/.

Cohen, Julie, Lydia Pallas Loren, Ruth Gana Okediji, and Maureen A. O'Rourke. *Copyright in a Global Information Economy*. New York: Aspen Law and Business, 2002.

Coleman, Brian. *Check the Technique: Liner Notes for Hip-Hop Junkies*. New York: Villard Books, 2007.

Cutler, Chris. "Plunderphonics." In *Sounding Off! Music as Subversion/Resistance/Revolution*, edited by Ron Sakolsky and Fred Wei-Han Ho, 67–86. Brooklyn, N.Y.: Autonomedia, 1995.

Dahlen, Chris. "David Byrne." *Pitchfork.com*, July 17, 2006, http://pitchfork.com/.

Dean, Katie. "Remixing to Protest Sample Ruling." *Wired.com*, September 22, 2004, http://www.wired.com/.

de Fontenay, Eric. "Should Artists Pay for Labels' Mistakes?" *Musicdish.com*, September 6, 2001, http://www.musicdish.com/.

Demers, Joanna. *Steal This Music: How Intellectual Property Law Affects Musical Creativity*. Athens: University of Georgia Press, 2006.

Demsetz, Harold. "Information and Efficiency: Another Viewpoint." *Journal of Law and Economics* 12, no. 1 (1969): 1–22.

DiCola, Peter. "Sequential Musical Innovation and Sample Licensing." In "Es-

says on Regulation of Media, Entertainment, and Telecommunications."
Ph.D. diss., University of Michigan, 2009, 76–112.

Diehl, Matt. "The Making of *Paul's Boutique.*" *Rolling Stone*, December 11, 2003, 138.

Digital Performance Right in Sound Recordings Act of 1995. Public Law No. 104–39, U.S. Statutes at Large 109 (1995): 336. Codified at *U.S. Code* 17 (2006), §§ 106, 114, 115.

Dixon, Willie. *I Am the Blues: The Willie Dixon Story.* With Don Snowden. New York: Da Capo, 1989.

Drumming, Neil. "How Kanye Got 'Down' without Lauryn." *Entertainment Weekly*, April 16, 2004, 78.

Drummond, Bill, and James Cauty. *The Manual (How to Have a Number One the Easy Way).* London: KLF Publications, 1989.

Dunn, Christopher. *Brutality Garden: Tropicália and the Emergence of a Brazilian Counterculture.* Chapel Hill: University of North Carolina Press, 2001.

Dyson, Frances. "The Ear That Would Hear Sounds in Themselves: John Cage, 1935–1965." In *Wireless Imagination: Sound, Radio, and the Avant-Garde*, edited by Douglas Kahn and Gregory Whitehead, 373–408. Cambridge, Mass.: MIT Press, 1994.

England, Phil. "That's Irritainment." *Wire*, June 2008, 22.

English, Timothy. *Sounds Like Teen Spirit: Stolen Melodies, Ripped-Off Riffs, and the Secret History of Rock and Roll.* New York: iUniverse Star, 2007.

Evolution Control Committee. "Past Releases: The Whipped Cream Mixes." Evolution Control Committee, http://evolution-control.com/.

Ewen, David. *Composers of Tomorrow's Music: A Non-Technical Introduction to the Musical Avant-Garde Movement.* New York: Dodd, Mead and Company, 1971.

Feld, Steven. "Pygmy Pop: A Genealogy of Schizophonic Mimesis." *Yearbook for Traditional Music* 28 (1996): 1–35.

Fisher, William W. III. *Promises to Keep: Technology, Law, and the Future of Entertainment.* Stanford, Calif.: Stanford University Press, 2004.

Frey, Darcy. "One Very, Very Indie Band." *New York Times Magazine*, March 4, 2007, 31.

Fricke, Jim, and Charlie Ahearn. *Yes Yes Y'all: The Experience Music Project Oral History of Hip-Hop's First Decade.* New York: Da Capo, 2002.

Frith, Simon. *Music and Copyright.* Edinburgh, U.K.: Edinburgh University Press, 1993.

George, Nelson. *Hip-Hop America.* New York: Viking, 1998.

Goldberg, David, and Robert J. Bernstein. "Reflections on Sampling: A Sampler of Issues." *New York Law Journal* (January 15, 1993): 3.

Gourley, Bob. "Pop Will Eat Itself." *Chaos Control Digizine*, 1994, http://www .chaoscontrol.com/.

Green, Jerry R., and Suzanne Scotchmer. "On the Division of Profit in Sequential Innovation." *RAND Journal of Economics* 26, no. 1 (1995): 20–33.

Hager, Steven. *Hip Hop: The Illustrated History of Break Dancing, Rap Music, and Graffiti*. New York: St. Martin's Press, 1984.

Hardin, Garrett. "The Tragedy of the Commons." *Science* 162, no. 3859 (December 13, 1968): 1243–48.

Harrington, Richard. "The Groove Robbers' Judgment: Order on 'Sampling' Songs May Be Rap Landmark." *Washington Post*, December 25, 1991, D1.

Heller, Michael. *The Gridlock Economy: How Too Much Ownership Wrecks Markets, Stops Innovation, and Costs Lives*. New York: Basic Books, 2008.

Henken, John. "Sounding Off by the Numbers: Making Music the MIDI Way." *Los Angeles Times*, October 16, 1988, Calendar, 66.

Hochman, Steve. "Judge Raps Practice of 'Sampling.'" *Los Angeles Times*, December 18, 1991, F1.

———. "Willie Dixon's Daughter Makes Sure Legacy Lives On." *Los Angeles Times*, October 8, 1994, F10.

Hughes, Justin. "Market Regulation and Innovation: Size Matters (or Should) in Copyright Law." *Fordham Law Review* 74 (2005): 575–637.

Jenkins, Mark. "In Negativland's Plus Column." *Washington Post*, September 20, 1998, G4.

Jones, Charisse. "Haven't I Heard that 'Whoop' (or 'Hoop') Somewhere Before?" *New York Times*, December 22, 1996, B44.

Jones, LeRoi. *Blues People: Negro Music in White America*. New York: Harper-Collins, 1963.

Kaplow, Louis. "Rules versus Standards: An Economic Analysis." *Duke Law Journal* 42 (1992): 557–629.

Katz, Mark. *Capturing Sound: How Technology Has Changed Music*. Los Angeles: University of California Press, 2004.

Katz, Zachary. "Pitfalls of Open Licensing: An Analysis of Creative Commons Licensing." *IDEA: The Intellectual Property Law Review* 46 (2006): 391–413.

Keyes, Cheryl L. *Rap Music and Street Consciousness*. Urbana: University of Illinois Press, 2002.

Klein, Joe. *Woody Guthrie: A Life*. New York: Delta Trade Paperbacks, 1980.

KLF Communications. "KLF Info Sheet: Jan 22 1988." *The Library of Mu*, http:// www.libraryofmu.org/.

Kun, Joshua. *Audiotopia: Music, Race, and America*. Berkeley: University of California Press, 2005.

———. "A Select History of Found Sound." *Option*, March-April 1997, 65–68.

Kurtz, Leslie A. "Digital Actors and Copyright—From *The Polar Express* to *Simone*." *Santa Clara Computer and High Technology Law Journal* 21 (May 2005): 783–805.

Kwall, Roberta Rosenthal. "The Attribution Right in the United States: Caught in the Crossfire between Copyright and Section 43(a)." *Washington Law Review* 77 (2002): 985–1033.

Landes, William M., and Richard A. Posner. *The Economic Structure of Intellectual Property Law*. Cambridge, Mass.: Belknap Press, 2003.

Last, Jonathan V. "The Samples: A Tale of Morality, Technology, Biggie, and the Law." *Weekly Standard*, March 31, 2006, http://weeklystandard.com/.

Lawrence, Tim. *Love Saves the Day: A History of American Dance Music Culture, 1970–1979*. Durham, N.C.: Duke University Press, 2003.

Lebrecht, Norman. "Echoes Strike a Chord." *Daily Telegraph*, May 11, 1996, 7.

Lee & Thompson. "Royalties: Other Uses." In *Guide to Music Industry Agreements*, § 3.10, http://www.leeandthompson.com/.

Leeds, Jeff. "Dispute over Sampling Fees Has George Clinton in a Legal Funk." *Los Angeles Times*, May 20, 2001, C-1.

LeRoy, Dan. *Paul's Boutique*. New York: Continuum, 2006.

Lessig, Lawrence. "Free(ing) Culture for Remix." *Utah Law Review* 4 (2004): 961–75.

———. *Remix: Making Art and Commerce Thrive in the Hybrid Economy*. New York: Penguin Press, 2008.

Levine, Robert. "Steal This Hook? D.J. Skirts Copyright Law." *New York Times*, August 6, 2008, http://www.nytimes.com/.

Library Copyright Alliance. Letter to Jule L. Sigall, Associate Register for Policy and International Affairs, March 25, 2005, http://www.copyright.gov/.

Lockwood, Lewis. *Beethoven: The Music and Life*. New York: Norton, 2003.

MacDonald, Malcolm. *Brahms*. New York: Oxford University Press, 2001.

Marshall, Wayne. "'Mad Mad' Migration: Caribbean Circulation and the Movement of Jamaican Rhythm." Paper presented at the Caribbean Soundscapes conference, March 11, 2004, Wayne&wax, http://www.wayneandwax.com/.

McGonigal, Mike. *Loveless*. New York: Continuum, 2007.

McLeod, Kembrew. *Freedom of Expression®: Resistance and Repression in the Age of Intellectual Property*. Minneapolis: University of Minnesota Press, 2007.

Merges, Robert P. "Of Property Rules, Coase, and Intellectual Property." *Columbia Law Review* 94 (1994): 2655–73.

Miles, Barry. *Paul McCartney: Many Years from Now*. New York: Owl Books, 1997.

Miller, Chuck. Liner notes to *Dickie Goodman and Friends, The King of Novelty: Greatest Fables*, vol. 2, Luniverse B00OY5D5YE CD, 1998.

Mills, Sherylle. "Indigenous Music and the Law: An Analysis of National and International Legislation." *Yearbook for Traditional Music* 28 (1996): 57–86.

Morse, Steve. "Setting the New Market in Sampling." *Boston Globe*, March 3, 2002, L1.

Moss, Mark D. "Who Owns the Songs the Whole World Sings?" *Sing Out! Folk Song Magazine* 42, no. 1 (spring 1998): 3.

Negativland. "Negativland and the RIAA." NegativWorldWideWebLand, http://www.negativland.com/.

Netanel, Neil Weinstock. *Copyright's Paradox*. Oxford: Oxford University Press, 2008.

Nimmer, Melville, and David Nimmer. *Nimmer on Copyright*. Rev. edn. 6 vols. New Providence, N.J.: Matthew Bender, 2009.

Ong, Walter. *Orality and Literacy*. New York: Routledge, 1982.

Oswald, John. "Creatigality." In *Sounding Off! Music as Subversion/Resistance/Revolution*, edited by Ron Sakolsky and Fred Wei-Han Ho, 87–90. Brooklyn, N.Y.: Autonomedia, 1995.

Passman, Donald S. *All You Need to Know about the Music Business*. 4th edn. New York: Simon and Schuster, 2000.

Perry, Imani. *Prophets of the Hood: Politics and Poetics in Hip Hop*. Durham, N.C.: Duke University Press, 2004.

Peters, Tamara C. "Infringement of the Adaptation Right: A Derivative Work Need Not Be 'Fixed' for the Law to Be Broken." *Journal of the Copyright Society of the U.S.A.* 53 (2006): 401–46.

Plant, Arnold. "The Economic Aspects of Copyright in Books." *Economica* 1, no. 2 (May 1934): 167–95.

Polansky, Larry. "The Early Works of James Tenney." In *The Music of James Tenney*, edited by Peter Garland, 119–294. Santa Fe, N.M.: Soundings Press, 1984.

Pouncey, Edwin. "Rock Concrete: Counterculture Plugs into the Academy." In *Undercurrents: The Hidden Wiring of Modern Music*, edited by Rob Young, 153–62. London: Continuum, 2002.

Prato, Greg. "Dickie Goodman: Biography." *AllMusicGuide.com*, http://www.allmusicguide.com/.

Recording Industry Association of America [RIAA]. "Gold & Platinum: Searchable Database." RIAA.com, http://www.riaa.com/.

Reighley, Kurt B. *Looking for the Perfect Beat: The Art and Culture of the DJ*. New York: Pocket Books, 2000.

Reilly, Tracy L. "Debunking the Top Three Myths of Digital Sampling: An Endorsement of the *Bridgeport Music* Court's Attempt to Afford 'Sound' Copyright Protection to Sound Recordings." *Columbia Journal of Law and the Arts* 31 (2008): 355–408.

Revill, David. *The Roaring Silence: John Cage—A Life*. New York: Arcade, 1992.

Ritz, David. *The Adventures of Grandmaster Flash: My Life, My Beats*. New York: Broadway Books, 2008.

Robert. "Ghostface Killah Wins Copyright Infringement Case." *Rap News Network*, October 27, 2003, http://www.rapnews.net/.

Rose, Mark. *Authors and Owners: The Invention of Copyright*. Cambridge, Mass.: Harvard University Press, 1993.

Rose, Tricia. *Black Noise: Hip-Hop Music and Black Culture in Contemporary America*. Hanover, N.H.: Wesleyan University Press, 1994.

Russcol, Herbert. *The Liberation of Sound: An Introduction to Electronic Music*. Englewood Cliffs, N.J.: Prentice-Hall, 1972.

Russell, Deborah. "Judge Clips Biz Markie on Sampling Issue." *Billboard,* January 4, 1992, 1.

RZA [Robert Diggs]. *The Wu-Tang Manual*. With Chris Norris. New York: Riverhead, 2005.

Sanjek, David. "Don't Have to DJ No More: Sampling and the 'Autonomous' Creator." *Cardozo Arts and Entertainment Law Journal* 10 (1992): 607–24.

Sanjek, Russell, and David Sanjek. *Pennies from Heaven: The American Popular Music Business in the Twentieth Century*. New York: Da Capo, 1996.

Sarig, Roni. *Third Coast: OutKast, Timbaland, and How Hip-Hop Became a Southern Thing*. New York: Da Capo, 2007.

Schumacher-Rasmussen, Eric. "Owners of P-Funk Catalog Sue over 500 Samples." *MTV.com*, June 11, 2001, http://www.mtv.com/.

Scott, Jeffry. "Will Federal Pact Slash CD Costs?" *Atlanta Journal and Constitution*, May 12, 2000, 1G.

Seeger, Anthony. "Ethnomusicologists, Archives, Professional Organizations, and the Shifting Ethics of Intellectual Property." *Yearbook for Traditional Music* 28 (1996): 87–105.

Shapiro, Peter. *Turn the Beat Around: The Secret History of Disco*. New York: Faber and Faber, 2005.

Shapiro, Samantha M. "Hip-Hop Outlaw (Industry Version)." *New York Times Magazine,* February 18, 2007, 29.

Sheffield, Rob. "Beat Pirates." *Blender,* April 2009, 40–41.

Sheppard, David. "What Kept You?" *MOJO Magazine*, May 2008, 62–67.

Shiver, Jube Jr. "Digital Double Trouble: From Rap Music to Medical Formulas, Little Seems Safe from Duplication." *Los Angeles Times*, April 11, 1994, A1.

Simpson, Paul. *The Rough Guide to Cult Pop*. London: Rough Guides, 2003.

Snowden, Don. "Sampling: A Creative Tool or License to Steal?" *Los Angeles Times,* August 6, 1989, Calendar, 61.

Soocher, Stan. "License to Sample." *National Law Journal* (February 13, 1989): 1–5.

Spoo, Robert E. "Ezra Pound's Copyright Statute: Perpetual Rights and the Problem of Heirs." *UCLA Law Review* 56 (2009): 1775–834.

Sprigman, Christopher. "Reform(aliz)ing Copyright." *Stanford Law Review* 57 (2004): 485–568.

Tape-beatles. "The Tape-beatles Undergo Severe Trauma, Depression." *Retro-Futurism*, no. 13 (July 1990): 1596–97.

Taylor, Sam. "Top Ten Lawsuits." *Observer*, January 31, 1999, 14.

Taylor, Shawn. *People's Instinctive Travels and the Paths of Rhythm*. New York: Continuum, 2007.

Toop, David. *Ocean of Sound: Aether Talk, Ambient Sound and Imaginary Worlds*. New York: Serpent's Tail, 1995.

——. *Rap Attack 2: African Hip-Hop to Global Hip-Hop*. London: Serpent's Tail, 1991.

Union Square Music. "The Story of Curtom." Union Square Music, http://www.unionsquaremusic.co.uk/.

U.S. Code 17 (2006).

U.S. Congress. House of Representatives. Committee on Energy and Commerce. Subcommittee on Telecommunications and the Internet. *The Digital Future of the United States: Part II, the Future of Radio*, 110th Cong., 1st session, March 7, 2007.

U.S. Constitution, art. I, § 8, cl. 8.

U.S. Copyright Office. "Mechanical License Royalty Rates." U.S. Copyright Office, http://www.copyright.gov/.

Vaidhyanathan, Siva. *Copyrights and Copywrongs, The Rise of Intellectual Property and How It Threatens Creativity*. New York: Fast Track, 2001.

Veal, Michael E. *Dub: Soundscapes and Shattered Songs in Jamaican Reggae*. Middletown, Conn.: Wesleyan University Press, 2007.

Vega, Suzanne. "Tom's Essay." *New York Times*, September 23, 2008, http://measureformeasure.blogs.nytimes.com/.

Watkins, Glenn. *Pyramids at the Louvre: Music, Culture, and Collage from Stravinsky to the Postmodernists*. Cambridge, Mass.: Belknap Press, 1994.

Weheliye, Alexander G. *Phonographies: Grooves in Sonic Afro-Modernity*. Durham, N.C.: Duke University Press, 2005.

Wu, Tim. "Jay-Z versus the Sample Troll." *Slate.com*, November 16, 2006, http://www.slate.com/.

INDEX

Page numbers with italics indicate tables.

tions assessment and, 204; alternative compensation systems and, 230; on artists' revenue, 291n15; on benefits of licensing, 157; on *Bridgeport*'s impact on licensing, 143–44; on bureaucracy in licensing, 166; on creativity and *Bridgeport*, 143–44; critical commentary and, 237–38; fair use doctrine and, 237–39, 241; on lawsuit effects on licensing, 137; on licensing, 83, 133; on licensing mash-ups, 180–81, 182; on structure and terms of licenses, 152–53; on substantial-similarity component, 293n8; on timing difficulties in licensing, 171; on transaction-facilitating institutions, 250, 251

Brown, James, 50, 70, 81, 88, 90–92, 94–95, 116, 119, 247

bureaucracy, licensing and, 165–69, 172

business: artists' experience and, 155–56; business models for licensing, 196–99, 297n6, 298nn8–9; of licensing, 148–58; of mash-ups, 178–85; music-business practices, 7, 93

Byrne, David, 9, 40–41, 50–51, 104–6, 108, 110, 118–19, 168–69

Campbell v. Acuff-Rose Music, Inc., 135–36, 138, 234–36, 294n17, 298n8

Castor, Jimmy, 131

Cepeda, Raquel, 21, 201

Chang, Jeff: on African American music tradition, 49; on artists' revenue and career revivals, 93; on expenses in licensing, 118, 162; on golden age of sampling, 20–21, 23–24; on intergenerational musical dialogues/tributes, 100, 101, 108; on licensing effects, 93; on negotiations, 151–52; on sound

collage, 45; on technology innovations, 34

Chuck D: album restrictions and, 201–2; assessment of licensing and, 213; on Black Atlantic influences, 52; on business of mash-ups, 178; on commodification of sound, 101; fair use doctrine and, 238; *Fear of Black Planet*, 23, 25; golden age of sampling and, 22–26; intergenerational musical dialogues/tributes and, 99; *It Takes a Nation of Millions to Hold Us Back*, 22–27, 213, 238; on James Brown samples, 90, 91; on lawyers' revenue from licensing, 85; on licensing, 27, 30, 124; on mash-ups, 174, 177; on replays/interpolations, 191; on technology and sampling, 60, 62; transaction costs of licensing and, 213. *See also* Public Enemy

Cibo Matto, 22

Clinton, George, 28, 64–65, 90, 93, 267

Coase, Ronald, 10, 267

Coldcut. *See* Black, Matt

collaborations, interdisciplinary, 94–95, 132, 267–68

commodification of sound, 101–2

competing interests in licensing, 75; artists as samplers/sampled musicians and, 121–24; artists' ethical support for flow of revenue and, 87; artists' refusal to be sampled and, 118–21; artists' revenue and, 78–79, 82–83, 88–89, 93, 94–95, 290nn6–9, 291n13, 291n15; commodification of sound and, 101–8; contradictions in licensing and, 95–98; copyright aggregators revenue and, 84–85; copyright law and, 7, 75–77; copyright ownership and, 78, 290n4; creative control and, 108; economic relationships competing interests in licensing, (*continued*)

in sampling and, 125–26, 293n48; economic rewards/claims by samplers/copyright owners and, 108–10; fair use doctrine and, 77; fees for licensing vs. lawsuits and, 110–18, 292n41; granting/obtaining licenses revenue and, 86–88; intergenerational musical dialogues/tributes and, 98–101; lawyers' revenue and, 85; music-business practices and, 7, 93; professionals' revenue and, 85; publishers' dealings with artists and, 121; publishers' revenue and, 83–85, 92–94; race/ethnicity issues in music industry and, 95–98, 106–8; rap and rock collaboration and, 94–95, 132; record companies' dealings with artists and, 122–23; record label revenue and, 81–82, 290nn8–9; rhythms protection and, 102–3; sound recordings and, 12, 284n15, 289n1; studio producers' revenue and, 81, 291n11; supporting/session musicians' revenue and, 79–81, 88, 89–92, 291n10; technology innovations and, 33–34; time limit on copyright and, 77–78, 289n2; traditional music protection and, 103–6; transformation/adaptation concept and, 102; voluntary unauthorized use and, 78. *See also* fees for licenses/licensing

compulsory licenses/mechanical licenses, 82, 225–29, 261–62, 291n13; mechanical royalties/mechanicals and, 82, 115, 209–10, 211, 299n19, 301n39; reform proposals and, 224–30, 300n19; reverse liability rule and, 265–66, 302nn6–7; transaction-facilitating institutions and, 166, 249, 254, 301n39

Constitution, U.S., 6, 14, 16, 215, 221, 237, 238

Coombe, Rosemary, 234

Copyright Act of 1919, cover versions and, 16

copyright law, 2, 129–30; cover versions and, 16; as cultural policy, 6; duration of, 13; fair use doctrine and, 80; file sharing and, 34–35, 138; fragmented literal similarity and, 130; limitations and exceptions in, 77, 144, 290n3; musical composition and, 2, 12, 75–77, 284n15, 289n1, 295n36; perpetual copyrights and, 259–61; pre-1923 recordings and, 289n2; pre-1972 recordings and, 76, 222, 289n2, 300n13; private motivation in balancing act of, 14–16; protected vs. freely viable elements of music and, 15–16; protection of samples under, 9–11, 284n10; quantitative approach to artist's work and, 130; reverse liability and, 261–66, 302nn6–7; rewards/losses and, 15, 108–10, 284n19; sound recordings and, 2, 12, 75–77, 140, 232–34, 284n15, 289n1; substantial-similarity component of, 130, 134–35, 293n8; technology innovations and, 34; transaction costs of licensing and, 12, 16. *See also* competing interests in licensing; compulsory licenses/mechanical licenses; copyright owners/ownership

copyright owners/ownership: authorization by, 29, 128–29, 136, 138, 209; choice between rules and, 265, 302n6–7; competing interests in licensing and, 78, 290n4; economic rewards for, 110, 284n19; greediness and, 162; lawsuits and, 29, 132–33, 136, 209, 294n15;

session/supporting musicians' revenue, 79–81, 88, 89–92, 291n10

settlements, out-of-court, 131–32, 134

Shanahan, Pat, 158–59, 161, 164, 170, 250

Sheffield, Rob, 132

Sherman, Cary, 81, 239, 290n9

Shock G, 64, 65, 123–24

Shocklee, Hank, 20, 22–24, 61–62, 78, 124, 142–44, 167–68, 238, 252–53. *See also* Public Enemy

Silverman, Tom: on album restrictions, 202; on artists' refusal to be sampled, 120; on beat biters, 66–67; on bureaucracy in licensing, 166; on compulsory licenses, 226–27; on copyright law, 75; on economic/commercial importance of licensing fees, 126; on expenses in licensing, 159, 160; on hip-hop DJs, 55–56; on licensing fees vs. lawsuits, 115; out-of-court settlements and, 131–32; on possessiveness of artists, 118; on technology of sampling, 63, 66–67; on underground sampling, 67–69, 289n76

similarity: fragmented literal, 130; substantial-similarity component, 130, 134–35, 293n8

sound collage, 60–62; African American music tradition and, 48–49; avant-garde, 37, 39–40, 42–45, 73, 117; Beatles and, 37, 39–40; Black Atlantic and, 48–53, 73; creativity and, 62–67, 258; cultural life and, 45–48; disco's role and, 57–59; hiphop DJs and, 53–57, 60; history of, 6, 37–41, 73–74; lawsuits and, 39; licensing conflicts with, 17; music traditions and, 45–47; *musique concrète*, 38, 39, 70, 177; popular music and, 37–41, 67–73, 289n76; technology and, 60–62; turntables and, 42, 53–54, 57–58, 213; underground, 41–44, 67–73, 289n76.

See also mash-ups; remix culture; sampling

sound recording rights, 2, 12, 75–77, 140, 232–34, 284n15, 289n1

Spoo, Robert, 259–61

Stafford, Bill: artists on fees for licensing and, 80; on assessment of licensing, 212; on compulsory licenses, 227, 229; on Creative Commons licenses, 246; fair use doctrine and, 239; on market incentives for licensing, 81; on relationships' importance in licensing, 163; on timing difficulties in licensing, 169; on transaction-facilitating institutions, 250–51

Steinski, 5, 67–70, 112, 117, 137–38, 289n6, 289n76

Stetsasonic, 20, 64, 90, 98

Stones Throw Records. *See* Alapatt, Eothen

structure and terms of licenses, 152–55, 296n7

Stubblefield, Clyde, 81, 88, 90–92. *See also* Brown, James

studio producers' revenue, 81, 291n11

supporting/session musicians' revenue, 79–81, 88, 89–92, 291n10

synchronization licensing, and films, 140, 295

Tape-beatles, 41–42, 65, 101

Tate, Greg, 4, 52, 55, 112, 131, 194–95

technology innovations, 5, 33–34, 60–62

T La Rock, 26–27, 53–54, 65–66, 288n59

3 Feet High and Rising (De La Soul), 19, 27, 29, 115, 131–32, 201

timing difficulties in licensing, 169–73

Tommy Boy Records. *See* Silverman, Tom

TradeMark Gunderson, 174

traditions, music, 45–49, 103–7

KEMBREW MCLEOD is a writer, a filmmaker, and an associate professor of communication studies at the University of Iowa. He has written and produced several books and documentaries on music, copyright, and popular culture. McLeod's previous book, *Freedom of Expression®: Overzealous Copyright Bozos and Other Enemies of Creativity* (2005), received the American Library Association's Eli M. Oboler Memorial Award. His co-produced documentary *Copyright Criminals* aired in 2010 on the Emmy Award-winning series Independent Lens on PBS, and his writing has appeared in the *New York Times*, the *Los Angeles Times*, the *Village Voice*, *SPIN*, and *Rolling Stone*.

PETER DICOLA is an assistant professor at the Northwestern University School of Law. He received his Ph.D. in economics and his law degree from the University of Michigan. As research director of the Future of Music Coalition, he co-wrote several reports and articles about the radio industry and the music industry. He currently serves on that organization's board of directors.

Library of Congress Cataloging-in-Publication Data
McLeod, Kembrew, 1970–
Creative license : the law and culture of digital sampling /
Kembrew McLeod and Peter DiCola.
p. cm.
Includes bibliographical references and index.
ISBN 978-0-8223-4864-1 (cloth : alk. paper)
ISBN 978-0-8223-4875-7 (pbk. : alk. paper)
1. Copyright—Music—United States.   2. Sampler (Musical instrument)
3. Plagiarism in music.   I. DiCola, Peter, 1976–   II. Title.
KF3035.M35 2011
346.7304'82—dc22
2010035883